This important book offers step-by-step coverage of the new mathematical procedures that are most likely to set the

MANAGEMENT TRENDS OF TOMORROW.

The authors—all experts in their fields—deal with a wide range of decision-making areas, from such general problems as the use of mathematical programing and econometrics . . . to strategies of diversification and techniques for selecting the most profitable products. Their detailed "how-to" discussions include actual instructions for working through several of the most useful procedures. Hundreds of examples, charts, illustrations, and a quick reference index add to the book's general business use and make it an invaluable teaching tool for company and management training programs. No forward-looking executive can afford to be unaware of these scientific techniques that are the latest and most important development in his profession.

"*New Decision-Making Tools for Managers* is a valuable addition to the library of the business executive who is concerned with new developments in his field."
—*Journal of Marketing Research*

Other MENTOR Books
for Executive Libraries

NEW DECISION-MAKING

TOOLS FOR MANAGERS

MATHEMATICAL PROGRAMING AS AN AID IN THE SOLVING OF BUSINESS PROBLEMS

EDITED BY
EDWARD C. BURSK
Editor, *Harvard Business Review*

JOHN F. CHAPMAN
Executive Editor, *Harvard Business Review*

A MENTOR BOOK from
NEW AMERICAN LIBRARY
TIMES MIRROR
New York and Scarborough, Ontario
The New English Library Limited, London

MENTOR TRADEMARK REG. U.S. PAT. OFF. AND FOREIGN COUNTRIES
REGISTERED TRADEMARK—MARCA REGISTRADA
HECHO EN CHICAGO, U.S.A.

SIGNET, SIGNET CLASSICS, SIGNETTE, MENTOR AND PLUME BOOKS
are published *in the United States* by
The New American Library, Inc.,
1301 Avenue of the Americas, New York, New York 10019,
in Canada by The New American Library of Canada Limited,
81 Mack Avenue, Scarborough, 704, Ontario,
in the United Kingdom by The New English Library Limited,
Barnard's Inn, Holborn, London, E.C. 1, England.

FIRST PRINTING, MAY, 1965

PRINTED IN THE UNITED STATES OF AMERICA

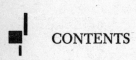

CONTENTS

CONTENTS

INTRODUCTION

In the years since the mid-1950's a trend toward a new and more scientific approach to the solution of business problems has been developing. It stems from the methods first suggested by the advocates of "operations research." But, it is already apparent that by drawing in depth both on mathematics and on the social sciences, and by utilizing intensively the high-speed electronic computer, researchers are beginning to give to the decision-making process a scientific base akin to the established methods which have long provided the bases for research in physics, biology, and chemistry.

Though claims of the progress already achieved are often exaggerated, it is significant that the developments of the last dozen years have so profoundly altered the businessman's thinking about the new decision-making tools that every alert executive feels he must become familiar with them as they are developed, and must learn as quickly as possible how he can utilize them to the advantage of his company.

Since one of the basic objectives of the *Harvard Business Review* is to bring to its management readers as quickly as possible news of developments which are of special interest to the administrator, the editors have followed this new trend toward a more scientific approach to decision making with special care.

Business organizations, schools of business administration, public and private research institutions, and specialized overseas publications have been contacted. In each case, claims that some new managerial tool had been discovered were examined and analyzed. Researchers and outstandingly successful managers were interviewed so that the editors would be familiar with the direction that research projects were taking and with the reactions of management to the theories which were being tested under real operating conditions.

A long series of articles was published as a result of these explorations. As is always true when writing about a new field, some of them have proved to be much more significant than others. In fact, in retrospect some of them turned out to be false leads—a groping for a new approach to the solution of a problem which failed to provide the desired answers, or which produced them by some circuitous and uneconomic method. In contrast, others have proved to be milestones along a route which leads in the direction of a far more scientific handling of the manager's job than is possible today.

The business administrator will become a true professional only when this trend progresses far beyond its present limits. In the meantime, the conscientious manager is attempting to keep abreast of each tested development which promises to sharpen his decision-making skills. In the competitive executive market in which he operates today, the highly motivated manager realizes that his progress through the executive hierarchy will depend importantly on his ability to supplement personal skills with the best of the new managerial tools.

In an age when the tempo of change is as great as it is today, no compilation of studies on "new" decision-making tools can expect to remain new for very long. But, a judicious selection of the articles which presented thoughtfully and accurately a basic concept that has stood the test of time can be of considerable value to the manager who is seeking to improve his skills and to the younger supervisor who aims to learn more about the tools of his profession.

The editors of the present volume have made such a selection. Out of 50 or more articles on decision-making tools, they have chosen 17 which give a well-rounded picture of a wide variety of decision-making theories which are still valid. Not all of them involve mathematical programing, but it is probably fair to say that all of them stem from the quality of thinking about a wide range of business problems which has been precipitated by the computer and by this new scientific approach to the analysis and solution of business problems.

Of the 17 articles which have been selected, all but three have appeared in the last five years. The three exceptions—on quality control, operations research, and mathematical programing—have proved to be so sound in the analysis of the basic function which they describe that the editors feel they can still serve a useful purpose. In each of these three cases, however, it should be made clear that the concepts have already undergone further refinements—as they will inevitably continue to do in the future.

In the case of the 14 more recent articles, all of them reveal an innovative approach to an old problem, or describe in thoughtful detail the elements of a new technique which it seems important for the alert executive to understand.

The editors have chosen to introduce the series with a basic discussion of "Operations Research for Management." This chapter provides a solid pattern of thinking for the young man not yet familiar with the problems of decision making or for the older executive who traditionally has counted on intuition, rather than on scientific analysis, to help him solve his management problems. It defines operations research as the application of the scientific attitude and the associated techniques to the study of operations. But, as the authors explain, before scientific analysis can be applied, the manager must be able to single out the segments of his business which make up an "operation." Then, he can begin to apply the new tools of analysis which will make it possible for him to correct faults in the individual units, and, ultimately, in the whole operation.

Operations research (popularly known as O.R.), when its methods are fully understood, helps a manager to single out the critical issues which require executive appraisal and analysis, and provides him with factual bases to support his executive judgment.

Though written almost nine years ago, "Mathematical Programing: Better Information for Better Decision Making" is a sound and especially clear presentation of a concept which every modern manager needs to understand if he is to utilize linear programing techniques for the solution of the wide range of intricate management problems to which they can be applied. Despite the fact that, since this article was written, mathematical programing has progressed far beyond the simple linear programing problems that it describes, the discussion provides one of the most significant chapters because it describes so lucidly the quality of basic thinking which is required before the successful programing of a business problem can be undertaken. Also, it makes clear the important relationship of the computer to many of the new mathematical techniques for solving business problems.

The last few years have seen the explosive growth of a new family of planning and control techniques adapted to the Space Age. Much of the development work has been done in the defense industry, but the construction, chemical, and other industries have played an important part in the story too.

Program Evaluation Review Technique (PERT) is the full name of one of the newest, most talked about, and least understood of these techniques for managing the operations of a business. In the chapter "How to Control with PERT," the reader will be introduced to:

(1) PERT's basic requirements, such as the presentation of tasks, events, and activities on a network in sequential form with time estimates.

(2) Its advantages, including greatly improved control over complex development and production programs, and the capacity to distill large amounts of data in brief, orderly fashion.

(3) Its limitations, as in situations where there is little interconnection between the different activities pursued.

(4) Solutions for certain difficulties, such as the problem of relating time needed and job costs in the planning stage of a project.

(5) Policies that top management might do well to adopt, such as taking steps to train, experiment with, and put into effect the new controls.

Another basic tool of decision making which is introduced in the "General" section of the present volume is econometrics—

economic models of vast operating problems which are designed and used by professional economists to help explain in telescoped form to top management just what is involved in a major economic change which is being proposed. While most older executives appear to be frightened by the very word "econometric," experience has proved that, skillfully used, these models can be relatively simple to understand. Once the basic elements of an econometric model are understood, they provide a greater insight into the nature of complicated problems and hence strengthen the manager's ability to exercise sounder judgment than would otherwise be possible.

Since accounting is said to be the language of business, the editors have included the chapter "Meaningful Costs for Management Action," because in it the author explains in especially clear detail how to measure what is going to happen to profits as a result of basic decisions by management. Profitability accounting and control, as described in this chapter, explains to the manager how he can hold all of these control tools in exact alignment so that he may be able to use them with maximum effectiveness in the increasingly intensive battle for profits.

Following the introduction to the new tools of decision making that is provided by the first group of articles, twelve chapters are presented under functional groupings.

For the financial specialists there is a chapter describing the "return-on-investment" method of evaluating a company's new investment projects, and showing the advantages it provides over the old "years-to-pay-out" concept. And in the chapter on "Mathematical Models in Capital Budgeting," managers in the financial end of a business have explained how a mathematical model can be set up which will allow them to evaluate the most profitable of a series of investment possibilities which is open to management.

Marketing managers will find help in four chapters. Simulation, one of the great advances in the science of business management that has developed in the last decade, provides the ability to operate some particular phase of a business on paper—or in a computer—for a period of time, and by this means to test various alternative strategies and systems. In a chapter by

Harvey N. Shycon and Richard B. Maffei, this new technique is described in detail, and with numerous examples drawn from actual experience in the H. J. Heinz Company.

The nagging problem of marketing costs, which is a perennial worry of many levels of management, is discussed in a thought-provoking chapter, "Marketing Costs and Mathematical Programing." Beyond demonstrating how marketing costs can be reduced and marketing efficiency increased through the use of a new approach to the problem, the chapter is likely to provoke interest also because it suggests other areas in the over-all distribution system in which mathematical programing may be used to advantage. Distribution may be the last area to yield to the statistical approach, but it also may offer the best opportunity for indicating where the marketing dollar should be spent to do the most good. The chapter includes an appendix with detailed formulas which can be applied to solve specific problems along lines proposed by the authors.

Because few businesses will introduce a new product without first testing its acceptance in a sample of its ultimate market, the editors have included a short but very useful chapter on "Tests for Test Marketing." Based on the assumption that it is crucial for the marketing manager to arrive at an early decision on the success or failure of a test-marketed product, Benjamin Lipstein has set up a method of testing brand-share trends, and presents a basic table on which results can be measured and analyzed. Since a successful method of measuring results at an early stage of the test will make it possible to move the product into national distribution more quickly if it is "accepted," the chapter will have special appeal for the distribution manager.

Just as important to the manager responsible for holding inventories to a minimum but, at the same time, for maintaining a high level of customer service, is "Less Risk in Inventory Estimates," by Robert G. Brown. How can the uncertainty facing a company be held to a minimum? How can that minimum be measured and accounted for in a well-designed inventory control system? Mr. Brown has three concrete proposals which have stood the test of time and wide usage. In a series of nine exhibits, the author demonstrates how his method has operated for such diverse products as copper tubing and fan belts.

Both marketing and production managers will find the three chapters on Product Strategy useful.

Gerald A. Busch, the vice president and director of market research at Lockheed Propulsion Company, provides the thought-provoking chapter on "Prudent-Manager Forecasting." Instead of allowing himself to be stymied because he was unable to forecast sales with certainty, Mr. Busch developed a method of working with probabilities—with the likelihood of certain potential markets and certain market penetrations occurring under certain conditions, the chances of other conditions developing which will affect the forecasts, and the probabilities of various alternative developments. Actually, what the author proposes is that management's aim should be to gain not a hard and fast outline of the future but an evaluation of probabilities on which it can make informed decisions. "Prudent-manager forecasting" developed out of this approach, and it is described in sufficient detail to help any forecaster apply it to his own forecasting problems.

H. Igor Ansoff, in "Strategies for Diversification," aims—both by qualitative and quantitative techniques—to relate diversification to the over-all growth perspectives of management, to establish reasons which may lead a company to prefer diversification to other growth alternatives, and to trace a relationship between over-all growth objectives and special diversification objectives. Managers whose companies are discovering that they may have overdiversified will find this text as useful as those who are just beginning to explore the possibilities of enlarging their operation through diversification.

Because most companies must continue to introduce new products if they are to sustain their long-run growth and profitability, the editors have included a chapter on "Selecting Profitable Products." The need for guidance in this area of management is evident when it is realized that between 75% and 95% of all new product introductions fail for reasons other than insufficient capital. In an elaborate but clearly defined procedure, the author outlines a method utilizing simple probability and weighting techniques which reduces the over-all new-product problem to a series of simpler ones which are more easily and objectively solved. The solutions of these smaller problems are then combined into three index numbers that represent an over-all rating for the potential of the new product. Detailed exhibits will help the reader to apply the method to the problems within his own company.

The final section of this volume includes three chapters selected especially to be helpful to production managers.

"Mathematics for Production Scheduling" reports the results of an intensive program of research which has brought about the development of new methods for improving the quality of production scheduling decisions and for helping managers make substantially better decisions than they could make by using prevailing rule-of-thumb and judgment procedures. Once the manager has mastered the technique and a general rule has been developed, the computations required to establish a monthly production schedule can be completed by a clerk in a few hours or on a computer in a few minutes. Because the broad implications of this study are likely to be of interest not only to production managers but also to a wide managerial group who may wish to apply the principles in other areas, an appendix of detailed, basic reference material is included with this chapter.

Since quality control is a matter of constant concern to production managers, two chapters are devoted to this topic. Practically all of the new methods which have been developed over the last 20 to 30 years to control the quality of products are both mathematical and technical in character. Only a few production managers are expert enough in both fields to understand how to choose one method over another. And yet, only when an administrator really understands why any method, or series of methods, secures the results it does will he be able to apply it effectively. In his chapter on "Quality Control," Professor Theodore Brown examines the basic theories of quality control with the objective of making clear to the businessman how to judge both the potentialities and the limitations of each method as it relates to his immediate problem. His presentation is designed specifically to serve as an introduction to the broad and developing science of quality control.

The chapter on "The Statistically Designed Experiment," by Dorian Shainin, describes briefly a technique he has developed to determine quickly and systematically why variations in quality develop on the production line, and explains the advantages of his technique over the conventional methods commonly used by production managers. Most importantly, he describes in considerable detail the kinds of problems that the statistically designed experiment can solve.

No single volume can encompass the full range of new decision-making tools which have developed in the last dozen years since the electronic computer opened the way to the large-scale application of mathematics to the solution of business problems. Neither would it be fair to evaluate the trend toward a more orderly and scientific solution of the manager's problem without including at least a sampling of the many nonmathematical but very valuable new methods of problem solving which have resulted from the mind-stretching questions that have developed as a part of the Space Age.

What it is most important to remember in this age of the almost monthly technological "breakthrough" is that no field of knowledge is standing still. In the face of this fact, the best that any manager can hope is to acquaint himself as thoroughly as possible with those new developments which seem to be establishing a new pattern of thinking on which a new body of knowledge and skills will be built.

This volume has been planned primarily to fill this need in the area of managerial decision making.

E. C. B.
J. F. C.

NEW DECISION-MAKING TOOLS FOR MANAGERS

1

"OPERATIONS RESEARCH" FOR MANAGEMENT

CYRIL C. HERRMANN AND JOHN F. MAGEE

Operations research has helped companies to solve such diverse business problems as directing salesmen to the right accounts at the right time, dividing the advertising budget in the most effective way, establishing equitable bonus systems, improving inventory and reordering policies, planning minimum-cost production schedules, and estimating the amount of clerical help needed for a new operation.

Operations research makes possible accomplishments like these and many others because (a) it helps to single out the critical issues which require executive appraisal and analysis, and (b) it provides factual bases to support and guide executive judgment. Thus, it eases the burden of effort and time on executives but intensifies the potential of their decision-making role. In this sense operations research contributes toward better management.

What is this thing called "operations research"? How does it work? How does it differ from other services to management? Where can it be used? How should management get it organized and under way? What are its limitations and potentials? These are all questions that we shall try to answer in the following pages.

Essential Features

Operations research apparently means different things to different people. To some businessmen and scientists it means only the application of statistics and common sense to business problems. Indeed, one vice president of a leading company remarked that if his division heads did not practice it every day, they would not last long. To others it is just another and perhaps more comprehensive term for existing activities like market research, quality control, or industrial engineering. Some businessmen consider it a new sales or production gimmick; some, a product of academic people interfering in the practical world. In truth, operations research is none of these things, as we shall soon see.

It should not be surprising that there has been this confusion. Operations research is not an explicit, easily identifiable concept that developed to meet the specific needs of industry. It was first applied in World War II by groups of scientists who were engaged by the government to help frame recommendations for the improvement of military activities. After the war a few soundly managed companies experimented with it and found that it worked successfully in business operations as well; and it has since gained a secure foothold in industry.

Early attempts by operations analysts to describe their activities, based on the objective of arriving at a precise and comprehensive definition of operations research, tended to be overly generalized, broad, and self-conscious, and suffered from emphasis on military applications. Some of the confusion surrounding the meaning of the term "operations research" has resulted from attempts at identification with special techniques or unnecessarily rigid distinctions between operations research and other management service activities.

Now, let us see if we can cut through some of this confusion.

The first point to grasp is that operations research is what its name implies, research on operations. However, it involves a particular view of operations and, even more important, a particular kind of research.

Operations are considered as an entity. The subject matter studied is not the equipment used, nor the morale of the participants, nor the physical properties of the output; it is the combination of these in total, as an economic process. And operations so conceived are subject to analysis by the mental processes and the methodologies which we have come to associate with the research work of the physicist, the chemist, and the biologist—what has come to be called "the scientific method."

The basic premise underlying the scientific method is a simple and abiding faith in the rationality of nature, leading to the belief that phenomena have a cause. If phenomena do have a cause, it is the scientist's contention that by hard work the mechanism or system underlying the observed facts can be discovered. Once the mechanism is known, nature's secrets are known and can be used to the investigator's own best advantage.

The scientist knows that his analogue to nature will never be perfect. But it must be sufficiently accurate to suit the particular purposes at hand; and, until it is, he must repeat the processes of observation, induction, and theory construction—again and again. Note that a satisfactory solution must be in quantitative terms in order that it can be predictive—the only accepted fundamental test of being physically meaningful.

The scientific method, in its ideal form, calls for a rather special mental attitude, foremost in which is a reverence for facts. Of course all modern executives are accustomed to using figures to control their operations. But they are primarily concerned with results and only secondarily with causes; they interpret their facts in the light of company objectives. This is a much different attitude from seeking out the relationships underlying the facts.

Thus, when an executive looks at sales figures, he looks at them primarily in terms of the success of his sales campaign and its effect on profits. By contrast, when the scientist looks at these same figures, he seeks in them a clue to the fundamental behavior pattern of the customers. By the process of induction he tentatively formulates a theoretical system or mechanism; then by the inverse process of deduction he determines what phenomena should take place and checks these against the observed facts. His test is simple: Does the assumed mechanism act enough like nature—or, more specifically in this case, does it produce quantitative data such as can be used for predicting how the customers will in fact behave?

For example, in a company manufacturing specialty products, examination of account records showed that customer behavior could be accurately described as a time-dependent Poisson process—a type of phenomenon found widely in nature, from problems in biology to nuclear physics. This concept yielded the key to establishing measures of the efficiency of the salesmen's work and of the effect of the promotion in building sales. On this basis a new method of directing promotional salesmen to appropriate accounts was constructed—and then tested by careful experiments, to see if sales increases resulted at less than proportionate increases in cost. (The results in this case were spectacular: an over-all sales rise in six figures, and a corresponding gain in net profits.)

Through the years mathematical and experimental techniques have been developed to implement this attitude. The application of the scientific attitude and the associated techniques to the study of operations, whether business, governmental, or military, is what is meant by operations research.

Newton was able to explain the apparently totally unrelated phenomena of planetary motion and objects falling on the earth by the simple unifying concept of gravity. This represented a tremendous step forward in helping men to understand and control the world about them. Again, more recently, the power of the scientific method was demonstrated by the ability of the nuclear physicists to predict the tremendous energy potential lying within the atom.

Here are a few summary examples of the way this same kind of approach has been applied to down-to-earth business problems.

A company with a number of products made at three different locations was concerned about the items to be produced at each location and the points at which the items would be warehoused. Freight costs constituted a substantial part of the delivered cost of the material. Operations research showed that what appeared to be a complex and involved problem could be broken into a series of rather simple components. Adaptations of linear programing methods were used to find the warehousing schedule which would minimize freight costs. The study is now being extended to determine the best distribution of products among manufacturing plants and warehouse locations in order to minimize net delivered cost in relation to return on investment.

A manufacturer of chemical products, with a wide and varied line, sought more rational or logical bases than the customary percentage of sales for distributing his limited advertising budget among products, some of which were growing, some stable, and others declining. An operations research study showed that advertising effectiveness was related to three simple characteristics, each of which could be estimated from existing sales data with satisfactory reliability: (a) the total market potential; (b) the rate of growth of sales; (c) the customer loss rate. A mathematical formulation of these three characteristics provided a rational basis for distributing advertising and promotional effort.

In a company making a line of light machines, the executive board questioned the amount of money spent for missionary salesmen calling on customers. Studies yielded explicit mathematical statements of (a) the relation between the number of accounts called on and resulting sales volume and (b) the relation between sales costs and manufacturing and distribution costs. These were combined by the methods of differential calculus to set up simple tables for picking the level of promotion in each area which would maximize company net profits. The results showed that nearly a 50% increase in promotional activity was economically feasible and would yield substantial profits.

An industrial products manufacturer wanted to set time standards as a basis for costs and labor efficiency controls. The operations research group studied several complex operations; expressed the effect of the physical characteristics of products and equipment and the time required to produce a given amount of output in the form of mathematical equations; and then, without further extensive time study or special data collection, set up tables of production time standards according to product characteristics, equipment used, and worker efficiency, which could be applied to any or all of the production operations.

A company carrying an inventory of a large number of finished items had trouble maintaining sound and balanced stock levels.

5

Despite careful attention and continued modification of reorder points in the light of experience, the stock of many individual items turned out to be either too high for sales or inadequate to meet demand. The problem was solved by a physical chemist who first collected data on the variables, such as size and frequency of order, length of production and delivery time, etc.; then set up an assumed system, which he tried out against extreme sales situations, continually changing its characteristics slightly until it met the necessary conditions—all on paper (a technique well known to physical scientists); and thus was able to determine a workable system without cost of installation and risk of possible failure.

These examples should serve to give some idea of how the scientific method can be applied. But they represent only a few of the many scientific techniques available (as we shall see when we examine further cases in more detail). Some practitioners even take the rather broad point of view that operations research should include the rather indefinite and qualitative methods of the social science fields. Most professional opinion, however, favors the view that operations research is more restricted in meaning, limited to the quantitative methods and experimentally verifiable results of the physical sciences.

Basic Concepts

There are four concepts of fundamental importance to the practice of operations research: (a) the model, (b) the measure of effectiveness, (c) the necessity for decision, and (d) the role of experimentation.

The most frequently encountered concept in operations research is that of the model—the simplified representation of an operation, containing only those aspects which are of primary importance to the problem under study. It has been of great use in facilitating the investigation of operations. To illustrate with some familiar types of "models" from other fields:

(1) In aeronautical engineering the model of an aeroplane is used to investigate its aerodynamic properties in a wind tunnel. While perfectly adequate for this purpose, it would hardly do for

practical use. It has no seats; it may not even be hollow. It is, however, a satisfactory physical model for studying the flight characteristics of the ship.

(2) Another, quite different kind of model, with which we are all familiar, is the accounting model. This is essentially a simplified representation on paper, in the form of accounts and ledgers, of the flow of goods and services through a business enterprise. It provides measures of the rate of flow, the values produced, and the performances achieved, and to that extent is useful (though it is hardly a realistic representation of operations).

(3) Many models are used in physics. Three-dimensional models of complex molecules are probably most familiar to laymen, but the most powerful models in this field are sets of mathematical equations.

There are several different types of operations research models. Most of them are mathematical in form, being a set of equations relating significant variables in the operation to the outcome. An example, illustrating how a company used a model to improve time standards on the production line, is provided in Exhibit I.

Another type of model frequently used is the punched-card model, where components of the operation are represented by individual punched cards; masses of these are manipulated on standard punched-card equipment. For example, in a study of a sales distribution problem, each customer, of thousands served by the company, was represented by a punched card containing significant information about his location, type of business, frequency of purchase, and average rate of business. The punched cards representing the customers could then be subjected to assumed promotional treatments, with the effects of the promotions punched into the cards. The resulting business could be calculated and an evaluation made of alternative sales-promotion campaigns.

Occasionally a model is physical like the ones often used by engineers. For example, the use of a hydrokinetic model has been proposed in the study of a mass advertising problem. The fluid flowing through the model would represent business of various types going to the company or to competitors as a result of various forms of the company's own and competitive promotional efforts (represented in the model by forces acting on the fluids).

7

Operations research models can also be distinguished as exact or probabilistic:

(1) An *exact* model is used in operations or processes where chance plays a small role, where the effect of a given action will be reasonably closely determined. Exact models can be used, for example, in long-range production scheduling problems in the face of known or committed demand. The exact model is sufficiently accurate since it can be assumed that, barring a major catastrophe, over the long run planned and actual production will be reasonably close.

(2) The *probabilistic* model, on the other hand, contains explicit recognition of uncertainty. Such models are of great use in the analysis of advertising problems, where the unpredictability of consumers plays a great role. And as Exhibit II indicates, they make extensive use of the highly developed theory of probability, which has come to be of such great value in the physical sciences. One customarily thinks of a physicist as dealing with rather exact concepts and highly predictable experiments. Yet physicists faced a problem equivalent to the advertising problem in predicting atomic activity. Methods developed for physical problems involving mass behavior under random conditions can be applied with great facility and value to operations.

The model is a major goal of the operations research analyst. In one sense, the construction of the model, or a faithful representation of the operation, is the scientist's primary job. In making it he develops a theory to explain the observed characteristics of the operation. In Exhibit III, for example, note how the investigators linked together the salient characteristics of such diverse and complicated operations as sales, promotion, manufacturing, and distribution. The remaining task is to interpret this theory through the manipulation of the model, whether mathematical or physical.

EXHIBIT I. USE OF MODEL IN MATHEMATICAL FORM

The Acme Products Company wanted to set time standards for cost accounting and labor control on the operations of a battery of taping machines. These machines wind a variety of protective tapes on steel cables. The cable is pulled through the center of a rotating disk, the "taping head," which carries a roll of tape; and this tape is unwound through a set of rollers and presented to the cable at an angle. Several kinds of metallic, paper, cloth, and rubberized tapes are used, and the diameter of the cable treated varies widely.

The machines used by the company had been purchased at different times and were felt to be rather varied in operating characteristics, although the principle of operation was the same in all. Time-study methods had failed to yield adequate standards because of the complexity and variability of the operators' tasks and the uncertain effects of changes in materials. Statistical (correlation) methods applied to job records of the time and character of jobs failed to explain the variations in time required, and there appeared to be substantial differences in efficiency among machines and operators.

Discussions with operators and foremen indicated that setup and starting time and complexity were largely the same for all jobs, but the workers set the machine speeds from experience and "feel" of what the tapes used would stand without undue breakage. Investigation indicated that the tension in the tape was proportional to its speed and the tensile strength was proportional to its width.

The simplest unit of production is the amount produced by the machine in one revolution of the taping head, the unit recorded on the work sheets as the "lay" of the tape. If the taping head turns at n revolutions per minute, the time required for a job is

$$T = t_o + \frac{L}{nl}$$

where t_o is setup time, l is the "lay," and L is the length of cable in the job.

From the geometrical relationship shown in Figure 1 the velocity of the tape is $n\sqrt{\pi^2 d^2 + l^2}$ and the maximum tension the tape will stand is $Kn\sqrt{\pi^2 d^2 + l^2}$ where K depends on the strength of tape used. The maximum speed of the machine is

$$n = \frac{Q_i w}{\sqrt{\pi^2 d^2 + l^2}}$$

where Q_i depends on the tensile strength of tape material.

FIGURE 1

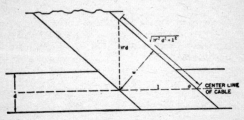

The cable diameter and lay are set independently and an appropriate tape width chosen. The required width, from Figure 1, is

$$w = l \sin \theta = l \frac{\pi d}{\sqrt{\pi^2 d^2 + l^2}}$$

and thus the maximum speed for the machine is

$$n = \frac{Q_i l \pi d}{\pi^2 d^2 + l^2}$$

The time required to cover a cable of diameter d and length L, with a tape of material type i at a lay l, is

$$T = t_o + \frac{L}{Q_i l} \left(\frac{\pi^2 d^2 + l^2}{l \pi d} \right)$$

Application of this formula to routine job-production records, with appropriate allowances for the types of tape material used, showed that the operation was surprisingly uniform and that the behavior of machines and operators was surprisingly similar. Apparent differences were due to unnoticed effects of differences in jobs handled. A direct basis was available for setting uniform and reasonable time standards.

EXHIBIT II. PROBABILISTIC MODEL

The classical newsboy problem discussed in Morse and Kimball, *Methods of Operations Research* (John Wiley & Sons, Inc., 1951), illustrates the construction of a simple probabilistic model. While the example itself is trivial, it illustrates how probabilistic considerations affect results.

A newsboy buys papers at two cents and sells them at five cents; he receives a one-cent allowance on unsold papers. He finds by experience he has ten customers a day, appearing at random; that is, he has no regular customers and one person passing is as likely to buy as the next. Under these circumstances, the Poisson law may be expected to describe the number of customers arriving. The chance that m customers will arrive on a given day is given by

$$P(m) = \frac{e^{-10} 10^m}{m!}$$

Suppose the newsboy buys k papers and m customers appear. If m is equal to or less than k, m papers are sold at a total profit of $4m - k$; if m is greater than k, k papers are sold at a total profit of $3k$. The newsboy's expected profit is

$$E_k = \sum_{m=0}^{k} (4m - k) P(m) + \sum_{m=k+1}^{\infty} 3k P(m)$$

10

The chance he will be able to service all the customers who will pass by is

$$S_k = \sum_{m=0}^{k} P(m)$$

Figure 2 shows how the newsboy's profit depends on the number of papers he buys, k, and Figure 3 how his ability to service customers depends on the papers he takes.

Because of chance variations in the number of customers available, if the newsboy buys ten papers every day, he will not average the expected three cents per paper or thirty cents per day and will meet the available demand less than 60% of the time. In fact, he can make a little more profit by buying not ten but twelve papers daily; if he

FIGURE 2

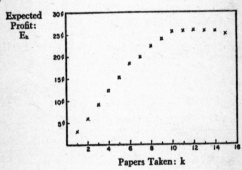

FIGURE 3

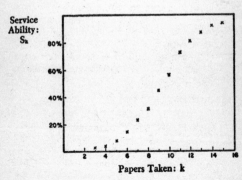

buys fifteen daily, he can make the same total profit on the average while meeting the available demand 95% of the time.

EXHIBIT III. INTEGRATING COMPONENTS OF A COMPLEX OPERATION

The Omega Machine Company sells portable industrial machinery, parts, and supplies to a large number of industrial users. Orders are received through a number of branch offices around the country, with missionary salesmen used to visit accounts to explain and promote use of the company's products. The company had tried to hold missionary sales expense to a fixed percentage of sales, with about 40% of the accounts receiving calls in any one quarter. Statistical methods based on previous business were used for selecting the accounts to be promoted.

Investigation showed the missionary sales expense to be proportional to the number of calls made rather than to the size of accounts called on, and because of the nature of the products, total volume from an account depended on the number of orders placed, since average order value was essentially the same from all accounts. Study of individual account records showed that if promoted in any quarter an individual account has a probability $P(n)$ of placing n orders in that quarter:

$$P(n) = \frac{e^{-c}c^n}{n!}$$

where c is the account's "ordering characteristic." While the ordering characteristics of individual accounts were unknown, mathematical analysis of sales records indicated that the fraction $Q(c)$ of accounts with an ordering characteristic equal or greater than c is

$$Q(c) = e^{-c/S}$$

where S is the average for the group of accounts. While the value of S varied somewhat from region to region and from year to year, the mathematical form of $Q(c)$ is remarkably constant. This knowledge permitted comparison of results in widely different regions and times, which yielded the results that:

(1) The group of accounts picked in any quarter for promotion by the company's procedure showed a distribution of ordering characteristics, c, of the form

$$Q'_p(c) = \frac{(1 - e^{-g/S})e^{-c/S}}{S}$$

where $g = a/1 - a$ and a is the size of the fraction selected.

(2) If an account was not promoted in any quarter, there was a 30% chance it would be completely inactive, but if active, it would order at a rate only 70% as great as if promoted; the net effect of lack of promotion was a cut of 50% in the potential value of the account.

These two results were summarized in an equation which showed how total business, $B(a)$, depended on the amount of missionary effort expended:

$$B(a) = NV\left\{\int_0^\infty \frac{c(1 - e^{-g/S})e^{-c/S}}{S}\, dc + .5\int_0^\infty \frac{ce^{-(c+g)/S}}{S}\, dc\right\}$$

$$= \frac{NSV}{2}(1 + 2a - a^2)$$

where N is the total number of accounts, V is the average order value, and Na is the number of accounts selected by the usual means for promotion. The cost of the promotional work would be expressible as pNa.

A detailed investigation of manufacturing and distribution operations resulted in the conclusion that the total manufacturing costs (including an interest charge imputed against capital employed in manufacturing and inventories) could be expressed simply, as shown in Figure 4. The break in the curve is due to the effect on costs of reaching capacity of existing plants, although operations are currently well below this level.

The facts learned about manufacturing and distribution costs could be combined with the information on sales and promotion to write down an equation for the profit $P(a)$ resulting from any given promotion effort

$$P(a) = m\frac{NSV}{2}(1 + 2a - a^2) - pNa - \{A - bB(a)\}$$

where m is the average gross profit and the last two terms are the manufacturing costs incurred when a volume $B(a)$ is produced. Then

$$P(a) = (m - b)\frac{NSV}{2}(1 + 2a - a^2) - pNa - A$$

By the methods of differential calculus, the profit $P(a)$ will be greatest when a is chosen so that

$$P'(a) = (m - b)NSV(1 - a) - pN = 0$$

or when

$$a = 1 - \frac{p}{(m - b)SV}$$

FIGURE 4

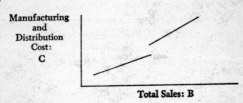

Manufacturing
and
Distribution
Cost:
C

Total Sales: B

The arbitrary method of setting the missionary sales budget as a fixed percentage of sales was replaced by a means for relating sales effort directly to profits through the impact on sales and manufacturing. The management had a numerical basis for increasing missionary sales effort by over 50% with expectation of a handsome return.

Related to the concept of a model or theory of operation is the measure of effectiveness, whereby the extent to which the operation is attaining its goal can be explicitly determined. One common over-all measure of effectiveness in industrial operations is return on investment; another is net dollar profit. Measures of effectiveness down the scale might be the number of customers serviced per hour, the ratio of productive to total hours of a machine operation, etc.

A consistent statement of the fundamental goals of the operation is essential to the mathematical logic of the model. (It does not matter if the goals are complex.) Just as the model cannot make two and two add up to five, so it is impossible to relate fundamentally inconsistent objectives and produce consistent and meaningful results.

Operations research has frequently brought to light inconsistencies in company goals. Take production scheduling, for instance. Very often its object has been stated as scheduling production to meet sales forecasts with minimum production costs, with minimum inventory investment, and without customer-service failure. Yet minimizing inventory investment typically requires the use of start-and-stop or at best uneven production plans, resulting in excessive production costs; and eliminating the risk of not being able to ship every customer order immediately requires huge inventories, in the face of fluctuating and at least partially unpredictable demand.

The solution is to combine and sublimate such otherwise inconsistent goals to a higher unified and consistent goal.

For example, the diverse goals of customer service, production economy, and investment minimization can be expressed in terms of costs—the cost of inefficient production (hiring, training, overtime, etc.), the cost of investment in inventory (the rate of interest the treasurer wishes to charge to conserve his funds or perhaps the

14

return on investment which can be earned through alternative uses of the available funds), and the cost of inability to meet a customer's demand (estimated loss of goodwill and future business). While the latter two costs are primarily policy costs, experience has shown that they are sufficiently determinable and realistic to afford a basis for management decision.

The three component costs can then be cast in an algebraic equation expressing their interrelationships in terms of total scheduling cost; and the minimum total scheduling cost becomes the one, consistent goal.

Note that, once set up, the algebraic equation can be worked in reverse. Thus, the sales manager might be told how much the company can afford to pay for an inventory large enough to avoid varying risks of failure to meet consumer demand.

This kind of clarification of goals is particularly important in relating subordinate and over-all company goals—as in the case of a department run efficiently at the expense of other departments or of a promotion budget based on a fixed percentage of sales without regard to the adverse effects on manufacturing budgets.

The statement of a complete and wholly consistent goal of company operations must be recognized as an ideal. Business goals are very complex, and to catch the full flavor of the objectives of an intricate business operation in any simple, explicit statement is difficult. Many business goals remain, and probably ever will remain, at least in part intangible—e.g., efforts to improve employee morale or contribute to the public welfare. To that extent, the objective of operations research must be more modest than the construction of a complete model and the measurement of the extent to which the operation is attaining the complete set of goals established for it. But it still can serve to clarify the interdependency of those intangibles with the company goals which in fact are measurable, thus providing a guide to executive decision.

The third concept inherent in operations research is that of decision and decision making. An essential element in all true operations research problems is the existence of alternative courses of action, with a choice to be made among them; otherwise the study of an operation becomes academic or theoretical. This should be clear from the cases already cited.

In sum, the objective of operations research is to clarify the relation between the several courses of action, determine their outcomes, and indicate which measures up best in terms of the company goal. But note that, while this should be of assistance to the executive in making his decision intelligently, in every case the ultimate responsibility still lies with him.

The fourth significant concept concerns the role of experimentation. Operations research is the application of experimental science to the study of operations. The theory, or model, is generally built up from observed data or experience, although in some cases the model development may depend heavily on external or a priori information. In any event, the theory describing the operation must always be verifiable experimentally. Two kinds of experiments are important in this connection:

(1) The first kind is designed simply to get information. Thus, it often takes the form of an apparently rather impractical test. In one case the operations analysts directed advertising toward potential customers the company knew were not worth addressing, and refrained from addressing customers the company typically sought—and for a very simple reason. There was plenty of evidence indicating what happened when advertising was directed toward those normally addressed but not enough about its effects upon those not normally addressed. To evaluate the effectiveness of the advertising, therefore, it was necessary to find out what happened to those normally promoted when they were not promoted, and what happened to those normally not promoted when they were.

(2) The other type of experiment is the critical type; it is designed to test the validity of conclusions. Again, what appear to be rather impractical forms of experimentation are sometimes used. Thus, in the most sensitive experiments of this type, the validity of the theory or model can often be tested most revealingly in terms of the results of extreme policies rather than in terms of the more normal policy likely to be put into practice.

Other Services

Now, before going on to discuss in more detail the administrative problems and uses of operations research, it may be well to make clear how it differs from other services to management. Many of these services have been proved of great value to the business community as a result of years of successful application to difficult problems. Are there significant differences that make it possible for operations research to extend the usefulness of these services? Let us examine some of the leading services briefly for comparison.

Statistics. Operations research is frequently confused with statistics, especially as applied to the body of specific techniques based upon probability theory which has grown up in recent years. This statistical approach originally developed in the fields of agriculture and biology but has now been extended into such areas as quality control, accounting, consumer sampling, and opinion polls.

The operations research analyst does use such statistical methods when applicable, but he is not restricted to them. Moreover, there is a difference in basic point of view. Statistics is concerned primarily with the relations between numbers, while operations research is concerned with reaching an understanding of the operation—of the underlying physical system which the numbers represent. And this may make a significant difference in results as well as approach. In a recent advertising study, the operations research team found the key to characterizing the way in which the advertising affected consumers in the results of a series of "split-run" tests. Earlier, these results had been presumed useless after statistical methods such as analysis of variance and multiple regression had failed to show meaningful conclusions.

Accounting. Operations research is also confused sometimes with accounting, particularly with the control aspects of accounting which have developed in recent years. In reality there are several differences. One springs from the fact that the fundamental and historical purpose of accounting methods has been to maintain a record of the financial operations of the company; and this is reflected in the training and attitude of many accountants. The growth of the accounting function as the interpreter of information for control purposes has been a fairly recent development, and the basic methods used and information provided are strongly influenced by the historical accounting purpose.

Accounting information is one of the principal sources of data to support an operations research study. Accounting data, however, require careful interpretation and organization before they can be used safely and efficiently. Businessmen tend to forget that accounting costs are definitions derived in the light of the fundamental accounting purpose, and sometimes they tend to confuse accounting figures with "truth." Operations research, using the same raw data, may make other definitions which serve the special needs of the particular study. One of the great stumbling blocks in the organization and implementation of an operations research study is the disentangling from accounting records of the costs appropriately defined and truly significant to the problem at hand.

It is true, however, that in the analysis and construction of measures of control, the functions of operations research and accounting do tend to overlap. Also, the men working in these functions have strong mutual interests. Accountants have served a useful purpose in bringing the importance of control measures to the attention of business management, while operations research has shown ability in building new methods for developing and implementing these concepts of control.

Marketing research. This management service is concerned with gathering and analyzing information bearing on marketing problems. Certain marketing researchers do go so far that in some instances they are performing services akin to operations research, but for the most part they are content to measure the market, by the use of questionnaires, interviews, or otherwise, and to gather factual data which management can use as it sees fit.

By contrast, operations research, when applied to marketing problems, seeks to gain a greater understanding of the marketing operation rather than of the market itself. Thus, it may rely heavily on marketing research sources for data; in one retail advertising study, for example, a consumer-interview program was used to obtain information on the frequency with which potential customers purchased outside their own towns. But the objective, even in quantitative studies, is usually to obtain a fundamental characterization of consumers for use in the model. Furthermore, much of operations research in marketing problems is directed toward clarifying the interdependencies between marketing and other company operations. Finally, it draws on a range of techniques and analytical methods that are well beyond the scope of the usual marketing research.

Engineering. Again, the boundary between operations research and engineering is frequently unclear. Some examples may serve to draw it more definitively:

(1) During the last war a great deal of effort went into the improvement of the effectiveness and efficiency of depth charges. The objective of engineering and physics research was the construction of a depth charge having the strongest explosive power. Operations research, however, was concerned with the effective use of the depth charges then available for the purpose of sinking submarines.

(2) In a recent industrial situation, the engineering problem was to construct a new railway control system which would get control information quickly and clearly to the railway engineer. By contrast, the associated operations research problem was to determine whether increased speed and clarity of control information would help the train engineer in his task of getting the train to its destination safely and quickly.

(3) More subtle distinctions can be found in the study of equipment that tends to break down in operation, such as aircraft or chemical-process equipment. The engineering problem may be to find out why the equipment breaks down and how the breakdowns can be prevented. The operations research assignment is likely to be finding the best way to run the operation in view of available information on the relation between breakdown and use.

19

Industrial engineering. Perhaps the most difficult distinction to make is that between operations research and modern industrial engineering. The pioneers in the field of industrial engineering did work of a character which operations research analysts would be proud to claim for their field.

In modern practice, however, industrial engineers usually apply established methodologies to their problems. Moreover, their work is generally restricted in scope to manufacturing activities and, in some cases, to distribution operations. Equally important, industrial engineering is not commonly characterized by the mental discipline and techniques of analysis that are commonly associated with the physical scientist; operations research is.

Perhaps the most significant difference marking off operations research from other management services lies in the type of people employed. Operations research people are scientists, not experts. Their value is not in their knowledge or business experience but rather in their attitude and methodology. It is indicative of the influence which the physical sciences have exerted on the people in operations research that they have a self-conscious concern with concepts and first principles and show a desire to generalize from specific examples to all-encompassing theories.

In any event, the important point is that, far from supplanting or competing with other management services, operations research has been shown by experience to be particularly successful in those areas where other services are active and well developed. Indeed, one useful contribution of operations research is frequently that of integrating other information, of using the expert opinion and factual data provided by other services in an organized, comprehensive, and systematic analysis. A soundly organized operations research group should have available the services and counsel of experts in these fields for most effective joint attack on management problems.

For example, in the continuing research program of one retail store chain operation, marketing research methods are used to provide field observations, opinions, and data on the behavior of consumers.

The accounting organization provides information on costs and capital requirements.

In the operations research models these data are combined and interpreted to yield information on cost control, staff incentives, merchandise policies, and credit management.

Management Problems

The task of establishing operations research in an industrial organization may be broken down into the problems of choosing the initial area for investigation, selecting personnel to conduct the work, and developing organizational plans for future growth. These problems raise many difficult and important questions to which there are no sound answers applicable to all companies, but which must be answered by each firm with particular reference to its own circumstances and needs. However, certain helpful suggestions may be drawn from experience in industrial operations research to date.

There are two kinds of starting places: (a) trouble spots where conventional techniques have failed and management feels the need for additional help and a fresh attack; (b) areas deliberately chosen to test the value of operations research because of its possible contribution to the general success of the company, i.e., without particular reference to an immediately pressing problem.

There are certain common characteristics of suitable problems on which to begin operations research:

(1) There should be an opportunity for decision between alternative courses of action.

(2) There should be a real possibility for quantitative study and measurement. Thus, a preliminary study to provide bases for predicting the acceptance of fabric styles had to be quickly dropped in one case because of the inability to construct within a reasonable period an adequate quantitative description of the complexities of fabric, style, pattern, and color.

(3) It should be possible to collect data. In one case, analysis of accounts receivable for the previous two years yielded the key to a knotty marketing problem. But, in another case, a study of maintenance problems was found to be uneconomical because

21

of the lack of available records showing maintenance and breakdown histories on equipment.

(4) It should be possible to evaluate results readily. In other words, the problem should not be so large that it is indefinite; there should be some specific aspect which lends itself to solution. Neither the analyst nor the most enthusiastic executive can expect operations research activities to be supported on the basis of faith alone.

The final choice is best made in cooperation with the research team. Executives have found it useful to map out the general area in advance; the research group can then comment on those aspects which are most amenable to study, to clear formulation of the problem, and to likelihood of progress with reasonable effort. On this basis a specific problem can be selected which meets the requirements both of the executive (for importance and use) and of the research group (for suitability of existing data for quantitative study).

Much frustration and dissatisfaction can be avoided when the research team and the executives keep in mind each others' needs. The research team must formulate a sufficiently understandable statement of the problem and method of attack to provide the executives with confidence in giving support. The executives, in turn, must recognize that in research advance specifications for a detailed program including scope and goals are frequently difficult and usually meaningless; they must provide the group with access to the necessary data and people; and they must maintain contact with the work, guiding and redirecting it along the lines of greatest value as it develops.

Most reasonably large industrial organizations can either employ operations research people from the outside as needs arise or develop their own team within the company.

Operations research groups attached to reputable consulting research organizations are the principal reservoirs of trained personnel at the present time. There are several advantages in using such consultants. Management is not committed to anyone if it decides ultimately to discontinue the work. Frequently outsiders have been found to have the stature or prestige required to effect necessary changes in internal attitudes or policies. Moreover, they bring a fresh viewpoint to the operation studied, since they are not steeped in the existing internal experiences and conceptions. And they are not so likely to be diverted by pressing but less important day-to-day problems.

With respect to the disadvantages of consulting organizations, there is the matter of fees, though this factor is often overemphasized. Particularly for the smaller corporations, the cost of using a consulting group does not appear to be high relative to the cost of maintaining an internal group of equivalent experience, diversity, and training; professional people have high pay scales, and there is usually a heavy overhead for a group of this type. If the cost of using an outsider is higher at all, it is likely to result from the outsider's lack of acquaintance with the organization and its operations. It takes time to get indoctrinated, and the fees that are charged reflect this fact.

Another possible disadvantage is that regular employees may resent "outsider" investigators dipping into the internal operations of the company. Management can minimize this disadvantage, however, by choosing members of reputable consulting organizations who are trained to approach their work with integrity and tact.

The establishment of an internal operations research group is more feasible for medium-size or large corporations than for small ones. If the large company is able to find the right kind of trained and experienced people (not an easy task these days) and to support a professional group with the associated clerical and computing services, it may realize some definite long-run advantages. The internal group may ultimately become more efficient and less costly, providing an opportunity for closer contact, greater awareness of problems, and deeper acquaintance with management objectives and needs.

A compromise solution has been the use of an outside consulting group to initiate the work and thereafter to provide assistance in getting an internal group organized. This pattern is similar to that frequently followed in the past in physical research. It provides an opportunity for the company to try out operations research before it commits itself permanently and to avoid setting it up on a basis restricted to the thinking of the department in which the first problems studied happen to occur. It also enable the company to draw on the experience of the outside group for the education of its management and analytical personnel.

In decisions about operations research, as in the case of other important decisions, it is vitally important for management to think ahead about the future implications. This applies with particular force to the question of organization. When the operation research group is organized, what should be its status in the company?

Some analysts have argued that the operations research group should hold a high position, acting in a staff capacity and advising the chief executive. This argument is based on the need for the operations research group to obtain the viewpoint of the company as a whole and to be aware of the objectives of top management. Unfortunately, the same argument can be made with great force for large numbers of other groups and services in the organization. They are all competing for the time of the top executives, and not all of them can have it.

A sounder course is for operations research to start modestly, at a lower point within the organization; and, as it proves itself, to develop and grow to a more prominent position. This has been the common pattern in physical research, where the research group was originally assigned to a rather low level in the organization but where today, as a result of research having proved itself, the chief research executive has risen to the vice-presidential level.

But operations research does have certain minimal requirements with regard to its authority and status even at the outset. It must be established at least at a level where decisions can be made and where there is access to the executives and the data bearing on the problems under study. If successful, the group should be given an opportunity to expand the area of its studies as it proves its case; it should not be shut off or restricted to specific and limited operating areas. Furthermore, the group needs the interest and encouragement of top management if it is to achieve its maximum level of usefulness within the company.

If a company undertakes operations research, it should gene

ally do so with the intention of continuing and expanding its use. The investment in knowledge and methodology, no matter how low the initial cost, is too valuable to be thrown away. Experience has shown that the problems first recognized and attacked do not generally turn out to be the most productive ones the group could study. There needs to be full recognition of the fact that operations research is not well suited to sporadic, offhand use.

A company undertaking operations research should be prepared to face the costs, not only the direct costs of the professional group but also the cost in time of executives available to the group. These costs may loom especially large in executives' minds in years to come because the return is not always visible and apparent; while operations research should pay for itself many times over in the end, yet because of the very nature of the work the payoff of specific projects is bound to vary and there will be occasional failures.

Certainly, the operations research group, if it is to realize the full potential of its particular point of view, needs freedom to initiate some problems on its own, to investigate alternative methods, and to elaborate its theories. This means that, from the point of view of the executive, the group must be free to "waste time" on subjects of little immediate or even of doubtful ultimate practical value. The successful case histories in operations research prove that with confidence, freedom, executive support, experienced and capable people, and the appropriate climate and diet of problems, operations research will survive and flourish.

Evaluation

In perspective, what is the current status of operations research? What are its contributions, its limitations, its future?

Case histories show that operations research provides a basis for arriving at an integrated and objective analysis of operating problems. Characteristically, operations research tends to force an expansion in viewpoint and a more critical, questioning attitude. It also stimulates objective thinking, partly because it emphasizes broad purposes and partly because the mathematical nature of the model and techniques limits the influence of personal bias.

The results of operations research studies are quantitative. They

provide an opportunity for sound estimates in terms of require
ments, objectives, and goals, and a basis for more precise planning
and decision making.

The contributions of operations research to business analysi
and planning have been important and substantial. Here are tw
worth singling out:

*The application of organized thinking to data already existing
within the company*—Frequently a major contribution has bee
the location, collection, and classification of existing data scattere
through widely separated branches of the company. In one recen
study, an operations research team found the same fundamenta
problem cropping up under various guises in a number of differen
parts of the company. Each division or section had its own poin
of view toward the problem, and each had significant informatio
bearing on it that was unavailable to the others. This sort of thing
happens despite the most sound and progressive management
operations research tends to rectify it.

*The introduction of new concepts and new methods of analy
sis*—Some of these concepts, such as information theory, contro
theory, and certain aspects of statistical mechanics have bee
carried over from other fields; the physical sciences, and in par
ticular modern physics, have been a very fruitful source of trans
planted analytical techniques. But there are also certain origina
contributions, such as the newborn theories of clerical organiza
tion and consumer behavior, which suggest the possibility o
developing further tools for attacking important business prob
lems. All these techniques make it possible to explore the effects o
alternate courses of action before management becomes com
mitted to one of them.

Operations research is hardly a cure-all for every business ill
neither is it a source of automatic decisions. It is limited to th
study of tangible, measurable factors. The many important factor
affecting business decisions that remain intangible or qualitativ
must continue to be evaluated on the basis of executive judgmen
and intuition. Often they make it necessary to adjust or modify
the conclusions drawn from the quantitative analysis of the re
searchers. Professional personnel in operations research strongly

26

emphasize this distinction between the operations research responsibility for analysis and the executive responsibility for decision. They point with approval to cases like the following one.

In a recent series of conferences called to implement the results of a long and major operations research investigation, the analysts emphasized that their conclusions were based in part on the assumption that the output of a plant in question could be increased substantially at the existing level of efficiency. The executive responsible for the operation of the plant felt that this assumption was a sound one. The official responsible for the ultimate decision, however, decided to follow a more conservative course of action than the one indicated by the study, primarily because of his estimate of the psychological effect that increases in volume would have on the plant personnel.

The fact that operations research is scientific in character rather than expert means that more time is required to achieve useful conclusions than in the case of normal engineering analyses. As an applied science, the work is torn between two objectives: as "applied" it strives for practical and useful work; as "science" it seeks increasing understanding of the basic operation, even when the usefulness of this information is not immediately clear. The executive who plans to support research work of this character must be fairly warned of the need for restraint. The natural tendency to require that the studies or analyses be "practical" can, if enforced too rigidly, result in the loss of substantial benefits. Also, the results of studies of this type are necessarily somewhat speculative. When operations research is purchased, neither the specific program to be followed, the precise questions to be answered, nor the successful achievement of results can be guaranteed.

Recognition of this difference between operations research and more conventional engineering methods is essential to the satisfaction of both the controlling executive and the analyst.

Thinking ahead about the future of operations research, the principal internal problem which it faces is the development of a reserve of manpower adequately trained and motivated. There is a serious need at the present time for trained personnel to carry forward even the present limited level of activity. Lack of manpower, even now, threatens the quality of the work. The insufficient supply of adequately trained and experienced men to meet the demand can create a vacuum, drawing in poorly trained persons and making maintenance of standards difficult. The growing interest among mathematicians, physicists, and others is easing this problem somewhat, however, and colleges and universities have taken the first steps in training young men to fill the gap. The problem the academic institutions face is primarily lack of sound case material and the current amorphous state of a subject with uncertain acceptance in industry generally. Industrial support of educational efforts by providing realistic case material and opportunities for field investigations would be of tremendous help.

The most serious problem in external relationships is probably the need to develop efficient means for communicating ideas and results of research to executive users. The more experienced operations research groups have come to realize that explaining or "selling" conclusions is just as important as arriving at conclusions, if they are in fact to be useful. The communication needs are simple: in short, an ability to express clearly and concisely conclusions based on lengthy studies, to organize results in terms of interest to the reader and user, and to recognize that executives' interests are more practical than the researchers'.

If operations research is to have a future, the professional groups and research workers in the field must ultimately establish "operations research" as something more than a catchword, by proving its continued usefulness to management in the solution of important business problems. The ten-year-old Operations Research Society of America will help in establishing the name by circulating case histories and information on methodology among professional workers and, at least implicitly, by establishing professional standards of competence and ethics. It is to be hoped that the activities of the Society will be sufficiently publicized in business circles to acquaint business executives with the meaning, responsibilities, and standards of the professional operations research field.

There is, unfortunately, already evidence of growing attempt to capture the term, to subordinate it to other established fields in he general areas of statistics or engineering, and to apply it to the ctivities of operators on the fringes of the established and reputa-le management and engineering consulting fields. The growth of uch tendencies, if unchecked by education and publicity, may vell threaten to send the term "operations research" along the vay of others, like "efficiency engineering," which sooner or later ecame victims of undiscriminating acceptance and careless sage.

In conclusion, the future of operations research appears reason-bly bright at the present time. Successful applications in industry re fulfilling the hopes of its early supporters, and the skepticism f businessmen is tending to break down as successful case istories pile up and become available for publication.

The areas of potential application of operations research appear road. The future holds possible extensions such as the develop-ent of strategic concepts through the applications of the much eralded (but as yet largely untested) theory of games and by he development of a fundamental understanding of the impact of dvertising and merchandising methods.

How will operations research help in the future to clarify the ole of the executive? Present indications are that it will live up o its expectations of helping executives to make decisions more ntelligently, but the decisions will always remain to be made. he possibility of removing all subjective and qualitative factors ust be deemed at the present time to be more a hope than a real ossibility, and the construction of completely consistent and gical goals, while a reasonable objective in decision making, is robably unattainable. The balancing of the responsibilities to ociety, consumers, owners, and employees will therefore still be he fundamental task of executives.

2

MATHEMATICAL PROGRAMING:

Better Information for Better Decision Making

ALEXANDER HENDERSON AND ROBERT SCHLAIFER*

In recent years mathematicians have worked out a number of new procedures which make it possible for management to solve a wide variety of important company problems much faster, more easily, and more accurately than ever before. These procedures have sometimes been called "linear programing." Actually, linear programing describes only one group of them; "mathematical programing" is a more suitable title.

Mathematical programing is not just an improved way of getting certain jobs done. It is in every sense a new way. It is new in the sense that double-entry bookkeeping was new in the Middle Ages, or that mechanization in the office was new earlier in this century, or that automation in the plant is new today. Because mathematical programing is still new, the gap between the scientist and the businessman—between the researcher and the user—has not yet been bridged. Mathematical programing has made the news, but few businessmen really understand how it can be of use in their own companies.

* The authors wish to express their gratitude to Charles A. Bliss, W. W. Cooper and Abraham Charnes for their invaluable assistance in the preparation of this article.

30

This paper is an attempt to define mathematical programing for businessmen, describe what it means in practice, and show exactly how to use it to solve company problems. We have divided the paper into four sections.

Part I is addressed specifically to the top executive. Here are the salient points about mathematical programing which the man who makes company policy needs to know.

Part II is addressed to executives directly responsible for the organization and administration of operations where mathematical programing could be used and to the specialists who actually work out the problems. This part is based largely on case examples which are typical of the kinds of problems that can be handled.

Part III shows management how to use mathematical programing as a valuable planning tool. In many situations programing is the only practical way of obtaining certain cost and profit information that is essential in developing marketing policy, balancing productive equipment, making investment plans, and working out rational decisions on many other kinds of short-run and long-run problems.

In addition, to be used in connection with Part II, there is an appendix providing actual instructions for working through the most frequently useful, quick procedure for solving a common class of business problems.

Part I. Basic Principles

Production men usually have very little trouble in choosing which machine tool to use for a given operation when there is free time available on every tool in the plant. Traffic managers usually have little trouble in choosing which shipping route to use when they are able to supply each of their customers from the company's nearest plant. The manager of a refinery usually has little trouble in deciding what products to make when he has so much idle capacity that he can make all he can sell and more.

Except in the depths of depression, however, the problems facing management are usually not this simple. Any decision regarding any one problem affects not only that problem but many others as well. If an operation is assigned to the most suitable machine tool, some other operation on some other part will have to be performed on some other, less suitable tool. If customer A is supplied from the nearest plant, that plant will not have sufficient capacity to supply customer B, who also is closer to that plant than to any other. If the refinery manager makes all the 80-octane gasoline he can sell, he will not have capacity to satisfy the demand for 90-octane gasoline.

Business Programs

The general nature of all these problems is the same. *A group of limited resources must be shared among a number of competing demands, and all decisions are "interlocking" because they all have to be made under the common set of fixed limits.* In part, the limits are set by machine-tool capacity, plant capacity, raw materials, storage space, working capital, or any of the innumerable hard facts which prevent management from doing exactly as it pleases. In part, they are set by policies established by management itself.

When there are only a few possible courses of action—for example, when a company with only two plants wants to supply three or four customers at the lowest possible freight cost—any competent scheduler can quickly find the right answer. However, when the number of variables becomes larger—when a company has a dozen factories and 200 or 300 customers scattered all over the country—the man with the job of finding the best shipping pattern may well spend many days only to end up with a frustrated feeling; though he thinks he is close to the right answer, he is not at all sure that he has it. What is worse, he does not even know how far off he is, or whether it is worth spending still more time trying to improve his schedule. The production manager who has 20 or 30 different products to put through a machine shop containing 40 or 50 different machine tools may well give up as soon as he has found any schedule that will get out the required production, without even worrying whether some other schedule would get out the same product at a lower cost.

Under these conditions business may incur serious unnecessary costs because the best program is not discovered. Another kind of cost is often even more serious. The few direct tests which have been made so far show that intelligent and experienced men on the job often (though by no means always) come very close to the "best possible" solution of problems of this sort. But since problems of such complexity can almost never be handled by clerical personnel, even these good cut-and-try solutions are unsatisfactory because they take up a substantial amount of the time of supervisory employees or even executives.

The time of such men is the one thing that management cannot readily buy on the market. If it is all used up just in getting the necessary information, there is nothing left for the next step, making sound decisions. Often this produces a sort of inertia against any change in the status quo; it is so hard to find out the cost or profit implications of a proposed change or series of changes that management simply gives up and lets existing schedules and programs stand unchanged. Conversely, if better information were available more easily, management would be less tempted to drop important questions without investigation or could make better decisions as a result of investigation.

Many of these complex and time-consuming problems can in fact be solved today by mathematical programing. The purely routine procedures of which it is comprised can be safely entrusted to clerical personnel or to a mechanical computer. Such procedures have already been successfully applied to practical business problems, some of which will be described in the course of this article.

The word "mathematical" may be misleading. Actually the procedures go about solving problems in much the same way as the experienced man on the job. When such a man is faced by a problem with many interlocking aspects, he usually starts by finding a program that meets the minimum requirements regardless of cost or profit, and then tries out, one by one, various changes in this program that may reduce the cost or increase the profit. His skill and experience are required for two reasons: (a) to perceive the desirable changes and (b) to follow through the repercussions of a single change on all parts of the program.

What "mathematical" programing does is to reduce the whole procedure to a simple, definite routine. There is a rule for finding

33

a program to start with, there is a rule for finding the successive changes that will increase the profits or lower the costs, and there is a rule for following through all the repercussions of each change. What is more, it is absolutely certain that if these rules are followed, they will lead to the best possible program; and it will be perfectly clear when the best possible program has been found. It is because the procedure follows definite rules that it can be taught to clerical personnel or handed over to automatic computers.

Cost Information

Quick and inexpensive calculation of the best possible programs or schedules under a particular set of circumstances is not the only benefit which management can obtain from this technique. The same complex situation which makes it difficult to find the best possible schedule for the entire operation makes it difficult to get useful cost information concerning details of the operation. When every operation in the shop can be performed on the most suitable machine tool, the cost of any particular operation can be obtained by the usual methods of cost accounting. But if capacity is short, then the true cost of using a machine for one particular operation depends in a very real sense on the excess costs incurred because some other part has to be put on a less suitable machine.

To illustrate further, if the production of 80-octane gasoline is carried to a point where less 90-octane can be produced than can be sold, the profits which failed to be made on 90-octane must certainly be kept in mind when looking at the stated profits on the 80-octane.

Or when a company is supplying some (but not all) of its eastern customers by bringing in supplies from the West Coast, additional cost will be incurred by giving one of these customers quick delivery from a nearby plant, even though the actual freight rate from the nearby plant is lower than the rate from the West Coast.

Any time that the programing procedure will solve the basic problem of determining the most profitable over-all schedule, it will also produce usable cost information on parts of the whole operation. In many cases this information may be even more valuable than the basic schedule. It can help management decide where to expand plant capacity, where to push sales, and where to expend less effort, or what sorts of machine tools to buy on a limited capital budget. In the long run, sound decisions in matters of this sort will pay off much more substantially than the choice of the best shipping program in a single season or the best assignment of machine tools for a single month's production.

Limitations

Mathematical programing is not a patented cure-all which the businessman can buy for a fixed price and put into operation with no further thought. The principal limitations of the technique lie in three areas:

Cost or revenue proportional to volume—Problem-solving procedures have been well developed only for problems where the cost incurred or revenue produced by every possible activity is strictly proportional to the volume of that activity; these are the procedures that belong under the somewhat misleading title of linear programing. This limitation, however, is not so serious as it seems. Problems involving nonproportional costs or revenues can often be handled by linear programing through the use of special devices or by suitable approximations, and research is progressing on the development of procedures which will handle some of these problems directly.

Arithmetic capacity—Even when the procedure for solving a problem is perfectly well known, the solution may involve such a sheer quantity of arithmetic that it is beyond the capacity even of electronic computing machinery. However, the problem can sometimes be set up more simply so that solution is practical. For instance, careful analysis may show that the really essential variables are relatively few in number, or that the problem may be split into parts of manageable size.

Scheduling problems—A third limitation is often the most serious, particularly in the assignment of machine tools. So far very little has been accomplished toward the solution of scheduling problems, where certain operations must be performed before or after other operations. Mathematical programing can indicate, within the limits of available tool capacity, which operations should be performed on which tools, but the arrangement of these operations in the proper sequence must usually be handled as a

35

separate problem. Again, however, research is attempting to find procedures which will reduce even this problem to a straight-forward routine, and some progress in this direction has already been made.

Application

In Part II we describe a series of cases which should suggest to the reader the sort of problems where mathematical programing can be of use in his own business. Included are both actual cases and hypothetical examples. The hypothetical examples are purposely made so simple that they could be solved without the use of these procedures; in this way the reader can better see the essential nature of the analysis which programing will accomplish in more complex problems.

Top executives may want to turn a detailed reading of this section over to specialists, but they will find the major points as set forth below of practical interest. Very briefly, the discussion of case examples will show that mathematical programing can be used to decide:

Where to ship—Here the problem is to find the shipping program that will give the lowest freight costs. It has been demonstrated by the H. J. Heinz Company that linear programing can save thousands of dollars on a single scheduling problem alone. By virtue of its greater ease and accuracy, linear programing has also enabled the company to schedule on a monthly rather than quarterly basis, thus taking advantage of new information as soon as it becomes available.

Where to ship and where to produce—A complete program to determine the most economical program of production or procurement *and* freight costs can be developed so quickly and inexpensively that every possible alternative can be taken into account without throwing a heavy burden on senior personnel.

Where to ship, where to produce, and where to sell—Here the problem is further complicated. Such factors as a management policy regarding minimum supplies for dealers and a varying price schedule should and can be taken into account.

What the most profitable combination of price and volume is— At present mathematical programing can provide the answers only under certain conditions, but progress is being made in broadening its applicability.

What products to make—Problems that can be solved range from the most economical use of scarce raw materials to the most profitable mix in gasoline blending. If automatic computers are necessary because of the sheer bulk of arithmetic, the small or medium-size firm can turn to a central service bureau; the company does not have to be so large that it can afford its own computers.

What products to make and what processes to use—This problem arises when machine capacity is limited. Here mathematical programing may produce surprising results. For example, a certain amount of idle time on one machine may be necessary for the greatest production. Without mathematical programing, there is a real danger that personnel will use every machine all the time to satisfy management pressure, and thus defeat the company's real objective.

How to get lowest cost production—Here the problem is to determine the most economical production when the company can produce all it can sell. In these days of growing cost-consciousness, mathematical programing may become one of management's really valuable cost-reduction tools.

The businessman who recognizes or suspects that he has a problem which can be solved by mathematical programing will usually have to consult with specialists to learn how to use the technique. But an even greater responsibility will remain with the businessman himself. Like the introduction of a variable overhead budget, each application of mathematical programing will require careful study of the particular circumstances and problems of the company involved; and, once installed, the technique will pay off only in proportion to the understanding with which management makes use of it.

Part II. Examples of Operation

The case examples to be presented here illustrate some of the uses of mathematical programing. Although limited in number, the examples are so arranged that the reader who follows them

37

through in order should gain an understanding of the situations in which mathematical programing can and cannot be helpful and of how to set up any problem for accurate solution. The exhibits accompanying the text set forth the mathematical solution of the problems posed in the cases, while the appendix gives specific directions on how to work through a procedure for handling some of the problems that may arise in the reader's own business.

Where to Ship

As our first example of the uses of mathematical programing, let us look at a case where the technique was put to use as a routine operating procedure in an actual company.

The H. J. Heinz Company manufactures ketchup in half a dozen plants scattered across the United States from New Jersey to California and distributes this ketchup from about 70 warehouses located in all parts of the country.

In 1953 the company was in the fortunate position of being able to sell all it could produce, and supplies were allocated to warehouses in a total amount exactly equal to the total capacity of the plants. Management wished to supply these requirements at the lowest possible cost of freight; speed of shipment was not important. However, capacity in the West exceeded requirements in that part of the country, while the reverse was true in the East; for this reason a considerable tonnage had to be shipped from western plants to the East. In other words, the cost of freight could not be minimized by simply supplying each warehouse from the nearest plant.

This problem can immediately be recognized as a problem of programing because its essence is the minimization of cost subject to a fixed set of plant capacities and warehouse requirements. It can be handled by linear programing because the freight bill for shipments between any two points will be proportional to the quantity shipped. (The quantities involved are large enough so that virtually everything will move at carload rates under any shipping program which might be chosen.)

This is, in fact, the simplest possible kind of problem that can be solved by this method. Certain complexities which make solution by trial and error considerably more difficult than usual—in particular, the existence of water-competitive rates, which make it practical to send California ketchup all the way to the East Coast—add no real difficulty to the solution by linear programing. Given the list of plant capacities and warehouse requirements, plus a table of freight rates from every plant to every warehouse, one man with no equipment other than pencil and paper solved this problem for the first time in about 12 hours. After H. J. Heinz had adopted the method for regular use and clerks had been trained to become thoroughly familiar with the routine for this particular problem, the time required to develop a shipping program was considerably reduced.

The actual data of this problem have not been released by the company, but a fair representation of its magnitude is given by the similar but hypothetical examples of Exhibits I and II, which show the data and solution of a problem of supplying 20 warehouses from 12 plants.

Exhibit I shows the basic data: the body of the table gives the freight rates, while the daily capacities of the plants and daily requirements of the warehouses are in the margins. For example, factory III, with a capacity of 3,000 cwt. per day, can supply warehouse G, with requirements of 940 cwt. per day, at a freight cost of seven cents per cwt.

Any reader who wishes to try his hand will quickly find that without a systematic procedure a great deal of work would be required to find a shipping program which would come reasonably close to satisfying these requirements and capacities at the lowest possible cost. But with the use of linear programing the problem is even easier than the Heinz problem.

Exhibit II gives the lowest-cost distribution program. For example, warehouse K is to get 700 cwt. per day from factory I and 3,000 cwt. per day from factory III. On the other hand, factory III ships nothing to warehouse A, although Exhibit I shows that factory III could ship at less expense to this warehouse than to any other. (The "row values" and "column values" are cost information, the meaning of which is explained on p. 70.)

One of the most important advantages gained by the H. J. Heinz Company from the introduction of linear programing was

EXHIBIT I. TABLE OF RATES, REQUIREMENTS, AND CAPACITIES

Factory	I	II	III	IV	V	VI	VII	VIII	IX	X	XI	XII	Daily requirements (cwt.)
					Freight rates (cents per cwt.)								
Warehouse A	16	16	6	13	24	13	6	31	37	34	37	40	1,820
B	20	18	8	10	22	11	8	29	33	25	35	38	1,530
C	30	23	8	9	14	7	9	22	29	20	38	35	2,360
D	10	15	10	8	10	15	13	19	19	15	28	34	100
E	31	23	16	10	10	16	20	19	17	17	25	28	280
F	24	14	19	13	13	14	18	9	14	13	29	25	730
G	27	23	7	11	23	8	16	6	10	11	16	28	940
H	34	25	15	4	27	15	11	9	16	17	13	16	1,130
J	38	29	17	11	16	27	17	19	8	18	19	11	4,150
K	42	43	21	22	16	10	21	18	24	16	17	15	3,700
L	44	49	25	23	18	6	13	19	15	12	10	13	2,560
M	49	40	29	21	10	15	14	21	12	29	14	20	1,710
N	56	58	36	37	6	25	8	19	9	21	15	26	580
P	59	57	44	33	5	21	6	10	8	33	15	18	30
Q	68	54	40	38	8	24	7	19	10	23	23	23	2,840
R	66	71	47	43	16	33	12	26	19	20	25	31	1,510
S	72	58	50	51	20	42	22	16	15	13	20	21	970
T	74	54	57	55	26	53	26	19	14	7	15	6	5,110
U	71	75	57	60	30	44	30	30	41	8	23	37	3,540
Y	73	72	63	56	37	49	40	31	31	10	8	25	4,410
Daily capacity (cwt.)	10,000	9,000	3,000	2,700	500	1,200	700	300	500	1,200	2,000	8,900	40,000

EXHIBIT II. LOWEST-COST DISTRIBUTION PROGRAM (DAILY SHIPMENTS FROM FACTORY TO WAREHOUSE IN CWT.)

Factory	I	II	III	IV	V	VI	VII	VIII	IX	X	XI	XII	Total	Row value
Warehouse A	1,820												1,820	16
B	1,530												1,530	20
C		2,360											2,360	28
D	100												100	10
E		280											280	28
F		730											730	19
G	940												940	27
H				1,130									1,130	28
J		4,150											4,150	34
K	700		3,000										3,700	42
L	1,360					1,200							2,560	44
M		140		1,570									1,710	45
N	580												580	56
P								30					30	51
Q		1,340			500				500			500	2,840	59
R	810						700						1,510	66
S								90				880	970	57
T												5,110	5,110	42
U	2,160							180		1,200			3,540	71
Y											2,000	2,410	4,410	61
Total	10,000	9,000	3,000	2,700	500	1,200	700	300	500	1,200	2,000	8,900	40,000	
Column value	0	−5	−21	−24	−51	−38	−54	−41	−49	−63	−53	−36		

relief of the senior members of the distribution department from the burden of preparing shipping programs. Previously the quarterly preparation of the program took a substantial amount of their time; now they pay only as much attention to this problem as they believe necessary to keep the feel of the situation, while the detailed development of the program has been handed over to clerks. Freed from the burden of working out what is after all only glorified arithmetic, they have this much more time to devote to matters which really require their experience and judgment.

An equally important gain, in the opinion of these officials themselves, is the peace of mind which results from being sure that the program is the lowest-cost program possible.

The direct dollars-and-cents saving in the company's freight bill was large enough by itself to make the use of this technique very much worth while. The first shipping program produced by linear programing gave a projected semiannual freight cost several thousand dollars less than did a program prepared by the company's previous methods, and this comparison is far from giving a full measure of the actual freight savings to be anticipated.

Shipping schedules rest on estimates which are continuously subject to revision. The capacity figures in part represent actual stocks on hand at the plants, but in part they are based on estimates of future tomato crops; and the figures for requirements depend almost wholly on estimates of future sales. The fact that schedules are now quickly and accurately prepared by clerks has enabled the company to reschedule monthly rather than quarterly, thus making much better use of new information on crops and sales as it becomes available.

Furthermore, the risk of backhauling is very much reduced under the new system. It had always been company practice early in the season to hold "reserves" in regions of surplus production, in order to avoid the danger of shipping so much out of these regions that it became necessary to ship back into them when production and sales estimates were revised. In fact, these reserves were largely accidental leftovers: when it became really difficult to assign the last part of a factory's production, this remainder was called the reserve. Now the company can look at past history and lecide in advance what reserve should be held at each factory and can set up its program to suit this estimate exactly. Since the schedule is revised each month, these reserves can be altered in the light of current information until they are finally reduced to nothing just before the new pack starts at the factory in question.

Many important problems of this same character unquestionably are prevalent in business. One such case, for instance, would be that of a newsprint producer who supplies about 220 customers all over the United States from six factories scattered over the width of Canada.

Similar problems arise where the cost of transportation is measured in time rather than in money. In fact, the first efforts to solve problems of this sort systematically were made during World War II in order to minimize the time spent by ships in ballast. Specified cargo had to be moved from specified origins to specified destinations; there was usually no return cargo, and the problem was to decide to which port the ship should be sent in ballast to pick up its next cargo. An obviously similar problem is the routing of empty freight cars, and a trucker operating on a nationwide scale might face the same problem with empty trucks.

Where to Produce

When ketchup shipments were programed for the H. J. Heinz Company, factory capacities and warehouse requirements were fixed before the shipping program was worked out, and the only cost which could be reduced by programing was the cost of freight. Since management had decided in advance how much to produce at each plant, all production costs were "fixed" so far as the programing problem was concerned.

The same company faces a different problem in connection with another product, which is also produced in a number of plants and shipped to a number of warehouses. In this case, the capacity of the plants exceeds the requirements of the warehouses. The cost of production varies from one plant to another, and the problem is thus one of satisfying the requirements at the least *total* cost. It is as important to reduce the cost of production (by producing in the right place) as it is to reduce the cost of freight (by supplying from the right place). In other words, management

43

must now decide two questions instead of one: (a) How much is each factory to produce? (b) Which warehouses should be supplied by which factories?

It is tempting to try to solve these two problems one at a time and thus simplify the job, but in general it will not be possible to get the lowest total cost by first deciding where to produce and then deciding where to ship. It is obviously better to produce in a high-cost plant if the additional cost can be more than recovered through savings in freight.

This double problem can be handled by linear programing if we may assume (as businessmen usually do) that the cost of production at any one plant is the sum of a "fixed" cost independent of volume and a "variable" cost proportional to volume in total but fixed per unit, and if these costs are known. The variable cost is handled directly by the linear programing procedure, while the fixed part is handled by a method which will be explained later.

Actually, the problem can be much more complicated and still lend itself to solution by linear programing. For example, we can bring in the possibility of using overtime, or of buying raw materials at one price up to a certain quantity and at another price beyond that quantity. (Although there is no longer a constant proportion between production and variable cost, we can restore proportionality by a device described in the Appendix, p. 92.)

Exhibit III shows the cost information needed to solve a hypothetical example of this sort. It is assumed that there are only four plants and four warehouses, but any number could be brought into the problem.

In our first approximation (which we shall modify later) we shall assume that no plant will be closed down entirely and, therefore, that "fixed costs" are really fixed and can be left out of the picture. Like Exhibit I, Exhibit III shows the freight rates from each plant to each warehouse, the available daily capacity at each plant, and the daily requirements of each warehouse; it also shows the "variable" (fixed-per-unit) cost of normal production at each plant and the additional per-unit cost of overtime production. The total capacity is greater than the total requirements even if the factories work only normal time.

EXHIBIT III. COST INFORMATION FOR DOUBLE PROBLEM

| | A—Warehouse requirements (tons per day) | | | | |
Warehouse	A	B	C	D	Total
Requirements	90	140	75	100	405

| | B—Factory capacities (tons per day) | | | | |
Factory	I	II	III	IV	Total
Normal capacity	70	130	180	110	490
Additional capacity on overtime	25	40	60	30	155

| | C—Variable costs (per ton) | | | |
Factory	I	II	III	IV
Normal production cost	$30	$36	$24	$30
Overtime premium	15	18	12	15
Freight rates to:				
Warehouse A	$14	$ 9	$21	$18
B	20	14	27	24
C	18	12	29	20
D	19	15	27	23

On the basis of these data, the lowest-cost solution is given by part A of Exhibit IV. It is scarcely surprising that this solution calls for no use of overtime. So long as fixed costs are taken as really fixed, it turns out that it is best to use the entire normal capacity of factories I, II, and III, and to use 25 tons of factory IV's normal capacity of 110 tons per day. The remaining 85 tons of normal capacity at IV are left unused. The total variable cost under this schedule (freight cost plus variable production cost) will be $19,720 per day.

Presented with this result, management would certainly ask whether it is sensible to keep all four factories open when one of them is being left about 80% idle. Even without incurring overtime, factory I, the smallest plant, could be closed and the load redistributed among the other plants. If this is done, the lowest-cost distribution of the requirements among factories II, III, and IV is that given by part B of Exhibit IV. Under this program the

45

EXHIBIT IV. LOWEST-COST DISTRIBUTION PROGRAM (DAILY SHIPMENTS IN TONS FROM FACTORY TO WAREHOUSE)

Factory	A—With all four factories open				
	I	II	III	IV	Total
Warehouse A			90		90
B		80	60		140
C		50		25	75
D	70		30		100
Idle normal capacity				85	85
Total	70	130	180	110	490

Factory	B—With factory I closed			
	II	III	IV	Total
Warehouse A		90		90
B	130	10		140
C			75	75
D		80	20	100
Idle normal capacity			15	15
Total	130	180	110	420

Factory	C—With factory IV closed			
	I	II	III	Total
Warehouse A			90	90
B		55	85	140
C		75		75
D	70		30	100
Total	70	130	205	405

total variable cost would be $19,950 per day, or $230 per day more than under the program of Exhibit IV, A, which depended on the use of all four plants. If more than $230 per day of fixed costs can be saved by closing down factory I completely, it will pay to do so; otherwise it will not.

It might be still better, however, to close down some plant other than factory I even at the cost of a certain amount of overtime. In particular, a very little overtime production (25 tons per day) would make it possible to close factory IV. A person asked to look into this possibility might reason as follows: Under the shipping schedule of Exhibit IV, A, the only use of factory IV's capacity is to supply 25 tons per day to warehouse C. Looking at Exhibit III for a replacement for this supply, he would get the following information on costs per ton:

Factory	Normal Cost of production	Overtime premium	Freight to warehouse C	Total
I	$30	$15	$18	$63
II	36	18	12	66
III	24	12	29	65

Apparently the cheapest way of using overtime, if it is to be used at all, would be to produce the needed 25 tons per day at factory I and ship them to warehouse C at a total variable cost of $63 per ton. Under the program of Exhibit IV, A, with all plants in use, warehouse C was supplied from factory IV at a total variable cost of $30 for production plus $20 for freight, or a total of $50 per ton. The change would thus seem to add a total of $325 per day (25 tons times $13 per ton which is the difference between $63 and $50 per ton).

But, in fact, closing factory IV need not add this much to the cost of the program. If we take factory IV out of the picture and then program to find the best possible distribution of the output of the remaining plants, we discover that the program of part C of Exhibit IV satisfies all requirements at a total variable cost of $19,995 per day, or only $275 per day more than with all plants in use. The overtime is performed by factory III, which does not supply warehouse C at all.

This last result deserves the reader's attention. *Once a change was made in a single part of the program, the best adjustment was a general readjustment of the entire program.* But such a general readjustment is impractical unless complete programs can be developed quickly and at a reasonable cost. It is rarely clear in advance whether the work will prove profitable, and management does not want to throw a heavy burden of recalculation on senior personnel every time a minor change is made. Mathematical

47

programing avoids these difficulties. Even minor changes in the data can be made freely despite the fact that complete recalculations of the program are required, because the work can be done quickly and accurately by clerks or machines.

We can proceed to compute the lowest possible cost of supplying the requirements with factory II or factory III closed down completely. We can then summarize the results for all alternatives like this:

Total freight plus variable production cost

All four factories in use	$19,720
Factory I closed, no overtime	19,950
Factory II closed, overtime at factory III	20,515
Factory III closed, overtime at factories I, II, and IV	21,445
Factory IV closed, overtime at factory III	19,995

Management now has the information on variable costs which it needs in order to choose rationally among three alternatives: (1) operating all four plants with a large amount of idle normal capacity; (2) shutting down factory I and still having a little idle normal capacity; (3) shutting down factory II, III, or IV and incurring overtime. Its choice will depend in part on the extent to which fixed costs can be eliminated when a particular plant is completely closed; it may depend even more on company policies regarding community relations or some other nonfinancial consideration. Mathematical programing cannot replace judgment, but it can supply some of the factual information which management needs in order to make judgments.

Problems of this general type are met in purchasing as well as in producing and selling. A company which buys a standard raw material at many different geographical locations and ships it to a number of scattered plants for processing will wish to minimize the total cost of purchase plus freight; here the solution can be obtained in exactly the same way as just discussed. The Department of Defense is reported to have made substantial savings by using linear programing to decide where to buy and where to send certain standard articles which it obtains from a large number of suppliers for direct shipment to military installations.

Where to Sell

In our first case, we considered a situation where management had fixed the sales at each warehouse and the production at each plant before using programing to work out the best way of shipping from plant to warehouse. In the second example, management had fixed the sales at each warehouse in advance, but had left the decision on where and how much to produce to be made as a part of the program. Let us now consider a case in which sales are not fixed in advance, and management wants to determine where to sell, as well as where to produce and where to ship, in order to give the greatest possible profits.

Such a problem often arises when sales would exceed a company's capacity to produce unless demand were retarded by higher prices, yet management does not wish to raise prices because of the long-run competitive situation. Under these circumstances some system of allocating the product to branch warehouses in the different market areas (or to individual customers) will be necessary. One way of doing this is simply to sell wherever the greatest short-run profits can be made. Often, however, management will not want to take an exclusively short-run view and will want to provide each warehouse or customer with at least a certain minimum supply, with only the remainder over and above these minimum allocations being disposed of with a view to maximum short-run profits.

One additional complication will often be present in real problems of this sort. The selling price of the product may not be uniform nationally, but may vary from place to place or from customer to customer. In addition, there may well be present the complication we dealt with in the last example: it may be desirable to have some plants working overtime while others are working at only a part of their normal capacity or are even closed down entirely.

Thus a production and distribution program must be prepared which answers all the following questions in such a way as to give the greatest possible profits, subject to the requirement of supplying certain warehouses with at least a specified allocation of product:

49

(1) How much shall be produced at each plant?

(2) How much, if any, above the predetermined minimum shall be delivered to each warehouse?

(3) The above questions being answered, which plants shall supply which warehouses?

As in the previous example, all three questions must be answered simultaneously; it is not possible to work them out one by one. The problem can still be handled by linear programing, however, despite the additional complications which have entered the picture; in fact, it is no harder to solve than the previous problem. The only difference is that we now look directly at the profit resulting from supplying a particular warehouse from a particular plant, rather than looking at the costs involved. We shall not even work out an example, since the solution would appear in the same form as Exhibit IV of the previous case, while the required data would look the same as Exhibit III with the addition of the selling price at each warehouse.

Price, Volume, and Profit

In all the previous examples it was assumed that management had set selling prices before the production and distribution program was worked out. The quantity to be produced and shipped followed from the predetermined prices. This is certainly a common situation, but it is also very common for management to want to consider the effect of prices on volume before prices are set. This means, of course, that sales volume must be forecast at each of a variety of possible prices, and we assume that such forecasts have been made separately for each of the branch warehouses of our previous examples.

Under these conditions the problem can no longer be handled directly by linear programing, since the margin, or difference between the selling price at a particular warehouse and the variable cost of producing at a particular plant and shipping to that warehouse, is no longer in a constant ratio to the quantity produced and sold. As quantities go up, prices go down, and the ratio of total margin to quantity sold declines. Even so, we can still use linear programing to solve the problem quickly, accurately, and cheaply if there is to be a single national selling price. We can compute the best program for each proposed price, determine the total profits for each program, and select the most profitable alternative.

However, linear programing becomes virtually impossible if prices can vary from place to place and management wishes to set each local price in such a way as to obtain the greatest total profits. Even if there are only ten distribution points for which price-quantity forecasts have to be considered, and even if each branch manager submits forecasts for only five different prices, we would have to compute nearly 10 million different programs and then select the most profitable one.

In practical cases it will often prove possible with a reasonable amount of calculation to find a program which is probably the best program or very close to it, but in general the solution of this problem of mathematical programing, like many others, depends on further research to develop methods for attacking nonlinear problems directly. As mentioned, progress in this direction is already being made.

What and How to Produce

All the cases discussed so far have involved problems of where (as well as how much) to buy, sell, produce, and ship. Mathematical programing can be of equal use in deciding what and how to produce in order to maximize profits or minimize costs in the face of shortages of raw materials, machine tools, or other productive resources. Some problems of this kind may be solved by clerks using procedures such as those previously discussed; others, however, may require new procedures and automatic computing equipment.

A representative problem in the first category is the following one, which involves the selective use of scarce raw materials.

A manufacturer produces four products, A, B, C, and D, from a single raw material which can be bought in three different grades, I, II, and III. The cost of processing and the quantity of material required for one ton of end product vary according to the product and the grade of material used, as shown in Exhibit V.

EXHIBIT V. COSTS, AVAILABILITIES, AND PRICES

| | A—Yields and processing costs | | |
Grade	I	II	III
Product	Tons of material per ton of product		
A	1.20	1.80	2.00
B	1.50	2.25	2.50
C	1.50	2.25	2.50
D	1.80	2.70	3.00
	Processing cost per ton of product		
A	$18	$30	$ 42
B	30	60	69
C	57	63	66
D	54	81	126

| | B—Material cost and availability | | |
Grade	I	II	III
Normal price per ton	$48	$24	$18
Quantity available at normal price (tons)	100	150	250
Premium price per ton	$72	$36	$24
Quantity available at premium price (tons)	100	150	400

| | C—Product prices and sales potentials | | | |
Product	A	B	C	D
Price per ton	$96	$150	$135	$171
Potential sales (tons)	200	100	160	50

If unlimited supplies of each grade of material were available at a fixed market price, each product would be made from the grade for which the total purchasing-plus-processing cost was the smallest; but the amount of each grade obtainable at the "normal" price is limited as shown in the exhibit. Additional quantities of any grade can be obtained, but only at the premium shown.

The products are sold f.o.b. the manufacturer's single plant; the selling prices have already been set and are shown in the exhibit, together with the sales department's forecasts of the amount of each product which can be sold at these prices.

The problem, then, is to determine what products to make and how much of each, and how to make them—in other words, which grade of material to use for which products. The solution is shown in Exhibit VI.

EXHIBIT VI. MOST PROFITABLE PRODUCTION PROGRAM

	Tons of product		Tons of material used		
Product	Sales potential	Production	Grade I	Grade II	Grade III
A	200	200		210	167
B	100	100	100		83
C	160	160			400
D	50	0			
Total material usage			100	210	650
Bought at normal price			100	150	250
Bought at premium price			0	60	400

It will be remembered that, in discussing the use of mathematical programing by the H. J. Heinz Company, we emphasized the fact that shipping programs are produced by a clerk with nothing but paper and pencil in a very reasonable amount of time. This is true even though the existence of about six plants and 70 warehouses makes it necessary to choose 75 routes for actual use from the 420 possible routes which might be used. This ease of solution, even in cases where a very large number of variables is involved, applies to the selective use of raw materials just discussed as well as to the other problems taken up in earlier sections. They are all problems which can be solved by what is known as the "transportation-problem procedure."

By contrast, other problems usually require the use of high-speed computing machinery. They are problems requiring the use of what might be called the "general procedure." While the mathematics involved here is at the level of grade-school arithmetic, the sheer bulk of arithmetic required is very much greater than under the transportation procedure. This means that, unless a skilled mathematician finds some way of simplifying a particular problem, it will be impossible for clerks to obtain a solution by hand in a reasonable amount of time when the number of variables is such as will be encountered in most practical situations.

Whether a given problem can be solved by the transportation-problem procedure or will require the use of the general procedure does not depend on whether the problem actually involves transportation or not, but rather on the form of the data. The raw material problem discussed just above, for example, could be solved as a transportation problem because any product would require 50% more material if grade II was used instead of grade I, or 67% more if grade III was used instead of grade I. But if the inferiority of yield of the lower grades had varied depending on the particular end product, it would have been necessary to use the general procedure.

The fact that the general procedure usually requires an automatic computer by no means implies that this procedure can be profitably applied only by very large firms with computers of their own. Fortunately, all problems which call for the use of this procedure are mathematically the same, even though the physical and economic meaning of each problem may be completely different. And since they are mathematically the same, a machine at a central service bureau can be coded once and for all to carry out the general procedure for any problem up to a certain size. The machine can then be used to solve the varying problems of many different companies promptly and inexpensively. Such a service can already be purchased from at least one source by the hour, and the time required to solve a problem is usually surprisingly short.

Now let us turn to a case requiring the use of the general procedure.

Gasoline sold as an automobile or aviation fuel is ordinarily not the product of a single refining process but a blend of various refinery products with a certain amount of tetraethyl lead added. To a certain extent each of the various constituents requires peculiar refining facilities. Consequently, the management of a refinery may well be faced with the following problem: given a limited daily supply of each of various constituents, into what end-product fuels should they be blended to bring in the maximum profits? The problem is made additionally complicated by the fact that there is no single "recipe" for any particular end product. In general, the end product may be blended in any of a large number of different ways, provided only that certain performance specifications are met.

This is clearly a problem of programing, both because the use of a given constituent in one end product means that less is available for use in another, and also because the use of one constituent to produce a given kind of performance in a particular end product means that less of other constituents is needed to produce that performance in the end product. But is the problem linear? We must look a little more closely at the relation between the characteristics of the constituents and the characteristics of the resulting blends.

The two most important measures of the performance characteristics of a gasoline fuel are its performance number (PN), which is a development of the octane number and describes antiknock properties, and its vapor pressure (RVP), which indicates the volatility of the fuel. In the case of most high-grade aviation gasolines there are actually two PN's specified: the 1-c PN, which applies to lean mixture, and the 3-c PN, which applies to rich mixture. Each of the various constituents has its own RVP and PN.

The PN and RVP required in the end product are produced by proper blending of the constituents and by the addition of tetraethyl lead (TEL) to improve the PN. The amount of TEL which can be used in any fuel is limited for various reasons; and since TEL is often the cheapest way of obtaining the desired PN (particularly in the case of aviation fuels), it is a common practice to use the maximum permitted amount of this chemical.

It appears from the above that the problem will be linear provided that the RVP and PN of any end product are simply weighted averages of the RVP's and PN's of the various constituents (each PN being calculated for the predetermined amount of TEL to be used in the end product). While not perhaps strictly true as regards PN, this proposition is close enough to the truth to serve as the basis for ordinary blending calculations. Therefore the problem can be handled in a straightforward manner by linear programing.

A. Charnes, W. W. Cooper, and B. Mellon have applied linear programing to the choice of the most profitable mix in an actual refinery; and although they were forced to simplify the problem somewhat in order to do the computation with nothing but a desk calculator, the results of their calculations were of considerable interest to the company's management.[1]

The figures which Charnes, Cooper, and Mellon present to show the nature of the calculations, and which we use below, are of course largely disguised.

The refinery in question is considered as having available fixed daily supplies of one grade of each of four blending constituents: alkylate, catalytic-cracked gasoline, straight-run gasoline, and isopentane. The quantities available and the performance specifications are shown in Exhibit VII. These constituents can be blended into any of three different aviation gasolines, A, B, or C, the specifications and selling prices of which are also shown in Exhibit VII.

EXHIBIT VII. QUANTITIES AVAILABLE AND PERFORMANCE SPECIFICATIONS

A—Product specifications

Product	Maxi-mum RVP	Mini-mum 1-c PN	Mini-mum 3-c PN	Maximum TEL cc. per gal. of product	Price per bbl. of prod-uct	Cost of TEL per bbl. of product
Avgas A	7.0	80.0	—	0.5	$4.960	$0.051770
Avgas B	7.0	91.0	96.0	4.0	5.846	0.409416
Avgas C	7.0	100.0	130.0	4.0	6.451	0.409416
Automobile	—	—	—	3.0	4.830	0.281862

B—Constituent specifications

Constituent	Supply bbl. per day	RVP	1-c PN 0.5 cc. TEL	1-c PN 4.0 cc. TEL	3-c PN 4.0 cc. TEL
Alkylate	3,800	5.0	94.0	107.5	148.0
Catalytic	2,652	8.0	83.0	93.0	106.0
Straight-run	4,081	4.0	74.0	87.0	80.0
Isopentane	1,300	20.5	95.0	108.0	140.0

[1] "Blending Aviation Gasolines—A Study in Programming Interdependent Activities in an Integrated Oil Company," *Econometrica*, April 1952, p. 135.

Any supplies not used in one of these three aviation gasolines will be used in premium automobile fuel, the selling price of which likewise appears in the exhibit. Performance specifications for automobile fuel are not shown since this product will be composed primarily of constituents not included in this study; these constituents will be added in the proper proportions to give the desired performance specifications.

Management has decided to use the entire available supply of the constituents in one way or another. Their costs can therefore be neglected in selecting the blending program since they will be the same whatever program is chosen. The costs of blending itself are also about the same whatever end product is produced and can, therefore, be neglected in solving this problem, too. The only variable cost factor is the TEL (since some end products use more of this than others), and its cost per barrel of product is shown in Exhibit VII.

The solution of the problem is given in Exhibit VIII. In the actual case, however, precise determination of the most profitable blending program was not the result which was of most interest to the management concerned. After all, the company's experienced schedulers could, given sufficient time, arrive at programs as profitable or nearly as profitable as those derived by mathematical programing—although the tests which seemed to show this were perhaps unduly favorable to the traditional methods because the schedulers were given the results of the programing calculations in advance, and thus knew what they had to try to attain.

EXHIBIT VIII. MOST PROFITABLE PRODUCT MIX

Product	Total amount produced	Composed of these constituents:			
		Alkylate	Catalytic	Straight-run	Isopentane
Avgas A	0	0	0	0	0
Avgas B	5,513	0	2,625	2,555	333
Avgas C	6,207	3,800	27	1,526	854
Automobile	113	0	0	0	113
Total	11,833	3,800	2,652	4,081	1,300

57

The indirect results were what really impressed management. For one thing, just as in the case of the Heinz Company, it was clear that the time and effort of experienced personnel would be saved if the job were routinized by the use of mathematical programing. This, in turn, now made it practical to compute programs for a variety of requirements and assumptions not previously covered.

For instance, the most profitable product mix as shown in Exhibit VIII contains no avgas A. However, company policy called for the production of 500 bbl. per day of this product for goodwill reasons. When the problem was recomputed taking this factor into account, it was found that the most profitable mix containing the required 500 bbl. of avgas A yielded profits about $80,000 per year less than those resulting from the program of Exhibit VIII.

This loss was considerably higher than management had believed. Presumably the cost could have been computed with adequate accuracy by the company's schedulers, but *when such calculations are expensive in terms of the time of senior personnel, they simply do not get made.*

The field of gasoline refining is perhaps the one in which the most extensive work has been done in trying out actual applications of mathematical programing to practical operations. One interesting type of nonlinear programing has been tried on actual data in this field. The method has been called "concave" programing.

In our gasoline case, the problem could be solved by linear programing because it was assumed that the RVP and PN of any product would be a simple weighted average of the RVP's and PN's of the constituents, the PN's being calculated for a predetermined amount of TEL in the product. We have already suggested that under some conditions this assumption is not strictly true. Linear programing is particularly inapplicable when the problem involves the blending of automotive rather than high-grade aviation fuels. In such a case it is not at all clear in advance that it will be economical to use the maximum permitted amount of TEL, and PN is definitely not proportional to the amount of TEL in the fuel.

The procedures which have been developed to cope with situations like this have at least approximately solved the problem in a number of actual cases. The results show the most profitable amount of TEL to use in various end products as well as the most profitable way to blend the refinery stocks.

What Processes to Use

Some of the most perplexing problems of limited resources which management commonly faces do not concern materials but the productive capacity of the plant. A good example is the problem of choosing what products to make and what processes to use for manufacturing them when a shortage of machine capacity restricts production. The problem may arise because of a shortage of only a few types of machine in a shop which is otherwise adequately equipped. The SKF Company, for example, has reported savings of $100,000 a year through the use of scheduling techniques developed from linear programing.

Rather than describing the SKF application, however, let us take a hypothetical example which will give an opportunity to show one of the ways in which setup costs can be handled by mathematical programing. Setup costs cannot be handled directly by linear programing because they are not proportional to volume of production. However, they can be handled indirectly by the same means used to deal with the fixed costs that can be avoided by closing down a plant completely (see the case described under the heading Where to Produce).

Here is an illustrative situation. A machine shop has adequate machine-tool capacity except for three types of machine, I, II, and III. These machines are used (in conjunction with others) to make three products, A, B, and C. Each product can be made in a variety of ways. It is possible, for example, to reduce the amount of time required for grinding by closer machining, but this requires more machining time. To be specific, let us suppose that for each product there are three alternate operation sheets, which we shall call processes 1, 2, and 3.

If sufficient time were available on all machines, the most economical process would be chosen for each product individually, and the company would then make all it could sell of that product. But because of the shortage of capacity the process to be used for any one product must be chosen with regard to its effect on machine availability for the other two products, and the quantity to be produced must be calculated for all products together in such a way as to obtain the greatest profit from the total production of all products.

The demands of each process for each product on the three critical types of machine are shown in Exhibit IX; these are per-unit times (standards duly adjusted for efficiency). For example, if product B is produced by process 3, each unit will require 0.2 hour on a machine of type II and 1.0 hour on a machine of type III, but no time on type I. The weekly available machine hours are also shown in the exhibit, after deduction of estimated allowances for repair and maintenance, but with no deduction for setup.

Exhibit IX also shows the number of units of each product which must be produced each week to fill orders already accepted, together with the "margin" which will be realized on any additional units that can be produced. This margin is the selling price less all out-of-pocket costs of production except the costs of operating the machines being programed. Since these machines are the·"bottlenecks," they will be used full time or virtually full time in any case, and, therefore, the costs of operating them will be virtually the same regardless of the program chosen.

To solve the problem, we start by neglecting the setup times for the machines (shown in Exhibit IX) just as we first neglected fixed costs in deciding where to produce ketchup. We simply deduct a roughly estimated flat six hours from each of the weekly machine availabilities and then develop a program based on the assumption that any program would involve exactly six hours total setup time on each type of machine. We can subsequently adjust for the number and kind of setups actually called for by the program.

Exhibit X shows the program which would be the most profitable if this assumption concerning setup were true. It calls for the production of only the required 100 units per week of product A and 200 units of B, but it calls for 394 units of product C instead of just the required 300. In other words, the calculation indicates that the most profitable use which can be made of the available capacity after fulfilling contractual obligations is to produce product C.

Checking to see how much setup time is actually implied by

EXHIBIT IX. MACHINE-SHOP REQUIREMENTS

		A—Per-unit machine times		
Machine type		I	II	III
Product	Process	Machine hours per unit		
A	1	0.2	0.2	0.2
A	2	0.4	—	0.3
A	3	0.6	0.1	0.1
B	1	0.2	0.3	0.4
B	2	0.1	0.1	0.8
B	3	—	0.2	1.0
C	1	0.2	0.1	0.7
C	2	0.1	0.6	0.4
C	3	—	0.8	0.2

	B—Total Machine hours available per week		
Machine type	I	II	III
Hours	118	230	306

C—Product requirements and "margins"			
Product	A	B	C
Minimum units required per week	100	200	300
Margin per unit on additional production	$10	$20	$30

		D—Machine setup times		
Machine type		I	II	III
Product	Process	Machine hours per setup		
A	1	2.4	0.6	1.2
A	2	1.8	—	1.8
A	3	1.2	1.8	1.2
B	1	3.0	1.2	2.4
B	2	0.6	3.0	1.2
B	3	—	3.6	1.2
C	1	2.4	1.8	3.0
C	2	1.2	1.2	1.2
C	3	—	2.4	2.4

this program, we discover that it exceeds the six-hour estimate on all three types of machine (see the totals shown in the table under B, Exhibit X). We could adjust for this by simply reducing the available machine hours accordingly and then recalculating the program, but examination of the program of Exhibit X brings to light another fact of which we ought also to take account. This is the fact that only eight units per week of product A are to be manufactured by process 3.

EXHIBIT X. MOST PROFITABLE USE OF CAPACITY ASSUMING SIX HOURS SETUP PER MACHINE

		A—Program based on six hours setup per machine			
Machine type		I	II	III	Units produced
Product	Process	Productive machine hours			
A	1	18.4	18.4	18.4	92
A	3	4.8	0.8	0.8	8
B	1	40.0	60.0	80.0	200
C	1	48.8	24.4	170.8	244
C	3	—	120.0	30.0	150
	Total	112.0	223.6°	300.0	
		B—Actual setup times implied by program			
Machine type		I	II	III	
Product	Process	Hours of setup time			
A	1	2.4	0.6	1.2	
A	3	1.2	1.8	1.2	
B	1	3.0	1.2	2.4	
C	1	2.4	1.8	3.0	
C	3	—	2.4	2.4	
	Total	9.0	7.8	10.2	

° Discrepancy from 306.0 due to rounding of figures.

Since these are bottleneck machines, we do not really need a cost calculation to decide that it is wasteful to tie them up in setup for this almost negligible amount of production. (This decision can be checked, as will be shown shortly.) Therefore we eliminate process 3 for product A before adjusting the available machine hours for the amount of setup time actually required, and then recalculate the program, again excluding the unwanted process.

One of the more useful features of linear programing is the fact that the calculation need not be purely mechanical, but can always be controlled to agree with common sense.

The resulting revised program is shown in Exhibit XI, together

EXHIBIT XI. MOST PROFITABLE USE OF AVAILABLE CAPACITY

	A—Revised program based on actual setup requirements				
Machine type			I	II	III	
Product	Process		Machine hours			Units produced
A	1	setup	2.4	0.6	1.2	100
		run	20.0	20.0	20.0	
B	1	setup	3.0	1.2	2.4	200
		run	40.0	60.0	80.0	
C	1	setup	2.4	1.8	3.0	238
		run	47.6	23.8	166.6	
C	3	setup	—	2.4	2.4	150
		run	—	120.2	30.0	
	Idle time		2.6	—	—	
	Total		118.0	230.0	305.6°	

B—Additional margin which would be made possible
by one additional machine hour

Machine type	I	II	III
Margin	—	$27.80	$38.80

C—Loss of margin which would result from production
of one unit by processes other than those selected†

		Process	
Product	1	2	3
A	—	$(1.70)‡	$(6.40)‡
B	—	10.00	20.80
C	—	2.20	—

D—Loss of margin which would result from production
of one extra unit of product other than product C

Product	Loss
A	$3.30
B	3.00

° Discrepancy from 306.0 due to rounding of figures.

† This table gives the loss which would arise from the running time of the process in question. The loss due to setting up for the additional process can be calculated from the value of one machine hour shown in the previous table.

‡ Minus quantity.

with some related cost information which corresponds to the "row values" and "column values" of the ketchup problems. This information will be discussed more fully in Part III. For the moment we may observe that it confirms our decision to reject process 3 for product A. Use of this process for 8 units would save running time worth $51.20 ($8 \times \$6.40$) but would cost nearly $100 in setup (1.8 hours on a type II machine worth $27.80 per hour plus 1.2 hours on a type III machine worth $38.80 per hour).

We could at this point ask whether it might also be better to use only a single process for product C. Common sense tells us, however, that the production of product C by each of the two methods is large enough to make setup cost negligible, and again this can be confirmed by analysis of the by-product cost information and other data on the worksheets underlying Exhibit XI. However, the argument is a little more complex than the one concerning process 3 for product A and will not be given here.

The final program still calls for only the required amounts of products A and B; proper choice of processes for all products makes it possible to produce 88 units per week of product C above the minimum requirements. This figure of 88 units is not greatly different from the 94 units shown in the first-approximation program (Exhibit X). That program, despite the rough-and-ready assumption on which it was based, proved in fact to be a very good guide to the proper use of the available capacity, and only minor refinements were required to make it into the genuinely most profitable program. A more complex problem might, of course, call for several successive approximations instead of just two as in this simple case.

One significant feature of the final program is the fact that it calls for a certain amount of idle time on machines of type I. Any program which used this type of machine fully would produce less profit than the program of Exhibit XI. In one actual application of mathematical programing to a machine shop, a result of exactly this sort proved to be of very considerable practical importance. Without some kind of provable justification, personnel were extremely hesitant to include idle time in the program when management was pressing for all possible production. There is a real danger under such conditions that personnel will produce a program less efficient than is possible simply because they concentrate their efforts on discovering a program which uses all machines 100% of the time.

Lowest Cost Production

The last few examples have involved the problem of getting out the most profitable production when a company can produce less than it can sell. Mathematical programing can also be of value when the problem is one of getting out the required production at the lowest possible cost. Here is an interesting example.

One of the large meat packers has been using linear programing to find the least expensive way of producing a poultry feed with all the required nutritive values. All that is needed to solve such a problem is: a list of the essential nutrients (minerals, proteins, and so forth) with the amount of each which should be contained in a pound of feed; a list of the possible materials which could be used to produce the feed, with the price of each; and a table showing the amount of each nutrient contained in a pound of each possible constituent for the feed.[2]

This problem is obviously very similar to the avgas problem discussed above, except that here the object of the program is to supply a fixed output at lowest cost rather than to choose the output which will maximize revenue.

Exactly the same kind of problem can arise when there is more than a single end product involved.

For instance, the manager of a refinery might be faced with this kind of problem: Suppose that instead of having inadequate supplies, this manager has ample capacity to make all he can sell. As we have seen, each of the products which he sells can be blended in a variety of ways from intermediate products such as alkylates and catalytic-cracked gasolines, and each of these intermediate products can be produced out of various crudes in various proportions. The manager of the refinery must decide which crudes to buy and how they should be refined so as to produce the required end products at the lowest possible cost.

[2] The use of mathematical programing in connection with a variety of problems in farm economics is described in a number of articles in the *Journal of Farm Economics*, 1951, p. 299; 1953, pp. 471 and 823; 1954, p. 78.

Charnes, Cooper, and Mellon have shown that it is possible to use linear programing to solve a still more complex problem than this, bringing in, for example, the possibility of using imported as well as domestic crudes, and considering even such factors as taxes, customs duties, and the cost differences between chartered and company-owned tankers.

Programing can also assist in cost reduction in a machine shop when there is sufficient capacity to produce all that can be sold of every product; it can indicate how to produce each product by the most economical process. All that is required for a programing problem to exist is that the capacity of the company's best or most economical machines of a given type—for example, its highest-speed screw machine—be less than sufficient for the entire production requirements.

To illustrate, suppose that a manufacturer wants to produce specified quantities of five different screw-machine parts, A through E, and has available three different screw machines, I, II, and III. Any of the machines can produce any of the parts, but the rates of operation are different, as shown by the per-unit times in Exhibit XII. If machine II were slower than machine I by the same percentage on all parts, and the same were true of machine III, this problem would not require much thought for its solution, but when the inferiority of a machine depends on the particular part, linear programing is of use.

The hourly variable cost (direct labor, power, repair and main-

EXHIBIT XII. PRODUCTION RATES, REQUIREMENTS, AND COSTS

Machine	I	II	III	
Part	Per-unit machine time (minutes)			Average weekly production (units)
A	0.2	0.4	0.5	4,000
B	0.1	0.3	0.5	9,000
C	0.2	0.2	0.4	7,000
D	0.1	0.3	0.3	9,000
E	0.2	0.3	0.5	4,000
	Variable operating cost (per hour)			
	$12	$9	$9	

tenance, etc.) of operating each machine is shown in the exhibit, since the machines are not all bottlenecks and the whole point of the problem is to avoid operating costs insofar as possible. The exhibit also gives the required average production of each part on a weekly basis, though we shall assume that management can make each part in long runs and thereby reduce setup cost to a point where it may be neglected in determining the program. Setup, maintenance, and repairs we shall assume to be performed on Saturdays, and therefore we take each machine as being available 40 hours per week.

The lowest-cost program which will accomplish the required production is shown in Exhibit XIII together with the usual by-product cost information. As previously stated, the production shown in the exhibit is in terms of weekly averages; the actual length of individual runs can be determined subsequently, in the usual way in which economic lot sizes are determined.

EXHIBIT XIII. LOWEST-COST PROGRAM AND BY-PRODUCT COST PRODUCTION INFORMATION

	A—Lowest-cost machine assignments					
	First Alternative Program			Second Alternative Program		
Machine	I	II	III	I	II	III
Part	Average weekly minutes					
A	600		500	467		833
B	900			900		
C		1,400			1,400	
D	900			900		
E		1,000	333	133	1,000	
Idle time			1,567			1,567
Total	2,400	2,400	2,400	2,400	2,400	2,400

	B—Cost of one additional unit of product				
Part	A	B	C	D	E
Cost	$0.0750	$0.0375	$0.0500	$0.0375	$0.0750

	C—Value of one additional machine hour		
Machine		I	II	III
Value		$10.50	$7.50	$0.00

PART III. COST AND PROFIT INFORMATION

Determination of the most profitable program under a particular set of circumstances is by no means the only advantage which management can derive from the intelligent application of mathematical programing. In many situations the technique will be of equal or even greater value as the only practical way of obtaining certain cost and profit information that is essential for sound decisions on both short-run and long-run problems of many kinds.

Need for Programing

What kind of cost information will mathematical programing provide? The gasoline blending case described in Part II is a good example.

In that instance the management learned that the manufacture of avgas A was leading to a reduction of nearly $80,000 a year in profits, far more than had been believed. Now, "cost" in this sense—the difference between the profit which results from one course of action and the profit which would result from another course of action—is obviously a completely different thing from cost in the accounting sense. Information regarding this kind of cost cannot be provided by ordinary accounting procedures. In fact, mathematical programing is the only way to get it quickly and accurately when there are many possible combinations of the various factors involved.

In some situations the need for looking at the effect of a proposed action on over-all profits rather than at its accounting cost or profit is perfectly clear. In our gasoline blending case, management knew very well that money was being lost by the production of avgas A even though the accounts showed a profit; it was only the extent of the loss that was unknown. In other situations, by contrast, accounting cost is really misleading in arriving at a sound decision, and it is easy to overlook this fact. An example should help make this point clear.

It would seem to be plain common sense that the cost of freight to a particular warehouse is simply the freight bill which is paid on shipments to that warehouse. But management will do well to think twice before acting on the basis of this "common-sense" view.

Suppose that the sales manager of the company whose shipping program is given earlier in Exhibit II finds that it is becoming very difficult and expensive to sell the supply allocated to warehouse E, whereas sales could easily be increased at warehouse T. Selling price is the same at both localities and, because of competition, cannot readily be changed. On inquiry the sales manager finds that warehouse E is being supplied at a freight cost of 23 cents per cwt., whereas freight to warehouse T is only six cents per cwt. He proposes, therefore, that supplies and sales be diverted from E to T, thus increasing the company's profits by the freight saving of 17 cents per cwt. as well as reducing the cost of advertising and other selling expense.

The traffic manager will probably counter that the two warehouses are not being supplied from the same factory, and that if the supplies now being sent from factory II to warehouse E are shipped to warehouse T instead, freight costs will not fall to six cents per cwt., but will increase from the present 23 cents to 54 cents, making a loss of 31 cents per cwt.

Actually, neither of the two would be right. In the event that supplies are diverted from warehouse E to warehouse T, there will in fact be an extra freight cost rather than a saving. But if the change is properly programed (the supplies formerly sent from II to E should be sent to Q, which can then take less from XII, which in turn can then supply the additional amount to T), then the extra cost will be only 14 cents per cwt. It is this cost which management should compare with the estimated extra cost of selling at warehouse E.

The example just cited and the gasoline blending case are typical of the way in which mathematical programing can be used to calculate the cost or profit which results or will result from a management decision. Generally speaking, any program is determined in such a way as to produce the greatest possible profits under a certain set of fixed conditions. If management wishes to consider a change in any of these conditions, a new program can be computed and profits under the two sets of conditions can then be compared.

In some cases it is not even necessary to compute a new program to find the cost or profit which applies to a proposed decision. The computation of the original program itself yields as a free by-product the cost or profit which will result from certain changes in the conditions underlying the program, provided that these changes are not too great in extent. In the jargon of the economists, these by-product figures are "marginal" cost or profit rates. To illustrate:

For diversion of sales from warehouse E to warehouse T, the marginal cost is given immediately by comparison of the "row values" shown in Exhibit II for the two warehouses. The value for E is 28 cents per cwt., the value for T is 42 cents, and the extra cost is therefore 14 cents per cwt. (42–28). We can be sure at once that this will be the extra cost if only a single cwt. is diverted from one warehouse to the other, but in order to find the cost of a larger diversion we must study the program itself. If we do so, we will find that the marginal rate will hold in this case even if the entire supply now allocated to E is diverted to T. If, on the contrary, we were considering diversion from warehouse G to T, we would find that the marginal rate of 15 cents (42–27) would apply only to the first 180 cwt.

The "column values" of Exhibit II give similar information concerning the cost or saving which will result from shifting production from one plant to another. If production is increased at factory V and decreased at factory VI, there will be a savings of 13 cents per cwt. (—38–[—51]) up to a certain limit, and study of the program shows that this limit is again 180 cwt.

The costs shown in Exhibits XI and XIII are marginal rates of this same sort. In fact, such information could have been given in connection with all the programs developed in this paper.

Probably the most important use of the marginal rates is that they immediately give a minimum figure for the cost of a change which reduces profits, or a maximum figure for the profitability of a change which increases profits. For example, when the program of Exhibit XI shows that an additional hour on a machine of type III is worth $38.80, we can be sure that ten additional hours will be worth no more than $388, although they may be worth less. Inspection of the marginal costs can thus be of practical value in limiting the range of alternatives which are worth further investigation.

Uses of Information

Now let us turn to consider a number of examples of particular kinds of cost and profit information which can be obtained by mathematical programing and which will be of use in making management decisions.

The gasoline blending case was as good an illustration as possible of the use of mathematical programing to find the true profitability of a particular product, but the technology of gasoline blending is so complex that it is not easy to see why the answer comes out as it does. Since it is difficult to make intelligent use of a technique without really understanding how it operates, let us look for a moment at a much simpler example of the same kind of problem.

In the first case involving the assignment of machine tools in Part II, there was idle capacity available after meeting the contractual commitments (see Exhibit XIII). Suppose that, after this schedule has been worked out, a customer places an order for an additional 1,000 units of screw-machine part D. What will be the cost of filling this order?

Machine III is the only machine with idle capacity; and if the additional quantity of part D is made on that machine, it will cost $75 (500 minutes at $9 per hour). The most economical course of action, however, is to produce the additional 1,000 units of D on machine I, obtaining the required 100 minutes by taking 500 units of part A off this machine and putting them on machine III. If this is done, the accounting cost of the 1,000 units of D will be only $20 (100 minutes at $12 per hour), but the actual addition to total cost will be $37.50 (250 minutes at $9 per hour to make the 500 units of A on machine III). Thus the true cost of the additional 1,000 units of D will be $0.0375 each, the value shown in Exhibit XIII. Any price above the sum of this figure and the material cost of the part will make a contribution to fixed overhead.

The example of the diversion of sales from warehouse E to warehouse T previously discussed shows how programing can be used to determine which customers are the most profitable in a situation where the only difference among customers lies in the cost of freight. The question would be no harder to answer if some customers were supplied from plants with higher production costs than others. Actually, of course, there is very little difference between determining the profitability of a product and the profitability of a customer.

Cost and profit information calculated by mathematical programing can be of use to management in deciding what products to make, what prices to set, and where to expend selling effort. We wish to emphasize, however, that we are not proposing that management should build its entire marketing program on the basis of short-run profit considerations. Programing provides information; it does not provide answers to policy questions.

On learning that certain products or certain customers are relatively unprofitable under present conditions, it is up to management first of all to decide whether the situation is temporary or likely to continue for some time to come. This means that management should forecast future costs and future sales potentials under a variety of reasonable assumptions, and then calculate the profitability of the various products or markets under various combinations of these assumptions. It is here that mathematical programing will make its real contribution, since it is only when such calculations can be easily and cheaply carried out that management can afford to investigate a wide range of assumptions.

After such calculations have been made, management can decide to change prices, refuse certain orders, accept them at a short-run loss, or install new capacity of such a kind and at such places that the products or markets under consideration will become profitable.

Another kind of cost which it is often important to know is the cost of an improvement in the quality of product or service rendered to the customer. A similar problem arises when it is necessary to decide whether improved materials acquired at higher cost will increase revenues or reduce other costs sufficiently to justify their higher cost. Here are some illustrative cases:

1. *Cost of quick delivery*—According to the shipping program of Exhibit II, warehouse M is to be supplied partly from factory II at a cost of 40 cents per cwt. and partly from factory IV at 21 cents per cwt. Suppose that stocks are low at this warehouse and that the manager would like to obtain some supplies quickly from the nearest source, factory V. Since this is the nearest plant, the freight rate to warehouse M, ten cents per cwt., is naturally lower than the rates from the factories currently supplying the warehouse; but use of this shorter route will necessarily result in an increase in total cost, since the program as it stands gives the lowest possible total cost.

Programing shows immediately that the extra cost will be 16 cents per cwt. for the first 140 cwt. shipped to M from factory V. The higher cost applying to additional quantities could be readily calculated if it were needed.

2. *Choice of process in a machine shop*—In the case of the machine shop with limited total capacity, Exhibit XI showed that the most profitable course of action was to produce product B by the use of process 1. Suppose that while an adequate product results from this process, a better quality would result from the use of process 3. Would it be worth using this process in order to increase customer satisfaction, or could the price be increased sufficiently to recover a part of the additional cost?

The program of Exhibit XI shows immediately that the extra cost resulting from the use of process 3 for product B will be at least $20.80 per unit. The cost arises because use of this process instead of process 1 takes up capacity which is being used for the production of product C, each unit of which produces a "margin" of $30 per unit. Up to 128 units of B can be made by process 3 instead of process 1 at the cost of $20.80 per unit. If 128 units are made, the entire capacity of the shop will be used up in producing the contractual commitments for the three products, and further use of process 3 for product B will be impossible.

3. *Cost of antiknock rating*—In the gasoline refinery studied by Charnes, Cooper, and Mellon, antiknock ratings (PN's) were specified for avgas B and avgas C for both rich and lean mixture. During the study an interesting question was raised as to the additional cost entailed by the rich-mixture specification. It was found to amount to over $1,000 per day. In other words, profits could have been increased by that amount if only a lean-mixture rating had been required in the products. A little further calculation with their data produced the equally interesting result that the lean-mixture requirement on these two fuels was costing nothing; satisfaction of the rich-mixture requirement automatically produced oversatisfaction of the lean-mixture requirement.

4. *Value of improved materials*—Engineers of this same refinery suggested that if the volatility of the straight-run gasoline being used in blending could be reduced, it would be possible to produce a product mix with a considerably higher market value. Again, programing provided significant and accurate information. It was able to show that if the RVP of this stock could be reduced by one unit, from 4.0 to 3.0, the market value of the products could be increased by $84 per day. Thus, if the improved stock could be produced at an additional cost smaller than this, it would pay to do so; otherwise it would not.

Some of the most important decisions that management has to make are those which involve the choice of the most profitable ways in which to invest new capital. The choice is usually made by comparing the cost of each proposed investment with the increase of income that it will produce. When several of the proposed investments are for use in the same productive process, and when this process produces a variety of different products, it may be extremely difficult to determine the additional income that will result from any one investment or from any combination of investments without the use of a systematic computing technique.

Machine tools. Consider, for example, the machine-shop case described in Part II in which sales were limited by machine capacity. Under the program of Exhibit XI, all machines of type II and type III are loaded to capacity; and while there is idle time on machines of type I, it is very small in amount and actually exists only because it was unprofitable to set up to produce just eight units per week of product A by process 3. Under these conditions what would be the return on an investment in an additional machine of one of the three types? It will be enough to work out the answer to this question for just one of the three types as an example, assuming that management has forecast that present demand and present costs and prices will remain unchanged in the future.

Suppose that if the shop acquires one additional machine of type III, it would be available for 38 hours per week (one shift with allowance for down time). We simply calculate a new program for the same conditions as shown in Exhibit IX, except that we increase the available time on machines of type III from 300 to 338 hours. The resulting program shows a $960 per-week increase in "margin"—selling price less all costs of production except the costs on the bottleneck machines. (To find the additional income produced by the new machine, we would have to subtract the labor and overhead costs of operating the machine and the depreciation and other costs of owning it.)

The result is due to the fact that the additional machine will make it possible to produce 32 additional units of product C per week. Note that the $960 margin on 38 hours of use amounts to only $25.30 per hour, considerably less than the $38.80 shown in Exhibit XI. As more time is made available on machines of type III, the bottleneck on this type becomes relatively less important and the bottlenecks on the other two types become relatively more important.

Raw materials. Without actually working out examples, we can point to either the gasoline refinery or the hypothetical case on the selective use of raw materials (both in Part II) as two other situations where the profitability of investment would be very difficult to calculate without the use of mathematical programing. The refinery problem discussed above involved only the most profitable way in which to blend existing supplies of materials. Mathematical programing would readily show the additional sales revenue which could be obtained (at present prices) if the refinery were to enlarge its facilities for production of one or more of the blending stocks.

In the case on selective use of raw materials, the materials had to be purchased in the market; and, as shown in Exhibit VI, it proved unprofitable to produce product D because of the limited supplies of materials available at normal prices. Programing could readily show how much the company could afford to invest in a source of raw materials in order to obtain them at more reasonable cost.

Programing and forecasts. In the case of investment decisions even more than in the case of the other types of decisions previously discussed, the relevant data are not so much the facts of the immediate present as they are forecasts of conditions which will prevail in the future. An investment decision cannot be made rationally unless it is possible to explore its profitability under a variety of assumptions about future costs and markets.

It is already difficult enough to make the necessary forecasts; without the use of a systematic technique for calculation, full exploration of their implications is virtually impossible because of time, trouble, and expense. It is for this reason that it seems likely that mathematical programing may be of even greater value to management in the field of planning than in the field of immediate operating decisions.

As in the case of its other applications, however, mathematical programing is not a cure-all. Management can use it to great advantage in planning and policy making, but executives must first understand it correctly and be able to use it intelligently in combination with the other tools of forecasting and planning. The fate of mathematical programing, in other words, lies today in management's hands. The scientists, the inventors, have done their work; it is now up to the users.

APPENDIX. DIRECTIONS FOR SOLVING PROBLEMS BY A USEFUL SHORT PROCEDURE

There are several alternate procedures available for solving problems of linear programing. One of these will work in all cases but takes a long time to carry out—the "general procedure," which is discussed toward the end of this appendix. The others are relatively quick, but will work only in certain cases—e.g., the "profit-preference procedure" and the "transportation-problem procedure."

A very restricted class of problems can be solved by hand with remarkable ease through the use of the "profit-preference procedure." A good example of its use is the scheduling of two classes of machine tools which formed a bottleneck in the operations of one actual company. The example has been published, with clear instructions for carrying out the procedure.[3]

By far the most frequently useful of the shorter procedures is the one known as the "transportation-problem procedure."[4] As pointed out in the preceding text, it got this name because it was developed to determine lowest-cost shipping programs, but it can be used for problems not involving transportation (just as certain problems involving transportation cannot be solved by it). Because of its simplicity, we shall give full directions for its use, first working through a simple example and then giving some suggestions for reducing more complex problems to such a form that they can be solved in the same way.

Transportation-Problem Procedure

Our example consists of assigning the production of three plants to fill the requirements of four warehouses in such a way that the total cost of freight will be at a minimum. This example involves so few variables that it could be solved far more quickly by common sense than by the use of a formal procedure. The example is adequate, nevertheless, to explain the procedure, and the procedure can then be used to solve much larger problems that would be extremely difficult to solve by common sense. Furthermore, the procedure itself can be considerably short-cut once it is understood; some suggestions for doing that will be given.

[3] See A. Charnes, W. W. Cooper, and D. Farr, "Linear Programming and Profit Preference Scheduling for a Manufacturing Firm," *Journal of the Operations Research Society of America I*, May 1953, pp. 114–129. (The reader should be warned that errors have crept into tables III and IV of this publication.)

[4] This procedure was developed by G. B. Dantzig: see T. C. Koopmans, *Activity Analysis of Production and Allocation* (New York, John Wiley & Sons, Inc., 1951), pp. 359–373.

Table A gives the data for the problem: the freight rates from each plant to each warehouse, the capacity of each plant, and the requirements of each warehouse. Now let us go through the various steps of the solution.

TABLE A. RATES, REQUIREMENTS, AND CAPACITIES

Factory	I	II	III	
	Freight rates (dollars per ton)			Warehouse requirements (tons)
Warehouse A	1.05	.90	2.00	35
B	2.30	1.40	1.40	10
C	1.80	1.00	1.20	35
D	1.00	1.75	1.10	25
Factory capacity (tons)	5	60	40	105

Getting a starting program. We first get a shipping program which satisfies the fixed requirements and capacities, regardless of cost, by the following procedure. Take factory I and assign its 5 tons of capacity to warehouse A. Fill the remaining 30 tons of this warehouse's requirements from factory II. Then use 10 more tons of factory II's capacity to satisfy warehouse B, and assign its remaining 20 tons in partial satisfaction of warehouse C. Complete C's requirements from factory III, and use the remainder of III's capacity to satisfy warehouse D. This produces the starting program of Table B. The procedure could obviously be used to assign warehouses to factories in a problem of any size.

A starting program can be based on a guess at the best solution

TABLE B. INITIAL PROGRAM OF SHIPMENTS (TONS)

Factory	I	II	III	Total
Warehouse A	5	30		35
B		10		10
C		20	15	35
D			25	25
Total	5	60	40	105

rather than on the "blind" procedure described in the text; and if the guess is any good at all, subsequent calculation will be materially reduced. Start with any factory at all and use its capacity to fill the requirements of those warehouses which it seems most economical to assign to this factory. When that factory's capacity has been used up, take any other factory; first use its capacity to complete the requirements of the warehouse which was left only partially satisfied at the end of the previous step, and then go on to fill any other warehouses which it seems sensible to assign to the second factory.

The only rule which should not be neglected is to finish filling the requirements of one warehouse before going on to a new one. If the number of plants is greater than the number of warehouses, it is perfectly legitimate, however, to reverse the procedure. Start by assigning one warehouse to a series of plants, and, when the warehouse's requirements are filled, take the next warehouse, use it to absorb the leftover capacity of the last factory previously used, and then go on to new factories.

The easiest way to do the work is on paper ruled into squares; and in the following discussion reference is made to locations in the tables as "squares"; for example, the number located in row B and column III is said to be in square B III.

Row values and column values. Next build up a "cost table" by the following procedure:

(1) Fill in the actual freight rates, taken from Table A, for those routes which are actually in use in Table B. This produces Table C except for the "row values" and "column values."

(2) Fill in the "row values" and "column values" shown in Table C. To do this, assign an arbitrary row value to row A; we have chosen .00 for this value, but it might have been anything. Now under every square of row A which contains a rate, assign a column value (positive or negative) such that the sum of the row and column values equals the value in the table. In column 1 we put a column value of 1.05, since 1.05 + .00 gives the value 1.05 found in square A I; in column II we put a value of .90, since .90 + .00 gives the .90 in square A II.

(3) We have now assigned all the column values which we can assign on the basis of the row value for row A. We must next as-

sign additional row values on the basis of these column values. We therefore look for rows with no row value but containing rates in squares for which column values exist. We observe that rows B and C both have rates in column II, which has a column value of .90. The row value for row B must be set at .50, since .90 + .50 = 1.40, which is the rate in B II. By the same reasoning, we arrive at .10 as the row value for row C.

TABLE C. RATES FOR ROUTES USED IN TABLE B (DOLLARS PER TON)

Factory	I	II	III	Row value
Warehouse A	1.05	.90		.00
B		1.40		.50
C		1.00	1.20	.10
D			1.10	.00
Column value	1.05	.90	1.10	

(4) No further row values can be assigned, so we go back to assigning column values by looking for rates which now have a row value but no column value. We observe that there is a 1.20 in square C III, which has a row value of .10 but no column value. The column value must be 1.10 in order to have 1.10 + .10 = 1.20.

(5) Finally, we assign the one missing row value. In row D there is 1.10 in square D III, with a column value of 1.10 and no row value. The row value must be .00 if the total of the row and column values is to equal the value in the square.

This procedure of alternately assigning row and column values can always be extended to fill in the row and column values for any cost table provided that "degeneracy" is not present in the corresponding route table. Degeneracy will be explained and a method of dealing with it will be described subsequently. In the absence of degeneracy, inability to complete the row and column values, or the existence of contradictory evidence on row and column values, indicates that an error has been made either in drawing up the table of routes (Table B) or in putting down in the cost table (Table C) the rates which correspond to the routes in Table B. On the other hand, it is not essential to derive the row values in the order A, B, C, D and the column values in the order I, II, III; they may be derived in any order that is possible.

The cost table. We now proceed to make Table C into a complete cost table, Table D, by filling in all the blank squares with the total of the appropriate row and column values. For example, the 1.55 in square B I is the total of the row value for row B (.50) and the column value for column I (1.05). The figures thus derived are shown in Table D in roman type, whereas the figures taken from Table C and corresponding to routes actually in use (in Table B) are shown in italic type. (In practice, the cost table can be made up directly without actually filling in the row and column values.)

TABLE D. COSTS FOR ROUTES USED IN TABLE B (DOLLARS PER TON)

Factory	I	II	III	Row value
Warehouse A	*1.05*	.90	1.10	.00
B	1.55	*1.40*	1.60	.50
C	1.15	*1.00*	*1.20*	.10
D	1.05	.90	*1.10*	.00
Column value	1.05	.90	1.10	

Revising the program. We now have a complete set of tables: a rate table, a route table, and a "cost" table. We proceed to look for the best change to make in the route table in order to reduce the cost of freight. To find this change, we compare the cost table, Table D, with the rate table, Table A, looking for the square where the figure in Table D is larger than the corresponding figure in Table A by the greatest difference. This is square B III. The fact that Table D shows 1.60 while Table A shows 1.40 tells us (for reasons to be explained later) that if we make shipments from factory III to warehouse B, and make the proper adjustments in the rest of our program, we shall save 20 cents for every ton we can ship along this new route.

The next problem is to find out what adjustments will have to be made in the rest of the program and, thereby, to find out how much we can ship along the new route from III to B. To do this, we construct Table E by first copying Table B (in actual practice there would be no need to copy the table) and then going through the following procedure.

TABLE E. CHANGES TO BE MADE IN ROUTES OF TABLE B (TONS)

Factory	I	II	III	Total
Warehouse A	5°	30°		35
B		$10-x$	$+x$	10
C		$20+x$	$15-x$	35
D			25°	25
Total	5	60	40	105

(1) In the square B III write $+x$: this is the as yet unknown amount which will be shipped over the new route from III to B. We have now overloaded the capacity of factory III by the amount x, and must therefore decrease by x the amount which III is to supply to some other warehouse. When this is done, it will be necessary to supply this warehouse from some other factory, and so on.

(2) To locate the factories and warehouses which will not be affected, look through Table E and put a star beside any number which is the only number in either its row or its column, but remember that the x in B III counts as a number. This leads to putting a star beside the 5 in A I and the 25 in D III. Considering the starred numbers as nonexistent, look through the table again and put a star beside any numbers which are now left alone in their row or column owing to the elimination of the starred numbers in the previous step. This leads to putting a star beside the 30 in A II, since with the 5 in A I starred, A II is alone in its row.

Now look through the table again for additional numbers which have been left alone in their row or column. In this case we can find none, so the operation is complete; otherwise, we would continue eliminating until no more isolated numbers could be found.

(3) Having completed the foregoing procedure, we now make all required adjustments by changing the amount to be shipped along those routes which have not been eliminated by a star. (Once a little experience has been gained, the routes affected by a change can easily be found without first starring the routes not affected.) The $+x$ in B III overloads factory III, so write $-x$ beside the 15 in C III. Warehouse C is now short by x, so write $-x$

beside the 20 in C II. Factory II is now overloaded, so write $-x$ beside the 10 in B II. This last $-x$ balances the $+x$ in row B with which we started, so that the effect of using the new route has been completely adjusted for throughout the program.

(4) Since we shall save 20 cents for every ton we ship along the new route from III to B, we wish to divert as much tonnage as possible to this route. We therefore look at all the squares in which we have written $-x$ and discover that the smallest number with $-x$ beside it is the 10 in B II. This is the limit to the diversion, and therefore the value for the unknown x. We now produce Table F by subtracting 10 in Table E wherever $-x$ was written

TABLE F. FIRST REVISED PROGRAM OF SHIPMENTS (TONS)

Factory	I	II	III	Total
Warehouse A	5	30		35
B			10	10
C		30	5	35
D			25	25
Total	5	60	40	105

and adding 10 wherever $+x$ was written. This is our first revised program of shipments. By multiplying the shipments along each route by the rate for that route, the reader can check that the reduction in total freight cost has in fact been 20 cents per ton times the ten tons diverted to the new route.

Repeating the process. The rest of the solution proceeds by mere repetition of the process already followed for the first improvement in the program. We build up a new cost table, Table G, by first copying from Table A the rates for the routes used in Table F (these rates are shown in italic type in Table G), then calculating the row and column values, and then filling in the other squares (roman type). We next compare Table G with Table A square by square and find that the square with the largest difference in favor of G is D I (1.05 against 1.00). We therefore put $+x$ in D I of Table H, remove the "isolated" squares with stars, and then follow around a circuit with $+x$ and $-x$ as indicated. The square with the smallest number with a $-x$ beside it is A I, with a value of 5, and we therefore add or subtract 5 as indicated by $+x$ or $-x$ to produce Table J.

TABLE G. COSTS FOR ROUTES USED IN TABLE F (DOLLARS PER TON)

Factory	I	II	III	Row value
Warehouse A	1.05	.90	1.10	.00
B	1.35	1.20	1.40	.30
C	1.15	1.00	1.20	.10
D	1.05	.90	1.10	.00
Column value	1.05	.90	1.10	

TABLE H. CHANGES TO BE MADE IN TABLE F (TONS)

Factory	I	II	III	Total
Warehouse A	$5-x$	$30+x$		35
B			10°	10
C		$30-x$	$5+x$	35
D	$+x$		$25-x$	25
Total	5	60	40	105

TABLE J. SECOND REVISED PROGRAM OF SHIPMENTS (TONS)

Factory	I	II	III	Total
Warehouse A		35		35
B			10	10
C		25	10	35
D	5		20	25
Total	5	60	40	105

TABLE K. COSTS FOR ROUTES USED IN TABLE J (DOLLARS PER TON)

Factory	I	II	III	Row value
Warehouse A	1.00	.90	1.10	.00
B	1.30	1.20	1.40	.30
C	1.10	1.00	1.20	.10
D	1.00	.90	1.10	.00
Column value	1.00	.90	1.10	

From Table J we make up a new cost table, Table K. Comparing Table K with Table A, we find that every lightface figure in Table K is smaller than the corresponding figure in Table A. There is no further improvement that can be made; in fact, any change made in the program of Table J would result in an increase in the cost of freight. Had there been squares where the figure in roman type in Table K was just equal to the rate in Table A, this would have indicated a route which could be used without either raising or lowering the total cost of freight.

Why the procedure works. To see why this method works, consider the map shown in Chart A. This map corresponds to the shipping program shown in Table B, with a solid line joining every factory to every warehouse where shipments are to be made. Beside each line is shown the tonnage moving along the route together with the freight rate applying to that route according to Table A. The map also shows a dotted line from factory III to warehouse B, corresponding to the x which we put in square B III in Table E.

CHART A. MAP OF ROUTES USED IN TABLE B

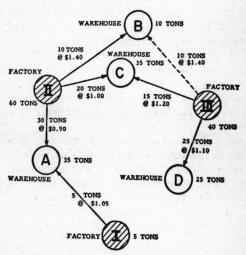

85

Now suppose that we ship x tons from factory III to warehouse B. Every ton that we ship will cost $1.40, the rate between these two points. But for every ton which B gets from III, one less ton from II will be needed, thereby saving $1.40 of freight. Factory III, on the other hand, cannot now supply both C and D as before, whereas factory II now has an excess. The simplest solution is to have III ship less to C, thus saving $1.20 per ton, while II makes up the deficit at a freight cost of $1.00 per ton. The net effect is a saving of 20 cents per ton, even though the shipments from III to B cost just as much as the previous shipments from II to B.

This saving of 20 cents per ton is exactly the difference between the $1.60 in square B III of Table D and the $1.40 in the same square of Table A. This is true in general; the figures in roman type in a "cost table" show the net savings on other routes which can be made by readjusting the program if direct shipments are made along the route in question. In other words, the figures in roman type show the cost of "not using" a route; the cost of using the route is, of course, simply the freight rate as shown in Table A.

The best possible program has not been reached until there is no unused route for which the cost of "using" is less than the cost of "not using." To be sure, at any stage in the process of arriving at a best program there may be more than one route for which the cost of not using is higher than the cost of using. We have given the rule of making the change by introducing the route for which the difference between the two costs is greatest. This rule is not necessary, but it is commonly believed that use of this rule will usually reduce the number of steps required to arrive at the best possible program.

Any program is a best possible program if there is no unused route for which the cost of using is less than the cost of not using. This is a rather important fact, since it means that a solution can be checked by simply building up the corresponding cost table. There is no need to check over the work which produced the solution. Furthermore, if there is an error in the solution, it is a waste of time to go back to find it; everything will come out all right if you simply go on making successive changes until the best possible program emerges. This is an additional reason why the transportation-problem procedure is really suited for hand computation while the general procedure is not; there is a reasonably simple check on the accuracy of the final solution obtained by the general procedure, but correction of any errors that may be present is far more difficult.

The map also shows why we arrived at the value 10 for the x in Table E. If we make direct shipments from III to B, we must reduce shipments from II to B and from III to C. We cannot reduce either of these below zero. The route from II to B carries the smaller traffic, 10 tons, and therefore 10 tons is the largest amount we can ship from III to B. Table E has $-x$ beside each route that will be reduced as a result of the change, and a $+x$ beside each route that will be increased. The routes which are starred in Table E are the routes which are not in the "circuit" III–B–II–C–III.

In some cases adjustments could be made which would give a greater saving per ton or make possible diversion of more tons than will result from the use of the rules given above. It is perfectly permissible to make more general changes in the program at any stage provided that they are made in accordance with the rule previously for starting the program. On the other hand, such general adjustments are never necessary, since it is absolutely certain that the step-at-a-time method described above will ultimately lead to the best possible program.

Coping with degeneracy. The procedure just described serves to solve any "transportation" problem of any size except when degeneracy appears in a route table at some stage in the solution of the problem.

A route table is degenerate if it can be divided into two or more parts each of which contains a group of factories whose combined capacity exactly satisfies the combined requirements of the warehouses assigned to them. Table L gives an example of such a situation which might have arisen in solving the example we have just worked out. Warehouses A and D exactly use up the capacity of factory II, while warehouses B and C exactly use up the capacity of factories I and III. Under such circumstances the procedure breaks down because it is impossible to build up the cost table corresponding to a degenerate route table; that is, in this instance, the cost table corresponding to Table L.

TABLE L. PROGRAM OF SHIPMENTS WHICH MIGHT HAVE OCCURRED BEFORE REACHING SOLUTION

Factory	I	II	III	Total
Warehouse A		35		35
B	5		5	10
C			35	35
D		25		25
Total	5	60	40	105

The following simple device will take care of this difficulty: If the number of plants is smaller than the number of warehouses, divide one unit of shipment by twice the number of plants. (If shipments are to be measured to the tenth of a ton, for example, we divide $\frac{1}{10}$ ton, not one ton, by twice the number of plants.) Take any convenient number which is smaller than this quotient and add it to the capacity of each of the plants; add the same total amount to the capacity of any one warehouse. If the number of warehouses is less than the number of plants, then reverse the rule.

In either case, solve the problem as if the additional quantities were real parts of the requirements and capacities; then when the problem has been solved, round all numbers containing fractions to the nearest unit of shipment. (A route carrying less than one-half unit is rounded to zero.) *The solution thus obtained is not approximate; it is exact.*

When to Use

In its original application, as illustrated in the example worked through above, the transportation problem consists of assigning a set of sources to a set of destinations in such a way that the total cost of transportation from sources to destinations will be a minimum. The capacity of each individual source and the requirements of each individual destination are fixed in advance, and the total capacity equals the total requirements. A unit of requirements at any destination can be filled by the use of a unit of capacity at any source, and only the cost of freight varies according to which particular source is used.

This can easily be generalized as a problem of assigning a set of inputs of any nature whatever to a set of outputs of any nature whatever in such a way that the total cost of conversion is a minimum. The inputs might be the available supplies of various raw materials, for example, rather than the capacities of various factories, while the outputs might be the quantities produced of various products rather than the quantities of a single product shipped to various warehouses.

There is no real change when the problem is one of maximizing profits rather than minimizing costs. Instead of a "rate table" giving the cost of converting one unit of any input into one unit of any output, we have a "margin table" giving the margin which will be realized by such conversion, the margin being the revenue from selling the unit of output less the variable costs of producing it. The program is developed in exactly the same way as in the example worked through above, except that new "routes" are introduced when the margin from not using the route is less than the margin from using it, rather than when the cost of not using it is higher than the cost of using it.

The formal characteristics which a problem must have if it is to be solved by the transportation procedure are the following:

(1) One unit of any input can be used to produce one unit of any output.

(2) The cost or margin which will result from conversion of one unit of a particular input into one unit of a particular output can be expressed by a single figure regardless of the number of units converted.

(3) The quantity of each individual input and output is fixed in advance, and the total of the inputs equals the total of the outputs.

If a problem cannot be put into the form specified by these three characteristics, it cannot be solved by the transportation procedure. However, these are formal characteristics, and it is often possible to find devices or tricks which will put a problem into this form even though at first glance it seems quite different. It is impossible to give a complete list of such devices, but we shall describe here the more common ones, which make it possible to solve by the transportation procedure all the problems discussed on pages 37–51.

Inputs and outputs not fixed in advance. In many problems all that we know in advance is how much of a given input is available or how much of a given output could be sold. We wish the program to determine how much of each it will be profitable to use or make. This violates the third requirement stated above, but the difficulty is easily overcome by the introduction of "dummy" inputs and outputs.

If, for example, total factory capacity exceeds total warehouse requirements, we create a dummy warehouse and treat it exactly as if it were real. The cost or profit which will result from supplying a unit to the dummy warehouse from any factory is set down in the rate table as zero, and the requirements of the dummy warehouse are set equal to the difference between total capacity and total real requirements. That part of any factory's capacity which the final program assigns to the dummy warehouse is capacity which is actually to be left idle.

If total potential output exceeds total available input, we create a dummy input equal to the difference between the two. The cost or margin resulting from supplying a unit of output from the dummy input is set at zero in the cost or margin table; where the final program calls for producing all or a part of some output from the dummy input, that amount of this potential output is not really to be produced at all.

In a case such as that described in Part II under the heading Where to Sell, it is possible that potential inputs may be left unused at the same time that potential outputs are left unfilled. This calls for the use of both a dummy input and a dummy output. Since neither the total amount of real inputs which will be used nor the total amount of real outputs which will be produced is known until the program has been computed, the quantity of the dummy input must be set equal to or greater than the total of the potential real outputs, and the amount of the dummy output must be set equal to or greater than the total of the potential real inputs. With this proviso, the quantities assigned to the dummies are arbitrary, except that the total of the real plus dummy inputs must equal the total of the real plus dummy outputs. The final program will show a certain amount of dummy output to be supplied from the dummy input, but this figure has no real meaning whatever and should be disregarded.

Inputs and outputs at varying prices. It may be that a factory can supply a certain amount of product at one cost and an additional amount at a higher cost (for example, by the use of overtime), or that a certain amount of a material can be obtained at one price and additional quantities at higher prices. Similarly it may be possible to sell a certain amount of product at one price and additional amounts only at lower prices. All such cases are handled by treating the input at each cost as a separate input, or the output at each price as a separate output. In this way we can still produce a cost or margin table which shows a single unchanging per-unit cost or margin for converting any particular input into any particular output.

Note that this method will not work if the price at which the entire output is sold depends on the quantity sold. As pointed out in Part II under the heading Price, Volume, and Profit, this is not a problem of linear programing.

Impossible processes. The first formal requirement set forth above demands that one unit of any output be producible from one unit of any input. In some cases particular input-output combinations may be completely or practically impossible. For example, freight service uniting a particular factory with a particular warehouse may be so poor that management will in no case permit its use, or it may be simply impossible to make a particular product from a particular material. This situation causes no difficulty at all in the solution of the problem, since all we need to do is to assign a fictitious, extremely high "cost" to the conversion of this input into output. In this way we can be sure that the unwanted process will not appear in the final solution.

Artificial units. In other problems, the amount of output which can be obtained from a unit of input depends on the particular output and input in question. In problems involving the selective use of raw materials, for example, the yield of any material may depend on the product, and the amount of material required for a particular product may depend on which material is used. Usually such problems cannot be solved by the transportation procedure, but in some cases the data can be reduced to such a form that they can.

This was true in the first raw-material problem discussed above. The trick here was to express each output not in terms of the quantity of product but in terms of the amount of grade I material which would be required to produce it, and to express the inputs of grade II and grade III material in terms of the amount of grade I material which they could replace. This made it necessary, of course, to make corresponding changes in the per-unit purchase cost of grades II and III material and in all per-unit processing costs. Table M shows the form to which Exhibit V had to be reduced before computing the program of Exhibit VI.

The reason why the subsequent cases discussed above could not be solved by the transportation procedure should now be clear. If the raw-material problem were changed so that the inferiority in yield of the lower-grade materials varied from product to product, it would no longer be possible to express these inputs in such a way that one unit of any input could produce one unit of any output. In the machine-shop problems, the amount of time on one machine which could be replaced by one hour on another varied according to the product and the process being used. The avgas problem is still more complex, since a single unit of any output is blended from several inputs.

Such are the problems which call for the use of the general procedure.

The General Procedure

"Simplex method" is the technical name for the general procedure. Actually there are two slightly different versions. The original version[5] will really work well only for rather small problems

[5] See A. Charnes, W. W. Cooper, and A. Henderson, *An Introduction to Linear Programming* (New York, John Wiley & Sons, Inc., 1953).

TABLE M. MARGINS, SALES POTENTIALS, AND AVAILABILITIES

Product	A	B	C	D	Quantity available (equivalent tons)
Material	Margin per equivalent ton				
I at $48/ton	$ 17	$ 32	$ 4	$ 17	100
I at $72/ton	(7)°	8	(20)°	(7)°	100
II at $24/ton	19	24	12	14	100
II at $36/ton	1	6	(6)°	(4)°	100
III at $18/ton	15	24	16 †	(5)°	150
III at $24/ton	5	14	6	(15)°	250
Potential sales (equivalent tons)	240	150	240	90	

° Minus quantity.

† *Derivation for product C and grade III material at normal price.* As shown by the yield table (Exhibit V), 2.5 tons of III replace 1.5 tons of I, so that 1 ton of III = .6 equivalent tons. As shown by the same table, 1.5 tons of I are required to produce 1 ton of C, so that 1 ton of C = 1.5 equivalent tons.

Material available: 250 tons, or $.6 \times 250 = 150$ equivalent tons.

Sales potential: 160 tons, or $1.5 \times 160 = 240$ equivalent tons.

Product price: $135 per ton, or $135/1.5 = $90 per equivalent ton.

Processing cost: $66 per ton of product, or $66/1.5 = $44 per equivalent ton.

Material cost: $18 per ton, or $18/.6 = $30 per equivalent ton.

Margin: $90 (selling price) — $44 (processing cost) — $30 (material cost) = $16 per equivalent ton.

because of the way in which rounding errors build up from step to step. Machine computation of large problems is better carried out by the modified method of Charnes and Lemke.[6]

The general procedure can be worked by hand with the aid of a desk calculator when the number of variables is small, as in the examples discussed in the main text. However, it requires the use of automatic computers in most practical problems owing not to the difficulty but to the sheer quantity of arithmetic involved. Even the simplified avgas problem discussed above required several days of hand computation to solve by the general procedure, while the answer to a problem with twice as many blending stocks and twice as many end products could be obtained in an hour or less on a good electronic computer.

There are still certain limitations on the size of problem which

[6] See *Proceedings of the Association for Computing Machinery* (Pittsburgh, Richard Rimbach Associates, 1952), pp. 97–98.

can be handled on existing computers with existing codes of instructions, and some problems which can be solved may cost too much time or money to be worth solving. In many cases, nevertheless, skilled mathematical analysis of a very large problem will show that it can be simplified or broken into manageable parts.

Some problems will undoubtedly remain intractable, but until many more practical applications have been made, it will not really be known whether this will prove to be a frequent obstacle or a very rare one. It should be remembered that rapid progress is being made both in mathematical research and in the design of computers and computing codes. If business finds that it is important to solve problems of linear programing, it seems almost certain that means will be found of solving the great majority of the problems that occur.

3

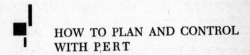

HOW TO PLAN AND CONTROL
WITH PERT

ROBERT W. MILLER

The last three years have seen the explosive growth of a new family of planning and control techniques adapted to the Space Age. Much of the development work has been done in the defense industry, but the construction, chemical, and other industries have played an important part in the story, too.

In this paper we shall consider what is perhaps the best known of all of the new techniques, Program Evaluation Review Technique. In particular, we shall look at the following features of PERT.

PERT's basic requirements, such as the presentation of tasks, events, and activities on a network in sequential form with time estimates.

Its advantages, including greatly improved control over complex development and production programs, and the capacity to distill large amounts of data in brief, orderly fashion.

Its limitations, as in situations where there is little interconnection between the different activities pursued.

Solutions for certain difficulties, e.g., the problem of relating time needed and job costs in the planning stage of a project.

Policies that top management might do well to adopt, such as taking steps to train, experiment with, and put into effect the new controls.

Leading Features

The new techniques have several distinguishing characteristics:

(1) They give management the ability to plan the best possible use of resources to achieve a given goal, within over-all time and cost limitations.

(2) They enable executives to manage "one-of-a-kind" programs, as opposed to repetitive production situations. The importance of this kind of program in the national and world economy has become increasingly clear. Many observers have noted that the techniques of Frederick W. Taylor and Henry L. Gantt, introduced during the early part of the century for large-scale production operations, are inapplicable for a major share of the industrial effort of the 1960's—an era aptly characterized by Paul O. Gaddis as the "Age of Massive Engineering."

(3) They help management to handle the uncertainties involved in programs where no standard cost and time data of the Taylor-Gantt variety are available.

(4) They utilize what is called "time network analysis" as a basic method of approach and as a foundation for determining manpower, material, and capital requirements.

A few examples may serve to indicate for top management the current status of the new techniques.

The Special Projects Office of the U.S. Navy, concerned with performance trends in the execution of large military development programs, introduced PERT on its Polaris Weapon Systems in 1958. Since that time, PERT has spread rapidly throughout the U.S. defense and space industry. Currently, almost every major government and military agency concerned with Space Age programs is utilizing the technique, as are large industrial contractors in the field. Small businesses wishing to participate in national defense programs will find it increasingly necessary to develop a PERT capability if they wish to be competitive in this field.

At about the same time the Navy was developing PERT, the

DuPont company, concerned with the increasing costs and time required to bring new products from research to production, initiated a study which resulted in a similar technique known as CPM (Critical Path Method). The use of the Critical Path Method has spread quite widely, and is particularly concentrated in the construction industry.

A very considerable amount of research now is taking place on the "extensions" of PERT and CPM time-network analysis, into the areas of manpower, cost, and capital requirements. As an ultimate objective, "trade-off" relationships between time, cost, and product or equipment performance objectives are being sought. This research is being sponsored in two ways—directly by the military and privately by large companies. Anyone familiar with the current scene will be impressed by the amount of activity taking place in this field. For example, at least 40 different code names or acronyms representing variations of the new management controls have come to my attention.

Applications of the new techniques, beyond the original engineering-oriented programs for which they were developed, are increasing every day. The PERT approach is usefully introduced in such diverse situations as planning the economy of an underdeveloped nation or establishing the sequence and timing of actions to effect a complex merger.

What Is PERT?

Now let us turn to PERT in particular. What are its special characteristics and requirements?

The term is presently restricted to the area of time and, as promulgated by the Navy, has the following basic requirements:

(1) All of the individual tasks to complete a given program must be visualized in a clear enough manner to be put down in a network, which is comprised of events and activities. An event represents a specified program accomplishment at a particular instant in time. An activity represents the time and resources which are necessary to progress from one event to the next. Emphasis is placed on defining events and activities with sufficient precision so that there is no difficulty in monitoring actual ac-

complishment as the program proceeds. Exhibit I shows a typical operating-level PERT network from the electronics industry.

(2) Events and activities must be sequenced on the network under a highly logical set of ground rules which allow the determination of important critical and subcritical paths. These ground rules include the fact that no successor event can be considered completed until all of its predecessor events have been completed, and no "looping" is allowed, i.e., no successor event can have an activity dependency which leads back to a predecessor event.

(3) Time estimates are made for each activity of the network on a three-way basis, i.e., optimistic, most likely, and pessimistic elapsed-time figures are estimated by the person or persons most familiar with the activity involved. The three time estimates are required as a gauge of the "measure of uncertainty" of the activity, and represent full recognition of the probabilistic nature of many of the tasks in development-oriented and nonstandard programs. It is important to note, however, that, for the purposes of computation and reporting, the three time estimates are reduced to a single expected time (t_e) and a statistical variance (σ^2).

(4) Depending on the size and complexity of the network, computer routines are available to calculate the critical path through it. Computers can also calculate the amount of slack (viz., extra time available) for all events and activities not on the critical path. A negative slack condition can prevail when a calculated end date does not achieve a program date objective which has been established on a prior—and often arbitrary—basis.

Interpretation of the concepts of optimistic, most likely, and pessimistic elapsed times has varied over the past few years. The definitions which, in my opinion, represent a useful consensus are as follows:

Optimistic—An estimate of the *minimum* time an activity will take, a result which can be obtained only if unusual good luck is experienced and everything "goes right the first time."

Most likely—An estimate of the *normal* time an activity will take, a result which would occur most often if the activity could be repeated a number of times under similar circumstances.

Pessimistic—An estimate of the *maximum* time an activity will take, a result which can occur only if unusually bad luck is ex-

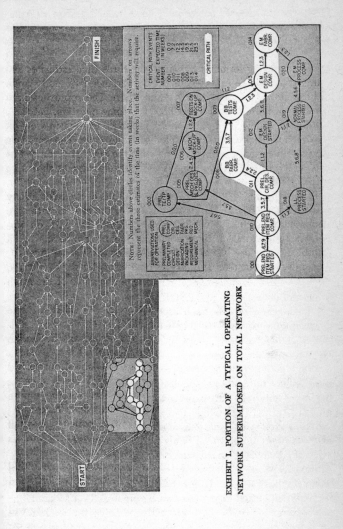

EXHIBIT I. PORTION OF A TYPICAL OPERATING
NETWORK SUPERIMPOSED ON TOTAL NETWORK

99

perienced. It should reflect the possibility of initial failure and fresh start, but should not be influenced by such factors as "catastrophic events"—strikes, fires, power failures, and so on—unless these hazards are inherent risks in the activity.

The averaging formulas by which the three time estimates are reduced to a single expected time (t_e), variance (σ^2) and standard deviation (σ) are shown in Appendix A. The approximations involved in these formulas are subject to some question, but they have been widely used and seem appropriate enough in view of the inherent lack of precision of estimating data. The variance data for an entire network make possible the determination of the *probability of meeting an established schedule date,* as shown in Appendix B.

In actual practice, the most important results of the calculations involved in PERT are the determination of the critical path and slack times for the network. Exhibit II contains data on the critical path and slack times for the sample network shown in Exhibit I (they are based on the method of calculation given in Appendix C). The data are shown in the form of a slack order report (lowest to highest slack), which is perhaps one of the most important output reports of PERT.

Other output reports, such as event order and calendar time order reports, are also available in the PERT system.

The actual utilization of PERT involves review and action by responsible managers, generally on a biweekly basis. Because time prediction and performance data are available from PERT in a "highly ordered" fashion (such as the slack order report), managers are given the opportunity to concentrate on the important critical path activities. The manager must determine valid means of shortening lead times along the critical path by applying new resources or additional funds which are obtained from those activities that can "afford" it because of their slack condition. Alternatively, he can re-evaluate the sequencing of activities along the critical path. If necessary, those activities which were formerly connected in a series can be organized on a parallel or concurrent basis, with the associated trade-off risks involved. As a final, if rarely used, alternative, the manager may choose to

EXHIBIT II. SLACK ORDER REPORT

	PERT SYSTEM		Airborne Computer — Slack Order Report			
Date 7/12/61		Week 0.0		Time in Weeks		Page 1
Event	T_E	T_L	T_L-T_E	T_S	P_r	
001	0.0	0.0	0			T_E = Expected event date
010	7.2	7.2	0			
011	12.2	12.2	0			T_L = Latest allowable event date
008	14.5	14.5	0			
009	19.5	19.5	0			T_L-T_E = Event slack
013	21.5	21.5	0			T_S = Scheduled event date
014	23.5	23.5	0	23.5	.50	P_r = Probability of achieving T_S date
020	20.6	21.5	+ .9			
019	15.6	16.5	+ .9			
012	14.4	15.3	+ .9			
018	9.4	10.3	+ .9			
007	18.2	20.3	+2.1			
006	16.0	18.1	+2.1			
005	13.2	14.3	+2.1			
003	14.2	19.5	+5.3			

change the scope of work of critical path activities in order to achieve a given schedule objective.

It should be pointed out that the PERT system requires constant updating and reanalysis; that is, the manager must recognize that the outlook for the completion of activities in a complex program is in a constant state of flux, and he must be continually concerned with problems of re-evaluation and reprograming. A highly systematized method of handling this aspect of PERT has been developed. An example of the input transaction document involved is given in Exhibit III.

Perhaps the major advantage of PERT is that the kind of planning required to create a valid network represents a major contribution to the definition and ultimate successful control of a complex program. It may surprise some that network development and critical path analysis do, in fact, reveal interdependencies and problem areas which are either not obvious or not well defined by conventional planning methods. The creation of the network is a fairly demanding task, and is a sure-fire indicator of an organization's ability to visualize the number, kind, and sequence of activities needed to execute a complex program.

EXHIBIT III. INPUT TRANSACTION DOCUMENT

PERT REPORT OF TIME INTERVAL ESTIMATES & PROGRESS				CLASSIFICATION:					Revision No. 2 13 February 1959	
From: (Name & Location of Contractor)				To:				Flow Chart No.		Report Period From:
								Contract No.		To:
For office use only (A)				Activity Identification		Time Interval Estimates			Completion Date	Remarks
				Beginning Event No. (B)	Ending Event No. (C)	Opti-mistic (weeks) (D)	Most Likely (weeks) (E)	Pessi-mistic (weeks) (F)	(G)	(H)
(1)	(2)	(3)	(4)	18 — 26	34 — 42	44 — 47	48 — 51	52 — 55	60 — 65	
12	13 — 16	17							Mo. Day Yr.	
1				010	003	5.0	6.0	7.0	— — —	New Activity
1				003	007	0	0	0	— — —	New Activity
1										
2				010	018	1.0	1.0	2.0	— — —	Re-estimated Activity (Change)
2				018	019	5.0	6.0	8.0	— — —	Re-estimated Activity (Change)
Signature of Responsible Official:					Date Signed:			CLASSIFICATION:		

* Columns D, E, and F. These estimates should be given for the full activity even though the activity has already started.

Another advantage of PERT, especially where there is a significant amount of uncertainty, is the three-way estimate. While introducing a complicating feature, this characteristic does give recognition to those realities of life which cause difficulties in most efforts at planning the future. The three-way estimate should result in a greater degree of honesty and accuracy in time forecasting; and, as a minimum, it allows the decision maker a better opportunity to evaluate the degree of uncertainty involved in a schedule—particularly along the critical path. If he is statistically sophisticated, he may even wish to examine the standard deviation and probability of accomplishment data, which were mentioned previously as features of PERT. (If there is a minimum of uncertainty in the minds of personnel estimating individual activity times, the single-time approach may, of course, be used, while retaining all the advantages of network analysis.)

And, finally, the common language feature of PERT allows a large amount of data to be presented in a highly ordered fashion. It can be said that PERT represents the advent of the management-by-exception principle in an area of planning and control where this principle had not existed with any real degree of validity. An additional benefit of the common language feature of PERT is the fact that many individuals in different locations or organizations can easily determine the specific relationship of their efforts to the total task requirements of a large program.

This particular benefit of PERT can represent a significant gain in the modern world of large-scale undertakings and complex organizational relationships.

Coping With Problems

A new and important development like PERT naturally is attended by a certain amount of confusion and doubt. PERT does indeed have its problems. However, they are not always what businessmen think they are, and often there is an effective way of coping with the restrictions. In any event, it is time to compare the situations in which PERT works best with situations in which real (or imagined) troubles occur.

One key question concerns the unknowns of time and resources that management frequently must contend with.

In PERT methodology an available set of resources including manpower and facilities is either known or must be assumed when making the time estimates. For example, it is good practice to make special notations directly on the network when some special condition (e.g., a 48-hour rather than a 40-hour week) is assumed. Experience has shown that when a well-thought-through network is developed in sufficient detail, the first activity time estimates made are as accurate as any, and these should not be changed unless a new application of resources or a trade-off in goals is specifically determined. A further caution is that the first time estimates should not be biased by some arbitrarily established schedule objective, or by the assumption that a particular activity does not appear to be on a critical path. Schedule biasing of this kind, while it obviously cannot be prevented, clearly atrophies some of the main benefits of the technique—although it is more quickly "discovered" with PERT than with any other method.

Because of the necessity for assumptions on manpower and resources, it is easiest to apply PERT in project-structured organizations, where the level of resources and available facilities are known to the estimator. PERT does not itself explicitly resolve the problem of multiprogram planning and control. But there is general recognition of this problem, and considerable effort is being devoted to a more complete approach to it. Meanwhile, in the case of common resource centers, it is generally necessary to undertake a loading analysis, making priority assumptions and using the resulting data on either a three-time or single-time basis for those portions of the network which are affected. It should be pointed out, however, that in terms of actual experience with PERT, the process of network development forces more problems of resource constraint or loading analysis into the open for resolution than do other planning methods.

Although PERT has been characterized as a new management control approach for R & D effort, it has perhaps been most usefully applied in those situations where there is a great deal of interconnection between the activities of a network, or where there are interface connections between different networks. Certainly, network development and critical path analysis are not too appropriate for the pure research project, where the capabilities of small numbers of individuals with highly specialized talents are being utilized at a "constant rate" and where their activities really have no significant dependence on other elements of the organization.

One of the most frequently raised objections to PERT is the cost of its implementation. A fundamental point to examine here is whether or not a currently established planning system is giving value commensurate with its cost—or perhaps more basic still, whether the system is used at all effectively to pinpoint and control problem areas. It is quite true that, by the very nature of its logical requirements for networking, the PERT approach calls for a higher degree of planning skill and a greater amount of detail than is the case with conventional methods. In addition, the degree of detail—or the "level of indenture," as it is called—is a function of what is meaningful to the person or persons who will actually execute the work, and the depth of analysis that is required to determine the valid critical path or paths.

It is perhaps more appropriate to view the implementation of PERT as costing initially something in the order of twice that of a conventional planning system. This figure will vary significantly with such factors as the degree of planning capability already available, the present effectiveness and homogeneity of the organization, and the amount and quality of PERT indoctrination given.

The advocates of PERT are quick to point out that the savings achieved through better utilization of resources far outweigh the system's initial implementation costs. This better utilization of resources is achieved through concentration on critical path activities—for example, limiting overtime effort to these key activities as opposed to across-the-board use of overtime. Even more important are the "downstream" savings which are achieved by earlier and more positive action on the part of management to resolve critical problems.

Because of the considerable impact of PERT on many organizations where detailed planning has not had major emphasis, a trend has recently developed which can be characterized as "model or standard networking." This has to do with efforts to use the typical or established pattern of carrying out a new program in a particular industry. Model networking has many advantages (particularly in handling the large amounts of data involved in PERT), but it may also compromise one of the real objectives of PERT—i.e., *obtaining a valid network which is meaningful to the person or persons who will actually execute the work.* In the area in which PERT is used most effectively, no two programs are ever exactly the same, and no two individuals will have exactly the same approach to the development of a network. Therefore, model networks should be introduced with this caution: management should always allow for the possibility of modifications which will match the realities of the program.

In addition, the introduction of so-called "master plan networks" and the top-down structuring of networks for large programs involving many different firms, while very necessary from the point of view of long-range planning and the ultimate management of such programs, should be handled with a philosophy of flexibility. The cardinal principle is that a management control structure is no better than the adequacy and accuracy of the data at its base. In the future, the top-down structuring approach—which is already evident on some major defense and space programs—will probably increase; but internal objectives, at least, will be subject to reconfirmation or realignment at the level of industry, depending upon the development of actual operating networks. The top-down structuring approach is necessary, however, in order to preserve the mechanics of network integration; it is important that the data from lower level networks be properly and meaningfully summarized into higher level management data.

A final problem, and one that is often viewed as a disadvantage of the PERT technique, is the system's lack of applicability to all of the manufacturing effort. As has been stated, PERT deals in the time domain only and does not contain the quantity information required by most manufacturing operations. Nevertheless, PERT can be, and has been, used very effectively through the preliminary manufacturing phases of production prototype or pilot model construction, and in the assembly and test of final production equipments which are still "high on the learning curve." After these phases, established production control techniques which bring in the quantity factor are generally more applicable.

Note, however, that many programs of the Space Age never leave the preliminary manufacturing stage, or at least never enter into mass production. Therefore, a considerable effort is going forward at this time to integrate the techniques of PERT within some of the established methods of production control, such as line-of-balance or similar techniques that bring in the quantity factor.

As a result of the Navy's successful application of PERT on the Polaris program, and other similar applications, there is a common impression that the technique is only applicable when large-scale data-processing equipment is available. This is certainly true for large networks, or aggregations of networks, where critical path and slack computations are involved for several hundred or more events. It is as desirable to have a computer handle a PERT problem when a large volume of data is involved as it is to use a computer in any extensive data-processing assignment.

Probably equally significant is the fact that several ingenious manual methods have been developed in industry by those organizations which have become convinced of PERT's usefulness. These manual methods range from simple inspection on small networks to more organized but clerically oriented routines for determination of critical path, subcritical path, and slack times on networks ranging from fifty to several hundred events.

This is sufficient proof that PERT can be applied successfully to smaller programs wherever the degree of interconnection and problems of uncertainty warrant it. For those organizations practiced in the technique, both the creation of small networks and the formation of time estimates and their reduction to critical path and slack analyses can be done in a matter of hours. Exhibit I shows the network for a relatively small electronics program. Developed in less than a day, the whole network required only two hours for manual computation.

It seems clear that the small business organization which wishes to participate in national defense and space programs, or to improve its own internal schedule planning and control, should not hesitate to adopt PERT merely because it does not possess large-scale data-processing equipment.

Variations of PERT to accommodate multiproject and manufacturing situations have already been mentioned, and these are merely representative of a basic movement to extend the approach into the areas of manpower, cost, and the equipment performance variable. The ultimate objective of these efforts is to quantify the trade-off relationships which constantly come up in development programs but are rarely acted on with explicit data in hand.

Though none of these extensions have as yet attained as much maturity and acceptance as PERT, anyone familiar with the current scene will be impressed by the amount of effort being given to them throughout the country in both the military and industry. One healthy offset to this particular trend is the fact that the U.S. Air Force has withdrawn its code name PEP (Program Evaluation Procedure), which was an equivalent for PERT. There remains, however, a great need for the various agencies to standardize ground rules for networking, and input and output requirements, if a uniform PERT system for government procurement is to be the long-run objective. As of July 1962, both the Department of Defense and NASA issued a joint PERT/COST Guide which outlines basic PERT/COST concepts, and provides a starting point in this direction.

PERT/COST

Much of the research effort on the new management controls which has taken place throughout the country is concentrated on the problem of manpower and cost. This is probably a reflection of certain facts well known to most managers of complex development programs:

108

(1) The job-costing structures generally found in industry on such programs need a great deal of interpretation to relate actual costs to actual progress. They are rarely, if ever, related in any explicit manner to the details of the scheduling plan.

(2) Cost constraints, either in the form of manpower shortages or funding restrictions, have a great deal to do with the success with which a program of this type can be managed.

It seems clear that both of these problems must be solved in any valid PERT cost approach.

The first problem means that an explicit relationship must be established between the time network and the job-cost structure, either on a one-to-one basis for each network activity, or for a designated chain of activities. As a minimum, it seems clear that more detailed job-cost structures are required than are currently in general use, although this requirement should present no serious limitation for organizations which possess modern data-processing methods and equipment.

With regard to the development of actual cost figures from the time network, an estimate of manpower requirements, segregated by classification, is usually considered the easiest place to start, since these requirements were presumably known at the time the network was established. In fact, however, the actual summation of such data often reveals a manpower or funding restriction problem, and forces a replanning cycle if no alternatives are available. (The summation may also reveal inefficiencies in personnel loading which can be removed by proper use of slack activities.)

Three other problems that should be mentioned are:

Handling of nonlabor items—The costs for these items are often aggregated in a manner quite different from that which would result from analysis of a time network. For example, there is a tendency to buy common materials on one purchase order for a number of different prototypes, each one of which represents a distinct phase of progress in the program. A refined allocation procedure may be needed to handle this problem.

Coordination and control efforts (e.g., those carried out by project or systems engineering)—These are often not indicated on time networks unless they result in specific outputs. For PERT

109

costing, the network in all cases must be complete, i.e., it must include all effort which is charged to the program. This is one of the areas of deficiency in many present-day networks, and one which must be overcome before an effective PERT cost application can be made.

Handling of cost uncertainties—A number of different approaches may be required to handle the problem of cost uncertainty, as opposed to the problem of time uncertainty. As we have seen, basic PERT handles the problem of time uncertainty, but does not necessarily cover all costs which may be incurred on a program. One approach which can be used to handle this problem is the development of alternative networks of varying degrees of completeness, i.e., varying numbers of planned activities, including contingency activities. Another approach is to assign "probability multipliers" to activities which may become unnecessary as the program proceeds, based upon the projected success of completion of a preceding activity or set of activities. Cost uncertainty as it relates to time, in the case of a fixed level of resource, can be handled by different cost estimates for significant three-time differences.

Each of the foregoing problems can be handled if there is an underlying PERT networking capability in the organization, and program objectives can be reasonably well defined. Currently, a number of "basic PERT/COST" approaches are being attempted in the development of costed networks which have as their objective the association of at least one cost estimate with a known activity or chain of activities on the network.

The ultimate objective of all this is not only improvement in planning and control, but also the opportunity to assess possibilities for "trading off" time and cost, i.e., adding or subtracting from one at the expense of the other. It is generally assumed that the fundamental relationships between time and cost are as portrayed in Exhibit IV. Curve A represents total direct costs versus time, and the "U" shape of the curve results from the assumption that there is an "optimum" time-cost point for any activity or job. It is assumed that total costs will increase with any effort to accelerate or delay the job away from this point in the case where resource application varies.

EXHIBIT IV. ASSUMED TIME-COST RELATIONSHIPS FOR A JOB

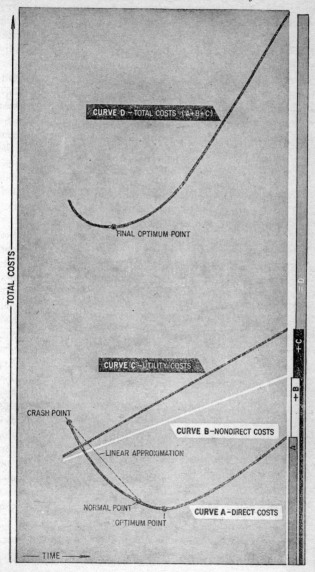

Some companies in the construction industry are already using such a time-cost relationship, although in a rather specialized manner. In one application, an assumption is made that there is a normal job time (which might or might not coincide with the theoretical optimum), and that from this normal time, costs increase linearly to a crash time, as indicated in Exhibit IV. This crash time represents the maximum acceleration the job can stand. On the basis of these assumptions, a complete mathematical approach and computer program have been developed which show how to accelerate progress on a job as much as possible for the lowest possible cost. The process involves shortening the critical path or paths by operating on those activities which have the lowest time-cost slopes.

Making time-cost data available for each activity in usable form is one of the fundamental problems in using PERT in development programs. At the planning stage, in particular, it is often difficult to determine time-cost relationships in an explicit manner, either for individual activities or for aggregates of activities. (There are often good arguments for characterizing time-cost relationships at this stage as nonlinear, flat, decreasing, or, more likely, as a range of cost possibilities.) If alternative equipment or program objectives are added as a variable, the problem is further compounded. While posing the problem, it should be pointed out that solutions for the technical handling of such data, in whatever form they are obtained, have recently been developed.

Curve B of Exhibit IV indicates total nondirect costs, which are assumed to increase linearly with time. Clearly, accounting practices will have to be reviewed to provide careful (and probably new) segregations of direct from nondirect costs for use in making valid time-cost trade-off evaluations.

Curve C is a representation of a utility cost curve, which is needed to complete the picture for total time-cost optimization (indicated as the final optimum point on curve D). The utility cost curve represents a quantification of the penalty for *not accomplishing the job at the earliest possible time*, and is also shown as a linear function increasing with time.

The difficulties of determining such a curve for many programs, either in terms of its shape or dollar value, should be obvious. But it is significant to note that in certain industrial applications such utility cost data have already been developed, typically in the form of "outage" costs or loss-of-profit opportunities, and used as the basis for improved decision making. Further, in the military area, utility cost is the converse of the benefit concept in the benefit-cost ratio of a weapon system; this factor varies with the time of availability of a weapon system, even though judgments of benefit are made difficult by rapidly changing circumstances in the external world.

Conclusion

It is clear that there are difficulties yet to be overcome in advancing the new management controls—particularly in the new areas into which PERT is being extended. Yet it is equally clear that significant progress has been made during the last few years. Assuming that developments continue at the rate at which they have taken place up to this time, what position should top management adopt today with regard to its own internal policies on the new management controls? Here are the most important steps:

(1) Management should review its present planning and scheduling methods and compare their effectiveness with that of the PERT system. (I refer here to time networks only—not time-and-cost networks.) If the company has no direct experience with PERT, it will certainly want to consider training and experimentation programs to acquaint the organization with the technique. Management may even decide to install PERT on all of its development or one-of-a-kind programs (as some companies have done), even though it has no contractual requirement to do so.

(2) Management may wish to enter directly into research efforts on the new management controls or, if such efforts are already underway in the organization, place them on a higher priority basis. As a minimum, it will probably want to assign someone in the organization to follow the numerous developments that are taking place in the field.

(3) Executives should consider carefully the problem of organization to make the most effective use of the new management controls. They should consider the responsibilities of the level of management that actually uses PERT data in its working form, and the responsibilities of the levels of management that review PERT in its various summary forms. Clearly, the usefulness of the new management controls is no greater than the ability of management actually to act on the information revealed. It should be realized that problems of "recentralization" will probably accompany the advent of the new tools, particularly when applied to the planning and control of large projects throughout an entire organization.

(4) Finally, management may wish to assess the longer range implications of the new management controls, both for itself and for the entire industrial community, since the forces calling for centralization of planning and control within the firm can apply equally well outside it. In the Age of Massive Engineering, the new controls will be utilized to an increasing extent in the nation's defense and space programs, which are in turn increasing in size and complexity. It seems clear that the inevitably closer relationships between government and industry will require the establishment of new guidelines for procurement and incentive contracting where these management control techniques are used.

APPENDIXES

Readers interested in applying PERT may find it helpful to have a more precise formulation of certain calculations mentioned earlier in this article. The mathematics involved is basically simple, as the following material demonstrates.

Appendix A. Expected Time Estimate

In analyzing the three time estimates, it is clear that the optimistic and the pessimistic time should occur least often, and that the most likely time should occur most often. Thus, it is assumed that the most likely time represents the peak or modal value of a probability distribution; however, it can move between the two extremes. These characteristics are best described by the

Beta distribution, which is shown in two different conditions in the figures that follow.

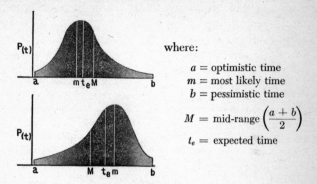

where:

a = optimistic time
m = most likely time
b = pessimistic time
M = mid-range $\left(\dfrac{a+b}{2}\right)$
t_e = expected time

As a result of analyzing the characteristics of the Beta distribution, the final approximations to expected time t_e, variance σ^2, and standard deviation σ were written as follows for a given activity:

1.
$$t_e = \frac{1}{3}(2m + M)$$
$$= \frac{1}{3}\left(2m + \frac{a+b}{2}\right)$$
$$= \frac{a + 4m + b}{6},$$

2.
$$\sigma^2 = \left(\frac{b-a}{6}\right)^2,$$

3.
$$\sigma = \frac{b-a}{6}.$$

The first equation indicates that t_e should be interpreted as the weighted mean of m (most likely) and M (mid-range) estimates, with weights of 2 and 1, respectively. In other words, t_e is located one third of the way from the modal to the mid-range values, and represents the 50% probability point of the distribution, i.e., it divides the area under the curve into two equal portions.

NOTE: The Beta distribution is analyzed in the PERT Summary Report, Phase I (Special Projects Office, Department of the Navy, Washington, D.C., July 1958).

Appendix B. Probability of Meeting Schedule Times

On the basis of the Central Limit Theorem, one can conclude that the probability distribution of times for accomplishing a job consisting of a number of activities may be approximated by the normal distribution, and that this approximation approaches exactness as the number of activities becomes great (for example, more than ten activities along a given path). Thus, we may define a curve which represents the probability of a meeting on established schedule-end date, T_s:

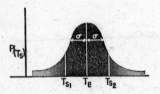

where:

$$T_E = \Sigma t_{e_1} + t_{e_2} + \cdots + t_{e_n}$$
$$\sigma^2(T_E) = \Sigma \sigma^2(t_{e_1}) + \sigma^2(t_{e_2}) + \cdots + \sigma^2(t_{e_n})$$
$$T_{S_1} = \text{Scheduled time (earlier than } T_E)$$
$$T_{S_2} = \text{Scheduled time (later than } T_E)$$

The probability of meeting the T_S date when given T_E and σ^2 for a chain of activities is defined as the ratio of (1) the area under the curve to the left of T_S to (2) the area under the entire curve. The difference between T_S and T_E, expressed in units of σ, is:

$$\frac{T_S - T_E}{\sigma}.$$

This will yield a value for the probability of accomplishing T_S by use of the normal probability distribution table. Thus:

$$\frac{T_{S_1} - T_E}{\sigma} = -1.2\sigma, \ P_r(\text{accomplishment of } T_{S_1}) = 0.12$$

$$\frac{T_{S_2} - T_E}{\sigma} = +1.2\sigma, \ P_r(\text{accomplishment of } T_{S_2}) = 0.88.$$

Appendix C. Determining Critical Path and Slack Times

The computation steps required to determine the critical path and slack times for the network shown in Exhibit 1 are as follows:

Step 1. Determine t_e for every activity on the network in accordance with the equation:

$$t_e = \frac{a + 4m + b}{6}$$

Step 2. Starting with event no. 001, determine T_E (or cumulative T_E) for all succeeding events by summing small t_e's for each activity leading up to the event, *but choosing the largest value for the final T_E figure in those cases where there is more than one activity leading into an event.* For example, Exhibit I indicates three activities leading into event no. 013 (EM design complete). The three preceding events are no. 007 (test on mock-up complete), no. 009 (breadboard tests complete), and no. 012 (EM design started). The cumulative T_E figures for these three preceding events, as can be seen from Exhibit II, are 18.2 weeks for event no. 007, 19.5 weeks for event no. 009, and 14.4 weeks for event no. 012. Now, add the respective activity times between these three events and event no. 013 and examine the results:

Event no.	T_E	Activity Time t_e to event no. 013	Total weeks
007	18.2	1.2	19.4
009	19.5	2.0	21.5
012	14.4	6.2	20.6

The largest figure, which represents the longest path or earliest time at which event no. 013 can be completed, is 21.5 weeks, and this path leads through event no. 009. As will be noted from Exhibit I, events no. 009 and no. 013 are on the critical path, since the T_E values of all other paths leading into final event no. 014 are smaller.

Step 3. Having determined the critical path through the network of Exhibit I to be 23.5 weeks, we can now set the final date of event no. 014 at 23.5 weeks, or we can use some arbitrary scheduled time. The process covered in step 2 is now reversed. Starting with the final event, we determine the *latest allowable time*, T_L, for each event so as not to affect critical path event times. For example, event no. 007, with a T_E of 18.2 weeks, can be delayed up to a T_L of 20.3 weeks, before it will affect critical path event no. 013.

Step 4. The difference between T_L and T_E, known as slack, is next computed for each event. These computations are shown in Exhibit II in the form of a slack order report, i.e., in order of lowest to highest values of positive slack. Note that along the critical path there is zero slack at every event, since by definition there is no possibility of slippage along the critical path without affecting the final event date. In this example, if the end schedule date of event no. 014 were set at 23.0 weeks rather than at 23.5 weeks, there would be 0.5 weeks of negative slack indicated for every event along the critical path.

Step 5. The computation of variance and of standard deviation for this network is optional and involves adding the variances for each activity along the critical path, which are obtained from the formula:

$$\sigma^2 = \left(\frac{b - a}{6}\right)^2$$

The interested reader may verify that the variance for final event no. 014, with a T_E of 23.5 weeks, is 1.46 weeks.

4

MEANINGFUL COSTS FOR
MANAGEMENT ACTION

ROBERT BEYER

As business becomes more complex and competition becomes
more intense, the hunger of business managers for better management information systems becomes insatiable. The days are certainly gone forever when a businessman—even the manager of a
very small business—could control his operation by confining his
attention to the balance in his checking account. It is quite generally conceded by businessmen that anyone doing business in
this manner would not survive very long in today's competitive
business world.

Although we can probably agree that businessmen now are
more sophisticated and knowledgeable about the ways of the
business world than were their forefathers, we can probably likewise agree that despite their gain in sophistication, many are less
well prepared than were their ancestors to wage war in the competitive business jungle.

What are the reasons for this state of affairs? Probably there are
many, but it is the thesis of this article that one of the most
important contributing reasons is the failure of accounting—the
language of business—to keep pace with developments in manu-

facturing, distributing, engineering, and general business practices. A positiveness with respect to implications for the future is necessary in accounting today, whereas post-mortems sufficed in the past; hence, the hunger of businessmen for better management information systems, of which accounting heads the list.

Modern Needs

In today's business world accounting must do at least two very important things: (a) it must tell the story of what has happened, and (b) it must tell why it happened. In doing the latter, it must portray as vividly as possible danger signals for the future and make it as easy as possible for the manager to select a proper course of action. It seems to me that accounting has allowed itself to be so concerned with accurately telling the story of what has happened that it has lost its perspective, its ability to assist a manager in determining why it happened and what should be done about it.

The accounting process of telling the story of what has happened might be called, "custodial accounting." Specifically, it concerns itself with the accountability for assets and liabilities and with the determination of over-all corporate income in accordance with sound accounting principles. This custodial accounting supplies the needs of most shareholders, creditors, governmental regulatory agencies, and the Internal Revenue Service.

In this area we have done well enough. There are, to be sure, many serious disagreements among theorists and practitioners on important bodies of thought in custodial or financial accounting, but there always seem to be new developments and fresh attempts to keep up with the times which give one the feeling, at least, that progress is being made, however slow it may seem at times.

We can perhaps find comfort in the thought that changes in concepts of the determination of business income and the bases for the recording of assets and liabilities must necessarily change slowly because of their importance. A prerequisite to such decisions must be a period of time during which the changes are thoroughly discussed and tested and after which substantial agreement slowly emerges.

Internal Concerns

Now let us turn to accounting for the internal manager, the manager who cares comparatively little about learned philosophies of income measurement and asset and liability accounting. He is interested in making decisions based on the information he can secure from an accounting system, decisions which will increase the returns he can produce on the capital he is employing.

His concept of income for certain purposes may not jibe with that of the custodial accountant, but that does not make him wrong. The fact of the matter is that he has a different point of view, one which lends itself much more easily to precise measurement, and which is narrowly confined in its objective to the well-being of his company and its shareholders. The broad social and economic implications of his decisions for the most part concern him but little.

Since World War II, there have been only two significant developments in the technique of internal profit measurement, i.e., the substantial interest displayed in (1) direct costing and (2) return on investment. Neither of these concepts was new in the postwar period. Each had been discussed in textbooks for many years. The significant point is, however, that in neither case have we exploited the advantages for good internal accounting and control which are inherent in both of the concepts. Thus direct costing has frustrated many managers because of its clash with the principles of custodial accounting and its lack of acceptability by the Securities and Exchange Commission and the Internal Revenue Service. And return on investment as a tool has not made the headway it should because of the inability of most accountants and managers to integrate it with internal accounting procedures.

The result has been that internal accounting limps along, to a great extent mimicking custodial accounting by making one pattern of figure recording do for two end products which by their very nature have widely varying purposes. Examine for a moment the earnings statement of the hypothetical company shown in Exhibit I. It is typical of earnings statements which are published by many companies today—the product of custodial accounting.

121

EXHIBIT I. CONVENTIONAL STATEMENT OF NET EARNINGS

	1959	1958
Revenues		
Net sales	$39,500,000	$37,500,000
Miscellaneous income	60,000	85,000
	$39,560,000	$37,585,000
Costs and expenses		
Cost of products sold, exclusive of depreciation	$27,200,000	$26,300,000
Selling and administrative expenses	3,100,000	3,200,000
Depreciation	1,800,000	1,700,000
Interest and debt expense	300,000	240,000
Federal and state taxes on income	3,700,000	3,500,000
	$36,100,000	$34,940,000
Net earnings	$ 3,460,000	$ 2,645,000

There is nothing wrong with it for that purpose, but the unfortunate point is that in all too many companies this same type of earnings statement is also presented to internal management.

It is quite understandable that competition in our economy is intense and that no company is interested in giving away, through a published report, valuable information which would enable competitors to neutralize any advantage they may have. Does that mean, however, that as internal managers we must likewise keep it away from ourselves? Almost as if to recognize that figures presented in this manner are inadequate to appraise performance, many companies include last year's comparable figures in an adjoining column, as if they were some sort of a yardstick.

Decision-Making Accounting

What has been wrong here during all these years is that there has been lacking the courage on the part of many accountants to deal with corporate results on any other than the custodial basis. They must be convinced that it is not only possible but proper to deal with accounting figures from more than one point of view. They must be convinced of the desirability of being able to wear two hats, to take the cold, dead results of custodial accounting and breathe life into them. In large part it means that the shackles must be taken off of accounting. Accounting must be adapted more for the businessman and less for the accountant because, again, it is the language of business.

The purpose of this paper is to describe briefly a technique called profitability accounting and control which has been developed recently in an effort to meet this problem. Its purpose is to integrate into one system all of the most modern and effective managerial control tools in such a way that the reporting under the system not only tells the manager what has happened, but also highlights important areas for future consideration and attention by management. And it is to report at the same time the results of operations for internal purposes in such a way that they are fully reconcilable with results under custodial accounting, so that in a sense management can have its cake and eat it too.

A central theme pervading the entire structure or system of profitability accounting is incremental costing and marginal contribution analysis. The acceptance of the incremental cost and profit contribution philosophy does not mean that this type of accounting is just another synonym for direct costing. It does heartily approve of the decisiveness of the direct costing approach, but it also disapproves of some of the fundamental principles of accounting which are generally associated with direct costing. Profitability accounting seeks to build on the central idea of incremental cost and profit contribution for internal reporting without destroying our traditional custodial accounting principles of income determination and inventory pricing.

One of the very important terms in the definition of profitability accounting is the word integration. We have all seen standard cost systems and budgetary control systems, as two examples of time-honored managerial control tools. Recently, we have also been hearing a great deal about profit planning, direct costing, target pricing, return on investment, and make-or-buy determinations.

Very rarely, however, have we seen all of these tools integrated into one decision-compelling approach to all management problems—an approach which results in a hard-hitting set of management reports that not only embrace the entire philosophy of accounting control but also provide the basis for decisions heretofore requiring "nonaccounting" techniques. This cannot be accomplished in either the custodial approach to accounting or the direct costing philosophy.

Thus, while many individual aspects of this general philosophy of accounting have been discussed for some years, the integrated approach described here should prove helpful to businessmen who, at present, are receiving little assistance from the conventional accounting reports. If it does nothing more than to cause them to think about the limitations of conventional accounting as an aid in decision making, this article will have served a worthwhile purpose.

Income Determination

At the very beginning it must be emphasized that there is no difference in fundamental principles of income determination between profitability accounting and traditional custodial accounting. Profitability accounting accepts the prevailing principles of inclusion of overhead in inventories. This is an important consideration because the usual rabid advocate of direct costing (which is actually a popular variant of the basically sound and long recognized marginal contribution accounting principle) will argue that traditional custodial accounting is theoretically wrong in its concept of inventory pricing and income determination. He would have us believe that inventories should contain no element of fixed manufacturing overhead, because that portion of manufacturing cost is a period cost and all period costs should be charged to earnings directly as they are incurred.

A favorite cliché of the direct coster is that "you must segregate the costs of being in business from the costs of doing business, and the costs of being in business have no place in the inventories." This is an attractive bit of reasoning on superficial analysis, but it just does not stand up under real probing. As a matter of fact, there may be some basis for running all of our overhead, including the commercial overhead, through the inventories so that its incidence on earnings would vary more directly in relation to shipments.

There can be no fine line of distinction between manufacturing overhead and commercial overhead. In the first place, there never will be unanimity of thinking as to what is included in manufacturing overhead as against commercial overhead. In the second place, the thought that we are always entitled to have in inventory only those costs which are required to bring production to the point of shipment and therefore only manufacturing costs may be included is another piece of specious reasoning. A portion or all of the administrative, engineering, research, personnel, and sometimes even selling expenses are incurred in advance of the income earned from these efforts. This is not a plea to change our inventory costing principles from what they have been for many, many years. However, if the time ever does come when we agree that a change is needed, let us be sure at least that we proceed in the right direction.

Cost Determination

We already have all kinds of trouble agreeing on what is to be included in manufacturing overhead. Imagine the confusion we would have if we compounded our frustration by trying to break down manufacturing overhead into that part which is variable and accordingly is to be included in inventories, and that part which is period cost and accordingly is to be charged directly to earnings.

Very shortly we would have no standards at all, and we would be even less able than we are today to compare one company with another because the concepts of period or fixed costs are almost as numerous as the theorists who discuss them. The different proportions of overhead that we would have in company inventories, depending on management's concept of fixed cost, would make the idea completely unsound.

Profitability accounting accepts the tenet that costs have different characteristics and that it is not only possible but useful for managerial purposes to develop the breakdowns of costs into standby and variable components. Profitability accounting, however, does not accept the philosophy that costs per se may be classified into two clear-cut groups: fixed and variable. It suggests rather that most costs have an element of variability and also a standby or fixed complement. It advocates determination of the incurrence of cost, account by account, at all volume levels and at shutdown and the use of these data as a basis for the budgetary control of overhead.

On this basis, only that cost which remains under conditions of significant shutdown comparable to a strike is termed fixed or standby. All increments of cost over and above that level are in the variable category. In discussing this concept, many people have asked how it is possible to forecast in advance to what extent an organization would be trimmed in the event of a shutdown. No forecast can be completely accurate, of course, but useful determinations can be made. Certainly the steel companies knew to what level they could cut costs when they were anticipating the latest steel strike. If the shutdown becomes so severe that the basic organization must be destroyed, then new determinations must be made. But that possibility should not deter us from organizing the facts in such a manner that they will be useful to us in most circumstances.

Exhibit II illustrates four overhead accounts which are different in incidence of incremental cost but which, nevertheless, are typical of operating department expenses. Each account must be

EXHIBIT II. FOUR TYPICAL OVERHEAD ACCOUNTS

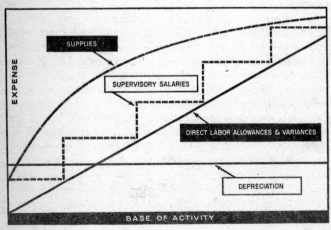

graphed according to its own characteristics of cost incurrence to determine the departmental budgetary cost allowances. In order that these same cost allowances may be useful for product cost purposes, however, they must be summarized in terms of a combined standby allowance and a composite variable rate applied to each common base of activity. This is done simply by cumulatively adding the allowances at many points of activity for all the accounts regardless of how cost increments occur. This will give a scattergraph of points through which a line of best fit may be drawn as shown in Exhibit III.

The line of best fit is drawn so that it is hinged to the exact total of the cost allowances at shutdown. Also, by eye testing, it is made to produce the best fit in what is known as the "zone of applicability." This is the area bounded by roughly one third less than and one third more than normal activity. The rate which is determined by the slope of the line forms the standard variable cost which is used for product cost purposes.

Standby cost, which is determined as a result of the graphing technique of anchoring the line of best fit to shutdown activity,

EXHIBIT III. FINDING STANDARD VARIABLE COSTS

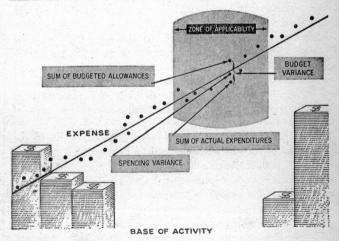

127

is the same absolute amount at all volume levels. To unitize it in product cost would require the assumption of a volume level and would freeze the cost at the assumed volume point. Profitability accounting regards this as objectionable for purposes of many managerial decisions which must be made in connection with product pricing, volume considerations, and make-or-buy determinations. It suggests rather that an incremental cost approach be taken in which standby cost is entirely eliminated from unit product cost and is assessed directly to the total product line as such. Some standby cost categories may be assessed entirely to individual product lines because they are specific to individual lines, but other standby cost groupings must be assessed to two or more product lines on an appropriate basis.

At this point, we must discuss one of the facets of profitability accounting where its close integration becomes clearly evident. As discussed above, we are using the same overhead breakdowns for budgetary control purposes, for input to and output from inventories, and also for product cost purposes. The summation of individual budgetary control allowances is used for all budget purposes without modification.

This is vital to measure accurately departmental performance, since a department head should only be responsible for costs in the manner in which they occur and not on the basis of their conversion to a straight linear variable. However, the conversion of these allowances to a linear variable form by means of the line of best fit enables us to determine the standard variable cost for inventory accounting and product costs purposes. How do we bridge the gap between these two sets of computations in the management reports where we will want to use both of them?

This is done by determining the dollar difference between the two computations and setting it forth in management reports as a so-called budget variance in addition to the usual performance variances. If the variable portion of all actual costs moved in direct proportion to the volume of base activity, there would be no budget variance, only a performance variance. Thus, the costs for three purposes are tied together and reconciled in the management reports by the use of these two types of variance accounts.

In profitability accounting there is another important category of cost which we have not touched on. This is so-called programed cost. It is a cost that varies in accordance with a management decision, and therefore it cannot be controlled by the techniques we have described above for variable and standby costs. Good examples of this type of cost are research and development cost and advertising expense. They are budgeted and controlled by means of appropriations. They are never unitized in product cost, and they are assessed to product lines in the same manner as standby cost.

Profitability accounting also deals with the problem of assessing service department expenses such as those incurred in a toolroom where almost all of the work is done for another department. In such cases, it is never appropriate to charge directly to the department served. First the charges must be collected by the home department in order that the efforts of the supervisor of that department may be appraised. An important principle which is carefully followed at all times is that all overhead must first be charged to department spending, then to department charged, and finally to the product line. The first two charges are actually made on the books of account while the third is made only on work sheets for the presentation of management reports.

It is never in order to make arbitrary allocations on the books of account. This would destroy the principle of responsibility for the costs which underlies the entire structure. If we must make assessments of cost to other departments in order that the costs may be eventually identified with product lines, that work is done on a work sheet basis in connection with the profit plan work before the start of the year.

The space limitations of this paper do not permit the discussion of the principles which underlie the assessment of overhead to departments and product lines. Let it suffice to say that once the assessments have been made in connection with the construction of the profit plan, they are not changed for the year, except under very unusual circumstances.

Thus, product lines will always incur the same amount of standby overhead from month to month unless the spending or performance variances can be clearly and specifically identified with particular product lines. In most cases overhead performance variances will be identified with people, because people are generally the cause of the variances, not the inherent nature of the product lines.

The Profit Plan

One of the cardinal features of profitability accounting is profit planning. Planning for future profits of course should be a daily affair in all companies, but in profitability accounting it takes on a very formal aspect several months in advance of the start of each year. It involves making detailed forecasts of shipments by product line and mix within the product lines. It involves assembling all the facts which have been discussed in the foregoing paragraphs and putting them together in one picture so that the forecasted results may be appraised before the year starts. A typical profit plan is presented in Exhibit IV.

Naturally it would be a rare occurrence if the profit plan were satisfactory the first time it was prepared for a particular year. Rather, it should provide the springboard for the rechallenge of volume, sales mix, production planning, inventory levels, cost allowances, and a host of other management considerations.

There can be little question but that the portrayal of profit contribution, standby, and programed expenses by product lines is a valuable tool in planning for greater profit periods.

For example, if it is decided to alter the sales volume or mix of a particular line, the entire cost planning does not have to be redone, because the standby and programed costs are not unitized in the product cost. Or if it is decided to spend some money for certain spot programs in order to accomplish a specific objective on a short-term basis, the cost can easily be provided for as a programed cost without altering the entire product cost structure.

After the profit plan has been finally approved, it is incorporated into the management reporting forms for the year to which it is applicable. Exhibit V shows a typical earnings statement which is used in connection with profitability accounting. It incorporates, on a monthly trend basis, the profit plan and the results of actual operations. There may appear to be accounting heresy here in

EXHIBIT IV. A TYPICAL PROFIT PLAN

Income and costs	Totals	Product lines		
		A	B	C
Gross sales	$10,000,000	$6,000,000	$2,000,000	$2,000,000
Variable costs				
Specific sales deductions				
Trade discounts	$ 500,000	$ 400,000	$ 100,000	—
Commissions	750,000	600,000	—	$ 150,000
Freight out	50,000	—	50,000	—
Allowances	10,000	—	5,000	5,000
Cash discounts allowed	40,000	—	20,000	20,000
Direct materials	2,500,000	1,600,000	300,000	600,000
Direct labor	1,200,000	600,000	200,000	400,000
Variable manufacturing expense	1,000,000	700,000	100,000	200,000
Variable commercial expense	300,000	200,000	70,000	30,000
Total variable costs	$ 6,350,000	$4,100,000	$ 845,000	$1,405,000
Profit contribution	$ 3,650,000	$1,900,000	$1,155,000	$ 595,000
Standby expenses				
Specific	$ 700,000	$ 350,000	$ 120,000	$ 230,000
General	400,000	200,000	100,000	100,000
	$ 1,100,000	$ 550,000	$ 220,000	$ 330,000
Programed expenses				
Specific	$ 600,000	$ 200,000	$ 125,000	$ 275,000
General	300,000	100,000	150,000	50,000
	$ 900,000	$ 300,000	$ 275,000	$ 325,000
Forecasted operating earnings	$ 1,650,000	$1,050,000	$ 660,000	$ (60,000)

Note: ( ) indicate unfavorable or negative figure; otherwise favorable

131

EXHIBIT V. PROFITABILITY ACCOUNTING: STATEMENT OF NET EARNINGS

(IN THOUSANDS)

1960	GROSS SALES OVER (UNDER)	GROSS SALES ACTUAL OR FORECAST*	STANDARD PROFIT CONTRIBUTION OVER (UNDER)	STANDARD PROFIT CONTRIBUTION ACTUAL OR FORECAST*	EXPENSES STANDBY FORECAST	EXPENSES PROGRAMED FORECAST	EXPENSES VARIANCES ACTUAL OR FORECAST*	OPERATING EARNINGS OVER (UNDER)	OPERATING EARNINGS ACTUAL OR FORECAST*	PROFIT SHARING CONTRIBUTION OVER (UNDER)	PROFIT SHARING CONTRIBUTION ACTUAL OR FORECAST*	TAXES ON INCOME OVER (UNDER)	TAXES ON INCOME ACTUAL OR FORECAST*	NET EARNINGS OVER (UNDER)	NET EARNINGS ACTUAL OR FORECAST*	EARNINGS PER SHARE ACTUAL OR FORECAST*
JAN	(35)	535	(12)	193	91	90	(21)	(33)	(9)	3	–	(18)	(5)	(15)	(4)	
FEB	40	780	20	280	91	68	18	38	139		11	20	67	15	61	.10
MAR		920*		330*	91	80			159*		14*		75*		70*	.12*
APR		1,160*		380*	91	82			207*		19*		97*		91*	.15*
MAY		850*		340*	92	50			198*		18*		92*		88*	.15*
JUN		900*		325*	92	52			181*		18*		86*		77*	.13*
JUL		890*		340*	92	48			200*		19*		95*		86*	.14*
AUG		1,000*		350*	92	60			198*		19*		92*		87*	.15*
SEP		970*		325*	92	70			183*		16*		76*		71*	.12*
OCT		750*		280*	92	82			106*		10*		52*		44*	.07*
NOV		770*		290*	92	99			99*		9*		47*		43*	.07*
DEC		800*		225*	92	119			14*		–*		8*		6*	.01*

YEAR TO DATE	5	1,295	8	473	182	158	(3)	8	130	3	11	2	62	–0–	57	.10
ORIGINAL FORECAST		10,000		3,850	1,100	900			1,650		150		780		720	1.21
CURRENT FORECAST		10,005		3,658	1,100	900	(3)		1,655		153		782		720	1.21

	MONTH	YEAR TO DATE
FORECASTED OPERATING EARNINGS	101	125
TOTAL VOLUME AND MIX VARIANCES	20	8
EXPENSE VARIANCES	18	(3)
ACTUAL OPERATING EARNINGS	139	130

	ORIGINAL FORECAST	CURRENT FORECAST
AVERAGE MONTHLY TOTAL CORPORATE ASSETS	$9,004	$9,010
CAPITAL TURNOVER	1.11	1.11
× RETURN ON SALES	7.20	7.19
RETURN ON CAPITAL EMPLOYED	7.99	7.98

Note: ( ) indicate unfavorable or negative figure; otherwise favorable;
° indicates forecast figure; otherwise actual.

that the profit plan amounts for standby and programed expenses and the forecasted percentages of profit contribution on the actual shipments are incorporated in the actual operating statement. All expense variances are reported in one column.

Naturally this is not a statement that the average accountant would prepare for custodial accounting purposes, but it is not intended to serve that purpose. It is intended to focus management's attention on the deviations from plan which require prompt decisions.

EXHIBIT VI. PROFITABILITY ACCOUNTING: SUMMARY OF EXPENSE VARIANCES

1960 MONTH	PERFORMANCE	TRADE DISCOUNTS	COMMISSIONS	FREIGHT OUT	ALLOWANCES	CASH DISCOUNTS ALLOWED	PURCHASE PRICE	YIELD	BUDGET VARIANCE	PROGRAMED	TOTAL
JAN	(10)	(12)	13	4	(8)	(5)	(6)	(7)	4	6	(21)
FEB	8	(4)	10	5	1	2	(4)	(2)	(2)	4	18
MAR											

YEAR TO DATE											
JAN	(10)	(12)	13	4	(8)	(5)	(6)	(7)	4	8	(21)
FEB	(2)	(16)	23	9	(7)	(3)	(10)	(9)	2	10	(3)
MAR											

Note: ( ) indicate unfavorable or negative figure; otherwise favorable.

From a glance at the small box at the bottom left of Exhibit V, the reader can quickly see to what extent the company is operating on plan. The statement tells us that earnings for the year to date were greater than those indicated in the profit plan for two major reasons: sales volume and mix differences accounted for a gain of $8,000 over the profit plan, and spending variances accounted for a loss of $3,000. Both of these differences can be referenced to the body of the earnings statement.

If sales are made at other than regular prices, there would also be a sales price variance as a reason for profit variance. If the alteration in price is made by changing an established discount structure, the variance is automatically reported in the trade discount variance as shown in Exhibit VI. Where there is no discount structure, however, the price variance would automatically be included in the mix variance, unless some additional effort were expended to determine it. In the many cases where this would prove worthwhile, the price variance would then be grouped in the top earnings statement, along with volume and mix variances.

Exhibit VII is a summary of all the product line statements of earnings, there actually being one statement for each product line

EXHIBIT VII. PROFITABILITY ACCOUNTING: CONSOLIDATED PRODUCT LINE STATEMENT OF EARNINGS

(IN THOUSANDS)

1960	GROSS SALES FORECAST	GROSS SALES ACTUAL	STANDARD PROFIT CONTRIBUTION FORECAST	PER CENT	ACTUAL	PER CENT	STANDBY SPECIFIC	STANDBY GENERAL	PROGRAMED SPECIFIC	PROGRAMED GENERAL	STANDARD PRODUCT LINE EARNINGS	ORDERS RECEIVED 1960	ORDERS RECEIVED 1959	ORDER BACKLOG 1960	ORDER BACKLOG 1959
JAN	670	535	205	35.9	193	36.0	59	32	67	23	12	650	600	1600	1580
FEB	720	760	280	36.1	280	36.8	59	32	49	19	121	1200	1050	2050	1880
MAR	920		330	35.8			59	32	56	24			1180		2980
APR	1,180		380	32.7			59	32	59	23			1080		3110
MAY	850		340	40.0			58	34	35	15			800		3060
JUN	900		325	36.1			58	34	36	17			600		2560
JUL	890		340	38.2			58	34	34	14			650		1860
AUG	1,000		350	35.0			58	34	40	20			580		1740
SEP	970		325	33.4			58	34	49	21			550		1650
OCT	750		280	37.3			58	34	50	32			400		1580
NOV	770		290	37.6			58	34	76	23			500		1560
DEC	600		225	45.0			58	34	50	69			300		1480
YEAR TO DATE	1,290	1,295	465	36.0	473	36.5	118	64	116	42	133				
ORIGINAL FORECAST	10,000		3,650	36.5			700	400	600	300	1,650				
CURRENT FORECAST	10,005		3,658	36.5			700	400	600	300	1,658				

RECONCILIATION OF STANDARD PROFIT CONTRIBUTION ON FORECASTED SALES TO STANDARD PROFIT CONTRIBUTION ON ACTUAL SALES

MONTH		
FORECASTED		260
VOLUME VARIANCE	14	
MIX VARIANCE	6	20
ACTUAL		280

YEAR TO DATE		
FORECASTED		465
VOLUME VARIANCE	1	
MIX VARIANCE	7	8
ACTUAL		473

	ORIGINAL FORECAST	CURRENT FORECAST
AVERAGE MONTHLY TOTAL ASSETS	$9,004	$9,010
CAPITAL TURNOVER —×—	1.11	1.11
RETURN ON SALES	16.50	16.56
RETURN ON CAPITAL EMPLOYED	18.31	18.38

subsidiary to this statement. This statement shows that a gain in volume alone of $5,000 accounted for $1,000 of additional profit, and a more favorable product mix accounted for $7,000 of the combined favorable volume and mix variance of $8,000.

It should be noted that there is no allocation of any spending or performance variances to the product lines because it is assumed, in this hypothetical case, that none of the variances is specific to a product line. In actual practice there will be cases where certain spending or performance variances may be specific to individual product lines. In such cases, two additional columns are required after "Standard Product Line Earnings" on the product line statement of earnings. One column would show variances specific to the line and the other would show the net amount after those variances.

It is neither impossible nor prohibitive in clerical effort to develop actual variances by product line in certain of the specific sales deductions, such as trade discounts, commissions, outbound transportation, and so on. In such event, they also should be shown on the product line statement. The variances in this particular case are shown functionally in Exhibit VI and again can be referenced to the box in Exhibit V. The variances summarized in Exhibit VI are supported by departmental budget reports to responsible personnel and their superiors. They are not, however, included in the report to managers whose attention is directed to policies and the functioning of people.

Exhibit VIII shows the balance sheet on a trend basis. The inventories in this case include an unchanging complement of standby manufacturing overhead for all 12 months of the year because it has been forecasted that the inventories will be approximately the same at the end of the year as they were at the beginning. If there were to be a significant change, an amount representing the change in standby cost in the inventory could be provided for in programed expenses. This would then make the profitability accounting results exactly the same as the custodial accounting results.

Another important feature of the system is its emphasis on return on capital employed. Exhibits V and VII show how the earnings are evaluated on a return-on-capital-employed basis. There

EXHIBIT VIII. PROFITABILITY ACCOUNTING: BALANCE SHEET SHOWING TRENDS

ASSETS (IN THOUSANDS)

1960	Cash		Notes and Accounts Receivable		Inventories		Prepaid Expenses		Net Property, Plant and Equipment		Investments and Other Assets	
	FORECAST	ACTUAL	FORECAST	ACTUAL	FORECAST	ACTUAL	FORECAST	ACTUAL	FORECAST	ACTUAL	FORECAST	ACTUAL
JAN	365	375	1,050	1,059	3,900	3,860	50	54	3,520	3,580	22	20
FEB	297	260	1,100	1,120	3,990	3,980	49	50	3,510	3,560	24	21
MAR	208		1,120		4,070		49		3,500		24	
APR	238		1,300		4,160		50		3,490		23	
MAY	363		1,250		4,140		55		3,470		20	
JUN	455		1,170		3,990		60		3,500		21	
JUL	428		1,180		3,990		61		3,510		18	
AUG	514		1,190		3,860		58		3,480		19	
SEP	360		1,250		3,910		52		3,460		21	
OCT	590		1,160		3,730		50		3,500		24	
NOV	807		1,150		3,640		49		3,510		23	
DEC	656		1,160		3,580		50		3,550		22	

LIABILITIES AND STOCKHOLDERS' INVESTMENT

1960	Notes Payable		Accounts Payable		Accrued Expenses		Income Taxes		Long-Term Debt		Stockholders' Investment		Current Ratio	
	FORECAST	ACTUAL	FORECAST	ACTUAL	FORECAST	ACTUAL	FORECAST	ACTUAL	FORECAST	ACTUAL	FORECAST	ACTUAL	FORECAST	ACTUAL
JAN	850	851	600	661	100	112	413	395	1,850	1,850	5,094	5,079	2.73	2.65
FEB	850	860	580	589	80	90	460	462	1,850	1,850	5,140	5,140	2.75	2.70
MAR	865		630		81		335		1,850		5,210		2.85	
APR	950		640		88		432		1,850		5,301		2.72	
MAY	925		520		90		524		1,850		5,389		2.82	
JUN	875		500		95		410		1,850		5,466		3.02	
JUL	700		500		80		505		1,850		5,552		3.17	
AUG	500		510		75		597		1,800		5,639		3.34	
SEP	500		450		70		523		1,800		5,710		3.61	
OCT	450		400		75		575		1,800		5,754		3.69	
NOV	450		430		80		622		1,800		5,797		3.57	
DEC	450		400		85		480		1,800		5,803		3.85	

is emphasis neither on percentage of return on sales nor on comparison to last year's results. These once popular yardsticks have very little usefulness in profitability accounting.

Other Uses

Thus far we have seen how completely profitability accounting integrates budgetary control and standard product costs with profit planning and management reports. But it might be said that these are all accounting processes and therefore relatively easy to integrate. What about some of the managerial problems which are not necessarily related to accounting such as product pricing, capital budgeting, and make-or-buy decisions? How does profitability accounting assist in these areas? It is felt that the incremental cost and profit contribution aspects of profitability accounting supply this need more completely than any other approach to managerial accounting does.

The time has passed into history when target prices or products were set by summarizing all costs—variable, standby, programed, specific sales deductions, and prime costs—and adding thereto a factor related to the total of such costs for profit. Even though cost factors may not have been known by such sophisticated terms, they certainly for many years were summarized this way as a basis for determining mark-on.

With today's more intensive competition, however, we must be able to adjust our thinking quickly to take account of the results of the interaction of supply and demand upon profits. Accordingly, we must know accurately what the cash cost of a product is in order that we may know what the effect of a contemplated adjustment in price on profit will be. Furthermore, we must know the answer quickly, as a by-product of the regular accounting process, not as a result of time-consuming, crash-type studies which convert custodial bookkeeping information to managerial uses.

Here lies one of the great benefits of profitability accounting, since its medium of communication is incremental cost and profit contribution—a by-product of the build-up of costs for budgetary control purposes. No longer is the sales manager required to wrestle with computations of "whole" cost and "gross profit" in his attempts to determine price policy. He now is presented with the same unit cost of product at any level of output, and he can make intelligent decisions to maximize profits.

Furthermore, today the modern division manager is being required to earn a target return on the capital he employs. This means that his sales manager must be determining his pricing policies so that aggregate results of pricing individual products will produce desired returns on capital. Target pricing policies developed in conjunction with profitability accounting have incorporated the return-on-capital-employed concept into the pricing of individual products so that management may be assured that all decisions in this area will contribute to maximizing—not necessarily absolute profit—but rather profit related to the capital required to produce it.

Lastly, target pricing formulas under profitability accounting have been so constructed that they recognize the difference between conversion cost and capital cost in a product. Hardly anyone would deny that the economically justifiable price of an article with 75% conversion cost and 25% material cost should be determined in a different manner than the price of an article with 25% conversion cost and 75% material cost, even though the total absolute costs of the two products were identical.

We should also consider briefly the advantages that regular incremental cost accounting offers managers confronted with make-or-buy decisions. It is not too uncommon to see companies strive to make in their own plants as much of the end product as their capacity will allow. Recently, however, there has been increasing sophistication in determining whether or not this is actually advisable.

Here, again, incremental cost comes into play, together with return on capital employed. Profitability accounting supplies the needs for determinations such as these. It enables management to compare the cash costs of manufacture with the costs of purchase and to relate both to the investment required on each basis.

Conclusion

The general approach to providing management with information on the results of operations should, first of all, permit no measure of disagreement on fundamental principles of accounting as between custodial accounting requirements and internal reporting principles. While it may be necessary to withhold from the general public certain information which is highlighted in reporting to management, the end results should at all times be the same for both purposes.

Secondly, internal reporting must speak in a language which is understandable and readily convincing to profit-minded managers, and not only to accountants. It must be alive and conducive to effective decision making at all levels. This article has sought to show that incremental cost and profit contribution are vital considerations in just about all management decisions that involve figures. For that reason, these concepts must pervade the entire framework of control techniques within a company.

Finally, profitability accounting and control emphasizes that all of the various control techniques which management uses in an effort to maximize its returns on the capital it employs must be effectively tied together. They must be integrated in such a way that the manager is not frustrated, but is assisted in the continuous and simultaneous manipulation of all his tools for profit maximization.

Just as there is always interaction between the forces that the manager is struggling to control, so likewise is there interaction between the tools that he uses on these forces. A change in the method of cost accumulation may require a change in pricing policy; a change in budgeting procedures may require a change in product costing. Profitability accounting and control holds all of the manager's tools in exact alignment so that he may use them with maximum effectiveness in the increasingly intensive battle for profits.

5

ECONOMETRICS FOR MANAGEMENT

EDWARD G. BENNION

In the management community there is a curious attitude toward the use of econometrics and programing as decision-making aids in business. Among people who possess a passable understanding of these aids and have given serious thought to the use of them in industry, few entertain any real doubts about the genuine value of the techniques. It is something of a paradox, therefore, that business has been singuarly slow and reluctant to make anything like an optimum use of them—if any use at all. Indeed, it is safe to make the even stronger assertion that more businessmen than not are highly skeptical of, if not downright antagonistic toward, such decision-making aids.

Reasons for Skepticism

Why does this paradox persist of business's reluctance to make full use of techniques which almost inevitably have a potential value substantially in excess of their cost? Here are six factors that have been important:

(1) Most decision-making aids are inherently more valuable to large organizations than to small ones, but effective communi-

cation is invariably slower and more difficult in larger organizations than in smaller ones.

(2) Because the aids are mathematical to the point of a rather formidable level of abstraction, it is quite difficult to acquire even an oversimplified understanding of them unless one has followed the unlikely course of carrying into his business career a continuing understanding and recollection of mathematics. Quite understandably, no intelligent businessman wants to back a considerable expenditure on techniques he does not understand.

(3) To illustrate with models possessing a formidable degree of abstraction, while trying to keep their general nature as understandable as possible, one must choose superficial and drastically oversimplified problems—a course which fortifies the businessman's instinctive feeling that there is nothing very new in these models, except that they have been unnecessarily glorified by being put in mathematical form.

(4) Intuitively, the businessman realizes that models derived from these techniques can be no better than the assumptions and judgments plugged into the models' circuits. These assumptions and judgments are largely the very things he has been plugging into his own handmade, less sophisticated "models" for years, and it is hard for him to believe (although in this case he is almost certainly wrong) that the more sophisticated models can improve much on his own versions.

(5) As a corollary to this last objection, the businessman is fearful—and with real justification—that misuse of any mathematical model can do more harm than good.

(6) Unconsciously, he may well resent such models as a challenge to his unique contribution of making decisions in complex and uncertain situations—although in truth the models actually tend to accentuate, rather than to diminish, the importance of top management's most unique contribution.

These reasons are not the only ones in the picture, but it is my view that they underlie management's skepticism concerning the value of econometrics and programing as decision-making aids. Almost invariably, management's reaction to a discussion of either an econometric model for predicting final demand or a programing model for, say, maximizing profits is something as follows: "These are simply elaborate mathematical expressions to get at the very things we have always taken into account; and the uncertainties involved in the measurement of variables and parameters, as well as in the assumptions on which we must all proceed, make it unlikely that these expensive and elaborate methods will constitute any real improvement over methods already in use."

Unfortunately, such a conclusion is, I believe, erroneous. The fact that it is understandably erroneous does not make the error any less so. And to correct this regrettable state of affairs, I am prone to feel that the econometrician and the programer, rather than the businessman, must accept responsibility for the first step. The econometrician and the programer have concentrated too heavily on turning out the answers yielded by their models—and the businessman knows perfectly well that the odds are heavily against turning out "the" answer in an uncertain world. They have given too little attention to the most valuable aspects of their models, namely:

(1) The capacity of the models to improve management's understanding of highly complex problems, which can scarcely fail to enhance the quality of the necessary value judgments management makes.

(2) The undeniable fact that the most valuable use of such models usually lies less in turning out the answer in an uncertain world than in shedding light on how much difference an alteration in the assumptions and/or variables used would make in the answer yielded by the models.

The principal purpose of this paper is to attempt to bring these aspects into sharper relief. I shall discuss econometric models—what they are and what they can do to help with decisions; linear programing models—their nature and advantages; and the vital role of executive judgment.

PART I. ECONOMETRIC MODELS

To understand how to improve the use of econometric models, let us begin with a simplified sketch of what these devices constitute. In the interest of further simplicity, let us focus on linear models, although the nonlinear variety is sometimes both preferable and possible.

How They Work

In the broad sense of the term, an econometric model might be defined as a mathematical description of some economic entity, varying in size all the way from rather small to vast. The primary objective of such models is generally considered to be that of predicting the future behavior of the economic variables encompassed by the model. It is obvious that the simpler the model, the easier it is to construct and to understand—but the less information it is likely to yield and the smaller its predictive value is likely to be (assuming, of course, that the more complex model is wisely interpreted and used).

Now, consider—as a starter—a highly oversimplified, two-equation econometric model of the United States economy:

$$(1) \qquad GNP_t = G_t + I_t + C_t$$
$$(2) \qquad C_t = \alpha + \beta \, GNP_t,$$

where GNP_t = gross national product, G_t = government purchases, I_t = gross investment, and C_t = consumption—all in time period t. The first equation is merely a definitional equation which says that gross national product in time period t is equal to the sum of government purchases, gross investment, and consumption. The second equation posits that consumption in time period t is some linear function of gross national product in t, the parameters α and β simply being constants (which we do not yet know) describing the precise nature of this linear function.

The construction and use of this model (or any other econometric model) customarily involves four broad steps.

Specification—This refers simply to the expression of an economic theory in mathematical terms. Thus, in the second equation just presented we have hypothesized, for example, that consumption is a linear function of gross national product.

Estimation—This is the attempt to determine parameters—in our second equation, for example, the true numerical values of the parameters α and β. This might be done by the conventional least-squares correlation method, by the Cowles Commission's "simultaneous-equation approach,"[1] or by any other method we might think would yield the most reliable estimate of these parameters.

Verification—A knotty problem involving some rather complex theory of mathematical statistics, this is the choice of criteria for accepting or rejecting the results of the specification and estimation processes as reasonable approximations to the truth.

Prediction—This is merely the projection into the future of the economy's behavior on the strength of the results of the preceding first three steps. In the next section we shall examine it in some detail.

To exemplify the prediction process in our simple little example, suppose we were able to specify, estimate, and satisfactorily verify a third equation:

$$(3) \qquad I_t = \pi + \phi\,(GNP_{t-1} - GNP_{t-2}),$$

which says that gross investment in t is a linear function of the increase (or decrease) in gross national product from time period $t-2$ to time period $t-1$.

At this point we have a more complete econometric model. It is still extremely oversimplified, but this is done in order to illustrate readily certain points, without encumbering the model with unnecessary details. In following this course, one naturally lays oneself open to the perfectly valid charge that this model could not be a very accurate one. (For example, I_t is an aggregate comprised of several important subaggregates such as plant and equipment expenditures, residential construction, and change in business inventories. One would not really expect any one of these subaggregates, let alone all of them, to be a very good function solely of GNP_{t-1} and GNP_{t-2}.) But as long as both the author and readers are fully aware of the limitations of this oversimplified model, there is much to be said for illustrations of such a simple nature.

---

[1] See E. G. Bennion, "The Cowles Commission's 'Simultaneous-Equation Approach': A Simplified Explanation," *The Review of Economics and Statistics,* February 1952, p. 49, for a comparison of these methods.

In the lingo of the econometrician, our three-equation model is comprised of four types of variables:

(1) C_t and I_t in the second and third equations respectively are *endogenous* variables; i.e., the behavior of these two dependent variables is assumed to be *induced* by the behavior of GNP_t, in the one case, and by the behavior of GNP_{t-1} and GNP_{t-2}, in the other case.

(2) GNP_{t-1} and GNP_{t-2} are *lagged* or *predetermined* variables; i.e., by the time that period t arrives, we do not have to estimate these variables, since by then their values are given data.

(3) G_t is a current *autonomous* variable; i.e., its behavior is induced by no other variables in our model, but it is also not a given datum, so we have to have some method of estimating G_t, if we are to predict the course of economic events by solving our three-equation model.

(4) C_t, in addition to being an edogenous variable, is, along with GNP_t, a *jointly determined* variable. Thus, as we shall see in our model, we can solve simultaneously for the values of C_t and GNP_t.

GNP_t (and, hence, C_t also) will give us no trouble, if we are in a position to predict (from various government budgets, say) the value of G_t with reasonable accuracy. Indeed, if real economic life were as simple as our three-equation model, and if we could satisfactorily predict G_t, we should now be in a position to become famous and much in demand! Let us consider briefly why this is so.

Since GNP_{t-1} and GNP_{t-2} are known data in time t, once we have estimated the π and ϕ parameters, we could readily estimate I_t from the third equation. Therefore, looking at the first and second equations (and assuming we have estimated α and β), if we could predict G_t, we would then have estimates for α, β, G_t, and I_t, leaving only C_t and GNP_t unknown. Having, then, only two unknowns and two equations in which those unknowns appear, we could readily solve simultaneously for C_t *and* GNP_t. Not only that, but having obtained GNP_t, we could go on to estimate I_{t+1}, simply by viewing the third equation as $I_{t+1} = \pi + \phi\,(GNP_t - GNP_{t-1})$. Then, by viewing the first and second equations as

$GNP_{t+1} = G_{t+1} + I_{t+1} + C_{t+1}$ and $C_{t+1} = \alpha + \beta \, GNP_{t+1}$, we could solve simultaneously for C_{t+1} and GNP_{t+1}.

Indeed, if we could predict successive G_t's, in theory we could turn the crank again and again, forecasting the course of economic events from today until doomsday!

This simple econometric model not only illustrates the general nature of such a device; it also helps to demonstrate the basis for much of the businessman's skepticism. Even admitting that economic life is much more complex than our little three-equation model implies, if it were possible to put together a much larger and more complex model which was highly reliable from a predictive viewpoint, this would long since have been done. Therefore, reasons the businessman, how much value does a set of predicted economic-variable numbers really have, irrespective of whether they are derived from a simple or from a complex econometric model? This is a fair question and, at least in my view, the answer is far more favorable than one might think at first blush; and the favorable nature of this answer turns around the problem of *how one should use such econometric models.*

The question to be asked is most certainly not that of whether an econometric model can always (or even usually) predict economic events accurately; for the answer to that question is that neither an econometric model nor any other known method can accomplish this. Implicitly or otherwise, however, some assumption about future economic events must be made for business decisions involving commitments into the future.

The real question, therefore, is whether there is any better-known method (or even any other method as good) for formulating such assumptions than by the use of an econometric model. In my opinion, the answer to this last question is a clear negative, provided one makes the most intelligent use of an econometric model.

Advantages from Econometrics

There are at least two highly valuable contributions that an econometric model (properly used) can make to many business

145

decisions; and, in one sense, these contributions are virtually inseparable.

First, the user gains a qualitative-quantitative insight into the economy's possible behavior that he is unlikely to be able to get from any other method. This follows from the fact that, in order to derive a predicted set of economic-variable numbers from the econometric model, it is first necessary to specify explicitly the full set of variables to be included in the full set of equations constituting the model, to estimate the parameters for those equations, to recognize which variables are autonomous, to formulate some basis for estimating those autonomous variables, and (through the verification process) to recognize approximately how strong (or weak) our criteria for acceptance are.

Whatever set of predicted numbers the model yields, unless we succumb to the temptation of thinking our set of predicted numbers is the gospel (which is, admittedly, something of an occupational disease among the unwary), the econometrician can scarcely fail to realize fairly well (a) how strong or weak his reed may well be and (b) how and where his reed is most vulnerable. Such a realization is surely a powerful asset in the intelligent use of any decision-making aid, and it is not obvious that any other known means of prediction is capable of providing this asset in anything like a comparable degree. *In brief, the very process of model formulation virtually forces on us both a better understanding of complex problems and a rational critique.*

The second contribution of an econometric model is closely related to the first one. There are some times when the econometrician will have much greater confidence in the predicted set of numbers than at other times. Usually on those occasions when his confidence is low, he will be able to pinpoint the reasons (i.e., the areas in his model) for his low confidence. It is then a simple matter to substitute alternative assumptions—about assumed values for autonomous variables, for example—and determine how much difference the alternative assumptions make in the predicted set of numbers.

Here too, then, it is far from obvious that any other known means of prediction can begin to compete successfully with an econometric model as a basis *for testing assumptions and for evaluating the sensitivity of one's results to alterations in those assumptions.*

To illustrate the very real and practical contribution made through better understanding, let me take an actual historical example.

In late 1950 there were some people who, despite Korea, forecasted an inventory-cycle recession for 1951—a somewhat less foolish forecast than it now looks with the benefit of hindsight. Indeed, it is a fact that business inventories did decline through 1951, though increases in other components of gross national product more than compensated for this decline in increments to business inventories, thus making the trend upward in total economic activity in 1951.

Our forecast at the General Economics Department of Standard Oil Company (New Jersey) in late 1950 was for a continued rise in the Federal Reserve Board index of industrial production from the third quarter of 1950 to the end of 1951. I was asked to defend that forecast vis-à-vis an outside economist's forecast of an inventory recession (of substantial magnitude) in 1951. At that time we had a fair-to-good econometric model. The inventory equation of this model, however, was rather poor (to put it charitably); and, indeed, this is an important problem we have yet to see solved decently by anyone.

Because of the weakness of our inventory equation and the extraordinary buying pressures of that time, we readily conceded that there might be a decline in the change-in-business-inventories component of gross national product during 1951. But we took the position that, even if this proved to be the case, unless government purchases for national security purposes fell well short of their target, (a) the worst that could happen would be a leveling off of economic activity from the third quarter of 1950 through 1951, with an upward resumption in 1952, and (b) at least a moderate rise in economic activity was an even greater probability.

The moral of this story is that even a fair-to-good econometric

147

model is better than no model at all. Even a model which falls far short of perfection has the decided advantages of making it possible to evaluate the over-all picture more accurately and to formulate a much better idea as to how far one's best estimate may go astray than would be otherwise possible. In the preceding case, for instance, the forecasters could recommend bold confidence in the future; in another case, confronted with a situation for which the outlook seems much less clear-cut, they might recommend tempered caution. Thus, whatever the situation, there can be little doubt about the value of a model's contribution to better understanding of the economy's potential behavior.

Using the same example just described, let me turn now to the capacity of an econometric model to help management deal readily with alternative assumptions, with probability coefficients assigned to the resultant alternative "forecasts."

In the 1951 episode, we made no explicit attempt to introduce an alternative assumption as to the course of government purchases for national security purposes—largely because time was at a premium and electronic computers were not then available. Suppose we had done so, however, and the alternative assumption had led to the conclusion that the economy would level off from the third quarter of 1950 to the end of 1951. We should then have had two forecasts, the original one calling for a 7% rise in the Federal Reserve Board index and the alternative one calling for neither an increase nor a decrease.

Suppose we had pushed our reasoning one step further and asked ourselves what sort of assumption about the course of government purchases for national security purposes would be necessary to generate, say, a 7% decline in the Federal Reserve Board index. We should then have had three forecasts, and we might have asked ourselves what probability coefficients we should assign to each of them.

With the benefit of hindsight, it is hard to give an unprejudiced answer to at least part of this question, although a probability coefficient of zero (and certainly no more than very slightly better than zero) would be an unbiased answer as far as the 7%-decline forecast is concerned. Certainly, too, we would never have assigned a greater probability coefficient than 0.5 to the leveling-off forecast, leaving a probability coefficient definitely no smaller than 0.5 to be assigned to the 7%-rise forecast.

What actually happened was that there was a 6% rise in the index between the third quarter of 1950 and the fourth quarter of 1951.

Now the fact that our initial and only explicit forecast for 1950–1951 was for a 7% rise, which turned out to be almost a centered bull's-eye, is irrelevant. Any time anyone comes this close, even with a first-rate model in a period as easy to forecast as that five-quarter period was, he is walking hand in hand with Lady Luck. What is relevant is the fact that in this situation requiring alternative-assumption forecasts, we could have provided, for each alternative, probability estimates of its actually occurring—estimates accurate enough to aid the decision-making process. Not only could we have done this explicitly (if we had known how, at that time) and with a reasonable degree of precision, but in effect we actually did do this *implicitly* and rather roughly.

More important still, this job, roughly done as it was, could not have been done satisfactorily at all had we had no econometric model on which to erect the analysis. *In short, the model permitted us to link possible outcomes to relatively simple probabilities*—a contribution of no mean proportions.

PART II. PROGRAMING MODELS

Something of a semantic debate might be produced as to the real distinction between econometric models and programing models. Certainly both are mathematical descriptions of economic entities. Certainly, too, an econometric model can be changed into a programing model with little more than a switch in objectives, and vice versa. For our purposes in this article, the essential difference between an econometric model and a programing model can be stated as follows.

An econometric model is basically a device with the primary objective of predicting what the future values of a set of certain variables (such as gross national product, producers' capital expenditures, and the like) will be.

A programing model is related but different, since it is basically a device with the principal objective of maximizing (or minimizing) some functional element such as profits or costs by determining what the future values of certain variables (over which one has some control) should be in order to maximize (or minimize) that element.

To see how and why this is so, suppose we begin by considering the relationship between econometric models and programing models.

Maximizing Profits

Assume we have an econometric model from which we have derived a single set of predicted values for the various components of gross national product. (It would be more desirable to assume that we have derived alternative sets of values or forecasts, but that would unnecessarily complicate our story. However, now that management has electronic computers to use, it should realize that it is almost as easy to turn out several alternative forecasts as it is to develop just one.)

From these predicted general-economic values one is usually able to derive predicted industry and then company values which are consistent with them. For example, in the petroleum industry, the consumption of the various products derived from crude oil is, among other things and frequently to a considerable extent, a function of various general-economic variables. Thus a consistent forecast of the future consumption of the various products of the petroleum industry should be derived, in part, from the general-economic forecast. Similarly, an estimate of a particular company's sales can be derived which is consistent with the predicted sales for the whole industry.

When the forecast of a particular company's sales of its various products has been made, linear programing enters the picture. To illustrate, I shall again take the petroleum industry.

Many petroleum companies are fully integrated. As such, they inherently tend to be highly complex and with geographically widespread interests. They must produce oil, refine it, market it, and transport it through its various stages to the ultimate consumer. Such a petroleum company will have alternative areas from which it can derive its crude oil; it will have alternative areas from which it can transport, and sometimes alternative methods of transporting; it will have alternative place in which the crude oil can be refined; it will generally have alternative methods of refining; and so on.

Now, before going further I want to emphasize two things. In the first place, an illustration of the nature of a programing model needs to be given; and the simpler this model can be made, the more easily can the fundamental nature of such models be grasped. Secondly, and equally important, the point needs to be made clear that optimizing profits for single operations of single refineries (known as *sub*optimization) is by no means the equivalent of optimizing profits for an integrated company in which these suboptimization problems are only small parts of the integrated company's total problem. Indeed, if each unit comprising the integrated company pursued a course of optimizing its own profits, the probability that profits of the integrated company would be optimized is virtually nil. This statement is far from obvious, but our second illustration in the following discussion will provide some insight into its validity.

Turning, first, to the purpose of illustrating a programing model, let us consider a small suboptimization problem, since this offers us our only hope of keeping our illustrative model down to reasonably simple proportions. Let us look at the following situation.

A refinery produces, as a by-product, 1,000 gallons per hour of virgin pitch in its crude distillation operation. Commercial fuel oil, having a sales value of five cents per gallon, can be derived from the pitch in one of two ways. The pitch can be blended directly with flux stock, which has a cracking value (and hence represents a cost) of eight cents per gallon, to make commercial fuel oil. The flux stock thus constitutes a cost of producing the commercial fuel oil, but we arbitrarily assign a zero cost value to our by-product, the pitch. Or the pitch can be blended indirectly with flux stock, either wholly or in part, by being first sent to a visbreaker unit capable of breaking the pitch (or visbreaker feed) down into an 80% yield of tar, which tar can then be blended with flux stock to make commercial fuel oil. The cost of this additional operation, in conjunction with the different viscosity- and gravity-blend numbers of the resultant tar, is such that we can assign a zero value to the tar, despite the fact that the quantity of tar derived is only 80% as great as the quantity of pitch. (The viscosity- and gravity-blend numbers vary with varying viscosity and gravity in the opposite direction from that which one would think most logical; i.e., the higher the viscosity and gravity-blend numbers, the less viscous and the lighter is the product.)

The viscosity and gravity-blend numbers of the pitch, tar, and flux are invariant at the figures shown in Exhibit I. The viscosity-

EXHIBIT I. VISCOSITY AND GRAVITY-BLEND NUMBERS

	Quantity available (gallons/hour)	Value (cents/gallons)	Viscosity-blend number	Gravity-blend number
Pitch	P = 1,000 − V	0	5	8
Visbreaker feed	V	0		
Tar	T = 0.8V	0	11	7
Flux	F = any amount	8	37	24
Fuel oil	P + T + F	5	21 (min.)	12 (min.)

and gravity-blend numbers of the fuel oil can be varied by varying the proportion of flux stock used in the blending process, but we specify minimum viscosity- and gravity-blend numbers for the commercial fuel oil of 21 and 12, respectively.

The complete information at our disposal is listed in Exhibit I. We pose as our problem that of determining the most profitable mixture of pitch, tar, and flux stock to obtain commercial fuel oil, which either meets or exceeds the minimum viscosity and gravity specifications:

Numbers 21 and 12 are, respectively, the minimum viscosity- and gravity-blend numbers we want to specify. But we might be able to maximize profits better by letting one (or both) of these blend numbers exceed this minimum. Similarly, we might be able to maximize our profits better by not using all (i.e., by throwing away some of the hourly output of pitch (P). Therefore, we let

$y_1 =$ the implicit excess in our viscosity specification,
$y_2 =$ the implicit excess in our gravity specification,
$y_3 =$ the amount of hourly output of pitch not used,

and these three y's are known as "slack variables."

Since this problem is treated elsewhere in great detail,[2] perhaps the reader will take it on faith that the foregoing table of information can ultimately be boiled down to the following model:

$$
\begin{aligned}
(1)\quad & 2P + V - 2F + y_1 && = 0 \\
(2)\quad & P + V - 3F && + y_2 && = 0 \\
(3)\quad & P + V && + y_3 = 0 \\
& \text{Maximum Z (profits)} = 5P + 4V - 3F
\end{aligned}
$$

We now have a set of three-requirement equations involving six variables. For these equations we must find that set of non-negative values for the variables (negative values for any of our variables would have no economic meaning) which maximizes our functional element, profits. Assuming that there is not only a non-negative solution to the equations but probably an infinite number of such solutions, ours is the task of finding the particular solution(s) which will maximize the profit function.

Such is the general nature of the linear programing problem. And in our example the optimal solution is actually

$$P = 0; \ y_1 = 0; \ y_3 = 0; \ V = 1,000; \ F = 500; \ y_2 = 500.$$

In words, this solution tells us:

Since $P = 0$, $y_3 = 0$, and $V = 1,000$, *all* of the pitch should go to the visbreaker unit to yield 800 gallons per hour of tar (remember, $T = 0.8V$).

Since $F = 500$, the 800 gallons of tar should then be blended with 500 gallons of flux to obtain commercial fuel oil.

[2] See E. G. Bennion, *Elementary Mathematics of Linear Programming and Game Theory* (East Lansing, Bureau of Business and Economic Research, Michigan State University, 1960).

Since $y_1 = 0$, the minimum viscosity specification is in fact met

Since $y_2 = 500$, the minimum gravity specification is exceeded (In fact, it is exceeded by a shade more than 1.5 points, since the flux part of the blend is 5/13 and has a gravity of 24, while the tar part of the blend is 8/13 and has a gravity of 7, which results in a fuel oil gravity of 13.5 plus.)

And since, as previously stated, Z (profits) = $5P + 4V - 3F =$ $0 + 4,000 - 1,500 = 2,500$, profits are maximized at $25 per hour

It is beyond the scope of this paper to explain the method of solving linear programing problems, let alone to explain the rationale for that method. There is no doubt, however, about the above solution constituting the optimum solution. The fact that this is by no means obvious, even in this relatively simple little problem, without first resorting to linear programing method both to discover and to prove this the optimal course of action bears silent witness to the potential value of linear programing models.

Levels of Profitability

Earlier I indicated that suboptimization at the level of the plant or even of the large affiliate is not equivalent to optimization at the integrated-company level. It is clearly not feasible to illustrate this on a large scale in this article since a realistic model would run to between 100 and 200 equations, and to perhaps two to three times as many variables as equations—a truly formidable undertaking. Fortunately, we can get at least an intuitional feel for the problem by relying primarily on a verbal and graphic description of a small hypothetical case.

Suppose we have an integrated company engaged in a two stage manufacturing process, this company having just two plants: plant A, which manufactures a semifinished product, and plant B, which finishes the semifinished product.[3] Both A and B can improve their technology (thus reducing operating costs) by investing in new capital equipment; and both A and B must pay the same fixed rate of return on any money received for such

[3] The basic idea for this illustration is drawn from an unpublished paper by L. A. Rapoport and W. P. Drews, "Mathematical Approaches to Long-Range Planning and Integrated Operations Scheduling," Esso Research and Engineering Company, October 1959.

additional investment. Thus Exhibit II gives, for A and B, a graphic description of the courses of total interest costs, total operating costs (clearly not a linear function, but programing models do not necessarily have to be linear to be soluble), and the sum of total interest and operating costs, as additional investment increases from zero to various positive figures.

It is clear from Exhibit II that, if plant A and plant B are each interested in minimizing their own total costs alone, then A should invest an additional amount am_1 to minimize its costs at $m_1\alpha_1$, while B should invest an additional amount bm_2 to minimize its costs at $m_2\beta_1$.

Suppose, however, that the company as a whole can obtain only a limited amount of total investment funds, T, and that T is smaller than $am_1 + bm_2$. In that event, as we can see from Exhibit III, the company can minimize its total costs only by not minimizing costs for either plant A or plant B. Thus, in Exhibit III, $ba = T =$ the total amount of funds available for additional investment. And total company costs (the curved line $\gamma_1 0\gamma_2$) are the summation of plant A's and plant B's total costs (the curved

EXHIBIT II. INTEREST AND OPERATING COSTS

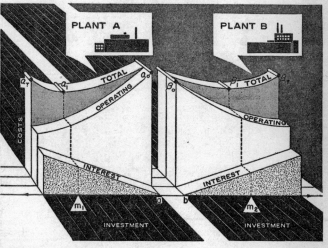

155

EXHIBIT III. TOTAL COMPANY COSTS COMPARED TO PLANT COSTS

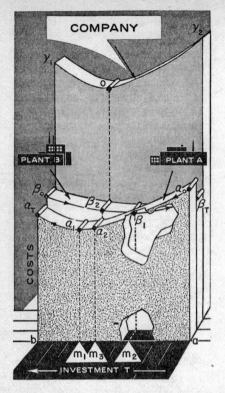

lines $\alpha_o\alpha_1\alpha_T$ and $\beta_o\beta_1\beta_T$) obtained graphically by superimposing plant A's cost diagram in Exhibit II on plant B's. Thus, in Exhibit III, $b\gamma_1$ is total company costs if all available investment funds, $T = ba$, are absorbed by plant A so that plant B obtains no additional funds for investment; and $a\gamma_2$ is the reverse cost picture, with plant B getting all the available investment funds; while all intermediate points on the $\gamma_1 0\gamma_2$ curve, running from left to right, represent costs associated with giving A less funds and giving B more funds.

From the viewpoint of minimizing total company costs, the optimum course of action is clearly to divert am_3 amount of funds to A and bm_3 amount of funds to B for a minimum company cost figure of $m_3 0$. This means individual cost figures of $m_3 \alpha_2$ and $m_3 \beta_2$ for A and B, respectively, and neither of these figures is a minimum cost figure for the individual plants.

There is no doubt about the validity of the conclusion we have just reached; but if it is to make real economic sense, certain other conditions must implicitly be true. Since $m_3 \alpha_2$ and $m_3 \beta_2$ are total costs for A and B, respectively, when both are operating at capacity with particular scales of plant which are of less-than-optimum size (from a total cost viewpoint), one of two things must be true for our illustration to make economic sense: either (1) the output of A must be precisely the output required by B when both are operating at capacity, or else (2) one of the two plants must operate at less than capacity.

The first of these two possibilities is not a likely one. It is, in fact, an apt illustration of the superficial or unreal nature of examples that are difficult to avoid adopting in the interests of simplicity and ease of understanding. The second possibility does, however, seem probable.

It makes more economic sense to maximize profits than to minimize costs, and it would not be difficult to make realistic enough assumptions about such things as price elasticity, A's and B's immediate markets, distances of A's and B's alternative markets and suppliers, and the like to justify the conclusion that the profits of this integrated company would in fact be maximized by having B operate at capacity and A operate at something less than capacity. This would be a more complicated model than the one under the first possibility mentioned, but it could be constructed.

Thus, our analysis shows that suboptimization may well fall far short of assuring integrated-company optimization.

Advantages From Programing

We turn now to a general consideration of the principal contributions one might expect from programing models. These contributions are of the same general nature as those of econometric models. In particular, such models can contribute heavily to a better understanding and grasp of the highly complex problems of an integrated structure, and a much more easily grasped and much more precise analysis of the effects of alternative assumptions.

To illustrate the easier understanding one can derive from a programing model, take Exhibits II and III. It is immediately obvious from these charts that restricting available investment funds to the point where T is less than $am_1 + bm_2$ is responsible for our being unable to minimize total costs for A and B individually at the same time that we minimize company total costs. If we change this restriction to make $T = am_1 + bm_2$, we can simultaneously minimize costs for A and B individually and still minimize costs for the integrated company.

Changing our restriction to $T = am_1 + bm_2$ is equivalent to increasing the length of line ab in Exhibit III by an amount equal to the line segment m_1m_2. We can visualize this as pulling the two vertical axes further apart by an amount m_1m_2. As we pull the axes apart, the plant A cost curve, being fixed to the right axis, shifts to the right with the right axis; and the plant B curve, being fixed to the left axis, shifts to the left with the left axis. When we have pulled the axes apart to the exact amount m_1m_2, then α_1 will lie directly under β_1; and with α_1 and β_1 the minimum points on the two curves, the new minimum point, 0, will also lie directly above α_1 and β_1. Consequently, changing our investment restrictions has made it possible simultaneously to minimize all three costs.

Our case example also illustrates the comparative ease with which managers can ascertain the effects flowing from making an alternative assumption. This advantage may take one of two general forms:

(1) The benefit may be similar to that stemming from making alternative assumptions about an econometric model. For example, the objective might be to maximize profits in our programing model, but we might wish to assume (a) that some foreign country (or countries) will not raise taxes, or (b) that taxes will be raised by some given amount. These two assumptions would certainly yield different maximized profits, and our problem in

this respect would be similar to an econometric-model problem: namely, what are the best probability coefficients to assign to our two tax assumptions? Given such estimated probability coefficients under these alternative tax assumptions, we might well conclude that a previously contemplated investment in the foreign country (or countries) is a more dubious conclusion than we first thought.

(2) We might be able to derive from our programing model a rather precise estimate of the cost of adhering to some given policy. Assume, again, an objective of profit maximization, along with a set of requirements equations which does not include an explicit dividend-requirements equation; assume, in other words, that we maximize profits and then decide what dividend we can "afford" to pay in the short run.

Now assume that corporate policy is to maintain dividends at some given level, unless there are compelling motives to reduce dividends temporarily. If we then add an explicit dividend-requirements equation to the constraints of our original model, we may well get a different (and lower) figure for maximized profits, and we will also have some concrete measure of the "cost" of adhering to our policy of maintaining dividends.

Invariably, the crux of many such corporate problems is that of deciding whether a policy is worth what it costs. Our alternative models cannot tell us whether the policy is worth its cost (unless we can add specific criteria for this purpose to the models), but they can provide us with a comparative measure of the costs.

PART III. BETTER DECISION MAKING

With a reasonably extensive background on the nature and potential contributions of econometric and programing models, we should now be able to see more clearly the relationship between such models and that epitome of top-management functions, judgment.

Judgment & Jigsaw Puzzles

To see this relationship, it is perhaps best to start at the end of our progression of models, rather than at the beginning. Let us begin, therefore, with our end-product model: namely, a linear programing model of an integrated company with geographically widespread interests. And let us define our objective as being that of maximizing profits, along with the further stipulation that the requirements equations of the model include (at least initially) no limitation on funds available for new investment and no dividend-policy restrictions. In brief, we will initially assume that if we need to tap the outside capital market and/or to reinvest all (or any part) of the company's profits in order to maximize profits, we are free to do so.

In general terms, what will this model look like? Well, it will be comprised of enough requirements equations and variables, along with our profits-maximization functional, to resemble an almost hopelessly intricate jigsaw puzzle. But this puzzle will be comprised essentially of only two general types of variables:

Physical-input variables, such as the amount of investment required and (in the petroleum industry) the amounts of the various types of crude oil to be produced from the various reservoirs or the amounts of the various products to be refined from these various crudes at the various refineries.

Physical-output variables, such as the sum of the outputs of the crude and products it is estimated will be sold. Each of these two types of variables will have value coefficients—either *cost* coefficients, such as the estimated cost of producing one barrel of the various types of crude from the various reservoirs, or *revenue* coefficients, such as the estimated selling price of one barrel of the various types of crude and products to be sold.

Although the magnitude of such a model is so vast that no mortal mind could grasp and coordinate all the information it contains, without an efficient method of analyzing that information (and linear programing techniques are just such a method), the general nature of the problem, its complexities, and its objective are quite easy to understand. We have one set of variables which, when we multiply them by their coefficients, give us a set of cost figures; and we have another set of numbers which, when we multiply them by their coefficients, give us a set of revenue figures. (These figures constitute given data for the right sides of programing inequations. The optimum solution to the programing problem may tell us to reduce some of these given revenue figures—that is, to deviate from the forecast.)

Obviously, the difference between total revenue and total costs is profit. The revenue figures are given data in the linear programing model, but the cost figures can take a variety of numbers, since our model is basically an attempt to set down all of the alternative ways in which the given demand for crude and products can be met. And the purpose of the programing model is to find with absolute certainty (given the accuracy of the data and the assumptions used) the most profitable of the alternative ways to meet that demand. Sometimes there will be more than one way to maximize profits, but there can be only one maximized profits figure; that is, if, say, there are two different ways to maximize profits, both ways will lead to the same profits figure.

I have mentioned the awesome scope of data in the model. The outstanding value of linear programing techniques is that they are an extraordinarily efficient method of analyzing problems fraught with complexities beyond the firm grasp of any human mind. Indeed, in a sense this has really been the most important thesis of my article. I have stated that two of the principal contributions of econometric and programing models are (1) vastly to enhance one's understanding and grasp of highly complex problems and (2) to make possible a much more easily grasped and precise analysis of the effects of alternative assumptions being plugged into the models' circuits. In the final analysis these two statements are essentially a more detailed way of saying that the models are highly efficient methods, not for yielding "the" answer in an uncertain world, but for analyzing more clearly and more completely the necessarily complex problems of that uncertain world.

Stated more earthily, to use such techniques is greatly to reduce the need for buying a pig in a poke.

Once the model is ready to be solved, there is, of course, no room for judgment; an electronic computer grinds out the one and only conclusion compatible with the inputs. But there is much room for the exercise of sound judgment both before the model is ready for solution and after the computer has turned out "the" answer. To refer back to our example of the integrated company, how much difference would there be in the answer yielded if we included in the model a constraint in the form of some specific dividend policy? The new model can tell us the answers under both approaches, but it cannot tell management which answer is the best answer.

Management can get help, even on this latter point, from the model by providing it with additional pertinent information. But, again, what is pertinent is something that only management can decide. Consequently, whether management chooses to exercise its judgment without providing additional information or by providing additional information, it must still make the critical decisions. All that programing models can do is to provide concrete answers to whatever questions are asked of it, subject to the assumptions (and other constraints) fed into it. This is a tremendously important contribution, since it throws into much sharper relief than any other method can the "price" of alternative assumptions—but it is clearly only an aid to judgment, not a substitute for it.

Note, too, that the programing model takes as given the demand-forecast figures. These were derived from a succession of forecasts building up from (1) a forecast of general economic activity, through (2) a forecast of industry demand, to (3) an eventual forecast of company demand. As we have previously seen, none of these three steps is simple and all can involve alternative assumptions. At each stage management judgment is vital.

Clearly, too, this can involve an appalling number of total alternatives to be fed into a programing model as given demand data. There may be as many as three sensible general economic alternatives. These would generate three alternative industry and company forecasts, even if the industry and company forecasts depended on nothing but the general economic outlook. But industry and company forecasts do, in fact, also depend invariably on something more than general economic conditions. In consequence, there might be three alternative industry forecasts applicable to each of the general economic forecasts, for a total of nine industry alternatives. And there might be three company forecasts applicable to each of the nine possible industry forecasts, for a total of twenty-seven company alternatives. Thus we have, quite literally, jigsaw puzzles within jigsaw puzzles—and each requires real judgment.

Furthermore, these puzzles are genuine assets, rather than unnecessarily complicated liabilities. *For they are always present, even when we fail to recognize them explicitly.* Hence, models have the great advantage of forcing us to focus our attention on finding the "best" solution to important puzzles which we might otherwise ignore.

Conditions of Progress

After a substantial introduction, a rather long discourse on the nature of econometrics and programing, on the contributions which might be expected from them, and something of a digression on judgment, we should be in a position to draw some reasonably trenchant inferences for company action. It seems to me that three points stand out:

It is incumbent on the econometrician and programer to convince business of the value of their products. Highly trained professional people are reluctant to divert much of their time from their professional interests to the challenging (but to them generally less satisfying) task of selling the value of their particular talents and techniques. Nevertheless, one cannot expect business to accept these products on blind faith; and neither can one expect to sell the value of such complicated, abstract-level techniques to the businessman without a carefully planned effort calculated to interest and enlighten him.

Any effort to interest and help management should involve a good deal more than merely presenting a simplified discussion of the new techniques. Certainly a rudimentary understanding of them is almost as important to top management as, let us say, elementary accounting. But such an understanding is more a means to an end than it is an end in itself. The advantages of econometric and programing models do not lie in the fact that they can produce a precise answer; for this could be true only if they could generally produce the answer, and that is out of the question.

Consequently, a rudimentary understanding of econometrics

and programing would be valuable to top management primarily so that the models no longer should appear mystical, complicated, and frighteningly abstract creations of the devil. Once this illusion is shattered, it is a relatively simple matter to understand how the models improve one's insight into complicated problems and how, by making alternative assumptions, one can make a more precise evaluation of alternative courses of action. Indeed, the very fact that models have to be understood and "digested" is the key to one of their major contributions.

Econometric and programing models are no substitute (and never can be) for sound judgment in making decisions. Rather, they are aids calculated to give a greater insight into the nature of complicated problems and hence to strengthen one's ability to exercise sounder judgment than would otherwise be possible. This means that sound judgment is required at both the top-management level and the professional level.

Clearly, top management must, by definition, accept ultimate responsibility for whatever judgment is exercised by whomever, and this is a form of judgment in itself. But this should imply far more than a mere understanding of techniques and of judgments made by technicians in choosing alternative assumptions and in recommending some decision seeming to flow from such assumptions. For the technician is frequently in nowhere near as good a position as is top management to formulate judgments (or even to conceive many relevant assumption alternatives). Particularly in a complex integrated company, top executives are frequently the only ones with the breadth of grasp necessary to conceive and evaluate certain types of alternative assumptions effectively.

Making good judgments has always been the *ne plus ultra* function of top management. To fortify this function with the best available analytical techniques is not to weaken its foundations but to give them the greatest possible strength.

6

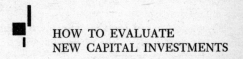

HOW TO EVALUATE
NEW CAPITAL INVESTMENTS

JOHN G. MCLEAN

In evaluating new investment projects, why are return-on-investment figures preferable to years-to-pay-out figures?

Of various possible methods for calculating return on investment, why is the discounted-cash-flow procedure likely to yield the best results?

What techniques and assumptions will help executives who want to make practical use of the discounted-cash-flow method?

Obviously, I cannot answer these questions satisfactorily for all companies. I shall attempt only to describe some of the answers developed by the Continental Oil Company. Faced with a need for better methods of evaluating investment proposals, management decided in 1955 to adopt the discounted-cash-flow method. The procedures adopted, the reasons for choosing them, and the results obtained during the past three years may serve as a useful "case example" for other companies to study.

Of course, the techniques that I shall describe were not invented by Continental. They have been used for centuries in the field of finance and banking and have been fully described in

165

many textbooks and articles in the field of industrial management and business economics during the past 25 or 30 years. It is only recently, however, that they have been applied in the industrial field, and their usage is still limited to a fairly small number of companies.

Management Concern

Prior to 1955, we had relied heavily—as many oil companies do—on years-to-pay-out figures as the primary means of judging the desirability of investments and as a yardstick for measuring one investment opportunity against another. We had also made use of return-on-investment figures computed in a variety of different ways, which I shall describe later.

In the latter part of 1954 our financial group, consisting of the controller, the financial vice president, and myself, undertook a comprehensive review of the techniques we were then using in making capital investment decisions. We were concerned about this matter because of the large amounts of new money we found it necessary to channel back into the oil business each year. Characteristically, oil companies have a very high rate of capital turnover because they operate assets which deplete at high rates, and large amounts of new funds must be reinvested each year if earnings are to be maintained and increased.

The capital expenditures of Continental Oil, for example, normally run in the neighborhood of $100 million per year, or about $385,000 each working day—roughly twice our net income, which is about $50 million per year. To the best of my knowledge, there are few, if any, other major industries with such a high ratio of capital expenditures to current net income.

In the oil business, therefore, the making of capital investment decisions assumes considerably more significance as a part of top management's job than is usually the case. In our own situation it was apparent that the management judgment exercised in directing the flow of new funds into our business had a very significant bearing upon current and future earnings per share and a profound influence on the long-term growth and development of our company. We decided, therefore, that we should make a maximum effort to develop the best possible yardstick for comparing one investment opportunity against another and for evaluating the returns that particular projects would earn on the stockholder's dollar.

New Techniques

As a background for outlining the new techniques which our financial group recommended as a result of its study and which were later implemented throughout the company, let me first outline the steps which are normally involved in the appraisal of new capital investments:

1. Estimate the volume of sales, prices, costs of materials, operating expenses, transportation costs, capital investment requirements, strength and nature of competition, rates of obsolescence or depletion, and other economic and business factors.

2. Summarize basic estimates of annual income, life of project, and capital investment in convenient form for appraisal purposes. (Commonly used yardsticks include years to pay out and return on investment.)

3. Exercise managerial judgment in determining whether or not (a) the anticipated return is large enough to warrant the business risks involved; (b) the investment opportunity is attractive in view of the various alternative opportunities for capital spending; (c) the timing of the investment is right relative to anticipated developments in the near future.

The discounted-cash-flow techniques which we introduced in 1955 had to do only with step 2; that is, with the way we did our arithmetic in adding up the basic estimates of annual incomes, life of project, and capital investments to arrive at payout and return on investment.

It was clearly recognized that there was nothing in the discounted-cash-flow method which would make it any easier to estimate the items listed in step 1 or which would improve the accuracy of those estimates. It was likewise recognized that there was nothing in the discounted-cash-flow techniques which would relieve management at any level of the responsibility for exercising judgment on the various matters listed under step 3. We were concerned fundamentally, at this time, with improving the mechanics of our capital investment analyses in order that management might render better judgments on the three points under step 3.

Our first recommendation was that we use the return-on-investment figures as the primary yardstick for evaluating new capital investments and pay much less attention to years-to-payout figures than had been our custom in the past.

Our reason for de-emphasizing payout figures was simply that they do not provide an adequate means of discriminating among new investment opportunities. They merely indicate how long it will take to recover the original capital outlay and do not tell us anything about the earning power of an investment. There is, of course, no point in making investments which just give us our money back. The true worth of an investment depends on how much income it will generate after the original outlay has been recovered, and there is no way that can be determined from a payout figure. Generally speaking, payout figures are reliable measures of the relative worth of alternative investments only when the income-producing life of all projects under consideration is about the same—which is far from the case in our particular situation.

To illustrate how misleading payout figures can be, I have prepared an example consisting of three different projects, each involving an investment of $125,000 (see Exhibit I).

The annual income generated by the investments begins at $25,000 and then declines in later years in each case as shown on the graph. Since the annual incomes are identical in the early years, each project has the same payout period; namely, five years. By this standard of measurement, therefore, the projects would be equal from an investment standpoint. But actually the returns on investment range from 12% per year for project A, which has the shortest life, to 20% per year for project B, which has the longest life.

At first glance, you might be inclined to say that this is all pretty simple—all you have to do is look at both the payout period and the total estimated life to reach a correct decision. And it is

EXHIBIT I. DIFFERENCES IN RATES OF RETURN WHEN PAYOUT PERIODS ARE EQUAL

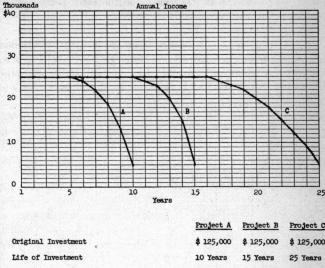

	Project A	Project B	Project C
Original Investment	$ 125,000	$ 125,000	$ 125,000
Life of Investment	10 Years	15 Years	25 Years
Payout Period $\frac{\$125,000}{\$ 25,000}$	5 Years	5 Years	5 Years
Return on Investment	12%	18%	20%

relatively easy if the payout periods are all the same, as they are in this example, or even if the payout periods are different but the total economic lives are the same.

Unfortunately, however, we are usually looking at projects where there is a difference in both the payout period and the project life. Under such circumstances, it becomes very difficult to appraise the relative worth of two or more projects on the basis of payout periods alone.

For example, consider the three projects shown in Exhibit II. The payout periods here range from eight years in the case of project A, which has a high initial income and a short life, to 11.5 years in the case of project C, which has a low initial income and a long life. On the basis of payout periods, therefore, project

169

A would appear to be the best of the three. Actually, however the true rates of return on investment range from 5% for project A to 8.5% for project C. The order of desirability indicated by payout periods is thus exactly the reverse of that indicated by return-on-investment figures.

It was for these reasons that our financial group recommended that in the future we make use of return-on-investment figures as our primary guide in evaluating new projects rather than the payout figures which had customarily been our main guide in the past.

EXHIBIT II. FAILURE OF PAYOUT PERIODS TO RANK INVESTMENTS IN ORDER OF DESIRABILITY

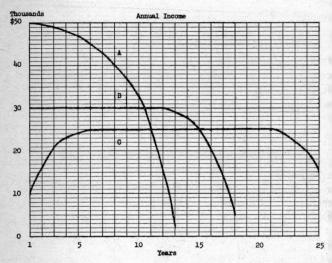

	Project A	Project B	Project C
Original Investment	$ 372,000	$ 267,000	$ 230,000
Life of Investment	13 Years	18 Years	25 Years
Average Annual Income, After Taxes Before Depreciation	$ 37,200	$ 26,700	$ 23,000
Payout Based on Average Income	10 Years	10 Years	10 Years
Payout Based on Actual Income	8 Years	8.7 Years	11.5 Years
Return on Investment	5%	8%	8.5%

Our second recommendation had to do with the procedures used in calculating the return-on-investment figures. There are at least three general ways to make the calculation:

(1) In the first method, the return is calculated on the *original investment;* that is, the average annual income from a project is divided by the total original capital outlay. This is the procedure we had been using in our producing, refining, petrochemical, and pipeline departments.

(2) In the second method, the return is calculated on the *average investment.* In other words, the average annual income is divided by half the original investment or by whatever figure represents the mid-point between the original cost and the salvage or residual land value in the investment. This is the procedure which was used in our marketing department for calculating returns on new service station investments.

(3) The third procedure—the *discounted-cash-flow* technique —bases the calculation on the investment actually outstanding from time to time over the life of the project. This was the procedure used in our financial department in computing the cost of funds obtained from various sources or in estimating the yields we might obtain by investing reserve working capital in various types of government or commercial securities.

These three methods will produce very different results, and the figures obtained by one method may be as much as twice as great as those obtained by another—i.e., a project that showed a return of 10% under the procedures used in our refining department could show as much as 20% under the procedures used by our marketing department, and might show 15% or 18% under those used by our financial department.

It was clear, therefore, that we must settle on one of these three methods and use it uniformly throughout all departments of the company. Otherwise, we would be measuring some investments with long yardsticks, others with short yardsticks, and we would never be sure exactly what we were doing.

Our selection of discounted cash flow was based on three primary considerations:

(1) It gives the true rate of return offered by a new project. Both of the other methods merely give an approximation of the return. The original-investment method usually understates the

171

return, while the average-investment method usually overstates the return. By contrast, the discounted-cash-flow method is a compromise and usually gives figures lying in between those that would be obtained by the other two methods.

(2) It gives figures which are meaningful in relation to those used throughout the financial world in quoting interest rates on borrowed funds, yields on bonds, and for various other purposes. It thus permits direct comparison of the projected returns on investments with the cost of borrowing money—which is not possible with the other procedures.

(3) It makes allowance for *differences in the time* at which investments generate their income. That is, it discriminates among investments that have (a) a low initial income which gradually increases, (b) a high initial income which gradually declines, and (c) a uniform income throughout their lives.

The last point was particularly important to us, because the investment projects which we normally have before us frequently have widely divergent income patterns. Refining projects usually have a relatively uniform annual income, because they must be operated at 75% to 100% of capacity from the time they go on stream in order to keep unit costs at reasonable levels. On the other hand, producing wells yield a high initial income, which declines as the oil reservoir is depleted; while new service station investments have a still different pattern in that they frequently increase their income as they gain market acceptance and build up their volume of business.

As an illustration of the usefulness of the discounted-cash-flow method in discriminating among investments with different income patterns, consider the three examples presented in Exhibit III. These three projects all require the same original outlay, have the same economic life, and generate exactly the same total income after taxes and depreciation. The return on the original investment would be 12%, and the return on average investment 24% in each case. By these standards, therefore, the projects would appear to be of equal merit. Actually, however, project A is by far the best of the three because it generates a larger share of its total income in the early years of its life. The investor thus has his money in hand sooner and available for investment in other income-producing projects. This highly important difference

EXHIBIT III. COMPARISON OF RETURN-ON-INVESTMENT CALCULATIONS

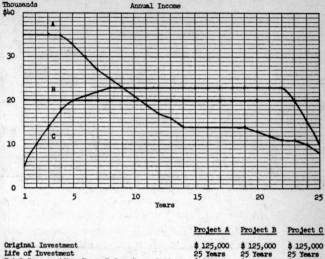

	Project A	Project B	Project C
Original Investment	$ 125,000	$ 125,000	$ 125,000
Life of Investment	25 Years	25 Years	25 Years
Total Income, After Taxes Before Depreciation:	$ 500,000	$ 500,000	$ 500,000
Average Annual Income, After Taxes Before Depreciation	$ 20,000	$ 20,000	$ 20,000
Deduct Depreciation ($125,000 ÷ 25 Years)	$ 5,000	$ 5,000	$ 5,000
Annual Income After Taxes and Depreciation	$ 15,000	$ 15,000	$ 15,000
RETURN ON ORIGINAL INVESTMENT $\frac{\$15,000}{\$125,000}$	12%	12%	12%
RETURN ON AVERAGE INVESTMENT $\frac{\$15,000}{\$62,500}$	24%	24%	24%
RETURN BY DISCOUNTED CASH FLOW METHOD	24%	15.5%	13%

is clearly reflected in the discounted-cash-flow figures, which show 24% for project A, 15.5% for project B, and 13% for project C.

Simple Application

To facilitate the adoption of the new system on a company-wide basis, we recommend a very simple application. Assumptions were made at many points in order to reduce the complexity of the calculations involved. In most instances, we found the range of possible error introduced by these simplifying assumptions to be negligible relative to that involved in the basic estimates of

173

income, costs, and economic life of a project. As a further means of facilitating the computations, we prepared a number of special arrangements of the discount tables.

The procedures that we developed for investments with a uniform annual income are illustrated in Exhibit IV. The payout period is computed in the usual manner by dividing the cash flow after taxes into the original investment. Then, since the life of the project is estimated at 15 years, the payout period is carried into the 15-year line of a cumulative discount table, and the column in which a matching number is found indicates the discounted-cash-flow rate of return. The numbers in this table are simply sums of the discount factors for the time periods and rates indicated. Thus, $4.675 is the present worth of $1.00 received annually for 15 years, discounted at a 20% rate.

It is apparent, therefore, that the discounted-cash-flow procedure involves nothing more than finding the discount rate which will make the present worth of the anticipated stream of cash income from the project equal to the original outlay. In this case, the anticipated cash flow of $20,000 per annum for 15 years has a present worth equal to the original outlay—$93,400—when discounted at 20%. Alternatively, it can be said that the discounted-cash-flow procedure simply computes the rate of return on the balance of the investment actually outstanding from time to time over the life of the project, as illustrated in Exhibit V.

The cash flow of $20,000 per annum, continuing over 15 years, is shown in column 1. Some part of this must be set aside to return the original outlay over the 15-year period, as shown in column 2. The remainder, tabulated in column 3, represents the true earnings.

On this basis, the balance of the original capital outlay outstanding (not yet returned to the investor) at the beginning of each year is shown in column 4. The ratio of the earnings to this outstanding investment is 20% year by year throughout the life of the project, as shown in column 5. The graph at the top of the form shows the declining balance of the investment and the division of the annual cash flow between repayment of principal and earnings.

EXHIBIT IV. APPLICATION OF DISCOUNTED-CASH-FLOW METHOD IN A SITUATION WITH UNIFORM INCOME

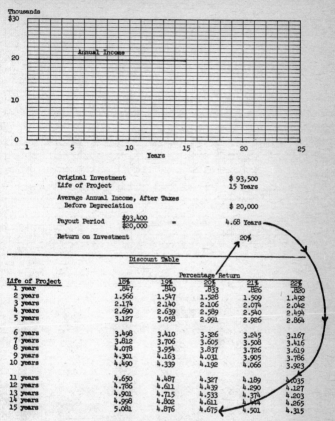

Original Investment	$ 93,500
Life of Project	15 Years
Average Annual Income, After Taxes Before Depreciation	$ 20,000
Payout Period $93,400 / $20,000 =	4.68 Years
Return on Investment	20%

		Discount Table			
			Percentage Return		
Life of Project	18%	19%	20%	21%	22%
1 year	.847	.840	.833	.826	.820
2 years	1.566	1.547	1.528	1.509	1.492
3 years	2.174	2.140	2.106	2.074	2.042
4 years	2.690	2.639	2.589	2.540	2.494
5 years	3.127	3.058	2.991	2.926	2.864
6 years	3.498	3.410	3.326	3.245	3.167
7 years	3.812	3.706	3.605	3.508	3.416
8 years	4.078	3.954	3.837	3.726	3.619
9 years	4.301	4.163	4.031	3.905	3.786
10 years	4.490	4.339	4.192	4.066	3.923
11 years	4.650	4.487	4.327	4.189	4.035
12 years	4.786	4.611	4.439	4.290	4.127
13 years	4.901	4.715	4.533	4.374	4.203
14 years	4.998	4.802	4.611	4.444	4.265
15 years	5.081	4.876	4.675	4.501	4.315

It will immediately be recognized that the mechanism of the discounted-cash-flow procedure here is precisely the same as that involved in a household mortgage where one makes annual cash payments to the bank of a fixed amount to cover interest and payments on the principal. This is the reason for my earlier statement; i.e., that the discounted-cash-flow procedure gives

175

EXHIBIT V. RETURN CALCULATED BY DISCOUNTED-CASH-FLOW METHOD

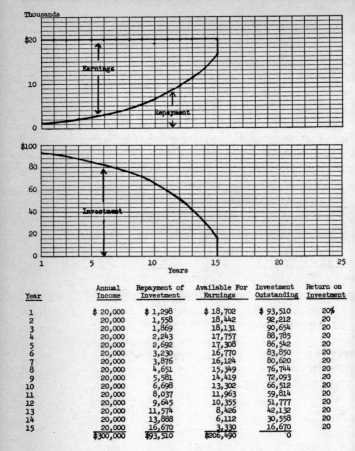

Year	Annual Income	Repayment of Investment	Available For Earnings	Investment Outstanding	Return on Investment
1	$ 20,000	$ 1,298	$ 18,702	$ 93,510	20%
2	20,000	1,558	18,442	92,212	20
3	20,000	1,869	18,131	90,654	20
4	20,000	2,243	17,757	88,785	20
5	20,000	2,692	17,308	86,542	20
6	20,000	3,230	16,770	83,850	20
7	20,000	3,876	16,124	80,620	20
8	20,000	4,651	15,349	76,744	20
9	20,000	5,581	14,419	72,093	20
10	20,000	6,698	13,302	66,512	20
11	20,000	8,037	11,963	59,814	20
12	20,000	9,645	10,355	51,777	20
13	20,000	11,574	8,426	42,132	20
14	20,000	13,888	6,112	30,558	20
15	20,000	16,670	3,330	16,670	20
	$300,000	$93,510	$206,490	0	

rates of return directly comparable to the interest rates generally quoted for all financial purposes. It is worth noting that in this particular case the conventional procedure of computing a return on the original investment would have given a figure of 15%. Had the calculation been based on the average investment, a figure of 30% would have been obtained (assuming straight-line depreciation in both cases and zero salvage value).

Our application of the discounted-cash-flow procedure in a situation with increasing income—e.g., investment in new service stations—is illustrated in Exhibit VI. In this case, we assume a build-up of income during the first five years, a twenty-year period of relatively stable income, and a five-year period of declining income at the end of the station's life (assumptions now undergoing modification in the light of recent statistical studies of volume performance).

To simplify the calculations and to avoid discounting the income on a year-by-year basis, however, we break the calculations into three parts. We assume that the income in the first to the fifth years is roughly comparable to a uniform series of payments of 60% of the normal level. We also ignore the decline in income at the end of the life, since it would have little effect on the results, and assume that the normal level of income will continue for the sixth to twenty-fifth years. And, finally, we assume that the land would, or could, be sold at the end of the twenty-fifth year at its original cost.

We have thus been able to make use of a special, and much simplified, discount table like the one shown at the bottom of Exhibit VI. The first column contains the sum of the discount factors for the first five years, and the second column shows the sum of the factors for the sixth to twenty-fifth years. The last column shows the present worth of $1.00 received 25 years from now. These factors may then be applied directly to the three segments of the anticipated cash flow from the project in the manner shown. The calculation proceeds by trial and error until a series of factors, and a corresponding discount rate, are found which will make the present value of the future cash flow equal to the original outlay.

Our application of the discounted-cash-flow procedure in a situation of declining income is shown in Exhibit VII. In this case—e.g., an investment in producing wells with a gradually depleting oil reservoir—we have found, again, that the cash flow

EXHIBIT VI. APPLICATION OF DISCOUNTED-CASH-FLOW METHOD IN A SITUA-
TION WITH INCREASING INCOME

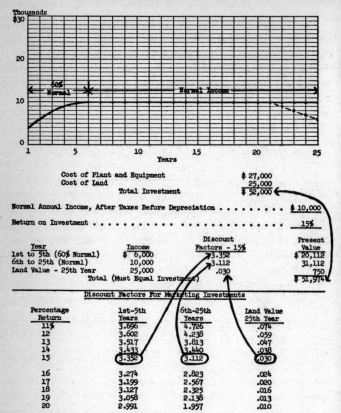

Year	Income	Discount Factors - 15%	Present Value
1st to 5th (60% Normal)	$ 6,000	3.352	$ 20,112
6th to 25th (Normal)	10,000	3.112	31,112
Land Value - 25th Year	25,000	.030	750
Total (Must Equal Investment)			$ 51,974

Cost of Plant and Equipment $ 27,000
Cost of Land 25,000
Total Investment $ 52,000

Normal Annual Income, After Taxes Before Depreciation . . . . $ 10,000

Return on Investment 15%

Discount Factors For Marketing Investments

Percentage Return	1st-5th Years	6th-25th Years	Land Value 25th Year
11%	3.696	4.726	.074
12	3.602	4.238	.059
13	3.517	3.813	.047
14	3.433	3.440	.038
15	3.352	3.112	.030
16	3.274	2.823	.024
17	3.199	2.567	.020
18	3.127	2.325	.016
19	3.058	2.138	.013
20	2.991	1.957	.010

can usually be divided into three pieces, with a uniform annual
income assumed for each. The first year must be treated separately, since the cash flow is usually high as a result of the tax
credits for intangible drilling costs. We then select a middle and
end period of varying lengths, depending on the characteristics
of the particular well, and simply assume an average annual income throughout each period.

These assumptions make it possible to use a simplified arrangement of the discount tables. The first line contains the discount factors for the first year alone, while the remainder of the table consists of cumulative factors beginning in the second year.

The factors for the first year and the middle period may then

EXHIBIT VII. APPLICATION OF DISCOUNTED–CASH–FLOW METHOD IN A SITUATION WITH DECLINING INCOME

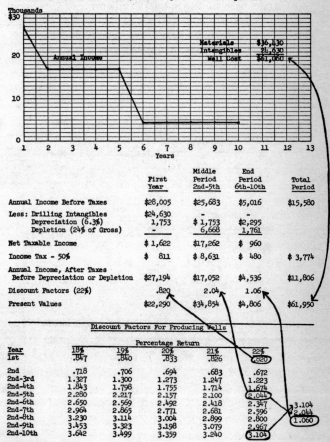

Annual Income, After Taxes, Before Depreciation and Depletion

	First Year	Middle Period 2nd-5th	End Period 6th-10th	Total Period
Annual Income Before Taxes	$28,005	$25,683	$5,016	$15,580
Less: Drilling Intangibles	$24,630	-	-	
Depreciation (6.3%)	1,753	$ 1,753	$2,295	
Depletion (24% of Gross)	-	6,668	1,761	
Net Taxable Income	$ 1,622	$17,262	$ 960	
Income Tax - 50%	$ 811	$ 8,631	$ 480	$ 3,774
Annual Income, After Taxes Before Depreciation or Depletion	$27,194	$17,052	$4,536	$11,806
Discount Factors (22%)	.820	2.04	1.06	
Present Values	$22,290	$34,854	$4,806	$61,950

	Discount Factors For Producing Wells				
			Percentage Return		
Year	18%	19%	20%	21%	22%
1st	.847	.840	.833	.826	.820
2nd	.718	.706	.694	.683	.672
2nd-3rd	1.327	1.300	1.273	1.247	1.223
2nd-4th	1.843	1.798	1.755	1.714	1.674
2nd-5th	2.280	2.217	2.157	2.100	2.044
2nd-6th	2.650	2.569	2.492	2.418	2.347
2nd-7th	2.964	2.865	2.771	2.681	2.596
2nd-8th	3.230	3.114	3.004	2.899	2.800
2nd-9th	3.453	3.323	3.198	3.079	2.967
2nd-10th	3.642	3.499	3.359	3.240	3.104

179

be read directly from the table, and the factor for the end period is obtained by deduction, as shown. The calculation proceeds by trial and error until discount factors are found which will make the present value of the cash flow equal to the original outlay—in this case 22%.

Somewhat more complicated applications of the discounted-cash-flow procedure occur whenever the cash flow is more irregular. To illustrate, here are two special situations:

Oil payment deals. Exhibit VIII shows the application when the problem is to analyze the profitability of acquiring a producing property under an oil payment arrangement.

EXHIBIT VIII. APPLICATION OF DISCOUNTED-CASH-FLOW METHOD IN A SITUATION WITH IRREGULAR CASH FLOW (A)

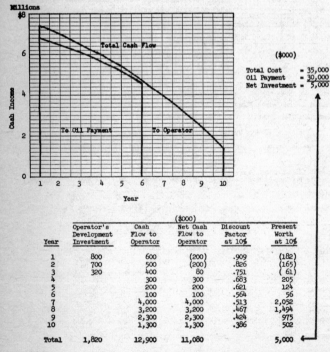

($000)

Total Cost = 35,000
Oil Payment = 30,000
Net Investment = 5,000

Year	Operator's Development Investment	Cash Flow to Operator	Net Cash Flow to Operator	Discount Factor at 10%	Present Worth at 10%
1	800	600	(200)	.909	(182)
2	700	500	(200)	.826	(165)
3	320	400	80	.751	(61)
4		300	300	.683	205
5		200	200	.621	124
6		100	100	.564	56
7		4,000	4,000	.513	2,052
8		3,200	3,200	.467	1,494
9		2,300	2,300	.424	975
10		1,300	1,300	.386	502
Total	1,820	12,900	11,080		5,000

The total cost of the property is $35 million, of which $30 million is supplied by an investor purchasing an oil payment. The terms of sale provide that he shall receive a specified percentage of the oil produced until he has recovered his principal and interest at 6%. The remaining $5 million is supplied by the new operator, who purchases the working and remaining interest and who agrees to do certain additional development drilling as shown in column 1.

The cash flow after expenses accruing to the operator from the properties is shown in column 2. Column 3 shows the operator's net cash flow after deduction of the development expenses in column 1. It is negative in the first two years, and remains small until the oil payment obligation is liquidated. Thereafter, it increases sharply and ultimately amounts to more than twice the original investment of $5 million. The discounted-cash-flow method recognizes that most of this income does not become available until late in the life of the project, and the resulting return on investment is 10% per annum. (If the same total income had been received in equal annual installments, the return would have been 15%.)

In situations of this kind, it is difficult to see how the analysis could be handled without resorting to the discounted-cash-flow approach. The conventional methods of calculating rates of return would give wholly misleading results.

Water flood project. Exhibit IX contains a second application of the discounted-cash-flow approach to situations in which the income generated by an investment is irregular. Normally, the free flow of oil from a reservoir (primary recovery) diminishes with the passage of time. In some cases, however, secondary recovery measures, such as injection of water into the reservoir, may result in a substantial increase in the total amount of oil produced.

The problem is to determine the profitability of acquiring a small producing property. The primary reserves have been nearly exhausted, and an investment of $2.5 million will be needed at the appropriate time for a water flood to accomplish recovery of the secondary reserves. No immediate payment will be made to the selling party, but he will receive a 12½% royalty on all oil produced from the property, whether from primary or secondary reserves.

181

EXHIBIT IX. APPLICATION OF DISCOUNTED-CASH-FLOW METHOD IN A SITUATION WITH IRREGULAR CASH FLOW (B)

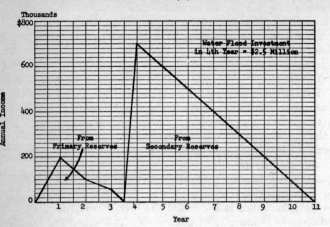

Water Flood in 4th Year   (Figures in Thousands)

Year	Cash Flow	Present Worth of Cash Flow At:						
		10%	20%	28%	30%	40%	49%	50%
1	$ 200	$ 182	$167	$156	$154	$143	$134	$133
2	100	83	69	61	59	51	45	44
3	50	38	29	24	23	18	15	15
4	-1,800	-1,229	-868	-671	-630	-469	-365	-356
5	600	373	241	175	162	112	82	79
6	500	282	167	114	104	66	46	44
7	400	205	112	71	64	38	24	23
8	300	140	70	41	37	20	12	12
9	200	85	39	21	19	10	5	5
10	100	39	16	8	7	3	2	2
Total	+650	+198	+42	0	-2	-8	0	+1

The calculations in Exhibit IX are made under the assumption that the water flood investment will be made in the fourth year. During the first three years all the primary reserves will be recovered, and income in the fourth to the tenth years will be attributable solely to the water flood project.

As shown by the table, the discounted-cash-flow analysis gives two solutions to this problem. At both 28% and 49%, the net present worth of the cash flow is zero; i.e., the present worth of the cash income is equal to the present worth of the $2.5 million investment. The correct solution is 28%, because the net present worth is declining as we move from the lower to the higher discount rates. The reverse is true at the 49% level.

In general, two solutions may arise whenever the net cash flow switches from positive to negative at some stage in the life of the project, possibly as a result of additional capital outlays required at that time, as in the case of secondary recovery projects. It is important, therefore, to recognize the possibility of two solutions and not to settle for the first one found. A false solution can easily be identified by noting the direction of change in the present worths as higher discount rates are introduced in the trial-and-error calculations.

As a final step in applying the discounted-cash-flow procedure to our business, it was necessary to develop some bench marks that could be used in appraising the figures resulting from the calculations.

As a starting point, we recommended that approximately 10% after taxes be regarded as the minimum amount we should seek to earn on investments involving a minimum of risk, such as those in new service stations and other marketing facilities. We further recommended that the minimum acceptable level of returns should be increased as the risks involved in the investment projects increased. Accordingly, we set substantially higher standards for investments in manufacturing, petrochemical, and exploration and production ventures.

We arrived at these bench-mark figures by considering:

Our long-term borrowing costs.

The returns which Continental and other oil companies have customarily earned on their borrowed and invested capital (substantially more than 10%).

The returns which must be earned to make our business attractive to equity investors.

The returns which must be earned to satisfy our present shareholders that the earnings retained in the business each year are put to good use.

In this latter connection, it may be noted that whenever we retain earnings instead of paying them out as dividends, we in effect force our stockholders to make a new investment in the Continental Oil Company. And clearly, we have little justification for doing that unless we can arrange to earn as much on the funds as the stockholders could earn by investing in comparable securities elsewhere.

Conclusion

The discounted-cash-flow method rests on the time-honored maxim that "money begets money." Funds on hand today can be invested in profitable projects and thereby yield additional funds to the investing company. Funds to be received at some future date cannot be profitably invested until that time, and so have no earning power in the interim. For this reason, a business concern must place a time value on its money—a dollar in hand today is much more valuable than one to be received in the distant future. The discounted-cash-flow method simply applies this general concept to the analysis of new capital investments.

The procedures which I have been describing in regard to the discounted-cash-flow method of analyzing new capital investments were adopted by Continental's top management in the fall of 1955 and were implemented throughout the company. Our subsequent experience in using the discounted-cash-flow approach may be summarized as follows.

We have found it to be a very powerful management tool. It is an extremely effective device for analyzing routine investments with fairly regular patterns of cash flow, and also for analyzing very complicated problems like those involved in mergers, acquisitions of producing properties under oil payment arrangements, and other ventures that require a series of capital outlays over a period of many years and generate highly irregular cash flows.

We have also found that the discounted-cash-flow techniques are far easier to introduce and apply than is commonly supposed. We had anticipated considerable difficulty in gaining acceptance of the new methods and in teaching people throughout the organization to use them; however, this turned out to be a very minor problem. Once the new methods were properly explained, they were quickly adopted throughout our operating and field organizations, and the mechanics of the calculations presented no problems of any importance.

There is one major theoretical and practical problem in using the discounted-cash-flow procedure for which we have not yet found a fully satisfactory solution. This problem is that of developing a return-on-investment figure for whole departments or groups of departments which may be computed year by year and compared with the returns calculated under the discounted-cash-flow procedures at the time individual investment projects were undertaken. Clearly, division of the cash income or the net income after taxes and depreciation by either the cost investment or the depreciated investment for the department as a whole will not produce statistics comparable to the discounted-cash-flow figures.

On the whole, our experience with the discounted-cash-flow techniques has been very satisfactory. To my mind, these techniques represent part of the oncoming improvements in the field of finance and accounting. Just as new technological discoveries continually bring us new opportunities in the field of exploration, production, manufacturing, transportation, and marketing, so too there are occasionally new techniques in finance and accounting that offer opportunities to improve operations. The discounted-cash-flow method of investment analysis falls in that category, and I would expect that steadily increasing application will be made of it by industrial companies in the years ahead.

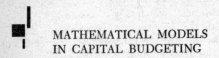

MATHEMATICAL MODELS
IN CAPITAL BUDGETING

JAMES C. HETRICK

Some of the major responsibilities of top management are in the fields of long-range planning and capital budgeting. Planning groups are constantly faced with such questions as:

> Should we build a new plant?
> If so, where is the best place to build it?
> And when should it be built?
> Or, instead of building, should we expand our existing facilities?
> Should we also modernize them?

This broad field of decision making for capital investment is one of the most difficult, one of the most recurrent, and one of the most controversial of management areas. And it is also an area where there are tremendous opportunities for basic improvements in operations and policies. Here are just a few of the shortcomings that show up again and again in corporate practice.

Many companies have never asked themselves such important questions as what the function of capital is in an industry.

Some managements pay only lip service to the idea that decisions should be made to the best advantage of the total enterprise and for the long term. All too frequently, short-term decisions are made that are crippling in the long term.

Capital is often allocated for the good of a department or for a cost center rather than for the company as a whole.

Confusion is likely to result if executives are asked to define the extent to which different investment decisions should be considered as being independent of each other.

It is rarely recognized that the proper rate of return may be different for various parts of the organization. In fact, many managements even fail to discount for differences in useful economic life.

In recent years operations research has been getting much publicity in the solution of the tactical problems associated with day-to-day decision making and immediate operations planning. However, the techniques of operations research can also help management face the issues and arrive at decisions in strategic areas such as those involved in planning and budgeting. The shortcomings just mentioned can be overcome, and many important factors in capital investment decisions can be taken into account in a model that truly represents corporate operations and can truly be solved with the computer technology of today.

The approach to capital budgeting that I shall describe in this paper is a new one. It has, however, been tested in a variety of situations, and I am convinced that it can be used profitably by a great many companies.

Making the Analysis

In explaining the new technique it will be helpful to refer to a company example. Let us assume that the company is in one of the process industries. The plant in question is physically adequate but technologically obsolete. Management is faced with the decision whether to invest capital in modernizing the plant or to scrap it for salvage and tax advantages.

If management modernizes the plant, it can take advantage of existing off-site facilities with several possibilities for expansion. If, on the other hand, the plant is scrapped, alternative sources of supply must be utilized. These in turn may involve additional capital investment in modernization, expansion, new transportation, storage facilities, and so on. Alternative possibilities may include purchasing, exchange, and processing agreements with other manufacturers.

In real life there are often thousands of possible combinations of manufacturing, transportation, and marketing investments in a case of this kind. In addition, the demographic changes in today's economy present a very real possibility of gross changes in the pattern of demand over as short a period as ten years, so that the operating configuration that is ideal for today's market may, in fact, be highly undesirable just a few years from now. In too many cases the existence of a problem of this complexity leads to total disagreement among members of top management. The disagreement is usually resolved by a compromise solution acceptable in the short term, but without enough regard for long-term corporate interests.

To meet the need, it is often possible to construct a model of the company's activities that permits a rational decision-making mechanism. The operations of our process plant, for instance, may be fairly represented as including manufacture, distribution, and sales. Each of these operations has cost components associated with it, which components in turn may be divided into capital costs, fixed operating costs, and variable operating costs. The system may be totally represented by a simple mathematical model, effectively balancing supply and demand on a detailed basis throughout the company's operations. The structure of such an operation might be developed along the lines indicated in the Appendix.

A system of this type is capable of being "optimized"; that is, an operating procedure consisting essentially of an allocation of production and supply can be found to minimize the total cost to the enterprise. This has long been known, and the method has been widely applied to operating problems such as the minimization of transportation costs.[1] It is possible, however, to use the same simple computing method as a guide in making investment decisions.

In order to do this, we must recognize that the first decision to

[1] See, for example, Chapter 2, above.

be made involves a definition of the function of capital in the company. What is the capital to do? To an investment banker, the function of capital is to make money, but not necessarily so for the chemical manufacturer. So far as the management is concerned, so far as the mode of operation is concerned, and so far as the investment policy is concerned, the function of a company is to get raw material manufactured into a finished product, distribute that product, and sell it to the customer. These are the operations; these are the objectives, the things to do.

The function of capital, then, is to permit management to meet the manufacturing and marketing objectives more efficiently. A measure of this efficiency is a lowering of the operating cost to the company. This means that the costs used in the model can be stated without consideration of any capital invested. They are, in fact, true operating costs for labor, raw materials, utilities, and so on. There are no charges for depreciation, taxes, or return on investment at this stage of manipulation.

We come now to a second important step in the construction of our model, or rather in the philosophy on which the model is based. This has to do with the treatment of production costs.

In many operations the unit cost of production decreases with the volume of the operation, and is generally taken as a variable operating cost. We need not consider it that way. We can define the true operating cost as the total cost of operating at full capacity, divided by the production at full capacity. Any cost higher than this is not a cost of production; it is a cost of *non*-production.

These two types of costs may be defined by a curve as shown in Exhibit I. (This is a very simple illustration, of course. In many cases the relationships might not be nearly so linear as portrayed here.) Note that the unit cost of nonproduction is zero at full capacity and 100% of the production cost when the machines are all stopped.

This treatment of costs is satisfying in that it places a penalty on failure to use a facility, the use of which would increase efficiency. It has a further mathematical advantage: whereas cost

EXHIBIT I. PRODUCTION AND NONPRODUCTION COSTS

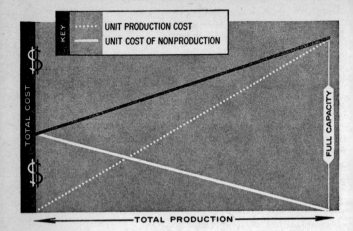

as usually defined is a variable, the two costs as now defined are true constants without approximation. This advantage promises an enormous simplification of the computing. The problem may now be solved and the optimal solution found by means of the simple calculation given in the Appendix. The steps are as follows:

(1) Find the cost associated with various modes of operation, taking into account available (or possibly available) manufacturing, transportation, and other facilities.

(2) Compare the differences in the operating costs with the differences in the capital investments required to achieve those costs.

(3) If the relationship is such that the savings in operating costs are at least as much as the return required on the capital investment, then the investment should be made. Preferably the return should be calculated on a discounted-cash-flow basis[2] so that the differences in economic life, in extent of obsolescence, and in book value may be fully taken into account.

In order to make a sound long-term decision, the problem should be studied at several points in time, the restrictions being

[2] For a discussion of the discounted-cash-flow approach see page 165, above.

assumed for as long a time period as possible. If we are extremely fortunate, we will find that the best modes of operation as calculated for different periods of time are compatible; that is, we will find that the best mode of operation for today can be logically expanded into the best mode of operation for several years from now. Unfortunately, in real cases this may not happen.

For example, in the case described in Exhibit II, it was found that a particular plant should be modernized and operated for three years, should then be placed on a stand-by basis and not enter the distribution system, and should then be reopened and expanded.

Such a solution, although mathematically valid, is totally impractical. In a case like this, one can define the practical strategies that most nearly fit the ideal. In the example given there are, in fact, three courses of action open to the management:

(1) The management may modernize the plant, keep it open, and adapt the distribution system to its existence in the middle years.

(2) It may modernize and operate the plant in the early term, then close it, and operate without it in the last period of years.

(3) It may shut the plant immediately and operate without it throughout the entire period.

The basic model may be re-solved to meet these practical requirements. The three modes of operation may then be compared by again taking differences in capital and in operating costs over the entire time period and discounting back to present value. The minimum cost alternative can thus be found and accepted.

EXHIBIT II. CASE IN PROGRAMING A CAPITAL INVESTMENT

A problem arose because of the existence of a manufacturing plant which, although physically adequate, was technologically obsolete and unable to supply the quality of products required in today's market. The plant in question was rather small compared to those then being built. Since it was argued that a plant of this size was at an inherent disadvantage for economic operation, there was considerable managerial controversy over the proper course of action—whether to modernize the operation by construction of better facilities or to scrap the existing plant and supply the area involved from facilities elsewhere, e.g., plants in adjacent states.

Possibilities Considered

Investigation of the managerial decisions to be made disclosed that the problem involved the choice of the best combination of facilities shown in Figure A.

The Jonesboro Plant was the one under consideration. It could have been closed, modernized at present capacity, or modernized and expanded in various degrees. The Smithville and Johnstown refineries could also have been modernized at present capacity; other possibilities for them were moderate expansion (enough to remove the bottleneck in existing facilities) or major expansion. Anderson, Boylstown, Charlestown, and Davis represented important market areas each of which, together with Jonesboro, could have acted as a terminal for secondary distribution of the product if transportation facilities were installed (see the dotted-line route) to supplement those existing from Smithville to Anderson and the available barging from Johnstown to Davis. Additional flexibility in operation was provided by the possibility of executing agreements for bulk purchase and sales, product exchange, and raw material processing with other manufacturers in the area.

In all, considering the various combinations of manufacturing and transportation facilities, plus agreements with other manufacturers, there were some hundreds of operating policies to be considered at any given time. Furthermore, the long-term consequences of immediate decisions were of major importance.

Available market forecasts indicated that various means of upgrading product quality would be required. Also, available forecasts of quantity demand, considered to be of acceptable accuracy for the first five years and of lesser accuracy for the next five, indicated that the demand pattern would shift considerably during the period, so that care had to be taken not to penalize operations at some later date so as to make an immediate good showing.

Expression of Problem

Analysis disclosed that, for any assumed management decision as to selection of facilities, the operating problem could be expressed as that of optimizing manufacture and distribution of products in a system consisting of approximately 200 destinations and 25 origins (plants, terminals, and points of exchange or purchase). It could therefore be defined as a transportation problem of the type given in the Appendix.

In the study of the costs involved, some peculiarities became evident. Rates for trucking, barging, or shipment were linear (i.e., the cost per unit was the same, regardless of the volume shipped). But pipeline

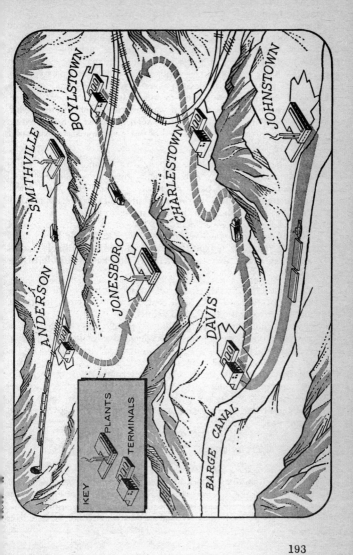

costs on a unit basis were nonlinear and varied in a manner which seemed to be dependent on the method of financing.

The major cost component—that of manufacture—was said to be a "step function." This meant that if a basic volume were produced at a certain unit cost, an additional "incremental" volume could then be produced at a lower unit cost per volume for that increment only, that a still lower unit cost then applied over a third range of volume, and so on. By appropriate devices these factors were introduced into the model, which became subject to optimization.

In constructing the cost tables, it was early apparent that the definition of costs could easily be varied in such a way as to favor certain types of investment and certain methods of operation. Two particular pitfalls existed:

(1) The divisions of the company—e.g., manufacturing, transportation, marketing—operated virtually autonomously, and internal accounting was on the basis of "transfer prices." Since these prices could include divisional overhead and profit, it was not appropriate to try to minimize them for the company as a whole.

(2) The existing investment was subject to various degrees of amortization, and it was known that new capital would be required at various times throughout the period studied. Accordingly, incautious use of capital investment charges could have led to fallacious answers.

To eliminate these dangers, all costs were constructed on the basis of true operating costs, with such components as interest, insurance, ad valorem taxes, and depreciation omitted.

Particular combinations of facilities were selected on the basis of an approximate balance of supply and demand throughout the period to be studied. The years at the beginning, end, and middle of the period were first studied, and the optimal mode of operation and distribution determined for each practical combination of manufacturing, transportation, and marketing facilities. This resulted in a series of cases for each of the key years. In order to compare these cases, decreases in operating costs were matched against increases in capital requirements.

Use of Model Technique

This step is a key point of the model technique. Recognizing that there is not an infinite pool of capital available for investment, we adopt the principal that the function of capital in industry is not only to earn a return but more specifically to earn the return by decreasing operating expenses. For example, typical results might be as listed in Figure B.

194

FIGURE B

Case	Operating cost (millions of dollars)	New investment (millions of dollars)
1	$53.0	$10.0
2	52.0	12.5
3	50.4	16.0
4	50.0	18.0
5	51.0	20.0

Here case 4, which has the lowest operating cost, is the one to start comparisons with. Case 5 is clearly not so good as 4 since both its capital requirement and operating costs are greater. In cases 1, 2, and 3 capital requirement is decreased at the expense of increased operating cost, as shown in Figure C.

FIGURE C

Case	Increase in cost compared to Case 4 (millions of dollars)	Decrease in capital compared to Case 4 (millions of dollars)	Ratio
1	$3.0	$8.0	0.375:1
2	2.0	5.5	0.364:1
3	0.4	2.0	0.200:1

These increases in operating cost may be looked on as the cost of the decreased amount of capital. Obviously the best of these is case 3, where $2 million of capital is obtained at an increased operating cost of only $400 thousand per year. That is, case 3 is the best of the alternative cases.

To determine whether it is absolutely preferable requires the establishment of bench marks for comparison. The bench mark is the acceptable return in this type of investment as defined by management. What we want to take into account is the less-than-infinite pool of money available, and the existence within the company of competitive opportunities for investment. The bench mark is properly set by an evaluation on a discounted-cash-flow basis by type of investment. Thus if a discounted return of 14% over a 25-year economic life is set, the ratio of the decrease in capital divided by the increase in cost is 0.255, or greater than the 0.200 for case 3. Case 3 is therefore preferable and should be chosen over case 4.

Let me put this in a slightly different way. In case 3 the company needs to invest $2,000,000 less capital than in case 4. At a discounted return of 14%, the company could earn $510,000 on this freed capital ($2,000,000 × 0.255). The price of earning this sum is $400,000, which is the increase in cost of case 3. Thus, the company is gaining $110,000 which it would not have if it chose case 4.

195

Solution

Proceeding in this fashion, optimal operating situations in our case example were chosen for the key years at the ends and the middle of the ten-year period. The results showed a curious effect. Because of the shifts in supply and demand during the period, the plant was scheduled to produce at base capacity initially but did not enter the solution (i.e., was closed) at the mid-period; it came in again for production at expanded capacity in the solution for the end period. That is, the computations showed that it would be desirable first to modernize the plant, then to close and "mothball" it, and finally to reopen and expand it. Investigation showed a three-year period over which the plant should be on stand-by.

Such a procedure was, of course, unthinkable from an administrative standpoint. Although a plant may be "moth-balled," people cannot be. Therefore, the practical alternatives were examined. The company could:

(1) Modernize the plant initially and operate until nonoptimal, then close for good and operate with the next-best arrangement of facilities during the final period.

(2) Modernize initially and operate over the entire period, using the next-best method of operation during the middle period.

(3) Close the plant immediately and operate according to the next-best method during the nonoptimal periods at the beginning and end of the time studied.

To make this choice, the possible investment schedules for each were determined and the model manipulated to find optimal operating costs for each alternative over the entire period of the study. The differences in operating costs and investments were then discounted over the entire period to enable comparison, and a choice was made as before. It appeared that the second alternative was best, and the third alternative next best. The advantage of the second over the third was that total investment was 16% lower, and the return, after discounting, higher.

The basic model gives a "rough cut" solution for a long-term pattern of investment designed to fit the changing conditions envisioned in the plant. The job is not yet finished, however. The model thus far will have considered broad operations without regard to the economic desirability of individual parts. To include this factor we proceed to a second stage of model building. From the results of our computations at this stage we construct a "tree of capital" which diagrams the relation of the various parts of the enterprise in the manufacturing-distribution-selling complex.

Such a tree is diagramed for a chemical company in Exhibit III. The structural relationships given in the tree do not depend on company organization. They are, in fact, input-output relations, the facilities at each level being supplied by the facilities at the next level below. The relationships also define two flows: the flow of product from bottom to top (like sap) and the flow of cash from top to bottom (like rain on the leaves).

Initially in the computations, no portion of the enterprise is permitted to earn anything; the cost of supplying the highest level is calculated with the costs that were used in the model. The cash generated is at first assumed to be associated with the highest level of the tree. The various facilities at this level may have very different values for the capital invested and the cash generated. We proceed as follows.

As a first step, we let the cash accrue only to each facility at the

EXHIBIT III. THE TREE OF CAPITAL

highest level and calculate the return on the investment at that point. Some one point will have the lowest rate of return. We now assume that this is a bench-mark rate of return for this type of investment, and we permit every facility at this level to earn at this rate.

All cash beyond the amount to be earned is reflected to a pool in a second-level facility and associated with that. The same type of analysis is performed at this level for the operations of the system.

The process is repeated at each of the various levels until eventually we come to the bottom of the tree and have a cash pool sufficient to pay off company expenses, overhead, and so on. If there is not enough money to do this, it is evident that some of the bench marks have been set improperly.

If it appears that some of the bench marks are in error, we eliminate the marginally productive facilities at various levels and reallocate our cash until eventually the system *is* in balance. If any major facility is eliminated, the basic model must be changed to reflect this fact and a new solution found to correct the structure of the tree.

The model thus gives us flexibility in a most important respect, viz., a balanced amount of parasitic capital is allowed to appear in the company. The value of this can be readily appreciated if we recall that many companies have a flat rule that a new facility costing, say, a million dollars must return at the appropriate rate on that million dollars, plus a certain percentage to go into company overhead. This rule does not allow for the attractive marginal investment which indirectly contributes to the total company. Also, in many cases representation in an area is desirable or even necessary for effective company operations.

There is no general rule, nor should there be any general rule, as to the extent to which facilities must support the enterprise. If, in fact, the investment is in balance on the tree of capital, we have a healthy enterprise.

As a further application of the model-building technique, we can devise another tree which represents not flow of goods but flow of decisions. This flow should closely resemble the scheme indicated by the company's organizational chart. We find here various levels of decision making, with a narrower range of activities and interests as we go to the lower levels. Requests for investment originate at all levels and are passed up to higher levels. At the very highest level top management is faced with the problem of budget allocation, and probably for the first time consideration is given to the question of return to the whole company rather than to a division or department.

Since in the usual case requests for funds exceed the funds available, there is a definite need for an optimum allocation. One procedure here is to begin at the lowest level of the enterprise, incorporate the planned facility into the company model, and determine the prospective return on the capital required. This should be done at the lowest level for each investment proposal, with those reporting to a common point on the second level being grouped together.

The return functions may now be compared. For example, suppose that management is considering one proposal to build unit A and another to build unit B, both in the same area of decision-making responsibility. Suppose further that if units A and B are given unlimited funds, the estimated rates of return will be as shown in Exhibit IV.

Now, the fact that the return for unit A is higher than that for

EXHIBIT IV. PROJECTED RATES OF RETURN FOR TWO PROJECTS

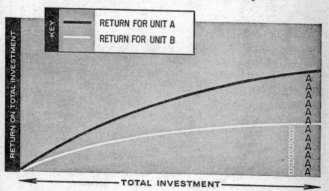

unit B at all levels does not imply that all available capital should be invested in unit A. Instead, the initial capital should go into unit A until the point where the incremental return falls below the initial rate of return for unit B (as happens in the last half of the unit A curve in Exhibit IV). At this point some funds should be diverted to unit B in order to maximize the return to the enterprise as a whole.

In fact, for any given level of investment there is an optimal allocation between the two units. With the necessary data at hand, this result could be expressed in curves as shown in Exhibit V. We see from this chart that all of the first million dollars of investment should go into unit A; in the case of the second million, however, somewhere around $950,000 should go into A and $50,000 into B; in the case of the third million, about $900,000 should go into A and about $100,000 into B; but after that A's share rises again.

Such a set of curves can be constructed for three or more competing investment opportunities. The result of them all, the output

EXHIBIT V. ALLOCATING FUNDS BETWEEN COMPETING PROJECTS

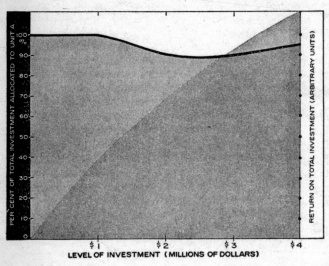

from the analysis of allocation at the lowest level, is the input to a similar analysis for the second level. At the second level, the return-on-investment curves define another set of enterprises competing for capital.

Such an analysis may be carried on step by step to top management, each decision-making level being in turn supplied with a plan for allocation of its funds.

One caution should be noted. No decision is better than the data available or the assumptions made. This is true for decisions based on a model as well as for those reached by any other means. The model approach, however, has two great virtues:

(1) Assumptions involved in defining a problem are necessarily made explicit when formulated mathematically, although this is not necessarily done in many other approaches.

(2) It is possible in many mathematical models to test the sensitivity of the results to the input data. Such sensitivity analysis may then indicate the areas where additional work in defining economic or operating quantities may be of importance.

Applications

How broadly applicable is the kind of analysis I have described? As we have seen, one kind of problem that can be solved is that presented in Exhibit II. But other kinds of problems, too, lend themselves to this type of solution. Let us look at some of them.

One such problem is that which production executives sometimes face when a company or plant is expanding. To illustrate, here is a situation that has recently come up.

A manufacturer is faced with a sales forecast which makes it necessary for him to expand facilities within a definite period of time. He has a proven process which may be used and which also is used by his competitor. He also has small-scale experimental information on two modifications which make patentable distinctions in the product and affect the economics of production. It is not certain in advance, however, that either of these modifications will apply favorably in large-scale production.

It has been found possible to design plants in various ways. Different designs are affected favorably or unfavorably by the existence in large-scale manufacture of effects observed in small-scale experimentation. A model of the system has been constructed and the theory of games applied to find the solution.

In solving the game, with quantities reflecting the advantage or disadvantage of the proposed process relative to the existent process, it has been found that there are several equally good alternatives. These represent the minimum return to be expected, regardless of what happens in large-scale work. The solution thus shows what is the least to expect in the face of uncertainty, with a high probability that a greater return will be achieved.

Other kinds of problems arise in the distribution system. Here are two illustrations, both from actual experience.

A problem in capital budgeting arose and was solved as a consequence of studying a large geographic area consuming 6% of a company's products but supplying only 3% of its marketing profit. The problem was to (a) find the reasons for the unprofitability and (b) determine if the region should be abandoned as a market or, if not, what steps should be taken to make it profitable.

The disproportion of profit to sales was found to be caused partly by the high cost of product and partly by improper marketing. The major sources of supply were plants which were among the company's oldest facilities with a high production cost relative to the company's other plants. This situation was aggravated by high-cost purchases in the area; and, in addition, high transportation costs prevailed.

The direct costs of marketing were comparable with those applying elsewhere, but unallocated expenses were lower. Thus, the region had a problem of inadequate margins.

So a mathematical model of the manufacturing and distribution system was constructed, and optimal operation under a variety of assumptions was studied. The results showed that the region could best be supplied by keeping one plant in its existing state, expanding another plant by approximately 25% of its capacity, and upgrading the product at the remaining plants while maintaining their then-current capacity. At the projected level for unallocated marketing expense, the over-all return to the system was less than the company's target but compared favorably with the company's achievement. Management saw that if these expenses could be reduced below the projected level, a very favorable over-all return could be achieved.

In another case, a major manufacturer of consumer goods is faced with the problem of deciding what to do about his distribution system. He currently distributes through a system of franchised distributorships, each of which independently controls field warehouse inventory levels, the intensity of marketing effort at the retail level, and to some extent the intensity of advertising in its locality. In the face of the projected expansion of sales during the foreseeable future, it is apparent that the existing facilities of the distributors will be inadequate.

A study of this problem has incorporated the factors of plant and field inventory, the freight costs required, distributor and dealer markups, and an elaborate forecast of the economic parameters or variables which affect sales. The data produced enable the company to make a decision between (a) systems based on distributorships, regional warehouses, and freight forwarding and (b) direct-to-dealer systems.

Still another kind of problem that lends itself to the analytical approach which I have described has to do with the composition of an investment portfolio. For instance, a large investment company has used the model-building technique to study the problem of constructing a portfolio of investments. At the same time that it has considered the factors of relative return and relative risk in various investment opportunities, it has incorporated not only management's desire for diversification but also the competitive necessity of producing both income in the form of dividends and capital gains in the form of appreciation.

The foregoing cases indicate something of the breadth of applicability of the model manipulation concept. The solutions found have already, in some cases, been applied for a sufficient period of time to show that the results predicted by the model can be achieved.

Conclusion

It must be emphasized that use of the model or of any of the mathematical techniques of the operations researcher does not imply management by computer. The mathematical model itself is a tool of management rather than a replacement for management. The factors to be considered in construction of the model are those which are and must be taken into account in any thorough decision-making process. These would include, for example:

(1) A description of the potential market over a given period of time in terms of the probable demand pattern for the entire area.

(2) The possible points for production distribution both already in existence and to be contemplated in planning.

(3) Typical production restrictions—for instance, whether or not a given plant may be considered as being tailor-made to produce one product or to be capable of flexible output.

(4) An estimate of the operation and distribution costs, classified as capital and/or noncapital charges and described preferably as a function of the volume of production. (These costs should include actual records as well as expenses projected and studies for new plants.)

(5) Any appropriate managerial restrictions such as a policy of constancy of employment; a decision on whether or not overtime or layoff dollars may be used; a decision on whether or not plant capacity must be fully or almost fully utilized at all times; a rule on whether or not labor productivity or capital investment is to be considered a prime objective; a preference for stating return in absolute dollars rather than as a rate on investment, or vice versa; a decision on whether or not control of a market is considered to have an economic value; or a policy committing the company to uniform exploitation of a broad area.

These quantities constitute the body of facts and assumptions on which the decisions must be made.

The concept of model building outlined in this paper has important advantages for modern business. For one thing, it enables the executive to probe more deeply and more thoroughly into the factors that affect a decision. Characteristically, managerial problems contain many more variables than restrictions, so that in a real case thousands of solutions may exist. The function of management lies in defining realistic assumptions and practical operating conditions. The computer can then perform its function of taking these restrictions and performing the detailed labor of investigating their consequences for the solution.

The output from the manipulation of the model is then a detailed plan of action which is only tentative over the period of study. Indeed, the solution itself may suggest to management introduction of modifications to recognize the effects of additional factors, changes in estimates, possibilities of diversification, and so on. In fact, the existence of the model, and of computers capable of dealing with the model, enables management to make an exhaustive study of possibilities rather than a comparison of some of the more obvious cases.

Of course, construction and manipulation of a model are not to be undertaken lightly, or in the expectation of achieving results overnight. Cost-wise, much depends on the excellence of existing data and the magnitude and complexity of the job to be done; but it is fair to say that data collection and refinement, the incorporation of economic analyses and forecasts, and mathematical analysis and computer operation may be a long and costly process, with costs running from $30,000 to $100,000 in some cases. It should be noted, however, that this figure is largely a "setup cost" and that the model, once constructed, may be kept current at a comparatively low expense so that successive applications can be made relatively cheaply.

To sum up, the use of mathematical models can supply management with a tool for decision making at virtually all levels, from daily operations to budget allocation and long-term capital investment programs. The full potential of the method has not yet been explored, but it is apparent that this technique can be of great aid in managerial decisions.

Appendix. Construction and Use of a Model

In this paper, and in the literature of mathematical programing generally, the terms "model" and "mathematical model" are used rather frequently. The usual meaning is that of a group of equations which purport to describe the problem under study in such fashion that all proper considerations are explicitly stated, so that the solution of the system of equations is in fact the solution of the real problem.

By way of illustration, let us construct a model for a relatively simple problem in distribution.

Mathematical Statements

Consider the problem of distributing a commodity in a system having balanced supply and demand, in which ten customers, 1 to 10, are supplied from four points, A, B, C, and D. In the broadest form of the case, any customer can be supplied from any one of the four points, and the problem is to determine that policy of distribution which minimizes the cost of transportation for the entire system. Data typical of such a situation might be as given in Table A. Here customer demands and warehouse supplies are shown under the columns and to the right of the rows respectively. The numbers in the body of the table represent the unit cost of supplying each customer from each warehouse.

Objectives and restrictions. The table is itself, in a sense, a model of the problem. A better and more generally expressive model can be constructed by a mathematical statement of objectives and restrictions—the objectives being statements of what is to be accomplished, and the restrictions being statements of all considerations which enter into the policy decision. To express these in equation form, the variable in the solution is defined as being the units of the commodity being supplied from each warehouse to each customer.

In Table B, x_1 indicates the (unknown) number of units to be supplied to customer 1 from warehouse A; x_{36} the number of units from warehouse D to customer 6; and so forth. This being so, any shipping schedule may be expressed by giving the numerical values associated with each of the x's. One such schedule might be:

$$x_1 = 2,114 \qquad x_{26} = 2,371$$
$$x_2 = 1,797 \qquad x_{27} = 612$$
$$x_3 = 532 \qquad x_{37} = 311$$
$$x_{13} = 270 \qquad x_{38} = 840$$
$$x_{14} = 2,032 \qquad x_{39} = 953$$
$$x_{15} = 2,760 \qquad x_{40} = 1,547$$
$$x_{16} = 209$$

All other x's would be zero, representing shipping combinations not used.

TABLE A. THE PROBLEM

Warehouse	Customer										Warehouse supply
	1	2	3	4	5	6	7	8	9	10	
A	4.41	4.60	1.50	2.85	3.82	3.75	3.10	3.97	2.95	3.19	4,443
B	5.56	5.41	2.38	3.31	5.36	4.96	4.36	4.83	3.87	3.25	5,271
C	4.28	5.00	2.10	2.50	3.59	3.65	3.03	4.64	2.91	2.86	2,983
D	6.87	6.63	3.21	4.51	5.98	6.11	5.75	6.53	4.60	6.55	3,651
Customer demand	2,114	1,797	802	2,032	2,760	2,580	923	840	953	1,547	16,348

TABLE B. THE VARIABLES

Warehouse	Customer									
	1	2	3	4	5	6	7	8	9	10
A	x_1	x_2	x_3	x_4	x_5	x_6	x_7	x_8	x_9	x_{10}
B	x_{11}	x_{12}	x_{13}	x_{14}	x_{15}	x_{16}	x_{17}	x_{18}	x_{19}	x_{20}
C	x_{21}	x_{22}	x_{23}	x_{24}	x_{25}	x_{26}	x_{27}	x_{28}	x_{29}	x_{30}
D	x_{31}	x_{32}	x_{33}	x_{34}	x_{35}	x_{36}	x_{37}	x_{38}	x_{39}	x_{40}

Similarly, the cost associated with any shipping schedule is given by the sum of all products of the values of the variables and the unit costs given in Table A. In equation form:

$$\text{Cost} = 4.41\, x_1 + 4.60\, x_2 + 1.50\, x_3 + \cdots + 6.55\, x_{40}.$$

This equation is the objective function, and the objective is to minimize this cost, while meeting all restrictions. The restrictions in this simple problem are easily stated: at all points supply and demand must balance. We write one group of equations stating that, for each warehouse, the sum of the variables associated with it (shipments out) must equal the amount available at that warehouse; another group of equations will similarly state that the sum of variables associated with each destination (shipments in) must equal the demand at that point. These restrictions are shown in Table C.

All of these equations together represent the model, and the problem as given is that of minimizing the objective function subject to the restrictions. The supply and demand restrictions are the only ones having meaning in the simple problem stated here. In real problems conditions of policy, legal requirements, capacity, physical or chemical properties of materials, and so on may be incorporated.

Solution

At first glance the technique of model construction may seem unnecessarily complicated, but it is not really so. The characteristic of management problems is that, when so stated, the number of variables involved is much greater than the number of equations required to express the restrictions. This is equivalent to the statement—certainly no news to most executives—that there are, in general, many ways to operate in a real system. Thus, even in the simple problem posed, there are many millions of shipping schedules that could conceivably be devised. And in any real case the least-cost solution may be by no means obvious. For the data as presented above, the optimum solution and the costs of departure therefrom are shown in Table D.

In this table, the numbers in italics represent quantities to be shipped from the indicated warehouse to the indicated customer.

208

TABLE C. RESTRICTIONS TO BE MET

1. Supply restrictions

$x_1 + x_2 + x_3 + x_4 + x_5 + x_6 + x_7 + x_8 + x_9 + x_{10} = 4,443$ (supply at warehouse A)
$x_{11} + x_{12} + x_{13} + x_{14} + x_{15} + x_{16} + x_{17} + x_{18} + x_{19} + x_{20} = 5,271$ (supply at warehouse B)
$x_{21} + x_{22} + x_{23} + x_{24} + x_{25} + x_{26} + x_{27} + x_{28} + x_{29} + x_{30} = 2,983$ (supply at warehouse C)
$x_{31} + x_{32} + x_{33} + x_{34} + x_{35} + x_{36} + x_{37} + x_{38} + x_{39} + x_{40} = 3,651$ (supply at warehouse D)

2. Demand restrictions

$x_1 + x_{11} + x_{21} + x_{31} = 2,114$ (demand by customer 1) $x_6 + x_{16} + x_{26} + x_{36} = 2,580$ (demand by customer 6)
$x_3 + x_{13} + x_{23} + x_{33} = 802$ (demand by customer 3) $x_7 + x_{17} + x_{27} + x_{37} = 923$ (demand by customer 7)
$x_4 + x_{14} + x_{24} + x_{34} = 2,032$ (demand by customer 4) $x_8 + x_{18} + x_{28} + x_{38} = 840$ (demand by customer 8)
$x_5 + x_{15} + x_{25} + x_{35} = 2,760$ (demand by customer 5) $x_9 + x_{19} + x_{29} + x_{39} = 953$ (demand by customer 9)
$x_{10} + x_{20} + x_{30} + x_{40} = 1,547$ (demand by customer 10)

TABLE D. THE SOLUTION

Warehouse	Customer									
	1	2	3	4	5	6	7	8	9	10
A	940	0.21	0.55	0.61	0.10	2,580	923	0.20	0.61	1.00
B	0.18	1,797	0.37	1,087	0.56	0.15	0.20	840	0.42	1,547
C	1,174	0.78	1.28	0.38	1,809	0.03	0.06	1.00	0.68	0.80
D	0.20	0.02	802	945	951	0.10	0.39	0.50	953	3.10

Thus warehouse A is to supply 940 units to customer 1; 2,580 to customer 6; and 923 to customer 7. The remaining table entries in all the warehouse-customer combinations not called for in the optimal solution represent penalty costs. Thus the 0.21 associated with A-2 indicates that the total cost of shipment will be increased by a minimum of 0.21 for each unit shipped from warehouse A to customer 2. The fact that all routes other than those called for in the solution have positive costs associated with them indicates that this is a least-cost, or optimal solution.

There are several surprising features to this solution. It will be noted, for example, that no one of the nine lowest-cost routes (A-3, A-4, A-9, B-3, C-3, C-4, C-7, C-9, and C-10) is actually used. Furthermore, of the ten customers, only customer 1 is totally supplied by the least-cost route available to him. Thus customer 3 is totally supplied from warehouse D, although the unit costs are lower from any one of the other warehouses; the apparent saving of 1.71 to be achieved by supplying customer 3 from warehouse A rather than from warehouse D becomes an over-all loss of 0.55 for the system. Yet it is to be emphasized that the solution as given is, over-all, that of minimum cost, as may be seen by computing the cost of alternative solutions.

Optimization Procedure

The construction of a mathematical model for such a simple problem as that presented by the assignment of a shipping schedule to the four warehouses and ten customers seems like an elaborate and formal procedure of little real value. However, if in large systems there is something to be gained by such an approach, the formal procedure may become more appealing. It will be readily seen that, even for the small problem earlier described, many shipping schedules may be devised; and in a real industrial situation, the magnitude may be such that literally billions of solutions to the problem may exist. Mathematical programing makes the claim that out of these billions of solutions the optimal solution can be found—the solution which is not only a good or even very good method of operation, but which is the best of all possible solutions. This claim may be verified with mathematics no more advanced than addition and subtraction.

Feasible solution. The first step in optimizing the system is to obtain a "feasible" solution—one that meets the restraints of the problem without regard to cost. In the case of the problem of Table A, this may be done systematically in simple fashion. Let the first customer have his demand filled as fully as possible from the first warehouse. If there is more at the warehouse than is needed to supply this first demand, the excess is supplied to the second customer; and so on until the warehouse supply is exhausted.

Generally the customer exhausting the warehouse will not have his demand fully met, in which case the difference is filled from the next warehouse; then the next customer is supplied. The process is continued until all demands are met and all supplies exhausted. For the illustrative problem this gives the shipping schedule shown in Table E (p. 213).

This schedule represents a managerial policy employing 13 of the 40 warehouse-customer combinations possible. Any simple departure from this policy involves use of one of the 27 unused warehouse-customer combinations. Whether or not such departures are good depends on the cost difference resulting from such a departure.

Departures. To evaluate a departure from this policy, we reason as follows. The designated solution represents a balance in supply and demand not only over-all but in each row or column separately and independently. A change in the value of any quantity must be compensated for by an equal and opposite change in another quantity in the same row and another in the same column. These two changes demand in turn two new changes, in a column and a row respectively; and so on.

The process terminates only when it is possible to satisfy both a row change and a column change simultaneously by finding a quantity which can be altered at the intersection of the row and the column. Further, since negative quantities cannot be introduced into the solution, the changes to compensate for introduction of a new variable—that is, employment of a hitherto unused warehouse-customer combination—can be made only by decreasing quantities in the solution.

For example, to depart from the policy defined by the solution given to Table E by supplying customer 1 from warehouse B demands that the supply to customer 1 from warehouse A be decreased by a corresponding amount, since otherwise customer 1 will be oversupplied. At the same time, the supply to one of customers 3, 4, 5, or 6 must be depleted to avoid demanding more than the total supply from warehouse B. Of these, it is seen that if customer 3 is the one whose supply from warehouse B is lowered, then increasing the supply to customer 3 from warehouse A compensates for both changes so that the solution need not be further disturbed.

Similarly, it may be seen that to depart from the indicated policy by supplying customer 2 from warehouse D (combination D-2) involves compensating decreases in A-2, B-3, C-6, and D-7, and equal increases in A-3, B-6, and C-7. In general, the compensating changes involved in utilizing a new route will be traced out by such a series of moves, and there will be only one such series of changes possible.

The economic consequences of such a departure from the assumed policy, in terms of the total change in cost of the shipping schedule, can be found by adding the unit cost associated with any route where the assignment is increased, and subtracting the unit cost if the assignment is decreased. Thus the effect on the first feasible solution of use of the combination B-1 (supplying customer 1 from warehouse B) is given by the figures

$$5.56 - 4.41 + 1.50 - 2.38 = 0.27,$$

and use of the combination D-2 (supplying customer 2 from warehouse D) changes the solution value by the following amount:

$$6.63 - 4.60 + 1.50 - 2.38 + 4.96 - 3.65 + 3.03 - 5.75 = -0.26.$$

Thus the first change increases the total cost, and is therefore unattractive; the second decreases the cost and might be incorporated into the solution. In this manner every possible change may be evaluated by calculating the associated change in cost for unit utilization. The solution may then be improved by incorporating the route having the largest associated saving, and doing this to the fullest possible extent.

The extent of incorporation (that is, the number of units to be assigned to this route) may in turn be judged from the compensat-

TABLE E. SHIPPING SCHEDULE

Warehouse	1	2	3	4	5	6	7	8	9	10
						Customer				
A	2,114	1,797	532							
B			270	2,032	2,760	209	612			
C						2,371	311	840	953	
D										1,547

TABLE F. TRANSPORTATION COST PER UNIT TO DESTINATION

Source	D_1	D_2	D_3	D_4	D_5	D_6	D_7	D_8	D_9	D_{10}	Available from source
					Destination						
R_1	1.45	1.15	0.21	2.54	1.98	0.49	1.00	0.36	2.35	3.00	6,500
R_2	1.67	1.45	0.50	2.80	2.15	0.80	1.26	0.75	2.75	3.25	2,000
R_3	1.48	1.20	0.30	2.59	2.00	0.60	1.10	0.55	2.40	3.00	4,800
R_4	0.85	0.65	0.10	2.00	1.25	0.38	0.89	0.25	1.75	2.25	4,800
Demand at destination	2,000	2,400	1,500	1,300	1,300	2,100	1,800	1,700	2,200	1,800	

ing changes made in evaluating the cost of unit utilization. Those changes which increase in magnitude need not be considered, since there is no upper limit on their magnitudes. Those which decrease in magnitude, however, may not go below zero, so that the largest change that may be made is equal to the smallest value of the group. When this value is determined, all the routes affected may be changed by the appropriate amount. This constitutes a new solution, corresponding to another policy of operation.

All possible departures from this policy may now be evaluated and the process repeated until a solution is obtained from which all changes are unprofitable. Such a solution is, of course, the optimum one.

Recapitulation. This process of evaluating departures from the first feasible solution has been reviewed in perhaps tedious detail in order to demonstrate two facts:

(1) The manipulation of the model is logical at an elementary level.

(2) The results of the manipulation is truly optimal; it is the best possible solution for the problem as stated.

Summarizing, it may be stated that the optimization procedure consists of certain definite steps:

(1) A model is constructed, consisting of a group of equations which explicitly describe all restrictive relations in the system.

(2) A feasible solution, or possible operational policy, is found without regard to value.

(3) All possible departures from the policy are identified and evaluated for their effects on the value of the policy.

(4) The departure with the greatest unit value is incorporated to the fullest possible extent, making a new feasible solution.

(5) Steps 2, 3, and 4 are repeated until a solution is found which cannot be improved on.

More Complicated Questions

The illustrative examples just presented have been simple in conception and represent what may be felt to be an idealized state. However, various degrees of complexity may be introduced.

Supply bottleneck. For example, consider another problem of four sources and ten destinations, with the appropriate quantities as given in Table F, and the solution as shown in Table G.

It will be noted that the solution calls for destination D_6, to be totally supplied from source R_1. Now, if in fact the capacity of the channel from R_1 to D_6 were limited to, say, 1,000 units, that fact could be reflected by constructing the original problem in the manner shown in Table H. Here the destination D_6 has been artificially split into two synthetic destinations, one of which can be supplied from R_1 and the other of which cannot be so supplied. The symbol "M" simply means a prohibitively large cost associated with the source-destination combination, and might have been carried, for example, as 9.99. Individual variable limitations, whether of fact or of policy, might be indicated in this fashion.

Supply-demand imbalance. Other costs may also be readily entered into the model. Thus assume that in the previous problem to the given transportation costs are added manufacturing costs of:

<table>
<tr><td>10.0 at R_1</td><td>10.2 at R_3</td></tr>
<tr><td>9.9 at R_2</td><td>11.1 at R_4</td></tr>
</table>

Then the total cost problem becomes as stated in Table I. This looks to be quite different. In the original problem, the transportation costs were such that the order of preference of sources for individual destinations was mixed, but with R_4 being first choice in all cases. In the combined cost problem, R_4 is *least* preferable, and the costs have been so chosen that in all cases the order of preference is R_1 over R_2, R_2 over R_3, and R_3 over R_4. Yet this is the same problem and has the same solution. Reflection will show this to be true in general, since in any situation of balanced supply and demand the transportation costs are the only quantities subject to optimization, for the total output of all plants is required, regardless of the cost level involved.

In a situation of unbalanced supply and demand, however, the model based on combined manufacture and transportation costs may give an optimal solution which is quite different from that based on transportation costs alone. Then the model technique may be used to assign the proper level of production at each of the plants, when not all the production of all plants is required. It is especially interesting to note that, when the "incremental" pro-

TABLE G. SOLUTION TO SECOND PROBLEM

Source	D_1	D_2	D_3	D_4	D_5	D_6	D_7	D_8	D_9	D_{10}
R_1	0.04	0.02	1,500	0.98	0.15	2,100	1,200	1,700	0.02	0.17
R_2	1,400	0.06	0.03	0.02	0.06	0.05	600	0.13	0.16	0.16
R_3	600	2,400	0.02	1,300	0.10	0.04	0.05	0.12	500	0.10
R_4	0.02	0.10	0.47	0.06	1,300	0.47	0.47	0.47	1,700	1,800

TABLE H. REVISED TRANSPORTATION COST SCHEDULE

Source	D_1	D_2	D_3	D_4	D_5	D_6	D'_6	D_7	D_8	D_9	D_{10}	Available from source
R_1	1.45	1.15	0.21	2.54	1.98	0.49	M	1.00	0.36	2.35	3.00	6,500
R_2	1.67	1.45	0.50	2.80	2.15	0.80	0.80	1.26	0.75	2.75	3.25	2,000
R_3	1.48	1.20	0.30	2.59	2.00	0.60	0.60	1.10	0.55	2.40	3.00	4,800
R_4	0.85	0.65	0.10	2.00	1.25	0.38	0.38	0.89	0.25	1.75	2.25	4,800
Demand at destination	2,000	2,400	1,500	1,300	1,300	1,000	1,100	1,800	1,700	2,200	1,800	

duction at different plants is at quite different price levels, it is not necessarily true that the lowest-cost production is to be used in the optimal solution.

Assume, for example, that in the previous illustration an imbalance of supply and demand is created by expanding demand by 10% at all destinations, and expanding supply by 20%. Further assume that the additional, "incremental" supply is available at a cost which is 80% of the cost of the basic supply at the same plant. The resulting distribution problem is represented by the schedule shown in Table J.

To represent the imbalance of supply and demand, a fictitious destination, D_{11}, can be introduced, with a fictitious demand equal to the difference between total supply and true demand. At the same time, the difference between production costs of the basic and incremental productions can be reflected by the difference in the cost entries for R_1 and for the increments for R_1, R_2, R_3, and R_4. Finally, the entry "M," having its previous meaning of a very large cost, associated with the fictitious destination for basic production and the zero entry for fictitious demand and incremental production, can be used to ensure that all basic production is employed before the incremental production, dependent on the basic production, enters the solution.

One solution to this problem (there are numerous solutions with equal costs, although none with lower cost) is shown in Table K. The numbers in italics represent costs to the destination.

Unexpected findings. Surprising things may transpire in investigating optimum costs with a model. For instance, under the particular cost conditions assumed in the preceding illustration, all the additional production required came from the least costly incremental production available. But such action is not always desirable. To demonstrate this, let us vary incremental unit costs only slightly, while keeping them in the same relative order. Let unit production costs of the additional 20% be as follows:

$$8.00 \text{ at } R_1 \quad (\text{Base capacity cost } 10.0)$$
$$7.95 \text{ at } R_2 \quad (\text{Base capacity cost } 9.9)$$
$$8.10 \text{ at } R_3 \quad (\text{Base capacity cost } 10.2)$$
$$8.55 \text{ at } R_4 \quad (\text{Base capacity cost } 11.1)$$

TABLE I. LAID DOWN COST PER UNIT TO DESTINATION

Source	D_1	D_2	D_3	D_4	D_5	D_6	D_7	D_8	D_9	D_{10}	Available from source
R_1	11.45	11.15	10.21	12.54	11.98	10.49	11.00	10.36	12.35	13.00	6,500
R_2	11.57	11.35	10.40	12.70	12.05	10.70	11.16	10.65	12.60	13.15	2,000
R_3	11.68	11.40	10.50	12.79	12.20	10.80	11.30	10.75	12.65	13.20	4,800
R_4	11.95	11.75	11.20	13.10	12.35	11.48	11.99	11.35	12.85	13.25	4,800
Demand at destination	2,000	2,400	1,500	1,300	1,300	2,100	1,800	1,700	2,200	1,800	

TABLE J. LAID DOWN COST PER UNIT TO DESTINATION WITH SUPPLY AND DEMAND UNBALANCED

Source	D_1	D_2	D_3	D_4	D_5	D_6	D_7	D_8	D_9	D_{10}	D_{11}	Available from source
R_1	11.45	11.15	10.21	12.54	11.98	10.49	11.00	10.36	12.35	13.00	M	6,500
R_2	11.57	11.35	10.40	12.70	12.05	10.70	11.16	10.65	12.60	13.15	M	2,000
R_3	11.68	11.40	10.50	12.79	12.20	10.80	11.30	10.75	12.65	13.20	M	4,800
R_4	11.95	11.75	11.20	13.10	12.35	11.48	11.99	11.35	12.85	13.25	M	4,800
Incremental supply at:												
R_1	9.45	9.15	8.21	10.54	9.98	8.49	9.00	8.36	10.35	11.00	0	1,300
R_2	9.59	9.37	8.42	10.72	10.07	8.72	9.18	8.67	10.67	11.17	0	400
R_3	9.64	9.36	8.46	10.75	10.16	8.76	9.26	8.71	10.56	11.16	0	960
R_4	9.73	9.53	8.98	10.88	10.13	9.26	9.77	9.13	10.63	11.13	0	960
Demand at destination	2,200	2,640	1,650	1,430	1,430	2,310	1,980	1,870	2,420	1,980	1,810	

TABLE K. SOLUTION TO DISTRIBUTION PROBLEM

Source		D_1	D_2	D_3	D_4	D_5	D_6	D_7	D_8	D_9	D_{10}	D_{11}
												Destination
R_1		0.04	190	1,650	0	0.13	2,310	1,780	570	0	0.15	M
R_2		2,000	0.04	0.03	0	0.04	0.05	0	0.13	0.14	0.14	M
R_3		0.02	2,450	0.04	1,430	0.10	0.06	0.05	0.14	920	0.10	M
R_4		0.04	0.10	0.49	0.06	1,430	0.49	0.49	0.49	1,390	1,980	M
Incremental supply at:												
R_1		0.04	0	0	0	0.13	0	0	1,300	0	0.15	0.21
R_2		200	0.04	0.03	0	0.04	0.05	200	0.13	0.14	0.14	0.13
R_3		0.02	0	0.04	0	0.10	0.06	0.05	0.14	110	0.10	850
R_4		0.11	0.07	0.56	0.13	0.07	0.56	0.56	2.06	0.07	0.07	960

The problem thus becomes that of optimizing the possibilities shown in Table L.

One solution (again there are numerous alternates) is shown in Table M.

Note that this solution calls for using fully the incremental output of R_4 although this is most expensive, while using none of the incremental output of R_2, which is seemingly the cheapest. Such a result may seem contrary to "common sense," but only because in the "common-sense approach" costs are separately defined and examined, without respect to the entire system.

This result, unexpected as it is, makes one wonder if it might not be desirable to reduce the "base" production at one plant while expanding the "incremental" capacity at another. This possibility can be examined in the model by discarding the concept of incremental capacity, recognizing only used and unused capacities, and assigning a cost to each. The cost of production becomes a fixed quantity, equal to the average unit cost at full production, regardless of the level of production actually used. The unit cost of unused capacity is also fixed and can be shown to be equal to:

(Unit cost of "base" capacity — unit cost at total capacity) ×
("base" capacity) ÷ ("incremental" capacity).

It will then be noted that unused capacity appears in the solution with a cost associated. Conceptually, this is important and intuitively satisfying. Failure to use an available facility, the employment of which will increase efficiency, is a neglect of opportunity which should be penalized. Under this concept, the costs of the various plants become those shown in Table N.

And the problem becomes that of optimizing production and distribution in the system. Table O shows the laid down cost per unit to destination.

Table P shows that not only should the cheap "incremental" production of R_2 not be used, but the base production should also be cut back, as should the base production of R_3, while the apparently expensive base and incremental production of R_4 should be fully utilized.

The simple model and optimization technique are thus seen to be capable of formulating reasonably complicated managerial questions—and of demonstrating rather surprising answers.

TABLE L. LAID DOWN COST PER UNIT TO DESTINATION

Source	D_1	D_2	D_3	D_4	D_5	D_6	D_7	D_8	D_9	D_{10}	D_{11}	Available from source
R_1	11.45	11.15	10.21	12.54	11.98	10.49	11.00	10.36	12.35	13.00	M	6,500
R_2	11.57	11.35	10.40	12.70	12.05	10.50	11.16	10.65	12.65	13.15	M	2,000
R_3	11.68	11.40	10.50	12.79	12.20	10.80	11.30	10.75	12.60	13.20	M	4,800
R_4	11.95	11.75	11.20	13.10	12.35	11.48	11.99	11.35	12.85	13.35	M	4,800
Incremental supply at:												
R_1	9.45	9.15	8.21	10.54	9.98	8.49	9.00	8.36	10.35	11.00	0	1,300
R_2	9.62	9.40	8.45	10.75	10.10	8.75	9.21	8.70	10.70	11.20	0	400
R_3	9.58	9.30	8.40	10.69	10.10	8.70	9.20	8.65	10.50	11.10	0	960
R_4	9.40	9.20	8.65	10.55	9.80	8.93	9.44	8.80	10.30	10.80	0	960
Demand at destination	2,200	2,640	1,650	1,430	1,430	2,310	1,980	1,870	2,420	1,980	1,810	

TABLE M. SOLUTION TO SECOND DISTRIBUTION PROBLEM

Source					Destination						
	D_1	D_2	D_3	D_4	D_5	D_6	D_7	D_8	D_9	D_{10}	D_{11}
R_1	0.04	0.02	1,650	0.02	0.15	2,310	1,520	1,020	0.02	0.17	M
R_2	1,540	0.06	0.03	0.02	0.06	0.05	460	0.13	0.16	0.16	M
R_3	660	2,640	0.02	1,430	0.10	0.04	0.03	0.12	70	0.10	M
R_4	0.02	0.10	0.47	0.06	1,430	0.47	0.47	0.47	2,350	1,020	M
Incremental supply at:											
R_1	0.04	0.02	0	0	0.15	0	0	850	0.02	0.07	450
R_2	0.21	0.27	0.24	0.21	0.27	0.26	0.21	0.34	0.37	0.27	400
R_3	0.17	0.17	0.19	0.15	0.27	0.21	0.20	0.29	0.17	0.17	960
R_4	0.02	0.10	0.47	0.06	0	0.47	0.47	0.47	0	960	0.03

TABLE N. COSTS OF USED AND UNUSED CAPACITY

Source	R_1	R_2	R_3	R_4
Unit cost, base capacity	10.0	9.9	10.2	11.1
Base capacity	6,500	2,000	4,800	4,800
Unit cost, additional capacity	8.0	7.95	8.10	8.55
Additional capacity	1,300	400	960	960
Average cost	9.666	9.575	9.860	10.675
Unit cost, unused capacity	1.666	1.625	1.750	2.125

TABLE O. LAID DOWN COST PER UNIT TO DESTINATION

Source	D_1	D_2	D_3	D_4	D_5	D_6	D_7	D_8	D_9	D_{10}	D_{11}	Available from source
R_1	11.12	10.82	9.88	12.21	11.65	10.16	10.67	10.03	12.02	12.67	1.67	7,800
R_2	11.25	11.03	10.08	12.38	11.73	10.38	10.84	10.33	12.33	12.83	1.63	2,400
R_3	11.33	11.05	10.15	12.44	11.85	10.45	10.95	10.40	12.25	12.85	1.75	5,760
R_4	11.53	11.33	10.78	12.68	11.93	11.06	11.57	10.93	12.43	12.93	2.13	5,760
Demand at destination	2,200	2,640	1,650	1,430	1,430	2,310	1,980	1,870	2,420	1,980	1,810	

TABLE P. SOLUTION TO REVISED DISTRIBUTION PROBLEM

Source	D_1	D_2	D_3	D_4	D_5	D_6	D_7	D_8	D_9	D_{10}	D_{11}
R_1	0.04	0.02	1,650	0.02	0.15	2,310	1,970	1,870	0.02	0.17	0.21
R_2	1,940	0.06	0.03	0.02	0.06	0.05	10	0.13	0.16	0.16	450
R_3	260	2,640	0.02	1,430	0.10	0.04	0.03	0.12	70	0.10	1,360
R_4	0.02	0.10	0.47	0.06	1,430	0.47	0.47	0.47	2,350	1,980	0.20

8

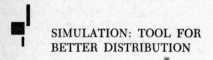

SIMULATION: TOOL FOR
BETTER DISTRIBUTION

HARVEY N. SHYCON AND RICHARD B. MAFFEI[*]

Recently a vice president of the H. J. Heinz Company, recognizing that proper warehousing was one of his company's biggest problems, asked himself these pertinent questions concerning his distribution system:

"How many warehouses should we have?"

"Where should the warehouses be located?"

"What customers should each warehouse service?"

"What volume should each warehouse handle?"

"How can we best organize our entire distribution function?"

In a firm like Heinz—with a dollar sales volume in the hundred millions, with several factories, with many mixing points where products from several factories are assembled for large shipments, with dozens of warehouses and thousands of customers—lowering the costs of distributing products to market, while still maintaining good customer service, is no easy trick. Moreover, the rising costs of distribution make maximum mileage from the distribution dollar absolutely essential.

[*] We wish to acknowledge the work of R. K. Bennett for programing, and C. C. Beymer, I. E. Zacher, J. W. Paschke, and A. E. Buekel of the H. J. Heinz Company for their contribution to our project.

How can answers to difficult questions like these best be obtained? The problem can be resolved through the use of simulation, one of the great advances in the science of business management developed in the past decade. Simulation provides the ability to operate some particular phase of a business on paper—or in a computer—for a period of time, and by this means to test various alternative strategies and systems. Distribution, sales and marketing, production problems—taken separately or in combination—have been solved in a remarkably accurate fashion by simulation. In the case of the H. J. Heinz Company, simulation worked with such effectiveness that a whole new approach to achieving the lowest practical costs of distribution resulted.

How Simulation Works

In this paper, we hope to describe the way we applied simulation to solve, to a considerable extent, Heinz's distribution problems. It should be of special interest, for this simulation is perhaps the most complete, comprehensive, and accurate study of a national distribution system ever carried out.

Some readers, of course, are much more sophisticated about simulation and its uses than are others. Those who are, we hope, will bear with us as we explain each step of our method. They should remember, also, that our object here is not to write a lofty treatise on simulation theory but to share with practical businessmen, in as clear and simple terms as possible, the logic of how we went about our simulation of Heinz's distribution system. While this information can hardly be expected to enable, say, a marketing executive to tackle a simulation study completely on his own, we do hope that it will enable businessmen to understand, in general, how such a procedure could be used to help their companies test various marketing and distribution strategies.

What we are describing is a general-purpose tool—a mathematical representation of a company's distribution system. It takes into account each of the important factors involved in the operation of a distribution system: transportation rate structures, warehouse operating costs, the characteristics of customers' demand for products, buying patterns of customers, costs of labor and construction, factory locations, product mix and production capacities, and all other significant elements. These factors, taken together, make up the distribution system. Each of these elements is represented in a way which simulates its actual effect in the national distribution pattern and its effect on costs, with proper weighting and consideration given to the interrelationships among the various factors.

Since the simulation represents the essential parts of the actual distribution system, it permits the operation of the system in such a way that a whole year's transactions can be run through under close scrutiny. "Goods" flow through the system, from factory to mixing point, to warehouses, to the customer; and transportation and operating "costs" are incurred, just as they would be under real working conditions.

But because it is only a synthetic representation, it permits the testing of various schemes for developing better distribution methods and achieving lower operating costs. Different cost trends incurred by the alternative distribution arrangements are compared, leading ultimately to a plan of distribution at lower cost to the company.

For the H. J. Heinz Company, the simulation has provided a unique tool for determining the number of warehouses and mixing points which should exist in the national distribution system. It also has determined where they should be located to achieve a minimal over-all operating cost. In addition, it has provided information on how best to service the many thousands of customers by an optimal combination of service direct from factory and service from area warehouses. Further, it has given a detailed plan for allocating merchandise to given warehouses and to particular customers for each product line and from each factory. With this cohesive national distribution plan in hand, management has now proceeded to make future marketing plans with assurance of lowest actual distribution costs.

The Heinz Problem

Heinz is typical of many manufacturers with large-scale distribution requirements. From multiple manufacturing plants across the nation, from a system of mixing points and warehouses spread across the country, the company must service all of the national marketing areas. As with many other manufacturers (both in the food and in the nonfood fields), Heinz's distribution setup has been undergoing substantial changes over the past few years.

Specific factors which have influenced traditional distribution methods are shifts in population centers and principal markets, the emergence of brand identification as a prime marketing factor, technological changes in distribution methods, the growth of large retail operations, and other changes in marketing. Added to these, of course, is the fact that the cost of physical distribution of product to market has been rapidly increasing.

As a result of these changes, the Heinz management recognized some years ago the need for a careful re-evaluation of its marketing plans and has had in process a program for streamlining and improving the marketing and distribution system nationally. More recently, it became evident that a re-examination of the transportation and warehousing system was required so that modern methods of physical distribution could be fitted to the new marketing plans in a way that would achieve a minimal over-all cost of distribution.

Heinz considered it important that a cohesive plan be developed which would combine the best features of direct plant-to-customer distribution with those of a national warehousing network. By an optimal combination of these, management hoped to minimize inclusive costs of distributing products to market and, at the same time, to maintain its policy of excellent service to customers.

Problems of distribution involving both the length of distribution time and the increasing cost of getting the product to market are felt in many major segments of industry. Heinz is hardly unique in this sense. Consumer products of all kinds—hard goods as well as soft goods, appliances, automobiles, electrical goods, clothing, the entire food industry—all are subject to increasing distribution costs.

The problem faced by the management of the Heinz company was even more complex than most. Not only were the costs of physical distribution of product to market growing, but the distribution system was increasingly being dated by a streamlined marketing program instituted at the company over the past few years to accommodate the needs of the market better and to provide improved service to customers. Included in this program were a greater recognition of the function of jobbers and distributors and a reorganization of the marketing program to build up the distributor's function in the marketing framework. Whole marketing areas had been converted from direct retailer selling to distributor areas, and, finally, an ever increasing portion of volume was moving through the distributor channels.

With changes of this nature taking place, it was inevitable that a warehouse system originally designed to handle one type of market would eventually require basic changes in order to service properly the new marketing system. Originally, the national market had been served by some 68 warehouses placed geographically to handle the many low-volume customers in the system. With the marketing structure changing, it became evident that some warehouses were located incorrectly in relation to the market now being served, and that some warehouses were simply no longer needed.

Management faced squarely the problem brought about by these changes, developed plans for the reallocation of customer volume to other warehouses, and closed some of the lower volume branches. This resulted in a reduction in the number of warehouses in the system. The company wanted to know if it had gone too far, if it had gone far enough, and, indeed, if it had retained the right locations in the system.

Management soon became convinced that the conventional methods were inadequate for analyzing (a) which warehouses to retain and (b) how best to allocate customer volume among warehouses, mixing points, and factories. In a large system of this kind changes in distribution pattern—even at the local level—tend to have chain reactions throughout the national system. A change which may appear to yield a lower cost of operation at the local level can, in fact, cause an increased cost of operation when all relevant costs are considered on a national basis.

For example, when a warehouse is placed close to a given customer, the cost of delivering merchandise to that customer may well become lower. But the over-all effect on cost of transportation of merchandise from the various factories to the warehouse, and costs of delivery to other customers still farther away—all these, combined with the cost of operating the given warehouse, make the problem complex indeed.

What was needed, management decided, was a bold new approach to studying the distribution system as a whole, on a national basis. The many interrelated costs, the many source points and many thousands of customers throughout the country, all had to be taken into account in establishing a distribution pattern of warehouses and mixing points which would yield the lowest overall cost.

Simulation Requirements

Our complete representation of Heinz's complex, high-volume national distribution system had to be detailed enough to handle each of the thousands of customers in the Heinz system. It had to take account of each customer's order sizes, his ordering patterns, the various types of shipments he receives, and his product mix. Provision had to be made for handling the costs of the various kinds of shipment made—i.e., carload, less-than-carload, truckload, less-than-truckload, and various shipment sizes within the lower classification. Variation in warehouse operating costs—i.e., labor costs, rentals, taxes for different geographical areas—had to be considered. The many different classifications of products which Heinz manufactures, the alternative factory source points for each of these products, and the factory capacity limitations on each— all had to be examined. Finally, when such a representation was designed, it had to be in such form that it could be synthetically operated, using real operating figures, for a year's time, over and over again.

In this way, various configurations of warehouses and mixing points could be tried so that costs might be observed for different conditions, and the lowest cost pattern achieved. And since the number of transactions required for one year's operation of the national system would be so great, the representation had to be in such form as to be operable on a high-speed computer.

Logic of Simulation

A distribution system exists in order to link production activity (which, of course, cannot exist everywhere) and consumption activity (which does exist almost everywhere). A company interested in studying its warehouse location problem could start by specifying where production takes place and where the majority of its customers are located. It could, initially, assume arbitrary locations of warehouses. If proper cost information, consumption information, and production information are available, then the costs of distribution associated with a given assumed configuration of warehouses could be determined. These results could be compared with costs accruing under other assumed configurations.

This idea is simple enough, but the question that immediately suggests itself is this: *How can sufficient detail be designed into such a representation to provide genuine assurance that the lowest-cost distribution plan developed on paper would be realized during actual operations?*

This question is not only legitimate but is of crucial importance when analysts talk of studying and simulating systems. The answer lies in the nature of the simulation developed. Properly designed, the simulation takes account of all relevant aspects of the problem as they interrelate with one another, and operates much as the real system does.

It might be said that simulation, in providing the means for testing the various alternative courses of action available, simply evaluates all of the "What if?" questions frequently asked. It tests those things that businessmen would like to try if time, money, and manpower permitted.

For example, without simulation, Heinz could have done a cost analysis for each of a number of distribution systems under various assumptions as to sales patterns. Each such analysis would have been rather costly to conduct. Analysis of a single national distribution configuration, yielding one year's operating results, required some 75 million calculations by the computer—and these were performed in less than one hour. By conventional methods, this would have taken two clerks almost 50 years!

Further, the number of alternatives which could be economically examined in this way would have nowhere nearly exhausted all of the possibilities. Analysis of just 20 such possibilities would have required 2,000 clerks working one year! Moreover, management could not feel any great confidence that its final decision was "correct," because of the probability of human error and the great passage of time during which things would change.

230

To assure that the results of this study would be meaningful, we first had to specify the characteristics of Heinz customers and factories. Each customer's characteristics were specified according to:

Geographic location.
Order sizes and frequency.
Volume of purchases.
Variety requirements.

And each factory's characteristics were specified according to:

Geographic location.
Production capacities by product line.
Product mix.

Between these two basic factors—customer location and needs, and factory location and production characteristics—lies the distribution system. The problem, then, becomes one of determining the number, size, and location of warehouses and additional mixing points which would properly serve customers at a minimum cost nationally.

In a dynamic distribution system of this type many forces exist which influence warehouse number, location, and size. The nature of each customer order—its product mix, its timing, the effect of special promotions and pricing policies on customer ordering and stocking, and other factors—all are influential. In similar fashion, every applicable freight rate from each geographic point to every other geographic point, the freight rate "breaks," and similar transportation specifications have their effect. The cost of operating a warehouse at each potentially alternate location has its influence. Finally, the precise product mix of each factory, along with the capacity limitations by product line, affects warehouse location and the cost of distribution.

To evaluate properly each of these characteristics—for the many thousands of customer orders, for the thousands of alternative sources and routings possible, for the multiplicity of alternate possibilities of warehouse and mixing point configurations—it was necessary to construct a mathematical "model" of the distribution system. Adding high-speed computing ability completed the requirements necessary to a solution of this problem.

Included in this "model" are all the essential parts of the distribution system which influence warehouse location. But which parts of the distribution system are essential and which are not?

The answers were found only after considerable research into the actual distribution records of the company. Specifically, these are the factors that had to be taken into account in setting up the model:

1. How frequently customers order, how much they order, what they order, where they are located, and how they prefer to take receipt of ordered goods.

2. The kinds of goods that can be supplied from any given factory point, the quantities that can be supplied, and the location of the factories.

3. The relationship between shipping rates and points of origin and destination, for truck and rail transportation, and for different types and sizes of orders.

4. The relationship between total handling costs and total volume handled at warehouses and mixing points.

5. The knowledge of where these relationships differ, so that adjustments to cost and volume estimates might be made.

Once this information was obtained, we then had to establish some basic working definitions of the terms *customer, factory, warehouse,* and *carrier.* And for our work at Heinz, the definitions had to be in precise numerical terms.

A. What is a customer? In terms of distribution requirements, a customer can be defined according to the following criteria:

By specific geographic location.

By business type (that is, whether it is a chain, distributor, wholesaler, jobber, vendor, or a hotel and restaurant distributor).

By product-mix consumption pattern—As a result of a thorough search of internal product records by customer account, some 50 different consumption patterns were isolated. Each customer in the national system was assigned that pattern which best reflected his product usage.

By frequency, quantity, and patterns of ordering—Each customer has his own way of ordering and of taking inventory. Some may accumulate requirements and take only large quantities; others may order frequently and in relatively small quantity shipments. The option is theirs. It was considered essential to reflect each customer's ordering patterns explicitly since this aspect was felt to have a great bearing on the distribution system.

By proximity to Heinz's various warehouses.

B. What is a factory? In terms of distribution requirements, a factory can be defined like this:

A geographic location that produces various company products.

A product-mix pattern—Not all factories turn out every product that the company makes. Therefore, in the Heinz study we defined a product as having both food and location characteristics.

In Exhibit I you will see that product 1 was defined as a class of varieties that were produced only at factory 1. Product 2 was a member of a class of products that were produced at factories 1, 2, 3, and so on for products 3, 4, and 5. This process of classification covered all the products in the Heinz line.

A production capacity pattern—Capacity by product lines is difficult to conceive and to measure in a multiproduct, multi-equipment plant. Therefore, in order to get an idea of system costs, production restraints must be imposed. This was done in the Heinz case, and a production capacity pattern was established for each of the factories in the system.

A controllable source—It is important to note that management has within its direct control the power to expand or contract capacity, to add or subtract product lines, and so on.

A cost area for transportation purposes—That is, the costs of shipping to an area of 100 miles around Chicago will probably not be the same as the costs of shipping to a 100-mile area around Denver.

With the simulation now completed, management has the means for testing various changes in production or marketing strategy. It can better answer questions as to whether additional factories should be allowed to produce a given product, or whether economies would result if certain products were removed from a given factory's production schedule. Let us take a simple example, and illustrate it with Exhibit I.

In the case of product 1, which currently is produced only at factory 1, we might wish to know what over-all costs would be if we were also to permit factories 2 and 5 to manufacture product 1. How do we find out? Simply by adding production capacity for

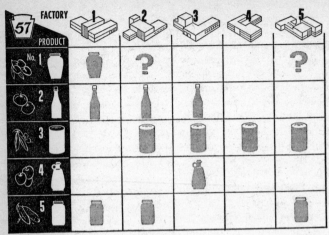

? To see how costs are affected when factories 2 and 5 are added see the explanation above.

product 1 to our simulated factories 2 and 5, and once again operating the system within the computer. A new cost of distribution will then indicate whether such a change is desirable.

We find this an excellent way to bring to management's attention the potential savings to be had under various assumed conditions.

C. What is a warehouse? For the purpose of our study, we defined a warehouse as:

A *geographic, gathering, sorting, and redistributing point*—A warehouse performs work, owns or rents space, employs people, pays taxes, and in general accumulates costs. In a study of this kind, it must be assumed that any geographic area in the United States is a potential location of a warehouse. And costs differ by geographic area.

A *cost accumulation point*—Geographic area cost differentials must be recognized in any study of warehouse numbers and locations. In a simulation of a national system it is most feasible to build into the model cost-adjustment factors by geographic area for the various cost elements.

For Heinz, the country was divided into a large number of "cost areas," and cost-adjustment factors were developed by area for warehouse labor, taxes, rentals, or depreciation. Hence, when a warehouse was placed in a given geographic area, its cost of operation was computed using the local area costs. When, in the study, the same warehouse was moved into another geographic area, the cost of operation was computed using the new area's costs. By this method a given warehouse might be more or less attractive for serving certain customers, based not only on the transportation cost for serving them, but also on the operating cost of that warehouse versus other warehouses in other areas which might have different operating cost structures.

D. What is a carrier? For our purposes, carriers were defined as:

Either a trucking firm or a railroad.

A cost for moving goods between geographic points; in effect, a geographic movement-cost relationship—It is extremely difficult to analyze transportation rate structures. Yet when we wish to determine distribution costs, we must draw together a pattern of freight costs which accurately reflect the national rate structure with all its differences depending on size of shipment, type of carrier, and other important factors.

Nevertheless, after much effort, basic regularities governing rate structure have been determined and have been made part of the simulation now accomplished. When, after careful consideration in the study that we made of the Heinz distribution system, it was decided to use relationships rather than point-to-point costs, we did this with the assurance that there was genuine regularity, and that the results were indeed authentic.

It is worthy of note that the transportation rate structures are frequently further complicated by other factors. Some customers cannot or will not accept certain types of shipments; some cannot accept rail. Some, for reasons of their own inventory policies, will not take shipments above certain sizes; others prefer not to accept small shipments. All these factors complicate the analysis problem and make necessary the use within the simulation program of fairly complex rate structure relationships based on type of shipment, shipment sizes, geographic area, and other pertinent factors.

Program Characteristics

A sequential flow of subcomponents and components representing the flow of raw materials and finished goods through the many processing and transfer points forms the simulated distribution system. Basically, customers place requirements on a system and the system responds. Demand thus usually "explodes" backwards through the production and procurement system. But this backward explosion of demand will vary somewhat in the channels used among different industries.

In the distribution of automobiles, customers in an area place orders first with dealers. The dealers then refer orders back to an assembly plant which, in turn, places demands for subcomponents back on suppliers and factories.

In the case of food and pharmaceuticals, on the other hand, customers place packaging demands back on warehouses or manufacturing plants of container companies. These companies then place orders with suppliers of raw materials or with other manufacturers.

In the Heinz system, as we conceived it, customers place orders with the company and the company responds by delivering in one of three basic ways, depending on which way or combination of ways offers the least cost. These three are: direct shipments from a given producing factory to large customers; shipments from various factories to a so-called mixing point located at a factory and then to customers; and shipments from factory points to a warehouse and then to the customer.

Let us focus our attention now on the warehousing aspect of the system and ask a basic question: Why do warehouses exist? Under what conditions might they be unnecessary? If all customers were very large, if all of them gave sufficient lead time when ordering, and if all factories produced the full line of the company's products, then all shipments to ultimate consumers could be made directly from the factory. Thus the main reasons why warehouses exist are that customers are not large enough to warrant direct

EXHIBIT II. ACTUAL AND SIMULATED VIEWS OF DISTRIBUTION

THE ACTUAL DISTRIBUTION PATTERN IN ABSTRACT FORM

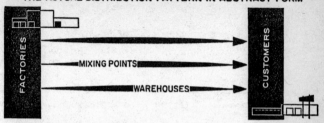

THE SIMULATION VIEW OF THE DISTRIBUTION PATTERN

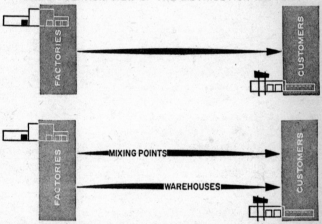

shipment, and do not all give sufficient lead time when ordering, and that individual factories are not always full-line.

Since our objective, however, is not only to determine the number and location of warehouses but, even more important, to design a total distribution system which will operate at lowest total cost, it is necessary that we assign customer shipment volume to its highest distribution classification. Thus, if a given customer's volume is such that he qualifies for shipments direct from producing factories, and if he is willing to accept shipments by this

237

method, then we should ship that way. Similarly, if part of a customer's volume might most economically be shipped from a mixing point, then this method is proper.

Hence, only after other volume has been allocated do we consider warehouses for shipment. And our simulation must be designed to make these determinations automatically.

Some customers in the system can take part of their total demand in direct shipments. Because shipments direct from producing factories to customers bypass the mixing point and warehouse system completely, direct shipments of this kind, as Exhibit II shows, have no effect on the optimal placement of mixing points and warehouses. Therefore, all direct shipment customers are eliminated from consideration when we are concerned with warehouse location.

Similarly, direct shipment volume is removed from the order patterns of those customers who take only part of their demand in direct shipments. That is, when the computer found a customer whose volume of given items was large enough to take shipments direct from producing factories, it made separate record of the volume so delivered and listed only the remaining volume for delivery from warehouses or mixing points.

This adjustment needs to be done only once and can be done by simulation. After removal of direct shipment volume for every customer, a single run on the computer will make available the resultant consumption patterns of the national system. This, then, is the information used to study the warehouse location problem.

The Computer Program

When talking in terms of large-scale computers, we should bear in mind one thing. Although computers are frequently called "electronic brains," they are by no means thinking machines in the human sense. A computer is merely a mathematical "beast of burden" which will do only what it is specifically told to do. But it does its assigned job with a speed and accuracy far beyond any other known means, human or mechanical. Instructions to the computer, therefore, must be precise and in detail. These instructions on how to proceed are called the computer "program."

In concept, the program for the simulation described is quite simple. Stored on tape is all information relating to transportation,

EXHIBIT III. SAMPLE OF COMPUTER OUTPUT

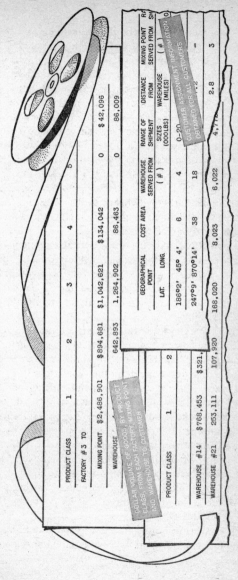

Note: Figures shown here are disguised and intended for illustration only.

handling, and delivery costs, geographic adjustment factors, factory locations, factory production specifications, and the volume remaining after elimination of direct shipment volume. Even the program itself is stored on tape.

The basic process is to vary warehouse configurations and to observe and compare the resultant effects on distribution costs. To do this, we must compute in detail the annual costs for operating the proposed nondirect distribution system for a year. Included are such costs as those for each of the warehouses and mixing points, for all shipments (both from factories to warehouses and warehouses to customers), and for each of the several thousand customers. Further, these costs must be broken down for each product class and each type of shipment.

Now the simulation is ready to accomplish its twofold objective: (1) to enable management to close in rapidly on the number and approximate locations of warehouses which will achieve lowest costs of distribution, and (2) to discover where changes can be made in warehouse locations which will lower costs still further.

When the simulated one-year operation of a complete warehouse configuration has been completed and all costs computed, the following results are shown in detail as computer output (see, for example, Exhibit III).

Costs are shown for all pertinent items indicated in accounting terminology familiar to management. For each factory, warehouse, and mixing point, there are three major categories of distribution costs determined in the simulation: (1) costs of direct shipments, factory to mixing point, mixing point to customer, and factory to warehouse shipments; (2) costs of operating both mixing points and warehouses at specified locations; and (3) costs of shipping from warehouses to customers.

All these costs are further classified by size of shipment, and include a volume-by-product-line breakdown for each warehouse.

Customer-warehouse affiliations are given so that accurate service areas are built up for each warehouse, mixing point, and factory. All this is based on a lowest cost for operating the entire distribution system.

In short, a great deal of useful information about any distribution configuration is provided by the simulation developed.

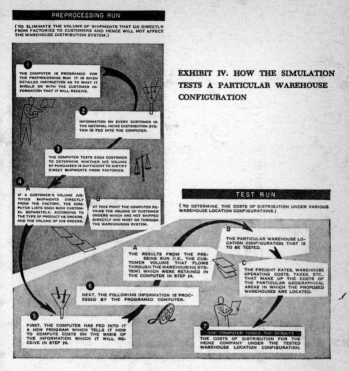

PREPROCESSING RUN

(TO ELIMINATE THE VOLUME OF SHIPMENTS THAT GO DIRECTLY FROM FACTORIES TO CUSTOMERS AND HENCE WILL NOT AFFECT THE WAREHOUSE DISTRIBUTION SYSTEM.)

1 THE COMPUTER IS PROGRAMED FOR THE PREPROCESSING RUN IT IS GIVEN DETAILED INSTRUCTION AS TO WHAT IT SHOULD DO WITH THE CUSTOMER INFORMATION THAT IT WILL RECEIVE.

2 INFORMATION ON EVERY CUSTOMER IN THE NATIONAL HEINZ DISTRIBUTION SYSTEM IS FED INTO THE COMPUTER.

3 THE COMPUTER TESTS EACH CUSTOMER TO DETERMINE WHETHER HIS VOLUME OF PURCHASE IS SUFFICIENT TO JUSTIFY DIRECT SHIPMENTS FROM FACTORIES.

4 IF A CUSTOMER'S VOLUME JUSTIFIES SHIPMENTS DIRECTLY FROM THE FACTORY, THE COMPUTER LISTS EACH SUCH CUSTOMER SEPARATELY, ACCORDING TO THE TYPE OF PRODUCT HE ORDERS, AND THE VOLUME OF HIS ORDERS.

5 AT THIS POINT THE COMPUTER RETAINS THE VOLUME OF CUSTOMER ORDERS WHICH ARE NOT SHIPPED DIRECTLY AND MUST GO THROUGH THE WAREHOUSING SYSTEM.

EXHIBIT IV. HOW THE SIMULATION TESTS A PARTICULAR WAREHOUSE CONFIGURATION

TEST RUN

(TO DETERMINE THE COSTS OF CUSTOMER ORDERS UNDER VARIOUS WAREHOUSE LOCATION CONFIGURATIONS.)

B THE PARTICULAR WAREHOUSE LOCATION CONFIGURATION THAT IS TO BE TESTED.

A THE RESULTS FROM THE PRESSING RUN (I.E., THE CUSTOMER VOLUME THAT FLOWS THROUGH THE WAREHOUSING SYSTEM) WHICH WERE RETAINED IN THE COMPUTER IN STEP #4.

C THE FREIGHT RATES, WAREHOUSE OPERATING COSTS, TAXES, ETC., THAT MAKE UP THE COSTS OF THE PARTICULAR GEOGRAPHICAL AREAS IN WHICH THE PROPOSED WAREHOUSES ARE LOCATED.

6 NEXT, THE FOLLOWING INFORMATION IS PROCESSED BY THE PROGRAMED COMPUTER.

5 FIRST, THE COMPUTER HAS FED INTO IT A NEW PROGRAM WHICH TELLS IT HOW TO COMPUTE COSTS ON THE BASIS OF THE INFORMATION WHICH IT WILL RECEIVE IN STEP #6.

7 THE COMPUTER ISSUES THE RESULTS THE COSTS OF DISTRIBUTION FOR THE HEINZ COMPANY UNDER THE TESTED WAREHOUSE LOCATION CONFIGURATION.

Exhibit IV may prove helpful at this point as a summary of the step-by-step action we took in using the simulation to test one particular warehouse pattern. A similar process, you will realize, took place for each warehouse and mixing point configuration we tested.

With the design of the simulation described, and the substantial research performed, the results showed a very distinct cost minimum. The cost of distribution which was minimized was that broad concept which includes costs of transportation between Heinz factories and warehouses, costs of operating the warehouses in various locations, and the cost of final delivery to the Heinz customer.

The results showed clearly that for the distribution requirement of the H. J. Heinz Company (a given optimal configuration of mixing points and warehouses, with given locations, and serving given customers in accordance with prescribed procedures) a lowest over-all cost of national distribution would be realized. The results are logical and attainable.

An area map is shown in Exhibit V to illustrate hypothetical warehouse locations obtained. For Heinz, a complete national map of actual warehouse locations recommended was drawn to provide a visual identification of the new distribution system. In addition, we were able to draw precise warehouse-to-customer assignments, specifying which warehouse would best serve each

EXHIBIT V. HYPOTHETICAL EXAMPLE OF CUSTOMER ASSIGNMENTS AND WAREHOUSE LOCATIONS OBTAINED FROM THE SIMULATION

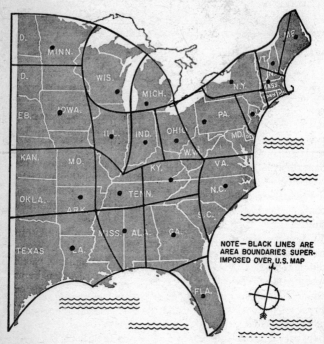

EXHIBIT VI. ARRIVING AT THE NUMBER OF HEINZ WAREHOUSES THAT WOULD MINIMIZE TOTAL DISTRIBUTION COSTS

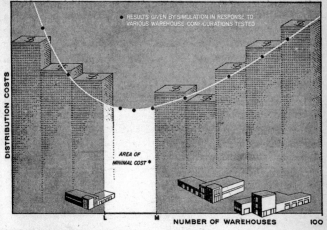

* RESULTS GIVEN BY SIMULATION IN RESPONSE TO VARIOUS WAREHOUSE CONFIGURATIONS TESTED

DISTRIBUTION COSTS

AREA OF MINIMAL COST *

L   M   NUMBER OF WAREHOUSES   100

* HERE MANAGEMENT MUST MAKE DECISIONS
AS TO WHETHER THE NUMBER OF WAREHOUSES SHOULD BE CLOSER TO THE L OR THE M LIMITS OF THE MINIMAL COST AREA

customer in the national system for each type of shipment received. Further, where shipments were large enough, we specified which mixing point should be used and, if a direct-from-factory customer, which factories should ship. These precise customer assignments then indicated exact area outlines for each warehouse. Samples of warehouse area assignments are shown in Exhibit V.

While the simulation does indicate such things as the optimal configuration of warehouses in exact figures, it is by no means a substitute for the judgment of management. As shown in Exhibit VI, for example, the results indicated clearly that for most efficient operation it was necessary to have M warehouses, but that it did not matter much, from a dollars-and-cents point of view, whether there were as few as L or as many as M. Costs were about equal under either alternative or any alternative in between. From the point of view of customer service, we recommended M, although a good case could have been made for some number in between. L and M differed by some few warehouses.

In making choices within ranges such as this, solid judgment, experience, and knowledge of local conditions in given areas come to the assistance of the simulation. And, as we did in the Heinz simulation, trends in the industry and economic arguments beyond the scope of the simulation should be examined carefully to determine whether the recommendations of the simulation were indeed proper ones.

Other Uses

The method for performing the Heinz study has provided great facility for studying other aspects of the business which are at least as important as the development of an optimal distribution system. When the simulation was developed, it was thought important to build a general-purpose tool, one which management could use at any time, future as well as present, to study questions of major concern. It was not, however, until the simulation was designed that it was fully realized that the tool provided such facility for studying a wide range of perplexing management problems, specifically listed here.

Distribution cost studies—Customers can be separated by areas, types, shipment sizes, salesmen, type of carrier, channels of distribution. We could get estimates of distribution costs on the basis of each or any combination thereof.

Locational studies—The number and location of factories could be changed, for example, rather than altering the warehouse configuration. Then, too, the effect on the company's operations of a sudden shift in customer type or location could be studied.

Studies related to products—The product mix at each factory can be changed arbitrarily to observe whether adding product capacity would change distribution cost appreciably. Similarly customer consumption patterns can be altered to see what effect such changes will have on distribution costs.

Studies related to time—Customer data can be altered in order to reflect gross annual volume changes by product line. These data would then be used to determine distribution costs. Thus, can be seen what effect proposed changes in sales policy, price, or new products would have on customer purchasing frequency, order size, or volume. The possible effect on distribution costs and on profitability can be estimated experimentally.

While the simulation is a remarkable management tool, it does have its limitations:

(1) Resources can only be stretched so far. Some compromises obviously have to be made, although any compromise that might seriously reduce the meaningfulness of major results must be avoided or the project may be worthless.

(2) The technical characteristics of the equipment set bounds. The program we used was written to be fast and versatile. This meant that much had to be stored in the computer's internal memory, and in a problem of this size it does not take too long to jam up against a 32,000-word ceiling.

(3) The accuracy and adequacy of input information impose limits on the program. If any one maxim developed out of this study, it was this: Know your customers (i.e., get control over your input data). Results are only as good as the data that are used to create them.

Conclusion

Great advances in the science of business management have taken place in the past decade on a scale unprecedented in the history of business planning. Perhaps one of the most useful techniques developed is simulation. Simulation provides the ability to operate some particular phase of the business, on paper or in a computer, for a period of time and by these means to test various alternative strategies. Distribution, sales and marketing, production, or even all in combination, can yield to this new science.

Every major decision-making executive has long wished he might, by some means, test the various alternatives open to him before making a final decision on a complex problem. With the development of simulation, a major breakthrough has been achieved in providing this insight into the future. To be able to test many alternative courses of action and to obtain documented evidence of the operating results of such proposed action, places in the hands of the aggressive businessman a tool of inestimable value.

The use of high-speed computers is a principal element contributing to the feasibility of examining the various alternatives. In order to put the problem on a computer, it is first necessary to express the problem and the characteristics of distribution in mathematical form, that is, to construct a mathematical model of the distribution requirements. Once it has been designed, however, the model may be looked on as a form of capital investment which makes possible economies in analysis, both present and future.

The importance of this accomplishment must be considered not only in the light of more profitable distribution, but also as a basic adjunct to policy determination and the study of profit achievement. Regardless of whether a company is in hard goods or soft, in food manufacturing or electrical appliances, in consumer or in industrial products, it can conduct, through simulation, a wide range of basic studies. Area profitability, product line and type of customer profitability, the effects of pricing "breaks," all these can be studied just as the factory and warehouse location problems have been by the Heinz company.

Certainly, though, we do not mean to imply that all the major logical difficulties of simulating a distribution system have now been solved. The remaining tasks of embellishment and increased accuracy are great. But we do want to assert that such simulations are powerful tools. In the business of the future, perhaps, every company will have one.

9

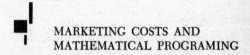

MARKETING COSTS AND
MATHEMATICAL PROGRAMING

WILLIAM J. BAUMOL AND CHARLES H. SEVIN

It is difficult to exaggerate the opportunities for reduced marketing costs and increased marketing efficiency, and hence greater profits, which are offered to management by the combined techniques of distribution cost analysis and mathematical programing. In the offing may be a revolution in the planning and execution of distribution that is fully comparable to the triumph of time and motion studies and cost analysis in the factory.

In the pages to follow we shall describe some of the more important techniques that management can profitably use, and we shall make the following points.

The misallocation of marketing effort in industry is greater than most people realize.

The separation of (a) fixed costs incurred in common for different types of sales effort, (b) separable fixed costs, and (c) variable costs which are related to different segments of the business is one of the key steps in analyzing a company's distribution problem.

The techniques of mathematical and linear programing can be used to derive approximately, on the basis of these cost data, the most profitable allocation of a firm's marketing expenditures and resources.

Once the needed data on cost-volume relationships are obtained and the computations are completed, the businessman can proceed to redirect his marketing effort in a way that is virtually guaranteed to increase his profits.

In a short appendix we shall suggest a few inexpensive computations that will help to improve a distribution cost analysis.

Tremendous Opportunities

In most businesses a very large proportion of the customers, orders, products, and territories brings in only a very small proportion of the sales. But selling, advertising, and other marketing efforts all too frequently are expended in proportion to the area covered, the number of customers, the number of orders, and so forth; management does not give enough explicit consideration to their actual and potential contribution to sales volume and profit.

Even the better-managed firms seldom realize how much of their marketing effort brings in only very small sales returns, since it is difficult to find out which sales can be ascribed to which selling and promotion work. They make little or no systematic attempt to evaluate the results of specific portions of marketing effort, and usually measure their success solely by the firm's total dollar sales in each product line. Moreover, the manufacturers of branded consumer goods with a national market typically follow a policy of 100% coverage of the market in order to support their national advertising.

For these and other reasons, there is widespread misallocation of sales effort. A business as a whole may be making a good profit; but if you analyze its costs and sales carefully, you will usually find that a large number of sales are not very profitable at all—at least, as compared with certain other sales.

Also, such sales are a heavy drain on potential profits. When time on an expensive television program is devoted to the promotion of a low-profit item, or a salesman spends time on an unpromising retailer, or limited warehouse space is tied up by large stocks of a low-turnover, low-markup item, the costs to the firm are high. Valuable television time, sales effort, and warehouse space are thereby withheld from more profitable uses. If a salesman divides his time between one product which earns the company $5 an hour and another which nets $12 an hour, then every hour spent promoting the former, in effect, costs the company $7. This is quite elementary, yet its lesson is ignored all about us every day. For instance, one company made a distribution cost analysis and found that 68% of its customers, bringing in only 10% of the volume, were responsible for a net loss of as much as 44% of sales. A distribution cost analysis in another firm revealed that 95% of all the customers in one territory were unprofitable—with losses ranging up to 86% of sales.

The substantial losses on unprofitable sales resulting from disproportionate spreading of marketing effort can be minimized or even eliminated simply by making certain that the marketing dollar goes where it can do the most good. This can be done with the help of two related tools—distribution cost analysis and mathematical programing. These tools can indicate to management where and how to apportion marketing effort to make the most of potential net profit possibilities. In fact, companies which have used just distribution cost analysis as a management tool—without the use of mathematical programing—have achieved startling reductions in their distribution costs by correcting only the more obvious maldistributions of market effort. For example, in one company marketing expenses were cut nearly in half, from 22.8% to 11.5% of sales, and a net loss of 2.9% on the books was turned into a net profit of 15%, after shifting some effort from the 68% of accounts which had been unprofitable. Another company shifted selling and advertising effort from less profitable to more profitable territories and achieved a 78% increase in average sales per salesman, a reduction of 33% in the ratio of selling and advertising expense to sales, and an increase of about 100% in the ratio of net profits to sales.[1]

How is management to find out what the different parts of the firm's marketing process contribute to its costs, its profits, and its

[1] These two cases are taken from Charles H. Sevin, *How Manufacturers Reduce Their Distribution Costs* (Washington, Government Printing Office, 1948).

sales? It is not so easy as it sounds. Prevalent accounting techniques for recording the results of marketing activities are insufficiently detailed; their information is distorted by arbitrary cost allocations, and their figures are only part of what is required.

The first step is a finer breakdown of the firm's average cost and profit data. The over-all distribution costs for the entire business must be allocated to *the specific segments of the business for which they are incurred.* For example, through distribution cost analysis we find that the sale of a thousand cases of product A through medium-size retailers located in the Chicago metropolitan area requires x dollars worth of salesman time, y dollars in transportation and warehousing costs, z dollars in advertising expenditure, and so on. We then get the production costs and figure the net profits or losses for each segment separately. This is not the place for an extended discussion of the principles and methods of distribution cost analysis, but two basic principles of the techniques used can readily be summarized:

(1) The distribution expenditures of a particular business, which are usually recorded on a *natural*-expense basis, are reclassified into *functional*-cost groups, which bring together all of the indirect costs associated with each marketing activity or function performed by that company.

(2) The functional-cost groups are allocated to products, customers, and other segments of sales on the basis of measurable factors, or product and customer characteristics which bear a cause-and-effect relationship to the total amounts of these functional costs.[2]

Treatment of Costs

Fixed (overhead) costs may be defined as those which, in the short run, do not change in total amount as sales increase (although, as we shall see later, costs which are fixed in one problem can be variable in another). This may be the result of contractual obligations assumed by the firm, or it may represent salaries, sunk or irrecoverable expenditures in buildings, equipment, and so forth.

[2] For further details on classification of distribution costs by functional categories and bases for their allocation to specific segments of a business, see Charles H. Sevin, *Manufacturers.*

Not all fixed costs should be treated alike, however. In fact, one of the crucial steps in distribution cost analysis is to distinguish between those costs which can be charged to specific types of sales and those which cannot. The management which is ready and able to do this well can confidently go on with the job of deciding where its unrealized potentials for profit lie.

Some fixed marketing costs are incurred in common for several different sales segments—for example, the advertising of a company's brand name, which must automatically influence the sale of all package sizes in one degree or another. Any breakdown of these advertising costs among the various package sizes must be arbitrary because the facts only entitle us to say that the advertising program is serving all of the package sizes at once.

Here we run into a serious problem. Two different methods of allocating such fixed costs can easily yield totally different results, and clearly both cannot be right. There is, in fact, no really correct method of allocating fixed costs incurred in common by sales for different products or customers.

The solution to this problem is simple: fixed costs which are common to several sales segments and whose magnitudes do not vary with the volume of sales in any one segment should be omitted from all cost and profit computations. Sales income should be viewed as a contribution to profit and fixed cost together. The situation is like a family debt; what each brother brings in helps both to support the family and to pay off the family's obligations, although it does not affect the size of the rent, food, and heating bills.

None of this applies, of course, to variable costs, which increase with sales and therefore can be allocated. For instance, more sales in Wisconsin help to pay the company's transportation bill, but they also increase the magnitude of this bill. It is a variable cost. The addition to the freight bill cannot be ignored in seeing how much these Wisconsin sales are worth to the firm. But a fixed cost of the sort we are discussing does not vary with sales. The added income from Wisconsin contributes to the payment of fixed costs but adds nothing to their size.

It follows, therefore, that an allocation of marketing costs which omits fixed elements can show how much a particular type of sale contributes to the well-being of the firm and can indicate how a

251

EXHIBIT I. RELATION OF PROFITS TO SALES UNAFFECTED BY FIXED COST

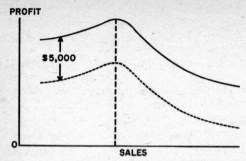

revision of the firm's distribution efforts can help sales and profits. Costs which include arbitrarily allocated fixed elements can be seriously misleading, and they do not add any useful knowledge to a management analysis of sales and profits.

To illustrate, suppose that a company correlates its sales and profits in a certain territory and finds a curve like the solid line in Exhibit I. It learns that the sales dollar is most profitable when total sales volume is at point x. Now suppose that warehouse rental goes up and adds $5,000 to fixed cost. This lowers the profit curve at every point; the dotted line now represents profits. But the highest point of the new curve still occurs at x, simply because warehouse rental is a fixed cost at all sales volumes. A change in such a cost does not tell management anything it did not know before about the sales-maximum profits relationship. It would be important to know only in the exceptional case where the increased fixed costs make it impossible for the firm to break even.

Of course, the elimination of fixed expenses from the allocation of costs is not quite so simple in practice as it may sound. It is often difficult to distinguish between variable and fixed marketing costs. For instance, warehousing cost, which is fixed when the warehouse is not used to capacity, becomes variable *when,* with all the storage space filled up, management considers the construction of more space to eliminate a bottleneck. A sales manager's salary may be a fixed cost *unless* the company considers firing him altogether rather than transferring his services from one product line to another. Most, if not all, costs which are fixed in the short run become variable after enough time passes, or if a large enough change in sales volume occurs. The costs of plant and equipment are usually fixed *until* the facilities wear out and have to be replaced.

In dealing with such questions, the nature of the problem is most often crucial in determining whether a cost is fixed or variable. If a firm is considering how many trucks it should use, the purchase cost of its truck fleet is clearly variable. But when the firm wishes to know how best to allocate the trucks which it already possesses, the assumption being that no new trucks are to be bought or old ones scrapped, then the nature of the problem dictates that the purchase cost of the truck fleet is fixed.

Again, if the problem is one of long-range planning, certain plant and equipment costs will be variable because the machines will wear out during the period under consideration, whereas these costs would be fixed for a problem in, say, short-run production programing or control. In any event, the segregation of fixed costs requires caution, skill, and experience; the job is an important one, but it is full of pitfalls for the unwary.

The fixed costs just considered are not the only kind of distribution costs which are fixed expenses for a company. In fact, most fixed marketing costs are different in the sense that they can and should be allocated to sales. These are what we shall call the separable fixed costs.

To illustrate: if the sales manager's job is not in question, his salary is, as we have seen, a fixed cost to the firm. No change in sales affects the magnitude of his salary (although it may affect his bonus). However, the time and effort which he spends on specific sales segments is variable. He can spend 5% of his time— or more, or less—working to promote sales in the New Orleans district. The more time he spends here, the less time he has left to spend on the promotion of other sales. Accordingly, we may be able to allocate his time with ease, even though his salary is a fixed cost. Similarly, the floor space in a warehouse for finished-goods inventory whose rental is fixed, or the capacity of a delivery truck fleet, is divided among the different products in terms of the space needed by each.

Such costs are not a direct deduction from the income which

accrues to the firm as its sales increase and need not enter the profit calculation any more than do fixed costs which are common to several sales segments. But they are nonetheless crucial for distribution cost analysis, for its purpose is to show where the firm's marketing effort can be used most effectively. Clearly the sales manager should devote his time to a sales sector which yields $50 per hour in preference to another sector which offers only $30 return for an hour of his effort.

As we shall see, it is this consideration which makes the methods of mathematical programing relevant to a distribution cost analysis. Separable fixed costs usually pertain to efforts or resources that are limited in total.

Accordingly, the marginal cost of separable fixed expenses—for instance, the cost of the manager's time which would be required to make additional sales in each segment of the business being costed—should be computed if possible. And these figures should be kept distinct from variable costs.

Changes in Sales Policy

Suppose now it is found that, on the average, the sale of a dollar's worth of product x through medium-size retailers in Kansas City contributes more to profits than a dollar sale of product y through small retailers in Richmond. It is tempting to jump to the conclusion that more sales effort should be allocated to the former and less to the latter. But does this follow? Suppose, for example, that sales of product X in Kansas City have saturated the market, while the Richmond market is ripe for development. Clearly, it would not be wise to shift effort to Kansas from Virginia.

Thus, the cost currently incurred by a specific segment of sales may be the right answer to the wrong question. It tells us how well the firm is doing now; but the firm wants to know whether it can do better in the future, and, if so, how and where. Accordingly, we must know the answer to the following hypothetical questions: What would happen to marketing costs if more effort were pointed in one direction rather than in another? More specifically, how are changes in total costs in each sales category related to changes in volume in the same category?

In effect, for each sales segment and each functional cost group, we want the kind of information contained in Exhibit II. We need these data for both variable costs and separable fixed costs. Once these figures are obtained, the businessman can proceed to apportion his distribution effort in a way virtually guaranteed to increase his profits.

This means that, in the simplest case where there is only one type of marketing effort in question (the more complicated—and more common—cases will be discussed later), effort should be reallocated as much as possible to those segments of sales where an additional unit of marketing effort will yield the highest contribution to net profits and overhead, after deduction of variable costs; i.e., effort should be increased in that sales sector where there is the highest value of the fraction:

$$\frac{\text{additional sales—additional variable costs}}{\text{additional effort or resource devoted to this sector}}$$

Further discussion and a rigorous derivation of this criterion are included in the appendix to this paper. However, here is a simple illustration. Suppose the figures show that in Boston an additional $2 in the field sales force's fixed budget will yield an additional $10 in sales and that the additional variable cost of those

EXHIBIT II. EXAMPLES OF SALES COST DATA NEEDED FOR STATISTICAL DECISION

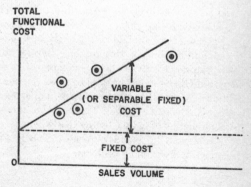

sales is $4. Then the value of the fraction in question will be $(10 - 4) \div 2 = 3$. If the corresponding figure for Oklahoma City is 2.6, it is clear that selling effort should be reallocated from Oklahoma to Boston.

Often, as shown in an example in the appendix dealing with use of a limited resource (warehouse space), the proper allocation of effort will actually be completely different from that indicated by the conventional approach via per-unit net profit.

How do we find out how the functional costs vary with sales? The obvious answer is to see what has happened to costs when sales changes occurred in the past. But past events are not controlled experiments; past sales changes are often the result of a variety of causes, many of which are no longer pertinent. Moreover, unlike most production costs, which are a function of volume, changes in distribution costs are often both a cause and an effect of changes in sales volume. Past experience may therefore be an unreliable test. There are, however, a number of techniques which will help us cope with this difficulty.

Mathematical Programing

Usually there are several types of distribution effort or cost which a company must allocate carefully. The funds available for advertising may be limited, the salesmen's time be fully occupied, and warehouse space constitute a bottleneck. The objective is to promote those sales which make the best use of all three of these factors.

No one sales segment is likely to use all three effectively. One product may use advertising dollars very efficiently because its sales can be increased with the aid of relatively little additional advertising expenditure. But if this product is also bulky, its inventory will employ relatively large amounts of warehouse space. Similarly, another product may yield much greater profits for each additional hour of the sales force's time but small returns on each additional advertising dollar. The problem, therefore, is to select that combination of sales activities that will make optimal use of the company's facilities and know-how. This is what the mathematician calls a programing problem.

What does programing do that other techniques cannot do?[3] In many cases the standard optimization technique, i.e., differential calculus, can, given adequate data, indicate precisely what is the maximum (profit) or minimum (cost) achievable. But in some problems of optimization there is a complication in that the outcome, to be acceptable, must meet certain specifications which the mathematician calls "side conditions."

For example, it may be most profitable for a firm to sell 10,000 pairs of shoes a week. This is, then, a sort of optimum. However, if the firm's warehouse can stock only 8,000 pairs of shoes, the optimum is an unattainable goal, and it becomes necessary to recompute a more modest and practicable target. The aim is to find the most profitable combination of outputs which do not violate the "inequality side condition" that production must be less than or equal to 8,000 pairs per week.

Programing is the mathematical method for analyzing and computing optimum output decisions which do not violate the limitations imposed by inequality side conditions. In other words, it attacks the same problem that distribution cost analysis seeks to solve. Its purpose is to find a pattern of sales which maximizes profits and yet does not exceed the available capacities of the firm.

The mathematical programing problem consists of two essential parts: (1) something which is maximized (e.g., profit) and (2) the inequality side conditions.

As for the first, it is generally assumed that the business is trying to maximize the sum of the gross (dollar) margins in the various segments of sales minus the sum of their variable costs. This is where our variable costs are used in the distribution cost analysis.

Next we examine the relevant inequality side conditions. These describe the various limitations imposed on the firm by a fixed advertising budget or sales force, limited warehouse space, and so forth. There will be an inequality which corresponds to each

---

[3] See Chapter 2, above, and Alexander Henderson and Robert Schlaifer, "Solution of Management Problems Through Mathematical Programming," *Cost and Profit Outlook*, May 1956, published by Alderson & Sessions, Philadelphia.

of these limitations. For example, one inequality will state that the amount of warehouse space used by the various sales segments must not exceed the available capacity. More specifically, if, say, the warehouse space used for finished-goods inventories is strictly proportional to the sales in each category, we will require that the warehouse space used up by the different categories of sales add up to an amount less than or equal to the available warehouse space. We can put all of this more comprehensively and concisely in mathematical terms:

$$a_1(W) + a_2(X) + a_3(Y) + a_4(Z) \leq A$$
$$b_1(W) + b_2(X) + b_3(Y) + b_4(Z) \leq B$$
$$c_1(W) + c_2(X) + c_3(Y) + c_4(Z) \leq C,$$

where A is the available warehouse space, B is the available sales force time, C is the budgeted advertising funds; and where $a_1(W)$ is the warehouse space used by W sales, $a_2(X)$ is the space used by X sales, $b_1(W)$ is the salesmen's time used by W sales, and so forth. (For illustration it is assumed that there are exactly four sales segments.)

It is here our separable fixed cost figures are used. We see now why these were not added to the variable cost statistics. The two types of figures play totally different roles in the analysis and appear in completely separate parts of the mathematical program. The variable cost represents a deduction from the firm's income; the separable fixed cost represents a drain on its limited marketing effort; and they must each be treated accordingly.

There remain two stipulations that must be made before the mathematician takes over:

(1) We must specify that sales in any segment can fall to zero but can never be negative, or:

$$W \geq 0, X \geq 0, Y \geq 0, \text{ and } Z \geq 0.$$

This may seem so obvious and unimportant that it is not worth mentioning; however, it turns out that this apparently trivial requirement is fundamental for the mathematical analysis. One reason is that the computations are usually done by electronic calculators, which are not really as bright as sometimes supposed. They may do computations quickly, but they do not realize (unless told so specifically) that negative sales are out of the question.

If some particular sales segment is especially unprofitable, the machine will figure out that the less the firm sells in that segment, the better off it will be. But, if so, why stop cutting down when we get to zero? Unless instructed otherwise, the machine is very likely to end up recommending negative sales in unprofitable segments!

(2) The nature of the problem may change so that a cost once fixed becomes variable and the corresponding capacity limitation disappears. In a planning problem, for instance, if present warehouses would be inadequate for increasing sales, the construction of new warehouses might be considered by the planners, and then the amount of construction would vary with the amount of sales. The effect on the mathematical program is simple; the corresponding inequality is dropped, and the variable cost figures in the profit expression are increased to include the new variable costs.

Linear Programing

The word "programing" most frequently occurs in the term "linear programing." When the facts of the situation state that costs will always be proportionate to sales so that, for example, a threefold increase in the level of sales in any one segment will always exactly triple all the costs incurred by the segment, the relevant program is said to be linear. This is because the graph showing the relationship between sales in a sector and the magnitude of some cost will then be a straight line, as in Exhibit II.

In a linear case there are great economies in data collection and computation. As Exhibit II indicates, it takes fewer dots or statistics to locate a straight line than to plot a curved line. The few dots shown on the graph would obviously not be sufficient to permit the fitting of a curved line with any degree of confidence; yet even these few are expensive to collect.

Linear programing has practical uses in distribution cost analysis, but to appreciate them it is necessary to look first at its limitations.

To begin with, it almost never fits the facts. If pursued to its logical conclusion, it is virtually certain to give the wrong answer. One reason is that in marketing various costs involve quantity discounts. For example, if we ship one-third of a carload of goods, the less-than-carload rates apply, and it will cost considerably more than one-third the amount required to ship a full carload. It is easy to think of other costs which do not rise strictly in proportion with sales. Inventory levels, and hence the costs of storage, do not usually rise exactly in proportion to sales volume; neither does the cost of sales management. One could make quite a list.

Moreover, linear programing has an inherent bias which often leads to seriously incorrect answers in distribution cost analysis. It usually suggests the elimination of a large number of sales categories; for example, it may suggest that a firm end up selling to only a certain type of retailer and in only a few major cities. This happens because of the basic theorem of linear programing, which in effect states that if there are, say, just three inequality side conditions in a problem, then maximum profits can be obtained by confining sales to no more than three sales segments.

To illustrate, if we are trying to get the most out of our warehouse capacity, our salesmen's time, and our advertising expenditure, linear programing would lead us to concentrate on three sales segments—one which produces large profits per square foot of warehouse space, another which returns large profits per salesman hour, and a third which yields high returns per advertising dollar. Any types of sales which are second best to these three would be eliminated.

Of course, this is all wrong. For one thing, there are diminishing returns to effort; markets become saturated. If one-twentieth of the national advertising budget is used in Chicago, moving the entire advertising effort to Chicago will not increase sales there twentyfold. The transfer of effort would be a good thing only up to a point, and it would be most profitable to devote much of the advertising budget to other market areas.

All of this is not to say, however, that linear programing has no uses. Quite the contrary. While a linear program usually will not compute a correct optimum because the changes it suggests will go too far, there is yet a very strong presumption that it will correctly indicate the best directions of change. It will identify correctly the sales segments to which more effort should be allocated. Accordingly, where it is too expensive to undertake a full-scale nonlinear programing analysis, or where the necessary data are simply not available, linear programing can still be exceedingly helpful.

Conclusion

In practice, the great bulk of the savings which distribution cost analysis has made possible can be ascribed to its ability to find those sales sectors to which marketing effort is most glaringly misallocated. Using this technique, many sales managements have been able to redirect their efforts and achieve very substantial additions to profits.

As most sales executives know, the data available are rarely so accurate that the analysts can trust a very refined calculation. But when their information points out a very costly case of misdirected effort, they can confidently proceed to take remedial action, for no small error in data and computation will normally account for the considerable losses which distribution cost analysis often reveals. In sum, even fairly inaccurate data and fairly crude computational techniques will usually turn up those inefficiencies which are most glaring and which constitute the most important opportunities to increase profits.

Accordingly, even though they may not have the data, the time, or the budget for a mathematical programing analysis, managers usually can still obtain much of the benefit of a full-scale distribution cost analysis by using a linear programing approximation or just the general approach outlined in this article. They can increase the accuracy of their information with only inexpensive modifications in distribution cost analysis procedures, as we indicate in the appendix to this article. Thus, the principles alone of mathematical programing will serve, when used in conjunction with a distribution cost analysis, to help management achieve from its marketing operations a marked increase in efficiency and substantially higher profits.

Appendix: Some Suggestions for Computations

Profit Computation for Allocation Decisions

When the firm is considering the allocation of the currently available amount of some type of marketing effort, it is posing a question which requires that the expenditure on that type of effort be treated as a fixed cost. In posing such a question the analyst is told, in effect, that the firm has, let us say, so many salesmen at its disposal, and he is then asked how the members of the sales force can best divide their time among products, customers, territories, and so forth.

In distribution cost analysis, the various separable fixed costs (e.g., the warehouse floor space) allocated to each sales segment are translated into money terms, and the sum of these and the allocated variable costs are subtracted from the dollar gross margins to obtain a net profit or loss figure for each segment of the business. The implication is that marketing effort ought to be decreased in the sectors which show a large net loss and increased in the sectors having the highest per-unit net profit figures. In many cases, however, this implication may be incorrect and misleading.

For simplicity, we will illustrate this with the linear case where variable and separable fixed costs per unit for any sales sector do not change with the volume of sales in that sector. We will also assume that warehouse space is the only separable fixed cost. We will deal with the sales W and X in two sectors.

Now, it is usually suggested that effort should be transferred from X to W if and only if W's per-unit net profit is greater than X's; that is, if and only if (formula I):

Gross margin of W — variable cost of W — separable fixed cost of W > gross margin of X — variable cost of X — fixed separable cost of X.

But formula I does not always correctly indicate the most profitable reallocation of marketing effort. The most profitable thing to do is to increase the effort devoted to the sector which yields the highest contribution to profit and overhead per dollar of warehouse space. That is because warehouse space is the separable fixed cost—the effort or resource factor which needs to be economized—and the best profit-making strategy is to use that space where it earns the most. This proposition is easily proved:

If A is total available warehouse space and is completely utilized, we have:

$$A = A_w W + A_x X$$
$$\text{or:} \quad X = A/A_x - A_w W/A_x,$$

where A_w and A_x are the respective number of square feet of warehouse space used up per unit of W and X. Now let T_w and T_x represent the contribution to profit plus overhead per unit of W and X respectively. Substituting the expression just obtained for X, the total contribution to profit plus overhead of both sectors then will be:

$$WT_w + XT_x = WT_w + A/A_x T_x - A_w W/A_x T_x$$
$$= A/A_x T_x + W(T_w - A_w/A_x T_x).$$

Thus an increase in W will add to this figure if and only if $T_w - A_w A_x T_x > 0$; i.e., if $T_w/A_w > T_x/A_x$. To put it in another way, an increase in W will add to the profit figure only if T_w/A_w, the contribution per unit of warehouse space from stocking W, is greater than T_x/A_x, the contribution per unit of warehouse space from stocking X.

The significance of all this for our main question is that actually more effort should be allocated to W from X if and only if the figure for W's contribution to profit and overhead in ratio to W's use of warehouse space is greater than the corresponding figure for X; that is, if and only if (formula II):

(Gross margin of W — variable cost of W) ÷ separable fixed cost of W > (gross margin of X — variable cost of X ÷ separable fixed cost of X.

Now the important thing to note is that formulas I and II will not always point in the same direction. For example, if both gross margins are equal to 1.0, if the unit variable cost of W is 0.3 and the separable unit fixed cost of W is 0.2, and if the variable cost of X is 0.1 and the separable fixed cost of X is 0.3, then the net profit computation under formula I yields less unit net profit for W, because:

$$1.0 - 0.3 - 0.2 = 0.5 < 1.0 - 0.1 - 0.3 = 0.6.$$

Thus, distribution cost analysis as often practiced would infer that effort should not be shifted from X to W, or that the shift should be in the other direction. But the correct computation under formula II shows that W's contribution to profit and overhead per unit of warehouse space is really greater than X's, because:

$$(1.0 - 0.3) \div 0.2 = 3.5 > (1.0 - 0.1) \div 0.3 = 3.$$

In other words, the firm should shift effort from X to W, in precisely the opposite direction from that indicated by the usual net profit computation of formula I.

It should be remembered, however, that the procedure which has just been shown to be correct is valid if there is only one category of fixed cost and one corresponding facility to be allocated optimally. Where the number of facility limitations is greater than this, it is necessary to utilize the standard mathematical programing computations discussed earlier in this article.

Marginal Versus Average Data

As we have seen, average costs per unit cannot tell us how to reallocate effort. The information needed to decide whether a shift of effort will be profitable is the addition to costs and sales which will result from such a shift; i.e., the marginal costs and revenues. In practice, however, it is much easier and less expensive to obtain average gross profit and cost figures than to acquire the corresponding marginal figures. Most distribution cost analysis, therefore, employs average data in its calculations. We believe that this often yields satisfactory approximations, but good practice requires that the data be corrected for the most glaring divergencies between the marginal and average cost figures. In many cases it should be possible to recognize such differences fairly easily.

Here economic analysis provides us with several simple rules:

(1) All fixed costs must be eliminated from the average cost figures. In particular, if there are setup costs which must be incurred in order for the firm to operate at all, these must be omitted. A perusal of the accounting practices of the firm may indicate gross profit or cost figures in which such costs enter heavily, and appropriate corrections should be made.

(2) If demand does not respond readily to effort, marginal

revenues will be considerably lower than average revenues. In effect, this is because there will be diminishing returns to effort in such markets, so that additional effort will normally yield smaller revenues than does most of the present effort. This means that if experience suggests that market *M* is pretty much saturated and will not respond readily to further marketing effort, the average gross profit figure for this market must be reduced to obtain a number closer to the marginal gross profit.

In a few cases, marginal revenues will be greater than average revenues because additional selling activity can increase the effectiveness of effort already expended. In such cases an upward adjustment of the average gross profit is called for.

Of course, it will not be possible to identify all of the sales segments requiring this sort of adjustment or to determine the precise magnitude of the required changes. But with a little experience one usually can recognize, on the basis of interviews with management and examination of the available records, the most extreme cases of divergence between marginal and average gross profit; the analyst can then eliminate the most serious sources of error.

(3) On the cost side we have a similar rule. Where there are seriously diminishing returns, increase the average costs; if demand does by any chance respond more readily to added sales effort, reduce the average costs. This rule applies in the same way to production and to distribution costs.

(4) The magnitude of the required change in an average gross profit figure and in an average cost figure can be inferred with the help of the following standard formulas:

(a) Marginal gross profit = average gross profit + sales × rate of change in gross profit per sale.

(b) Marginal cost = average cost + sales × rate of change in average cost per sale. The rate of change in average cost per sale would mean, for example, (average cost in sector *X* when sales are $1,001,000 − average cost when sales are $1,000,000) ÷ the increase in sales [$1,000].

10

TESTS FOR TEST MARKETING

BENJAMIN LIPSTEIN

It is crucial in marketing to arrive at an early decision on the success or failure of a test-marketed product and, if successful, to move the product into national distribution as quickly as possible. But this is easier said than done.

Certainly, if you take enough time and spend enough money, you can easily judge from a test-marketing project whether or not the product will gain sufficient consumer acceptance to warrant going ahead nationally. But in view of the risk that a competitor will beat you into the market with a variation of your product, as well as the danger that you will lavish more time and money on the test than the results are worth, you have to find ways of evaluating the incoming data as the test develops.

Therefore, I would like to discuss how brand-share data derived from store audits and consumer panels can be used to get an early and continuing evaluation of the market test, and thus make an early decision to take action on the product (either positively or negatively) or to wait for further findings.

Brand-Share Trends

There are two brand-share trends that can be observed in most test-market situations.

266

EXHIBIT I. TYPICAL MARKET TEST BRAND SHARE FOR TWO TRENDS

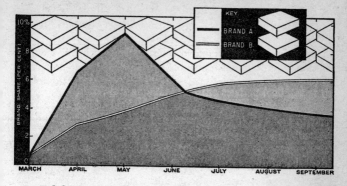

In Exhibit I you will see as a *black line* the so-called "typical" brand-share trend of new product introduction. Notice that this pattern is characterized by a sharp rise to a peak within the first two to three months, an equally sharp fall-off to a lower level, and a stabilization at this lower level.

While this kind of pattern is rather typical, it is by no means the only pattern that will appear in test marketing. The *white line* in Exhibit I shows another common pattern. Here there is a gradual rise in brand share, which eventually levels off at its highest point.

Being able early in the test-market situation to anticipate which of these two patterns your product will follow is the ultimate goal.

To see how these brand-share patterns operate in a real test-market situation, let us examine the test results from the mid-November 1958 introduction of Electra Oleomargarine in a western city.[1]

This particular product is, of course, quite fictitious. But the story behind its introduction is based on a real marketing situation—involving a food product possessing similar brand and repurchase qualities.

Look at Exhibit II and assume for the moment that data are available only through the end of December. The chart shows, at this point, that Electra has achieved a brand share well in ex-

[1] All brand names referred to in this paper are fictitious. The actual test involved a product with marketing characteristics similar to those of oleomargarine.

cess of our expectations. But will it hold at this level, as in the *color pattern* shown in Exhibit I? Or will it fall off sharply and hold at a much lower level, as the *black line* in Exhibit I? And, if so, how far will it fall off before it holds?

What is needed is a frame of reference for extracting the relevant facts. Only then is it possible to make reasonable projections of the product's direction. Our investigation revealed the following things.

During the first few months, the rate of new triers moved up very sharply, accounting for 15% of all consumers, as a result of the heavy introductory advertising campaign, coupon distribution, free product samples, and store promotions.

Closer scrutiny revealed that from the very beginning only 12% of these new triers bought the product a second time. Thus, it was the high rate of entry of new triers during these first few months that produced the sharply rising brand share. The rising brand trend was built on sand, and future events justified being cautious.

In the third month, as expected, our brand share took the turn down (thus following the pattern of the *black line* in Exhibit I). The rate of new triers diminished considerably—from 15% as of mid-December to a mere 5% in mid-January. This drop in new triers was the principal cause of the decline in brand share.

EXHIBIT II. INTRODUCTION OF ELECTRA OLEOMARGARINE IN A WESTERN CITY

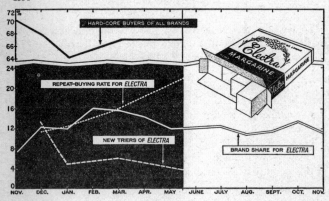

Compensating in part for the falling off of new triers was an increase in repeat buying. The repeat-buyer rate (made up of the percentage of customers who, having bought the brand in one period, buy it again in the next) rose from 12% in the first six weeks to 19% eighteen weeks after the initial introduction. This definite growth in repeat buyers assured us that the bottom had not really fallen out.

But even though the repeat-buying rate might generate some optimism, further investigation of the factors influencing it was necessary before any precipitate action could even be considered. For example, how did our share of repeat buyers compare with those held by competitive brands? We found out that prior to the introduction of Electra, the average repeat rate for competitive brands stood at 24%; and after eighteen weeks of introduction the average was 17% for all brands, compared to 19% for Electra.

Did this mean that we were passing competitive brands? Not exactly. But it did reveal that a very interesting phenomenon had occurred. In detail, before Electra was introduced in mid-November 1958, hard-core oleomargarine buyers (those who devoted three quarters of their purchases of oleomargarine to any single brand over a six-week period) made up 70% of the market. During the initial six weeks of introduction, hard-core buyers in the entire market declined to 65% primarily because some part of the total market had just become new triers of Electra.

Then, the hard core of competitors' brands was further shaken by our advertising campaign and coupon distribution (it dropped to 58%, in fact), but by now the repeat buyers of Electra were bringing up the total of hard-core buyers of all brands. So, even though the repeat rate for Electra was two percentage points above the market average at the end of four months, this was not necessarily promising. The reason? The total market, as measured by the level of hard-core buyers, was still in turmoil. A settling of the market was needed before a sound conclusion could be drawn.

During the next few months, Electra's share of the market continued to slide—but at a diminishing rate. Without the following supplementary information, this might have been cause for some concern. Specifically, while the new-trier rate leveled off at 3%, the repeat rate for our product continued to climb to 23%—just

EXHIBIT III. TABLE OF SWITCHING AND STAYING TENDENCIES BY CONSUMERS
OF VARIOUS BRANDS OF OLEOMARGARINE

READING ACROSS, YOU CAN SEE THE PERCENTAGE
OF ELECTRA BUYERS WHO SWITCHED TO OTHER BRANDS
DURING THE SECOND PERIOD

READING DOWN, YOU CAN SEE THE PERCENTAGE OF ORIGINAL BUYERS OF
OTHER BRANDS WHO SWITCHED TO ELECTRA DURING THE SECOND PERIOD

BUYERS OF THESE BRANDS IN THE FIRST PERIOD	BOUGHT THESE BRANDS IN THE SECOND PERIOD							TOTAL
	ELECTRA	GLORIA	MEADOWLARK	AUNT MARY'S	B-R PRIVATE LABEL	ALL OTHER	DID NOT BUY IN THE PERIOD	
ELECTRA	12%	5%	7%	4%	3%	28%	41%	100%
GLORIA	5%	25%	3%	2%	2%	26%	37%	100%
MEADOWLARK	3%	2%	21%	5%	3%	26%	40%	100%
AUNT MARY'S	2%	5%	1%	23%	4%	25%	40%	100
B-R STORES PRIVATE LABEL	4%	1%	3%	2%	22%	30%	38%	100%
ALL OTHER	3%	5%	3%	4%	5%	23%	57%	100%
DID NOT BUY IN THE PERIOD	5%	3%	4%	1%	2%	28%	57%	100%

one percentage point short of the product average prior to its
introduction.

By the end of May 1959, there was every reason to conclude
that our brand-share level would hold. (As the right-hand part of
Exhibit II shows, Electra's share did hold up within one percentage point during the remainder of the year.)

The minimum duration of test marketing had been completed.
The risk of erroneous evaluation of the new product had thus
been reduced. Now we were ready for the next move—testing in
other markets or an outright discontinuance of the product.

To help with our decision four basic sets of data derived from
store audits and consumer panels gave us information on (1)
brand shares, (2) new triers, (3) repeat-buying rates, and (4)
hard-core buyers. These data provided a relatively complete and
dynamic description of the behavior of the product's introduction
in the test market.

The data, furthermore, would help us answer the question,
"What happens to consumers who do not repeat the purchase of
Electra?" In Exhibit III, you will see the type of chart we compiled to answer this and other questions. The horizontal row for
Electra on the chart shows the percentage of consumers who
switched to other oleomargarine brands in the second week, as
well as those consumers who remained loyal to our product. It is
easy to see the effect of a brand's promotion or advertising on
competitors from a table of this type.

There is an additional class of information which is worth noting on Exhibit III. Reading down the Electra column under the second purchase period, you can see the percentage of the consumers of each brand who switched to Electra in the second week.

In effect, this table of staying and switching tendencies provides detailed information about where our buyers come from and where they go. This kind of information gives the product manager considerable insight into the market structure and at times affords unique opportunities for strategy development. Looking at the test market in this way, we uncovered an interesting and important characteristic of private-label buyers. Specifically, Exhibit IV compares the sources of business for Electra just after

EXHIBIT IV. SOURCES OF ELECTRA'S BUSINESS

Brand	Introductory period (November–December)	Five-to-six months later (April–May)
Electra	12%	23%
Gloria	5	5
Meadow Lark	3	2
Aunt Mary's	2	1
B-R Store's private label	4	0
All other	3	3
Did not buy in this period	5	5

introduction and six months later. The column of data identifying the source of Electra's business showed that 4% of private-label buyers switched to Electra during the introductory period of heavy promotion. The comparable figure five-to-six months later showed that virtually no private-label buyers switched to Electra when it was not being promoted. These two columns on sources of Electra business demonstrate rather effectively that while private-label buyers can be attracted by promotion, they do not represent business potential for a premium brand such as Electra during normal periods.

Conclusion

Perhaps the most essential point this type of analysis reveals is the way that the introduction of a new product disrupts the market and disturbs the usual patterns of hard-core buyers. When the heavy introductory campaign is reduced, the market—as reflected in buying patterns, loyalties, and hard-core buyers—will tend to return to equilibrium. However, now your new product (if successful) has become part of this market and has its own loyal consumers or hard-core buyers.

These marketing measurements apply to all products in the grocery category. Naturally, however, the definitions and criteria must be varied to fit the particular product category. For example, the hard-core buyer of ready-to-eat cereal buys the same brand less frequently than does the hard-core buyer of a product such as oleomargarine, because consumers typically use more than one kind of cereal during the same period of time. Furthermore, the evaluation of the repurchase rate is similarly conditioned by kind of product. A package of cleaning pads, for instance, may well have a repurchase cycle of six months, and repeat rates cannot be legitimately evaluated in less than one repurchase cycle.

In sum, with the accumulation of data on repeat-buying and hard-core buying patterns for a variety of food items, you are in a better position to make reasonably accurate advance estimates of the optimum length of a marketing test for a particular product type.

Of course, there will always be a risk in marketing decisions. Conventional techniques have helped minimize these risks of interpreting test markets by waiting to see how long-run trends of brand share establish themselves. Since competition or other circumstances often will not allow you to wait, however, evaluation of repeat-buying rates and hard-core buying levels as revealed in this article provides the earliest guides to the success or failure of the operation.

11

LESS RISK IN INVENTORY ESTIMATES

ROBERT G. BROWN

The future is uncertain. Only a company with a monopoly in an unsaturated market can be sure of what the future demand for its products will be. For managers concerned with inventories and customer service, this situation poses obvious problems. Accordingly, I shall discuss these questions: How can the uncertainty facing a company be kept to a minimum? How can that minimum be measured and accounted for in a well-designed inventory control system?

Forecasts & Predictions

Demand for a product is generated by the complex interaction of many factors. If it were possible to understand the effect of each of these factors, and how they interact, we could build a mathematical model that would give a very accurate estimate of future demand. Usually, however, this is not possible, since we do not fully understand the effect of competition, advertising, service, and substitutes for supplying the demand or for using the product.

We can nevertheless visualize some mechanism, some system of interacting factors, that does generate the demand; and we can use statistical theories to build a useful model of the total effect.

For example, a physicist studying a gas cannot know all the forces acting on a single, specific molecule, to predict its movement. He can, however, make very precise statements about the behavior of a large collection of molecules. Although the behavior of individuals is random, the ensemble has very stable statistical characteristics.

We might think of all the factors in our model that will generate the total demand during the next month. Some might be important, some unimportant; some might be fairly predictable, some unpredictable. But any factor could be put into one of two classes: (1) factors that generated customer demand in past months and are not new to the future; (2) factors that appear for the first time in affecting total demand.

There are many industries, and many types of products, for which the factors in the first class have most of the effect on total demand. In such cases, routine methods can be developed to forecast the effect of those factors, leaving management free to predict the effect of the few new influences. For other industries, by contrast, the future is almost entirely a change from the past; management predictions are more difficult and occupy a more central role. Here, as elsewhere in this article, I use the term "forecast" or "routine forecast" to mean the projection of the past into the future; and the term "predict" to mean management's anticipation of changes and of new factors affecting demand. While in practice both forecasts and predictions must be used, I shall concentrate my discussion on new developments in routine mathematical forecasting.

The difference between routine forecasting and prediction is important. Essentially, in forecasting we take a sequence of numbers and try to guess what the next number will be. Later we know what that next number was, and try to guess the following one, profiting by our mistakes in previous guesses. On the other hand, a prediction requires one to know a great deal about what the numbers represent—what the item is, how it is used, future marketing plans, the probable effect of competition, the economic climate, and so on.

Some people seem to have the ability to predict the future sales of an item, commodity, or stock fairly accurately if given enough time to study all the pertinent information. But it is not at all uncommon for a company to make hundreds or even thousands of items; and when one considers all the package sizes, colors, and locations, there may be a half-million SKUs (stock-keeping units) to be controlled. And the control of total investment, total service, and total cost is based on the control of the replenishment of one SKU at a time.

Since there are not enough skilled people who have the time to predict the demand for each SKU, the men who have the job must forecast instead, extrapolating past experience and making any necessary adjustments to account for predictions of general economic or competitive factors (e.g., a strike or recession).

In the routine forecasting of demand for hundreds or thousands of SKUs we must necessarily "play the averages" as best we can. There are different ways of doing this.

Suppose that, in effect, we have a game in which we are given a sequence of numbers—say, 64, 115, 101, 65, 126, and 111—and must guess what the next number (or numbers) in the sequence will be. We guess 97 (the average of the six numbers), actual demand turns out to be 150, and we sit down to guess again. What method shall we use? We could take the average of all seven numbers that we have now—104.6; we could take the average of the most recent six numbers—111.3; or—a little more complicated—we could adjust our next forecast on the basis of the difference between the last forecast (97) and the actual demand which materialized (150).

The first two ways of estimating are familiar averages; the third is newer. In some circumstances the first two are adequate, but frequently—especially in expanding markets—they are not. To illustrate: Let us suppose that the sequence had been 64, 65, 101, 111, 115, 126. Although the numbers are the same as before, the problem is different: each month the demand has been greater than the demand the previous month, so that it might be plausible to assume that the demand in the seventh month is going to be at least 126, and probably higher. Thus the simple average 97 would be a poor estimate of the next value in the sequence. Some allowance for trend must be made.

Many of the conventional procedures in use for routine forecasting do, in one way or another, compute an average; and a few recognize the problem of systematic trends by asking an analyst to "be on the lookout for a trend, and make the necessary adjustments." But, as we shall see shortly, routine computations can detect a trend more quickly than the eye can, and the necessary adjustments can be made automatically. There are a number of new procedures that can be helpful in this regard, and we shall discuss them in some detail.

There is a further dimension to this problem where conventional procedures are inadequate. It is the common practice to estimate a single number, which may represent the most probable or the expected eventuality—for example, 268,100 passenger miles or 23,500 conveyer belts. But this number is almost certain to be wrong, if only by a few units. On the other hand, by specifying a range of possibilities and making the range wide enough, we could achieve any reasonable percentage of successful estimates, even in markets subject to great change.

We shall see later how to estimate the expected value for future demand, and how to estimate the range necessary to insure any desired probability of being right—right, that is, in predicting that

EXHIBIT I. DEMAND FOR TEN-FOOT LENGTHS OF COPPER TUBING

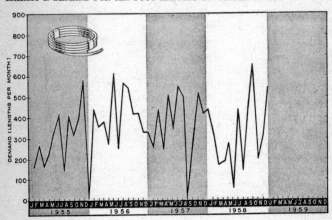

demand will not exceed a number equal to the expected demand, plus an allowance for uncertainty.

Warmdot Case

To illustrate the new, improved methods that can be applied to these problems, I shall use the fictional, but realistic "Warmdot Appliance Company." Through the paper I shall refer to four products that typify the problems posed by the thousands of SKUs stocked:

(1) Copper tubing is used by both heating and air conditioning contractors; and the demand for it is affected by strikes, the weather, building activity, and competitive sources. The demand for 3B1676, heavy duty ⅝" tubing, stocked in ten-foot lengths, is plotted in Exhibit I. On the average, in the past four years, Warmdot has sold 343 lengths of this item a month. The maximum was 657 in September 1958, and there were two months with no demand.

(2) A new line of general-purpose thermostats was introduced in 1954, and the demand has been growing steadily, as shown in Exhibit II for the 1D9120 model. The average demand in the past

EXHIBIT II. DEMAND FOR THERMOSTATS

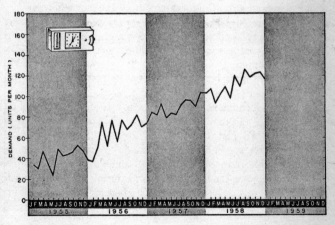

EXHIBIT III. DEMAND FOR EVAPORATOR PLATES

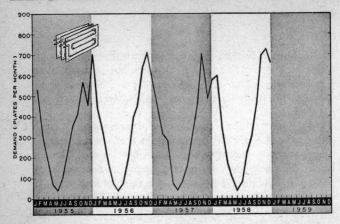

four years has been 77 units a month, and the maximum was 126. However, since there has been a steady upward trend in demand, the four-year average would be of little value in estimating demand during the first quarter of 1959.

(3) Evaporator plates are used only in furnaces, but need to be replaced every two or three years. Exhibit III shows how the demand for 1A9375 plates has a definite peak when cold weather sets in. The low sales level of about 30 is a good estimate of summer demand, and a peak of about 700 has occurred every fall—although in different months. So the long-term average of 338 plates a month must be modified according to the season of the year, if we are to have a useful forecast.

(4) Warmdot's fan belts are used primarily as replacements on furnace motors, but they are occasionally sold for all sorts of other uses. Exhibit IV plots the demand for the 2F2828 ½″ × 18″ V-belts. The average of 518 a month might at first glance seem to be a reasonable representation of the demand. Closer examination, however, reveals a tendency to peak during the summer with demand reaching 1,000 to 1,100 belts when most of the maintenance is done, and a winter low that reached zero in two years.

Note that demand for these four items, like so many other products and services sold by business, is characterized by:

Average demand, both long- and short-term.
Trends in the average, that may continue for a long time, or that may occasionally change direction.
Cycles, which repeat peaks and valleys in demand at nearly the same time every year.
Noise—i.e., the unpredictable fluctuations around the basic pattern described by the average, trend, and cycle.

The demand for any item manufactured at Warmdot can be thought of as a time series made up of the foregoing four components in varying proportions. The problem of statistical forecasting is to try to isolate and measure each component so that its sum can be computed for future months.

This brings us to the problem of computing trends and averages. I should like to outline this problem in a general way first, before returning to our case example.

Average Demand

When an inventory control system includes an objective method of forecasting demand item by item, the method is usually some form of moving average. Thus, one sixth of the total demand in the past six months may be a very good estimate of the average rate of movement for an item in coming months. This method is straightforward, and easily programed for punched-card machines or for electronic computers. Its disadvantage is that a record must be kept of the demand in each of the past six months—which can mean long files.

An alternative method is what I shall call "exponential smoothing." This is a very special kind of weighted moving average with the following features.

The new estimate of the average is updated periodically as the weighted sum of (a) the demand in the period since the last review and (b) the old average. Thus it is not necessary to keep any record of past demand, and the data processing under this "exponential smoothing" method becomes more economical.

EXHIBIT IV. DEMAND FOR FAN BELTS

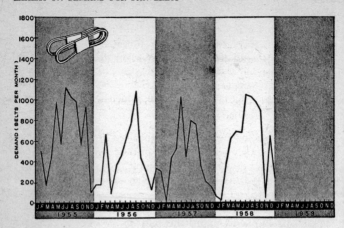

The average is a weighted sum of all the past demand, with the heaviest weight being placed on the most recent information.

The method can be extended, with little additional data processing effort, to detect, and compensate for, trends.

It can be made to respond smoothly, automatically, and accurately to any anticipated changes in the pattern of demand.

Using exponential smoothing, it is also very simple to calculate the necessary and sufficient allowance for uncertainty in management estimates of the future.

Allowing for Trend

The longer our series of numbers for past demand, the more accurate an estimate based on averaging should be—if there is any reason to believe that the market remains stable for a long period of time. But usually it does not, as we know only too well. If the average is computed over a short period of time, it is subject to a large "sampling error"; if it is computed over a long period of time, we may be averaging together several different markets.

In this situation the moving average is an attempt at compromise. A stock record for each item may show the actual demand in each of the past several months. Although a longer record may be available, we deliberately compute the average using only the most recent six months, or the most recent twelve months, or some other interval. The objective is to take a long enough base period to allow random fluctuations in demand to cancel each other out, but a short enough period to discard information that is no longer relevant to current conditions. (Items with a significant seasonal pattern of demand are a special case, which will be covered in some detail later.)

Further, even if conventional moving averages serve for smoothing out the fluctuations in a demand history to get a stable estimate of the expected rate of demand, they have the practical drawback of requiring extra work. Not only must the company keep extensive records of past demand, but accounting for trends, changes in trend, and the distribution of forecast error requires cumbersome computations.

Here we can put our special kind of moving average, exponential smoothing, to work.

Suppose that in our record we had stored only the average past demand computed last month, but had not stored any of the data used in computing the average. This month we have a new value for the demand, and so we want to get a new value for the average. It seems logical that if the demand this month is higher than the old average, we ought to increase our estimate. Conversely, if the demand is below our previous estimate, the new estimate should be lower. Furthermore, if the difference is small, the adjustment ought to be small! but if the new demand is far above the average, the new estimate ought to be increased by a sizable amount.

Now suppose we adopt a rule such as this: to get a new estimate of the average demand, take the previous estimate and add to it a fraction of the amount by which demand this month exceeds that estimate. (Demand below the estimate "exceeds" the estimate by a negative quantity; adding a fraction of a negative quantity would, of course, decrease the estimate.)

The fraction used is called a smoothing constant, and is conventionally represented by α, the Greek letter alpha. The value

281

for the smoothing constant must be a fraction between 0 and 1. We can abbreviate our rule as an equation:

New estimate = old estimate + α (new demand − old estimate).

It can be shown mathematically that we are justified in calling this estimate an average in the same sense as we use the term "moving average." Therefore, proceeding to rearrange the terms a little, we can write down the basic rule of exponential smoothing as

New average = α (new demand) + (1 − α) (old average).

The data-processing simplicity is obvious, because only one number has to be recorded instead of the actual demands in each of the past several months. For the typical large company, with 100,000 or more SKUs, a saving of only one-tenth of a second in the time required to process one item can reduce the total running time by almost three hours. In smaller companies, some of the other advantages listed above may have considerably greater relative importance.

Exhibit V compares the actual monthly demand for Warmdot's

EXHIBIT V. ACTUAL DEMAND FOR TUBING AND THE EXPONENTIALLY SMOOTHED AVERAGE

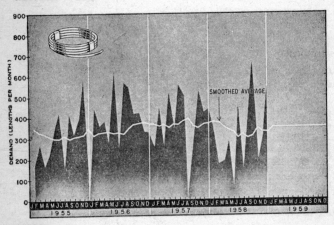

copper tubing with the average computed by exponential smoothing, using a constant, $\alpha = 0.1$. Notice that this estimate is stable, in spite of wide fluctuations in demand, but that it does change gradually when the demand changes.

The average thus computed by exponential smoothing will lag behind a demand that follows a steadily rising (or falling) trend. If we can estimate the magnitude of the trend, however, we can make the necessary correction to eliminate the lag.

An estimate of the trend is the difference between the new average and the old average. Random fluctuations in demand are, to be sure, bothersome; but a simple method is readily available for estimating the average of a fluctuating quantity. The formula for the new trend therefore looks very much like the basic rule of exponential smoothing:

New trend $= \alpha$ (new average − old average) $+ (1 − \alpha)$ (old trend).

This method of computing the trend is in fact the least-squares estimate of it, if the weights given to the demand in each previous month are the same as those used in computing the average.

The correction for the lag due to trend can be expressed as

Expected demand $=$ new average $+$ $\dfrac{(1 − \alpha)}{\alpha}$ (new trend).

Using these formulas, it is necessary only to store the previously calculated values for the average and for the trend, so that the data processing is still simple.

Exhibit VI shows the results of applying this calculation of expected value, as corrected for trend, to the data for Warmdot's thermostats, sales of which have been steadily increasing in the past four years. Note that, while the expected values computed from month to month were commonly under or over the demand which actually materialized, they stayed with the trend of demand all the way.

The value chosen for the smoothing constant α determines how much of the past demand figure has any significant effect on the

EXHIBIT VI. ACTUAL DEMAND FOR THERMOSTATS AND THE EXPONENTIAL
SMOOTHING EXPECTED VALUE

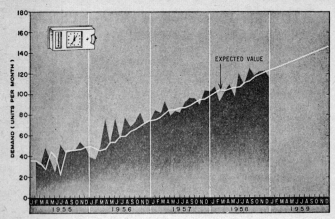

estimate of the average. As in the case of the moving average, the
more past data included in the average, the smaller will be the
error in the estimate—provided, of course, that the basic pattern
of demand does not change during the interval. On the other
hand, if fewer past months are included in the averaging process,
the response to the changes that do occur will be faster.

If a small value, say $\alpha = 0.01$, is chosen for the smoothing constant, the response will be slow and gradual, since it is based on
the average of approximately 199 past months used to compute
the expected demand figure. By contrast, a high value like $\alpha = 0.5$,
which corresponds to an average of three months' demand, will
cause the estimates to respond quickly, not only to real changes
but also to the random fluctuations. For instance, in Exhibit VI
the large changes in the first six months of 1955 are due to using
a smoothing constant, $\alpha = 0.3$; the remainder of the estimates
were made using $\alpha = 0.1$.

In practice, many companies have found that $\alpha = 0.1$ is a satisfactory compromise between a very stable system that fails to
track real changes and a "nervous" system that fluctuates with the

demand. This value corresponds to a moving average of 19 months' demand. Prediction of major changes in demand, as described below, can help improve the compromise.[1]

Most of the time, demand follows a very slowly changing pattern, so that a small smoothing constant is appropriate. But what if executives think an important change is coming because of the introduction of a new product, a promotional campaign, the discovery of a new use for an item, strikes, or a recession? If management can predict a development of this nature, it can increase the value of the smoothing constant to $\alpha = 0.3$ or even $\alpha = 0.5$, for a temporary period of, say, five or six months.

During that period, the routine calculations will respond quickly to whatever changes do materialize. Later, when the new pattern of demand is established, the smoothing constant can be dropped back to its original value to provide greater stability and accuracy.

Note that it is not necessary for management to predict the magnitude or even the direction of the change. *Management need predict only that a major change will occur shortly.* The routine calculations can detect and correct for the actual change that materializes in the demand for each item. In fact, a computer can probably make the corrections more accurately than could the men making the prediction.

Once we have recorded values for the average and for the current trend, then the exponential-smoothing formulas tell us how to update these values with the new demand data each month. For the first month, however, special steps must be taken to compute an initial condition for the average and for the trend. The average can be the average of last year's demand. As for the trend, it is frequently practical to assume that it is zero, and to let the system compute its own trend. I recommend starting with a smoothing constant, $\alpha = 0.3$. After six months, when the ups and downs of starting have begun to even out, the constant can be dropped back to 0.1.

[1] For greater detail on this and other aspects of mathematical forecasting, see Robert G. Brown, *Statistical Forecasting for Inventory Control* (New York, McGraw-Hill Book Company, Inc., 1959).

Seasonal Patterns

Some products (though fewer than commonly supposed) have a true seasonal pattern of demand—e.g., Warmdot's evaporator plates and fan belts, both of which sell in response to seasonal weather changes.

In deciding to use a seasonal method of forecasting, two principles are important:

(1) There must be a known reason for the heavy selling season to occur at about the same time every year, so it must be assumed that it can be depended on.

Thus, one company's products have a very definite annual pattern of demand at the plant, even though the actual consumption of the product is known to be remarkably stable from month to month throughout the year. The reason lies in the distribution system. The manufacturer decides on sales bonuses after he looks at the performance against quota for the fiscal year that ends in June. Also, many of the jobbers have to pay a tax on their inventories at the end of December. The net result is a demand on the plant that is light in November and December, and heavy in May and June.

(2) The seasonal variation in demand should be larger than the random variations, or "noise."

Failure to observe the first principle may lead management to provide a great deal of inventory when the demand is light, and to cut orders back just before a big, but random, surge in demand. Failure to observe the second may require a great deal of extra work with no results to show for it.

The Base Series

Most common methods of forecasting when there is a seasonal pattern depend on comparing the observed demand this year with historical or predicted figures called a "base series."

The best possible base series, of course, is one that has exactly the same pattern as the demand for the item being forecast will have. Short of this Utopian goal, however, we should settle for a series that is high when demand is high, low when demand is low, and that has about the same relative range of values. Commonly used series include:

Same month last year. Perhaps the most common base series, and the most obvious one, is the actual demand for the product during the corresponding month last year. The pattern of demand should show some rational change from year to year; if the changes are not too violent, the pattern observed last year can be used to advantage in forecasting the rest of this year. The evaporator plates in Exhibit III have such a demand pattern.

Average of surrounding quarter. If the demand for a product depends on weather, the peak demand may be earlier or later this year than it was last year. Notice the varying points for the fan belts in Exhibit IV. If the peak demand shifts back and forth by a month or so from year to year, then the average of the demand in the three months surrounding the corresponding month last year may prove to be a more stable base series to use in the case of a seasonal pattern.

Pattern for a line. Suppose that we have a large number of SKUs that are different sizes or colors of the same basic item (e.g., boys' school pants; pints, quarts, gallons, and drums of porch paint; stovepipe sections; or fan belts). There are random variations in the pattern of demand for each SKU, but when we examine the total demand for all related SKUs, we find that some of the upward fluctuations cancel some of the downward ones. Thus, the total demand for all related SKUs appears to provide us with a clearer picture of the basic pattern.

If we can identify such related items, we can use their total demand in the same month last year (or perhaps the average of their total demand in the quarter surrounding that month) as a base series. But note that the items so grouped must in fact be related. It is a mistake to use the total pattern for an entire business (unless only one product line is sold), because different seasonal patterns for different lines may cancel out in the same way the "noise" does, making the base series *too* general. For example, fan belts and evaporator plates should not be grouped.

There are several methods of applying the base series to get an item-by-item forecast of demand. A successful one is to smooth the

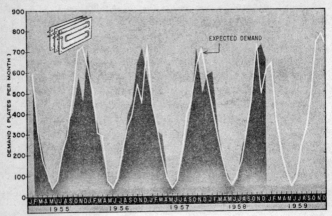

ratio of the demand in the current period to the corresponding
value of the base series. The procedure is simple:

(1) Each month, as the first step, compute the demand ratio.
This ratio equals demand in the current month divided by the
value of the base series for the current month.

(2) Next compute the average, trend, and expected value of
the demand ratio, as described earlier for the nonseasonal demand
itself. The expected demand for any future month is the expected
ratio multiplied by the value of the base series for that month.

Exhibit VII shows Warmdot's calculations for the evaporator
plates, using the same month last year as the base series. Exhibit
VIII shows similar calculations for fan belts, but with a base series
equal to the total of the quarter surrounding the corresponding
month in the previous year. The high forecast for 1959 results
from the fact that demand in 1958 was well above the corresponding months in 1957.

Here again, of course, the current demand ratio can be
smoothed with a moving average. Indeed, an often cited advantage of the moving average is its applicability to seasonal demand

EXHIBIT VIII. ACTUAL DEMAND FOR FAN BELTS AND THE EXPECTED VALUE

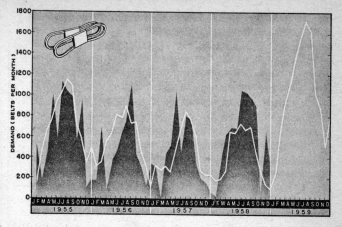

problems. Once more, however, the same kind of results can be accomplished by exponential smoothing—and with considerably less effort and cost.

Forecast Errors

We come now to the question of allowing for errors in the forecast. Barring mistakes in judgment and miscalculations, these errors arise because of the many "noise" factors which make forecasting the problem that it is—factors like the weather, the economic and political climate, competition, marketing strategy, popular styles, and so on.

The first part of this article has dealt with methods of estimating the expected demand that have some advantages over the more familiar moving averages. In an inventory control system it is necessary to estimate the maximum reasonable demand during the replenishment lead time, in order to provide enough stock to meet reasonable demand. The maximum reasonable demand is equal to the expected demand plus an allowance for error.

In most of the current systems, the allowance—commonly referred to as "safety stock"—is equal to a flat "one month's supply" for all items; a more refined system may have different allowances for different classes of items. Such an allowance will be too small for some items with a highly variable demand; it will be too large for others.

By measuring the variability of demand for each item, it would be possible to provide the necessary and sufficient inventory to satisfy demand. In our experience with some 40 corporations, the measurement of uncertainty item by item has made it possible to redistribute the inventory, with an improvement in service and a total reduction of $150 million in investment.

The uncertainty must be expressed in terms of a probability distribution, which may be either a convenient mathematical formula or an empirical curve.

The errors in forecasting demand are limited, of course. Generally speaking, the demand is never negative, and it never exceeds some upper limit; we can write down a number so large that no forecast error will ever be greater. However, it is usually convenient in the mathematical analysis not to have to worry about these physical upper and lower limits. My own experience indicates that the formulas used need only be designed to fit most of the errors that occur, and they allow only a negligible probability for very large errors.

In the formula stating the probability that a forecast error will be of any given amount, two numbers will usually be enough to tell us all we want to know about the whole distribution:

(1) *The mean or the average value of the distribution of error.* Because with any reasonably good method of forecasting the average forecast error should be zero, we need not think of the mean explicitly. (It is, of course, a good idea to check that the errors do have a zero mean.)

(2) *The standard deviation.* This is a measure of how much the errors cluster around the mean value. If most of the errors are very small positive or negative numbers, the standard deviation will be small. If there are several large errors, the standard deviation will be larger, indicating a greater scatter or dispersion of the values.

Exhibit IX shows the distribution of the errors in forecasting demand for Warmdot's products; the period covered is the same

EXHIBIT IX. DISTRIBUTION OF ERRORS IN FORECASTING DEMAND FOR
WARMDOT PRODUCTS

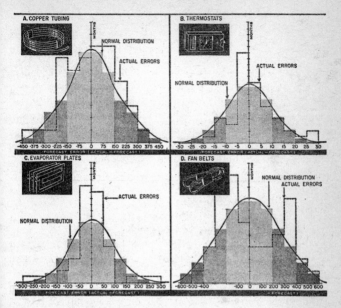

48 months as in previous exhibits. Thus, for copper tubing, one
standard deviation includes errors (in either direction) up to 150
units per month—units in this case being ten-foot lengths. Similarly, two standard deviations include errors of up to 300 units;
and three standard deviations, errors up to 450 units. (In the
graphs, one standard deviation is shown by the lightest shade;
two standard deviations extend through the bands of medium
shade; and three, through the darkest bands). Such figures can be
translated in two ways, whichever is more helpful to the forecaster:

(1) In only two or three months out of 48—or, extrapolated to
a longer period, in only about six months out of ten years, or only
5 times out of 100—will a forecast for copper tubing be off by
more than 300 units. Or, stating it in terms of the central tendency

291

rather than of the exceptions, about two thirds of the time actual performance will be within 150 units of the forecast; almost all of the time (95% of all forecasts), within 300 units. And, of course, over the long run, the differences will be distributed evenly between the high and the low sides.

(2) In inventory control we are concerned principally with demand that is larger than forecast—i.e., which may be difficult to service. There is only one chance in a thousand that demand will be 450 units higher than forecast. There is one chance in fifty that it will be more than 300 units above forecast, and four chances in twenty-five that it will be as much as 150 units above forecast.

For the other three products the errors have other normal distributions, i.e., with other values of the standard deviation. Note that only for the fan belts does the normal distribution turn out to be a poor approximation of the actual errors.

The standard deviation is an observable property of the demand and the method used for forecasting. The allowance for error is usually proportional to this standard deviation. The number of standard deviations used (e.g., for safety stock) is called a safety factor, which can be adjusted as a matter of policy to give the desired level of service.

Since the normal distribution is evidently a satisfactory approximation to the distribution of errors in forecasting, all we need is an estimate of the standard deviation. With this it is possible to reproduce the whole distribution whenever needed in the derivation of a decision rule, such as one for determining the best level of safety stock.

For the normal distribution, the average value of the absolute difference between the actual current demand and the previous calculation of the expected demand is proportional to this standard deviation. Therefore we can proceed as follows:

(1) Subtract the actual demand in the current month from the expected value that was calculated last month (which may be the result of smoothing the demand, or the statistical forecast modified by a judgment prediction).

(2) Call this difference the *current deviation.*

(3) The new mean absolute deviation can then be expressed in the formula

New mean absolute deviation = α |current deviation| + (1 − α) (old mean absolute deviation).

(The vertical bars surrounding "current deviation" indicate that the value is to be taken as positive without regard to actual sign.)

The standard deviation, which will appear in the derivation of safety-stock rules, is equal to 1.25 times the mean absolute deviation.

This method of estimating the standard deviation for each item is the only one that gives a practical current measurement of variation. The most sophisticated studies I have seen elsewhere depend on a special study of the distribution of error in the past demand, like the four years' history for Warmdot in Exhibit IX, which is used until the next study. (Some analysts assume a Poisson distribution, and take the standard deviation as equal to the square root of the average.) Now, for the first time, it is practical to measure the standard deviation routinely. This extension of exponential smoothing is actually being used in several large corporations today, and it gives a practical, sensitive, and current measurement of the variability of demand, by item.

Conclusion

To sum up, the points I have been trying to emphasize in the preceding discussion are:

New methods, especially adapted to modern high-speed electronic computers, can routinely measure the expected demand (including routine detection of, and correction for, trend).

For the first time it is possible and practical to measure the current distribution of error in the forecast, by item.

Sound inventory control systems require independent measurements of the expected demand, and of the distribution of error in these forecasts.

The expected demand, the distribution of forecast error, and decision rules must be used in combination. They are like the legs of a milking stool: you need them all.

12

PRUDENT-MANAGER FORECASTING

GERALD A. BUSCH

The practicality of long-range planning is a controversial question in industry today, and in the planning area itself one of the most disputed topics is long-range sales forecasting.

How, businessmen may argue, can a firm foretell the future with certainty? The answer, in the opinion of a growing number of executives, is that forecasts do not need to be certain. Then how, ask the critics, can long-range forecasting be of much help in planning? The answer is that long-range planning can be effective without dealing in certainties.

According to this thinking, it is enough if management can work with probabilities—with the likelihood of certain potential markets and certain market penetrations occurring under certain conditions, the chances of other conditions developing which will affect the forecasts, the probabilities of various alternative developments. In other words, management's aim should be to gain not a hard and fast outline of the future but an evaluation of probabilities on which it can make informed decisions.

This is the thinking that has animated an approach developed at Lockheed Aircraft Corporation. We have used the method, dubbed "prudent-manager forecasting," with some success for a

294

number of years. We believe that many other companies could also use it with profit, especially firms selling products and services to markets characterized by relatively small numbers of large buyers and sellers.

To apply this technique, management (a) brings together a small group of seasoned specialists representing such functions as marketing research, marketing, finance, engineering, and administration, and (b) asks them to assume the role of decision-making managers in a customer firm that is evaluating one of the firm's products for purchase. In effect, this group of specialists assumes the position of the customer's management. In so doing, it attempts to evaluate prudently the facts available and to arrive at the preferred procurement decisions—preferred from the customer's point of view.

In a way, this is very much like the "role playing" used in management training, in that company people put on the hat of somebody else and assume that "somebody else's" point of view. The origin of the idea probably lies in the sociodrama that has been used with some success by clinical and group psychologists in ironing out family problems.

Preparatory Steps

But prudent-manager forecasting cannot take place in a vacuum. It will not work unless it is preceded by a great deal of staff work. To be successful, those who are asked to serve as prudent managers must be provided with adequate, carefully organized information to draw on in the decision-making process. They should not be expected to make decisions without having the facts necessary for rational judgment. This is where the work of the market-research staff comes in.

Since the preliminary, analytical work is so vital to the successful application of the prudent-manager technique, I shall begin with a brief discussion of some of the major stages of preparation. Note that the steps described are actually those involved in the classic analytical approach to forecasting, and in themselves will provide a forecast that may be sufficient for certain purposes. However, when top management requires a longer term sales forecast, the addition of the prudent-manager technique is far more than frosting on the cake. As we shall see, it adds substance, acumen, and depth of viewpoint to management's expectations.

The main steps in forecasting can be illustrated from Lockheed's experience. Executives of other companies should not find it difficult to visualize data from their own studies in place of the specifics shown here.

It is typically necessary to narrow the scope of a study so that it will be compatible with the elapsed time, manpower, and other resource constraints surrounding the study. Accordingly, we start with certain ground rules which are tailored to the specific forecasting problem at hand. For example, in a study in 1959 having to do with our electronics sales outlook, we set forth three categories of ground rules and assumptions—economic, political, and technological (see Exhibit I). In each case we drew on the best thinking of both line and staff executives. To illustrate from Exhibit I:

(1) *Some of the points were derived from previous studies focusing on the subject at hand.* The last four items in the "economic" group are a case in point. Here we dealt with projections of the gross national product, total major national security expenditures, and certain components of the latter—for instance,

EXHIBIT I. MAJOR GROUND RULES AND ASSUMPTIONS

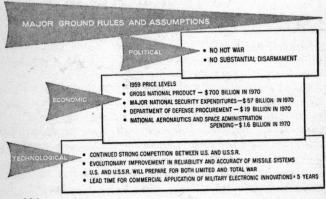

MAJOR GROUND RULES AND ASSUMPTIONS

POLITICAL
- NO HOT WAR
- NO SUBSTANTIAL DISARMAMENT

ECONOMIC
- 1959 PRICE LEVELS
- GROSS NATIONAL PRODUCT — $700 BILLION IN 1970
- MAJOR NATIONAL SECURITY EXPENDITURES—$57 BILLION IN 1970
- DEPARTMENT OF DEFENSE PROCUREMENT — $19 BILLION IN 1970
- NATIONAL AERONAUTICS AND SPACE ADMINISTRATION SPENDING—$1.6 BILLION IN 1970

TECHNOLOGICAL
- CONTINUED STRONG COMPETITION BETWEEN U.S. AND U.S.S.R.
- EVOLUTIONARY IMPROVEMENT IN RELIABILITY AND ACCURACY OF MISSILE SYSTEMS
- U.S. AND U.S.S.R. WILL PREPARE FOR BOTH LIMITED AND TOTAL WAR
- LEAD TIME FOR COMMERCIAL APPLICATION OF MILITARY ELECTRONIC INNOVATIONS • 5 YEARS

Department of Defense procurement and procurement by the National Aeronautics and Space Administration. These were all areas in our business warranting continued investigation. (In the case of a company selling, let us say, bearings to large manufacturers of diesel engines, a similar statement might be made about projections of the number of end users, transportation trends, gross national product, and related factors.)

(2) *Some assumptions were simply based on informed judgment.* For instance, our "political" assumptions were that there would be no hot war and no substantial disarmament. These appraisals may, of course, turn out to be completely wrong. And yet we had to make assumptions to begin with, and these seemed like the most reasonable ones.

(3) *Some assumptions were based on specialized technical knowledge.* Examples here are the "technological" estimates that the improvement in missiles would be evolutionary rather than revolutionary, and that a five-year lead time would be needed for commercial application. (In the case of the bearings manufacturer, comparable projections might concern the development of new materials affecting the use of bearings.)

You may quarrel with individual items in this list of ground rules; and, of course, we do not recommend them for other companies' programs. The point is that in long-term sales forecasting you generally cannot afford the luxury of a "womb to tomb" approach, so limiting ground rules are necessary. Management should make a practice of stating these explicitly.

The next stage requires a look at the historical characteristics of supply and demand in the markets that management is concerned with. Ordinarily this means studies not only of demand for different products but also of the buying behavior of different customers. At Lockheed, for example, we are deeply interested in such customers as the military services, other government agencies, and certain commercial buyers; and in the demand characteristics for aircraft, missiles, space vehicles, electronics, ground-handling equipment, and a host of other products.

Exhibit II shows a study we made last year in one area of importance to us—Air Force spending of its aircraft procurement

EXHIBIT II. HISTORICAL CHARACTERISTICS OF DEMAND FOR MANNED
AIRCRAFT BY THE U.S. AIR FORCE

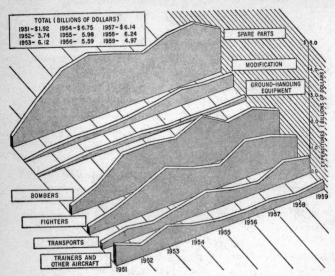

budget. This analysis gives us a picture of how these funds were
expended during the decade of the 1950's—for bombers, fighters,
transports, trainers, and other types of aircraft, as well as for spare
parts, ground-handling equipment, and modification. From this
type of study we can make comparisons and correlations with
concurrent operational, technological, political, and economic
events, and then develop appropriate forecast indicators. Per-
sonally, I am a great believer in the value to the forecaster of a
good hard look at history.

Next comes the development of economic indicators. Correlation analysis may be very helpful here. A case in point is a Lockheed study of the relation between cargo transportation and gross
national product. Exhibit III portrays (1) the effective demand
for cargo transportation service in the U.S. domestic market since
1929 as compared to (2) the gross national product in terms of
constant dollars.

The correlation between these two series is 0.97—high enough to permit us to project the demand for cargo transportation on the basis of our forecasts of gross national product. We at Lockheed are interested in the total cargo picture, of course, because the total demand is relevant to the demand for air cargo, in which we are more directly concerned.

I should add that it is seldom that we get such a high correlation as in Exhibit III. As forecasters know, the closer to the actual product an analysis gets, the lower is the correlation which is usually obtained.

EXHIBIT III. CORRELATION BETWEEN U.S. DOMESTIC CARGO TRANSPORTATION DEMAND AND GNP

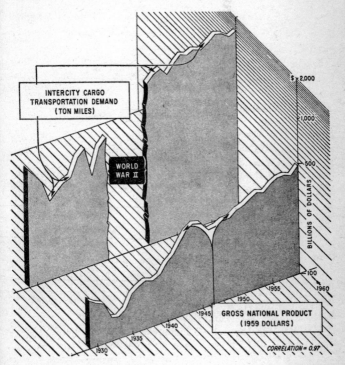

The next step is to derive a parameterized market projection. In such an analysis the aim is to look at the effect on the market of changes of the key variables. Briefly, the procedure is as follows:

1. For the problem at hand, the forecasters select the significant variables (like consumer income, price and availability of service, system performance) and decide what the "most likely" future levels will be.

2. Then, assuming that these "most likely" levels will turn out to be correct, they make an estimate of demand for the product or service.

3. But they must make allowances for other possibilities; the "most likely" levels may not in fact be realized. Therefore, they make projections of demand based on other levels that may reasonably occur.

4. When they have a range of demand or "output" figures correlated with different "input" levels for one variable, they take another variable and repeat the process.

5. The final result is a matrix of projections showing how sensitive the forecast is to various changes in each of the input variables.

Such a "sensitivity analysis," as it is called, is valuable to the prudent managers when, subsequently, they deliberate over the forecast. It is likely to show, for instance, that certain variables are more important to watch than others. Let me illustrate again from the experience of Lockheed:

Exhibit IV shows a typical "parameterized" forecast. At the left is the historical trend in the distribution of the demand for air, rail, and bus transportation in the United States. At the right are shown five alternative projections:

In projection A all of the inputs are at their "most likely" projected levels.

Projection B shows what demand would look like if we held all other inputs constant, but restricted the availability of air coach service to no more than what it was in 1953.

In projection C we have restricted the performance of the surface systems—bus and rail—to their 1953 levels.

In projection D we have increased the unit valuation on the time of the traveler by 50% over the projected levels.

EXHIBIT IV. DISTRIBUTION OF DEMAND FOR BUS, RAIL, AND AIR TRANSPORTA-
TION

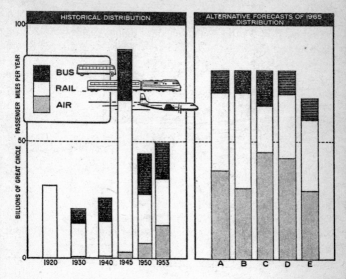

And in projection E we show what the effect on the picture is
in the event that the rate of expansion of the economy of the
United States should turn out to be somewhat less than our other
studies suggest.

Thus we see at a glance how variations in the input variables
will affect the total demand for air passenger transportation in
1965. Incidentally, the staff did not make firm conclusions or
choices among the several situations. We concluded that the
demand for airline transportation would increase between threefold and fivefold from 1953 to the early 1970's and that, *assuming
all inputs were at their "most likely" projected levels,* the potential
air transportation demand would be about 57 billion great circle
passenger miles per year at that latter time. But we pointed out
that this conclusion was highly sensitive to two of the inputs—
(1) the projected expansion of the U.S. economy, and (2) the
projected performance of the surface transportation systems.

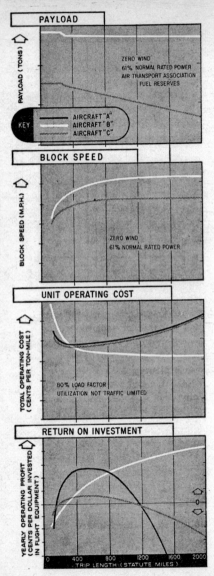

302

(Note that air transport is highest in projection C, where it is assumed that performance of surface transport systems will stay at the same level as in 1953.)

Comparisons With Competitors

The next step is to take an objective look at the company's product or service in comparison with its competition. It is important to select those characteristics for comparison which are of particular concern to the potential buyer. To illustrate, Exhibit V shows a few of the characteristics of competing transport-type aircraft of concern to Lockheed's customers. Here we see comparative data on speed performance, pay-load range performance, unit operating-cost performance, and return on investment. With comparative data such as these, the prudent managers can subsequently make judgments as to the relative importance in the eyes of the customer of, say, differences in block speed and return on invested capital.

Now, with all this work done, the market-research staff is able to make a forecast of sales of the Lockheed product—again preferably in parameterized form. This it does on a customer-by-customer basis, if feasible. The procedure is as follows:

(1) The major customer categories are separately analyzed. For instance, in making a study of the sales outlook for a certain type of electronic end equipment, the Lockheed staff looked at prospective sales to the government, including the Air Force, Navy, Army, and NASA, and to the nongovernment agencies.

(2) Within each customer category, the sales in each application are separately forecast, as in Exhibit VI. (To simplify this chart, I have shown the data in nonparameterized form.)

(3) The staff puts all of the individual forecasts together and comes up with an aggregate sales forecast.

(4) The aggregate figure is subjected to a test of reasonableness. After adding up all the individual forecasts, the staff asks itself, "Does the resulting total appear reasonable? Is it in consonance with our traditional percentage of the market? Does it appear too pessimistic or too optimistic? Is too much weight given to some factors and too little to others?" Only after the forecast has been subjected to questions like these and, if necessary, revised, is the stage set for the prudent managers.

EXHIBIT VI. ESTIMATED PROCUREMENT OF AN ITEM OF ELECTRONIC EN
EQUIPMENT FOR DIFFERENT APPLICATIONS

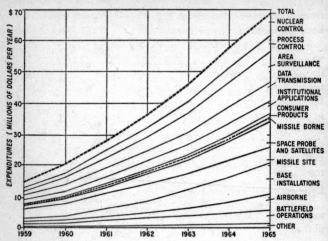

More Realistic Judgments

All of the steps and techniques I have described up to now are
part of the staff work of forecasting in many companies. A
Lockheed, some details may be changed or emphasized more i
anticipation of what comes later, but in the main the type of work
just outlined is essential to any intelligent type of forecasting, and
even by itself would lay the groundwork for informed manageria
decisions.

But it does have the disadvantage of inbreeding. It is done by
staff people like myself who sometimes may become bemused
with figures and, in their concentration on the tools and technique
of their craft, lose contact with the reality with which they should
be dealing and which, in effect, they are trying to forecast.

Therefore, to reintroduce this factor of outside reality and to
help assure that our sales forecast will give service to the com-
manding importance of the customer's point of view, we like to
expose the staff analysis to a balanced group made up predomi-
nantly of non-market-research people, and get their evaluation
This brings us to the essence of the prudent-manager approach

To begin, there is the question of how these non-marketing-research people should be organized. Our experience at Lockheed indicates that it is a good idea to try to make up a conference from a representative group, but we have found it essential to keep the number of participants small.

So far as it is practical to do so, we use Lockheed people. We will usually include a representative from finance who knows firsthand the financial situation of our customers, one or two representatives from marketing who are very knowledgeable of the market and the customers in question, and one or two managers from the technical side of the house who have a detailed knowledge of the product's performance. Occasionally, we include an outside consultant—an economist from a university, perhaps, or a business consultant. And we always include a senior market-research staff member who is familiar with all of the preparatory work done by the staff.

In general, the participants should be mature, seasoned in their areas of specialization, objective in their approach to problems, and able to both give and take in the negotiating process.

We have found that it is desirable, prior to the first get-together of the prudent managers, to provide each man with copies of the preliminary staff reports in order that he may do some "homework" on the subject beforehand.

At the first formal meeting, the prudent managers are briefed in detail on the staff work. Sometimes we devote as much as one day to this briefing so that the participants will know in detail how each input was developed, how the variables were integrated, and so forth. From there on, the group is on its own. I stress the importance of adequately briefing the prudent managers—for if this is not done well, there is the distinct danger that the group will resort to that insidious technique which I call "feet-on-the-deskmanship."

Now let us turn to the deliberative process itself. For the sake of being specific, let us suppose that the managers are considering the problem of arriving at a long-term sales forecast for a proposed new passenger transport airplane. How do they go about making their judgments?

To begin with, they put themselves in the place of each major potential customer in turn, starting with the larger airlines and later dealing with relatively homogeneous groups of small airlines. In this position, and generally accepting the analytical work done by the staff as "gospel," they carefully review the judgments made by the staff—and typically interject others which the staff may have overlooked.

To be more specific still, let us suppose that the customer under consideration is Air France, a major foreign airline. Each participant figuratively stands in the shoes of the manager of Air France and attempts to answer questions such as these:

> What new aircraft procurement policy must I pursue in order that my airline will remain competitive and retain or improve its standing in the market over the next decade?
>
> How does the proposed new Lockheed plane stack up against competitive offerings?
>
> Will I be able to finance my new aircraft?
>
> How many planes should I buy, say, in 1965?
>
> What will be my needs over short-haul routes, long-haul routes, and so on?
>
> How much money can I make with the Lockheed aircraft as compared to what I can make with competitive planes?
>
> What about return on investment?
>
> What about operations into marginal airports?

In pursuing this approach, each participant tries to appraise dispassionately the Lockheed product vis-à-vis competing products in each customer's application. The prudent managers must be hardheaded about this—just as hardheaded, we hope, as they would be if they were charged with the responsibility of actually running the company they are considering. Very often they know something about the personal failings and strengths, the preferences and prejudices, of the men whose positions they are assuming. For example, Mr. A likes pod-mounted engines, while Mr. B has been publicly thumping the drums for high-density coach configurations. All these items are taken into account as they argue out and discuss the probable buy the customer will make.

Next, the prudent managers work out a forecast of that customer's likely purchases of the Lockheed airplane. Then, having settled on what they think is the most probable purchase of one customer, they pass on to another and start the whole process over again.

When they have covered the whole field of potential customers, they total the probable purchases and come up with an aggregate forecast. This result is then compared with the staff results and, as in the staff procedure, is subjected to the general test of reasonableness.

The result, we think, gives a closer approximation to what may in fact actually happen than can mere staff work alone.

Tests of Effectiveness

How effective prudent-manager sessions are depends in part, of course, on the thoroughness of the staff work done in preparation for them, for a lot of the managers' thinking is based on this work. But effectiveness also depends on how well the talents and viewpoints represented mix together.

Generally speaking, the level of competence increases as the organizational level of the members of the team increases, because the men higher in the organization are generally those with the greatest knowledge and acumen, and the broadest point of view. But there are drawbacks to inviting men who sit too high in the organization. For one thing, they may not find it possible to stay with the group because of other demands on their time. For another, a vice president sitting with men two levels below may unknowingly tend to constrain valuable give-and-take discussion.

Beyond this, we have found that there are some people who have a natural talent for this sort of discussion. They have the imagination to put themselves in someone else's place, the ability to judge dispassionately and realistically, and the breadth to consider all phases of the problem. Generally speaking, we have found that people in senior staff jobs in the company measure up best in this respect.

Conclusion

To sum up, certain lessons based on experience in using the prudent-manager techniques should be emphasized.

In organizing a conference, these are the most important points for management to remember:

(1) Keep the number of participants small.

(2) Include a balanced representation of technical specialties. Bring in:

Selected "in house" specialists.

A senior market-research staff analyst.

An occasional outside consultant, as needed.

(3) Give the participants a detailed briefing on the background and results of the staff study.

To make the deliberative process a success, each prudent manager should:

(1) Assume the position of decision-making executives in the customer firm.

(2) Dispassionately appraise the performance of competing products that the customer firm might consider buying.

(3) Make a forecast of the purchases that he thinks the customer will make.

(4) When the individual forecasts are pulled together into an aggregate forecast, join with the other participants in testing its reasonableness.

Keep in mind throughout all this that prudent-manager sessions are not a substitute for sound staff forecasting; they are merely a refinement on it. Certainly they should never be used instead of such staff work. Management should also be forewarned that the technique is relatively costly—particularly in the early years of its application. As a rule, at Lockheed, we "roll over" our important long-term forecasts every year or two. The time and effort required in the second and subsequent passes is significantly less than in the original forecast.

I do not suggest that prudent-manager sessions are the answer to all forecasting problems or, indeed, that they should even be applied to all such problems. But I do suggest that, where the sales forecast is of particular importance to top management in its long-range planning, and where objectivity and realism are primary goals, this technique may be a useful addition to present forecasting methods. There is every reason to believe that the benefits gained at Lockheed can be duplicated at many other companies.

13

STRATEGIES FOR DIVERSIFICATION

The Red Queen said, "Now, *here*, it takes all the running *you* can do to keep in the same place. If you want to get somewhere else, you must run at least twice as fast as that!"[1]

So it is in the American economy. Just to retain its relative position, a business firm must go through continuous growth and change. To improve its position, it must grow and change at least "twice as fast as that."

According to a recent survey of the 100 largest United States corporations from 1909 to 1948, few companies that have stuck to their traditional products and methods have grown in stature. The report concludes: "There is no reason to believe that those now at the top will stay there except as they keep abreast in the race of innovation and competition."[2]

There are four basic growth alternatives open to a business. It can grow through increased market penetration, through market development, through product development, or through diversification.

A company which accepts diversification as a part of its planned

---

[1] *Through the Looking-Glass.*
[2] A. D. H. Kaplan, *Big Enterprise in a Competitive System* (Washington, The Brookings Institution, 1954), p. 142.

approach to growth undertakes the task of continually weighing and comparing the advantages of these four alternatives, selecting first one combination and then another, depending on the particular circumstances in long-range development planning.

While they are an integral part of the over-all growth pattern, diversification decisions present certain unique problems. Much more than other growth alternatives, they require a break with past patterns and traditions of a company and an entry onto new and uncharted paths.

Accordingly, one of the aims of this paper is to relate diversification to the over-all growth perspectives of management, establish reasons which may lead a company to prefer diversification to other growth alternatives, and trace a relationship between over-all growth objectives and special diversification objectives. This will provide us with a partly qualitative, partly quantitative method for selecting diversification strategies which are best suited to long-term growth of a company. We can use qualitative criteria to reduce the total number of possible strategies to the most promising few, and then apply a return on investment measure to narrow the choice of plans still further.

Product-Market Alternatives

The term "diversification" is usually associated with a change in the characteristics of the company's product line and/or market, in contrast to market penetration, market development, and product development, which represent other types of change in product-market structure. Since these terms are frequently used interchangeably, we can avoid later confusion by defining each as a special kind of product-market strategy. Let us begin with the basic concepts.

The *product line* of a manufacturing company refers both to (a) the physical characteristics of the individual products (for example, size, weight, materials, tolerances) and to (b) the performance characteristics of the products (for example, an airplane's speed, range, altitude, payload).

In thinking of the market for a product we can borrow a concept commonly used by the military—the concept of a mission. A *product mission* is a description of the job which the product is intended to perform. For instance, one of the missions of the Lockheed Aircraft Corporation is commercial air transportation of passengers; another is provision of airborne early warning for the Air Defense Command; a third is performance of air-to-air combat.

For our purposes, the concept of a mission is more useful in describing market alternatives than would be the concept of a "customer," since a customer usually has many different missions, each requiring a different product. The Air Defense Command, for example, needs different kinds of warning systems. Also, the product mission concept helps management to set up the problems in such a way that it can better evaluate the performance of competing products.

A *product-market strategy*, accordingly, is a joint statement of a product line and the corresponding set of missions which the products are designed to fulfill. In shorthand form (see Exhibit I), if we let π represent the product line and μ the corresponding set of missions, then the pair of π and μ is a product-market strategy.

With these concepts in mind let us turn now to the four different types of product-market strategy shown in Exhibit I.

Market penetration is an effort to increase company sales without departing from an original product-market strategy. The company seeks to improve business performance either by increasing the volume of sales to its present customers or by finding new customers for present products.

EXHIBIT I. PRODUCT-MARKET STRATEGIES FOR BUSINESS GROWTH ALTERNATIVES

MARKETS / PRODUCT LINE	μ_0	μ_1	μ_2		μ_m
π_0	MARKET *Penetration*	MARKET	DEVELOPMENT		
π_1					
π_2	PRODUCT DEVELOPMENT	DIVERSIFICATION			
π_x					

Market development is a strategy in which the company attempts to adapt its present product line (generally with some modification in the product characteristics) to new missions. An airplane company which adapts and sells its passenger transport for the mission of cargo transportation is an example of this strategy.

A *product development* strategy, on the other hand, retains the present mission and develops products that have new and different characteristics such as will improve the performance of the mission.

Diversification is the final alternative. It calls for a simultaneous departure from the present product line and the present market structure.

Each of the above strategies describes a distinct path which a business can take toward future growth. However, it must be emphasized that in most actual situations a business would follow several of these paths at the same time. As a matter of fact, a simultaneous pursuit of market penetration, market development, and product development is usually a sign of a progressive, well-run business and may be essential to survival in the face of economic competition.

The diversification strategy stands apart from the other three. While the latter are usually followed with the same technical, financial, and merchandising resources which are used for the original product line, diversification generally requires new skills, new techniques, and new facilities. As a result, it almost invariably leads to physical and organizational changes in the structure of the business which represent a distinct break with past business experience.

Forecasting Growth

A study of business literature and of company histories reveals many different reasons for diversification. Companies diversify to compensate for technological obsolescence, to distribute risk, to utilize excess productive capacity, to reinvest earnings, to obtain top management, and so forth. In deciding whether to diversify, management should carefully analyze its future growth prospects. It should think of market penetration, market development, and product development as parts of its over-all product strategy and ask whether this strategy should be broadened to include diversification.

A standard method of analyzing future company growth prospects is to use long-range sales forecasts. Preparation of such forecasts involves simultaneous consideration of a number of major factors:

> General economic trends.
>
> Political and international trends.
>
> Trends peculiar to the industry. (For example, forecasts prepared in the airplane industry must take account of such possibilities as a changeover from manned aircraft to missiles, changes in the government "mobilization base" concept with all that would mean for the aircraft industry, and rising expenditures required for research and development.)
>
> Estimates of the firm's competitive strength relative to other members of the industry.
>
> Estimates of improvements in the company performance which can be achieved through market penetration, market development, and product development.
>
> Trends in manufacturing costs.

Such forecasts usually assume that company management will be aggressive and that management policies will take full advantage of the opportunities offered by the different trends. They are, in other words, estimates of the best possible results the business can hope to achieve short of diversification.

Different patterns of forecasted growth are shown in Exhibit II, with hypothetical growth curves for the national economy (GNP) and the company's industry added for purposes of comparison. One of the curves illustrates a sales curve which declines with time. This may be the result of an expected contraction of demand, the obsolescence of manufacturing techniques, emergence of new products better suited to the mission to which the company caters, or other changes. Another typical pattern, frequently caused by seasonal variations in demand, is one of cyclic sales

EXHIBIT II. TREND FORECASTS

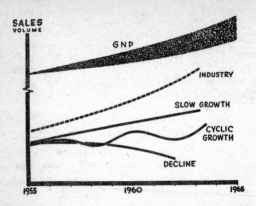

activity. Less apparent, but more important, are slower cyclic changes, such as trends in construction or the peace-war variation in demand in the aircraft industry.

If the most optimistic sales estimates which can be attained short of diversification fall in either of the preceding cases, diversification is strongly indicated. However, a company may choose to diversify even if its prospects do, on the whole, appear favorable. This is illustrated by the "slow growth curve." As drawn in Exhibit II, the curve indicates rising sales which, in fact, grow faster than the economy as a whole. Nevertheless, the particular company may belong to one of the so-called "growth industries" which as a whole is surging ahead. Such a company may diversify because it feels that its prospective growth rate is unsatisfactory in comparison to the industry growth rate.

Making trend forecasts is far from a precise science. The characteristics of the basic environmental trends, as well as the effect of these trends on the industry, are always uncertain. Furthermore, the ability of a particular business organization to perform in the new environment is very difficult to assess. Consequently, any realistic company forecast should include several different trend forecasts, each with an explicitly or implicitly assigned probability. As an alternative, the company's growth trend forecast may be represented by a widening spread between two extremes, similar to that shown for GNP in Exhibit II.

In addition to trends, another class of events may make diversification desirable. These are certain environmental conditions which, if they occur, will have a great effect on sales; however, we cannot predict their occurrence with certainty. To illustrate such "contingent" events, an aircraft company might foresee these possibilities that would upset its trend forecasts:

A major technological "breakthrough" whose characteristics can be foreseen but whose timing cannot at present be determined, such as the discovery of a new manufacturing process for high-strength, thermally resistant aircraft bodies.

An economic recession which would lead to loss of orders for commercial aircraft and would change the pattern of spending for military aircraft.

A major economic depression.

A limited war which would sharply increase the demand for air industry products.

A sudden cessation of the cold war, a currently popular hope which has waxed and waned with changes in Soviet behavior.

The two types of sales forecast are illustrated in Exhibit III for a hypothetical company. Sales curves S_1 and S_2 represent a spread

EXHIBIT III. A HYPOTHETICAL COMPANY FORECAST—NO DIVERSIFICATION

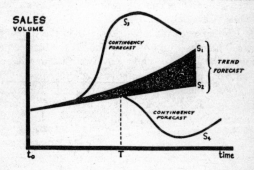

of trend forecasts; and S_3 and S_4, two contingent forecasts for the same event. The difference between the two types, both in starting time and effect on sales, lies in the degree of uncertainty associated with each.

In the case of trend forecasts we can trace a crude time history of sales based on events which we fully expect to happen. Any uncertainty arises from not knowing exactly when they will take place and how they will influence business. In the case of contingency forecasts, we can again trace a crude history, but our uncertainty is greater. We lack precise knowledge of not only when the event will occur but also whether it will occur. In going from a trend to a contingency forecast, we advance, so to speak, one notch up the scale of ignorance.

In considering the relative weight we should give to contingent events in diversification planning, we must consider not only the magnitude of their effect on sales, but also the relative probability of their occurrence. For example, if a severe economic depression were to occur, its effect on many industries would be devastating. Many companies feel safe in neglecting it in their planning, however, because they feel that the likelihood of a deep depression is very small, at least for the near future.

It is a common business practice to put primary emphasis on trend forecasts; in fact, in many cases businessmen devote their long-range planning exclusively to these forecasts. They usually view a possible catastrophe as "something one cannot plan for" or as a second-order correction to be applied only after the trends have been taken into account. The emphasis is on planning for growth, and planning for contingencies is viewed as an "insurance policy" against reversals.

People familiar with planning problems in the military establishment will note here an interesting difference between military and business attitudes. While business planning emphasizes trends, military planning emphasizes contingencies. To use a crude analogy, a business planner is concerned with planning for continuous, successful, day-after-day operation of a supermarket. If he is progressive, he also buys an insurance policy against fire, but he spends relatively little time in planning for fires. The military is more like the fire engine company; the fire is the thing. Day-to-day operations are of interest only insofar as they can be utilized to improve readiness and fire-fighting techniques.

So far we have dealt with diversification forecasts based on what may be called foreseeable market conditions—conditions which we can interpret in terms of time-purchased sales curves. Planners have a tendency to stop here, to disregard the fact that, in addition to the events for which we can draw time histories, there is a recognizable class of events to which we can assign a probability of occurrence but which we cannot otherwise describe in our present state of knowledge. One must move another notch up the scale of ignorance in order to consider these possibilities.

Many businessmen feel that the effort is not worthwhile. They argue that since no information is available about these unforeseeable circumstances, one might as well devote the available time and energy to planning for the foreseeable circumstances, or that, in a very general sense, planning for the foreseeable also prepares one for the unforeseeable contingencies.

In contrast, more experienced military and business people have a very different attitude. Well aware of the importance and relative probability of unforeseeable events, they ask why one should plan specific steps for the foreseeable events while neglecting the really important possibilities. They may substitute for such planning practical maxims for conducting one's business—"be solvent," "be light on your feet," "be flexible." Unfortunately, it is not always clear (even to the people who preach it) what this flexibility means.

The interesting study by The Brookings Institution[3] provides an example of the importance of the unforeseeable events to business. Exhibit IV shows the changing make-up of the list of the 100 largest corporations over the last 50 years. Of the 100 largest on the 1909 list (represented by the heavy marble texture) only 36 were among the 100 largest in 1948; just about half of the new entries to the list in 1919 (represented by white) were left in 1948; less than half of the new entries in 1929 (represented by the

[3] See note 2, above.

EXHIBIT IV. CHANGES IN LIST OF THE 100 LARGEST INDUSTRIAL CORPORA-
TIONS

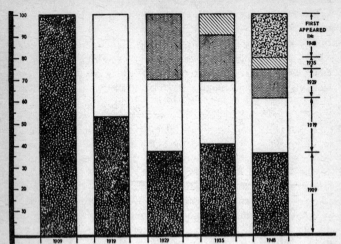

zigzag design) were left in 1948; and so on. Clearly, a majority of
the giants of yesteryear have dropped behind in a relatively short
span of time.

Many of the events that hurt these corporations could not be
specifically foreseen in 1909. If the companies which dropped
from the original list had made forecasts of the foreseeable kind
at that time—and some of them must have—they would very
likely have found the future growth prospects to be excellent.
Since then, however, railroads, which loomed as the primary
means of transportation, have given way to the automobile and
the airplane; the textile industry, which appeared to have a
built-in demand in an expanding world population, has been
challenged and dominated by synthetics; radio, radar, and television have created means of communication unforeseeable in
significance and scope; and many other sweeping changes have
occurred.

The lessons of the past 50 years are fully applicable today. The
pace of economic and technological change is so rapid that it is

318

virtually certain that major breakthroughs comparable to those of the last 50 years, but not yet foreseeable in scope and character, will profoundly change the structure of the national economy. All of this has important implications for diversification, as suggested by the Brookings study:

The majority of the companies included among the 100 largest of our day have attained their positions within the last two decades. They are companies that have started new industries or have transformed old ones to create or meet consumer preferences. The companies that have not only grown in absolute terms but have gained an improved position in their own industry may be identified as companies that are notable for drastic changes made in their product mix and methods, generating or responding to new competition.

There are two outstanding cases in which the industry leader of 1909 had by 1948 risen in position relative to its own industry group and also in rank among the 100 largest—one in chemicals and the other in electrical equipment. These two (DuPont and General Electric) are hardly recognizable as the same companies they were in 1909 except for retention of the name; for in each case the product mix of 1948 is vastly different from what it was in the earlier year, and the markets in which the companies meet competition are incomparably broader than those that accounted for their earlier place at the top of their industries. They exemplify the flux in the market positions of the most successful industrial giants during the past four decades and a general growth rather than a consolidation of supremacy in a circumscribed line.[4]

This suggests that the existence of specific undesirable trends is not the only reason for diversification. A broader product line may be called for even with optimistic forecasts for present products. An examination of the foreseeable alternatives should be accompanied by an analysis of how well the over-all company product-market strategy covers the so-called growth areas of technology —areas of many potential discoveries. If such analysis shows that, because of its product lines, a company's chances of taking advantage of important discoveries are limited, management should broaden its technological and economic base by entering a number of so-called "growth industries." Even if the definable horizons look bright, a need for flexibility, in the widest sense of the word, may provide potent reasons for diversification.

[4] Kaplan, p. 142.

Diversification Objectives

If an analysis of trends and contingencies indicates that a company should diversify, where should it look for diversification opportunities?

Generally speaking, there are three types of opportunities:

(1) Each product manufactured by a company is made up of functional components, parts, and basic materials which go into the final assembly. A manufacturing concern usually buys a large fraction of these from outside suppliers. One way to diversify, commonly known as *vertical diversification*, is to branch out into production of components, parts, and materials. Perhaps the most outstanding example of vertical diversification is the Ford empire in the days of Henry Ford, Sr.

At first glance, vertical diversification seems inconsistent with our definition of a diversification strategy. However, the respective missions which components, parts, and materials are designed to perform are distinct from the mission of the over-all product. Furthermore, the technology in fabrication and manufacture of these parts and materials is likely to be very different from the technology of manufacturing the final product. Thus, vertical diversification does imply both catering to new missions and introduction of new products.

(2) Another possible way to go is *horizontal diversification*. This can be described as the introduction of new products which, while they do not contribute to the present product line in any way, cater to missions which lie within the company's know-how and experience in technology, finance, and marketing.

(3) It is also possible, by *lateral diversification*, to move beyond the confines of the industry to which a company belongs. This obviously opens a great many possibilities, from operating banana boats to building atomic reactors. While vertical and horizontal diversification are restrictive, in the sense that they delimit the field of interest, lateral diversification is "wide open." It is an announcement of the company's intent to range far afield from its present market structure.

How does a company choose among these diversification directions? In part the answer depends on the reasons which prompt diversification. For example, in the light of the trends described for the industry, an aircraft company may make the following moves to meet long-range sales objectives through diversification:

1. A vertical move to contribute to the technological progress of the present product line.
2. A horizontal move to improve the coverage of the military market.
3. A horizontal move to increase the percentage of commercial sales in the over-all sales program.
4. A lateral move to stabilize sales in case of a recession.
5. A lateral move to broaden the company's technological base.

Some of these diversification objectives apply to characteristics of the product, some to those of the product missions. Each objective is designed to improve some aspect of the balance between the over-all product-market strategy and the expected environment. The specific objectives derived for any given case can be grouped into three general categories: *growth objectives,* such as 1, 2, and 3 above, which are designed to improve the balance under favorable trend conditions; *stability objectives,* such as 3 and 4, designed as protection against unfavorable trends and foreseeable contingencies; and *flexibility objectives,* such as 5, to strengthen the company against unforeseeable contingencies.

A diversification direction which is highly desirable for one of the objectives is likely to be less desirable for others. For example:

—If a company is diversifying because its sales trend shows a declining volume of demand, it would be unwise to consider vertical diversification, since this would be at best a temporary device to stave off an eventual decline of business.

—If a company's industry shows every sign of healthy growth, then vertical and, in particular, horizontal diversification would be a desirable device for strengthening the position of the company in a field in which its knowledge and experience are concentrated.

—If the major concern is stability under a contingent forecast, chances are that both horizontal and vertical diversification could not provide a sufficient stabilizing influence and that lateral action is called for.

—If management's concern is with the narrowness of the technological base in the face of what we have called unforeseeable

EXHIBIT V. DIVERSIFICATION OBJECTIVES

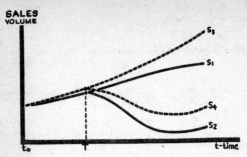

contingencies, then lateral diversification into new areas of technology would be clearly indicated.

Management can and should state the objectives of growth and stability in quantitative terms as *long-range sales objectives*. This is illustrated in Exhibit V. The solid lines describe a hypothetical company's forecasted performance without diversification under a general trend, represented by the sales curve marked S_1, and in a contingency, represented by S_2. The dashed lines show the improved performance as a result of diversification, with S_3 representing the curve for continuation of normal trends and S_4 representing the curve for a major reverse.

Growth. Management's first aim in diversifying is to improve the growth pattern of the company. The growth objective can be stated thus: Under trend conditions the growth rate of sales after diversification should exceed the growth rate of sales of the original product line by a minimum specified margin. Or to illustrate in mathematical shorthand, the objective for the company in Exhibit V would be:

$$S_3 - S_1 \geq \rho,$$

where the value of the margin ρ is specified for each year after diversification.

Some companies (particularly in the growth industries) fix an annual rate of growth which they wish to attain. Every year this rate of growth is compared to the actual growth during the past year. A decision on diversification action for the coming year is

STRATEGIES FOR DIVERSIFICATION

then based upon the disparity between the objective and the actual rate of growth.

Stability. The second effect desired of diversification is improvement in company stability under contingent conditions. Not only should diversification prevent sales from dropping as low as they might have before diversification, but the percentage drop should also be lower. The second sales objective is thus a stability objective. It can be stated as follows: Under contingent conditions the percentage decline in sales which may occur without diversification should exceed the percentage drop in sales with diversification by an adequate margin, or algebraically:

$$\frac{S_1 - S_2}{S_1} - \frac{S_3 - S_4}{S_3} \geq \delta.$$

Using this equation, it is possible to relate the sales volumes before and after diversification to a rough measure of the resulting stability. Let the ratio of the lowest sales during a slump to the sales which would have occurred in the same year under trend conditions be called the stability factor F. Thus, $F = 0.3$ would mean that the company sales during a contingency amount to 30% of what is expected under trend conditions. In Exhibit VI the stability factor of the company before diversification is the value $F_1 = S_2/S_1$ and the stability factor after diversification is $F_3 = S_4/S_3$, both computed at the point on the curve where S_2 is minimum.

EXHIBIT VI. IMPROVEMENT IN STABILITY FACTOR AS A RESULT OF DIVERSIFICATION FOR $F_1 = 0.3$

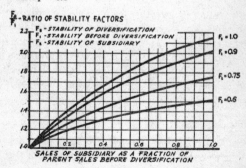

Now let us suppose that management is considering the purchase of a subsidiary. How large does the subsidiary have to be if the parent is to improve the stability of the corporation as a whole by a certain amount? Exhibit VI shows how the question can be answered.

On the horizontal axis we plot the different possible sales volumes of a smaller firm that might be secured as a proportion of the parent's volume. Obviously, the greater this proportion, the greater the impact of the purchase on the parent's stability.

On the vertical axis we plot different ratios of the parent's stability before and after diversification (F_3/F_1).

The assumed stability factor of the parent is 0.3. Let us say that four prospective subsidiaries have stability factors of 1.0, 0.9, 0.75, and 0.6. If they were not considerably higher than 0.3, of course, there would be no point in acquiring them (at least for our purposes here).

On the graph we correlate these four stability factors of the subsidiary with (1) the ratio F_3/F_1 and (2) different sales volumes of the subsidiary. We find, for example, that if the parent is to double its stability (point 2.0 on the vertical axis), it must obtain a subsidiary with a stability of 1.0 and 75% as much sales volume as the parent, or a subsidiary with a stability of 0.9 and 95% of the sales volume. If the parent seeks an improvement in stability of, say, only 40%, it could buy a company with a stability of 0.9 and 25% as much sales volume as it has.

This particular way of expressing sales objectives has two important advantages: (1) By setting minimum, rather than maximum, limits on growth, it leaves room for the company to take advantage of unusual growth opportunities in order to exceed these goals, and thus provides definite goals without inhibiting initiative and incentive. (2) It takes account of the time-phasing of diversification moves; and since these moves invariably require a transition period, the numerical values of growth objectives can be allowed to vary from year to year so as to allow for a gradual development of operations.

Long-Range Objectives

Diversification objectives specify directions in which a company's product-market should change. Usually there will be several objectives indicating different and sometimes conflicting directions. If a company attempts to follow all of them simultaneously, it is in danger of spreading itself too thin and of becoming a conglomeration of incompatible, although perhaps individually profitable, enterprises.

There are cases of diversification which have followed this path. In a majority of cases, however, there are valid reasons why a company should seek to preserve certain basic unifying characteristics as it goes through a process of growth and change. Consequently, diversification objectives should be supplemented by a statement of long-range product-market objectives.

For instance, one consistent course of action is to adopt a product-market policy which will preserve a kind of technological coherence among the different manufactures with the focus on the products of the parent company. For instance, a company that is mainly distinguished for a type of engineering and production excellence would continue to select product-market entries which would strengthen and maintain this excellence. Perhaps the best known example of such policy is exemplified by the DuPont slogan, "Better things for better living through chemistry."

Another approach is to set long-term growth policy in terms of the breadth of market which the company intends to cover. It may choose to confine its diversifications to the vertical or horizontal direction, or it may select a type of lateral diversification controlled by the characteristics of the missions to which the company intends to cater. For example, a company in the field of air transportation may expand its interest to all forms of transportation of people and cargo. To paraphrase DuPont, some slogan like "Better transportation for better living through advanced engineering," would be descriptive of such a long-range policy.

A greatly different policy is to emphasize primarily the financial characteristics of the corporation. This method of diversification generally places no limits on engineering and manufacturing characteristics of new products, although in practice the competence and interests of management will usually provide some orientation for diversification moves. The company makes the decisions regarding the distribution of new acquisitions exclusively on the basis of financial considerations. Rather than a manufacturing entity, the corporate character is now one of a "holding company."

325

Top management delegates a large share of its product-planning and administrative functions to the divisions and concerns itself largely with coordination, financial problems, and with building up a balanced "portfolio of products" within the corporate structure.

These alternative long-range policies demonstrate the extremes. No one course is necessarily better than the others; management's choice will rest in large part on its preferences, objectives, skills, and training. The aircraft industry illustrates the fact that there is more than one successful path to diversification.

Among the major successful airframe manufacturers, Douglas Aircraft Company, Inc., and Boeing Airplane Company have to date limited their growth to horizontal diversification into missiles and new markets for new types of aircraft. Lockheed has carried horizontal diversification further to include aircraft maintenance, aircraft service, and production of ground-handling equipment.

North American Aviation, Incorporated, on the other hand, appears to have chosen vertical diversification by establishing its subsidiaries in Atomics International, Autonetics, and Rocketdyne, thus providing a basis for manufacture of complete air vehicles of the future.

Bell Aircraft Corporation has adopted a policy of technological consistency among the items in its product line. It has diversified laterally but primarily into types of products for which it had previous know-how and experience.

General Dynamics Corporation provides a further interesting contrast. It has gone far into lateral diversification. Among the major manufacturers of air vehicles, it comes closest to the "holding company" extreme. Its airplanes and missile manufacturing operations in Convair are paralleled by production of submarines in the Electric Boat Division; military, industrial, and consumer electronic products in the Stromberg-Carlson Division; electric motors in the Electro Dynamic Division.

Selecting a Strategy

In the preceding sections qualitative criteria for diversification have been discussed. How should management apply these criteria to individual opportunities? Two steps should be taken:

(1) apply the qualitative standards to narrow the field of diversification opportunities; (2) apply the numerical criteria to select the preferred strategy or strategies.

The long-range product-market policy is used as a criterion for the first rough cut in the qualitative evaluation. It can be used to divide a large field of opportunities into classes of diversification moves consistent with the company's basic character. For example, a company whose policy is to compete on the basis of the technical excellence of its products would eliminate as inconsistent classes of consumer products which are sold on the strength of advertising appeal rather than superior quality.

Next, the company can compare each individual diversification opportunity with the individual diversification objectives. This process tends to eliminate opportunities which, while still consistent with the desired product-market make-up, are nevertheless likely to lead to an imbalance between the company product line and the probable environment. For example, a company which wishes to preserve and expand its technical excellence in design of large, highly stressed machines controlled by feedback techniques may find consistent product opportunities both inside and outside the industry to which it caters, but if one of its major diversification objectives is to correct cyclic variations in demand that are characteristic of the industry, it would choose an opportunity that lies outside.

Each diversification opportunity which has gone through the two screening steps satisfies at least one diversification objective, but probably it will not satisfy all of them. Therefore, before subjecting them to the quantitative evaluation, it is necessary to group them into several alternative over-all company product-market strategies, composed of the original strategy and one or more of the remaining diversification strategies. These alternative over-all strategies should be roughly equivalent in meeting all of the diversification objectives.

At this stage it is particularly important to allow for the unforeseeable contingencies. Since the techniques of numerical evaluation are applicable only to trends and foreseeable contingencies, it is important to make sure that the different alternatives chosen give the company a broad enough technological base. In practice this process is less formidable than it may appear. For example, a company in the aircraft industry has to consider the areas of technology in which major discoveries are likely to affect the future of the industry. This would include atomic propulsion, certain areas of electronics, automation of complex processes, and so forth. In designing alternative over-all strategies the company would then make sure that each contains product entries which will give the firm a desirable and comparable degree of participation in these future growth areas.

Will the company's product-market strategies make money? Will the profit structure improve as a result of their adoption? The purpose of quantitative evaluation is to compare the profit potential of the alternatives.

Unfortunately, there is no single yardstick among those commonly used in business that gives an accurate measurement of performance. The techniques currently used for measurement of business performance constitute, at best, an imprecise art. It is common to measure different aspects of performance by applying different tests. Thus, tests of income adequacy measure the earning ability of the business; tests of debt coverage and liquidity measure preparedness for contingencies; the shareholders' position measures attractiveness to investors; tests of sales efficiency and personnel productivity measure efficiency in the use of money, physical assets, and personnel. These tests employ a variety of different performance ratios, such as return on sales, return on net worth, return on assets, turnover of net worth, and ratio of assets to liabilities. The total number of ratios may run as high as 20 in a single case.

In the final evaluation, which immediately precedes a diversification decision, management would normally apply all of these tests, tempered with business judgment. However, for the purpose of preliminary elimination of alternatives, a single test is frequently used—return on investment, a ratio between earnings and the capital invested in producing these earnings. While the usefulness of return on investment is commonly accepted, there is considerable room for argument regarding its limitations and its practical application. Fundamentally, the difficulty with the concept is that it fails to provide an absolute measure of business performance applicable to a range of very different industries; also, t. e term "investment" is subject to a variety of interpretations.

But, since our aim is to use the concept as a measure of relative performance of different diversification strategies, we need not be concerned with its failure to measure absolute values. And as long as we are consistent in our definition of investment in alternative courses of action, the question of terminology is not so troublesome. We cannot define profit-producing capital in general terms, but we can define it in each case in the light of particular business characteristics and practices (such as the extent of government-owned assets, depreciation practices, inflationary trends).

For the numerator of our return on investment, we can use net earnings after taxes. A going business concern has standard techniques for estimating its future earnings. These depend on the projected sales volume, tax structure, trends in material and labor costs, productivity, and so forth. If the diversification opportunity being considered is itself a going concern, its profit projections can be used for estimates of combined future earnings. If the opportunity is a new venture, its profit estimates should be made on the basis of the average performance for the industry.

A change in the investment structure of the diversifying company accompanies a diversification move. The source of investment for the new venture may be: (1) excess capital, (2) capital borrowed at an attractive rate, (3) an exchange of the company's equity for an equity in another company, or (4) capital withdrawn from present business operations.

If we let i_1, i_2, i_3, and i_4, respectively, represent investments made in the new product in the preceding four categories during the first year of diversified operations, we can derive a simple expression for the improvement in return on investment resulting from diversification:

$$\Delta R = \frac{(p_2-p_1)(i_2+i_3+i_4)+(p_2-r)\ i_1-i_2r+(p_1-r)(i_2+i_3)^i 1/I}{I+i_2+i_3},$$

where p_1 and p_2 represent the average return on capital invested in the original product and in the new product, respectively, and

329

quantity I is the total capital in the business before diversification.

We can easily check this expression by assuming that only one type of new investment will be made at a time. We can then use the formula to compute the conditions under which it pays to diversify (that is, conditions where ΔR is greater than zero):

(1) If excess capital is the only source of new investment ($i_2 = i_3 = i_4 = 0$), this condition is $p_2 - r > 0$. That is, return on diversified operations should be more attractive than current rates for capital on the open market.

(2) If only borrowed capital is used ($i_1 = i_3 = i_4 = 0$), it pays to diversify if $p_2 - p_1 > r$. That is, the difference between return from diversification and return from the original product should be greater than the interest rate on the money.

(3) If the diversified operation is to be acquired through an exchange of equity or through internal reallocation of capital, $p_2 - p_1 > 0$ is the condition under which diversification will pay off.

The formula for ΔR just stated is not sufficiently general to serve as a measure of profit potential. It gives improvement in return for the first year only and for a particular sales trend. In order to provide a reasonably comprehensive comparison between alternative over-all company strategies, the yardstick for profit potential should possess the following properties:

(1) Since changes in the investment structure of the business invariably accompany diversification, the yardstick should reflect these changes. It should also take explicit account of new capital brought into the business and changes in the rate of capital formation resulting from diversification, as well as costs of borrowed capital.

(2) Usually the combined performance of the new and the old product-market lines is not a simple sum of their separate performances; it should be greater. The profit potential yardstick must take account of this nonlinear characteristic.

(3) Each diversification move is characterized by a transition period during which readjustment of the company structure to new operating conditions takes place. The benefits of a diversification move may not be realized fully for some time, so the

measurement of profit potential should span a sufficient length of time to allow for effects of the transition.

(4) Since both profits and investments will be spread over time, the yardstick should use their present value.

(5) Business performance will differ depending on the particular economic-political environment. The profit potential yardstick must somehow average out the probable effect of alternative environments.

(6) The statement of sales objectives, as pointed out previously, should specify the general characteristics of growth and stability which are desired. Profit potential functions should be compatible with these characteristics.

We can generalize our formula in a way which will meet most of the preceding requirements. The procedure is to write an expression for the present value of ΔR for an arbitrary year, t, allowing for possible yearly diversification investments up to the year t, interest rates, and the rate of capital formation. Then this present value is averaged over time as well as over the alternative sales forecasts. The procedure is straightforward (although the algebra involved is too cumbersome to be worth reproducing here[5]). The result, which is the "average expected present value of ΔR," takes account of conditions (1) through (5), above. Let us call it $(\Delta R)_e$. It can be computed using data normally found in business and financial forecasts.

This brings us to the final step in the evaluation. We have discussed a qualitative method for constructing several over-all product-market strategies which meet the diversification and the long-range objectives. We can now compute $(\Delta R)_e$ for each of the over-all strategies and, at the same time, make sure that the strategies satisfy the sales objectives previously stated, thus fulfilling condition (6), above.

If product-market characteristics, which we have used to narrow the field of choice and to compute $(\Delta R)_e$, were the sole

---

[5] See H. Igor Ansoff, *A Model for Diversification* (Burbank, Lockheed Aircraft Corporation, 1957); and John Burr Williams, *The Theory of Investment Value* (Amsterdam, The North-Holland Publishing Co., 1938).

criteria, then the strategy with the highest $(\Delta R)_e$ would be the "preferred" path to diversification. The advantages of a particular product-market opportunity, however, must be balanced against the chances of business success.

Conclusion

A study of diversification histories shows that a firm usually arrives at a decision to make a particular move through a multi-step process. The planners' first step is to determine the preferred areas for search; the second is to select a number of diversification opportunities within these areas and to subject them to a preliminary evaluation. They then make a final evaluation, conducted by the top management, leading to selection of a specific step; finally, they work out details and complete the move.

Throughout this process, the company seeks to answer two basic questions: How well will a particular move, if it is successful, meet the company's objectives? What are the company's chances of making it a success? In the early stages of the program, the major concern is with business strategy. Hence, the first question plays a dominant role. But as the choice narrows, considerations of business ability, of the particular strengths and weaknesses which a company brings to diversification, shift attention to the second question.

This discussion has been devoted primarily to selection of a diversification strategy. We have dealt with what may be called external aspects of diversification—the relation between a company and its environment. To put it another way, we have derived a method for measuring the profit potential of a diversification strategy, but we have not inquired into the internal factors which determine the ability of a diversifying company to make good this potential. A company planning diversification must consider such questions as how the company should organize to conduct the search for and evaluation of diversification opportunities; what method of business expansion it should employ; and how it should mesh its operations with those of a subsidiary. These considerations give rise to a new set of criteria for the business fit of the prospective venture. These must be used in conjunction with

$(\Delta R)_e$ as computed in the preceding section to determine which of the over-all product-market strategies should be selected for implementation.

Thus, the steps outlined in this article are the first, though an important, preliminary to a diversification move. Only through further careful consideration of probable business success can a company develop a long-range strategy that will enable it to "run twice as fast as that" (using the Red Queen's words again) in the ever-changing world of today.

14

SELECTING PROFITABLE PRODUCTS

JOHN T. O'MEARA, JR.

As businessmen know only too well, most companies must continue to introduce new products if they are to sustain their long-run growth and profitability. To this end a number of leading firms have established new-product or product-planning departments. Despite such efforts, however, the fact remains that most new products are doomed to failure before they reach the market. For example, a Ross Federal Research Corporation study shows that of the new products placed on the market by 200 leading packaged-goods manufacturers, 80% failed—for reasons other than insufficient capital.[1] Other sources show the failure rate varying between 75% and 95%, depending on the samples and definitions used.

The story behind these figures is one of loss—loss of time, of money, and of increasingly scarce technical and management resources.

How are companies attempting to cope with this problem? An investigation of systems for deciding on new products would, of course, reveal varying degrees of sophistication. At one end of the scale is the company in which a single person attempts to

[1] "The Introduction of New Products," survey made for Peter Hilton, Inc.

assimilate the pertinent data, make a decision, and then sell his recommendation to his associates. At the other end of the scale is the large company with a well-organized new-products department, where the desired information is collected and compiled into a myriad of charts, profile graphs, and estimate sheets for the consideration of those responsible for the final decisions. This potpourri of information is absorbed for comparison with like information on other potential products.

In this age of progress, one cannot help but feel that the first approach is too simple, too primitive. As for the second approach, one may suspect that, at best, it is the crude predecessor of more scientific decision-making processes.

Main Features

One helpful step in coping with the selection of new products for development can, I believe, be taken with an "assist" from techniques and concepts developed in other fields of management. The new procedure that I shall describe in this paper can be distinguished by several main features:

(1) By utilizing simple probability and weighting techniques, the procedure reduces the over-all new-product problem to a series of simpler ones which are more easily and objectively solved.

(2) The solutions to these smaller problems are then combined into three index numbers that represent an over-all rating for the potential of the new product.

(3) The first index number is a rating for intangible factors (not easily quantifiable), such as marketability, growth potential, productive ability, and durability; the second index number indicates the product's short-term profitability or payback potential; and the third number indicates the product's long-run profit potential.

Some readers will recognize the parts of this paper dealing with expected profits and payback tables. These ideas have been used in control, finance, and other fields. But the application of these techniques, and especially the proposed use of weights and probabilities, represents an attempt to venture into entirely new territory. Before going on, however, I want to emphasize two points:

335

(1) *This system in no way eliminates the necessity for managerial judgment.* It simply divides an overwhelmingly complicated problem into its component parts, and thus affords the opportunity to grasp and work with smaller segments. In fact it becomes a menace rather than an aid if managers begin to swallow its findings whole and stop thinking for themselves.

(2) *No company should consider buying the system exactly as it is presented here.* There ought to be as many modifications of the approach as there are organizations using it. This article attempts only to present a general method for attacking the new-product problem. It is left to the individual company to adapt the method to its particular needs.

Intangible Factors

As indicated above, of the three index numbers to be derived, the first is for intangible marketing factors. To illustrate the procedure, let us work through a hypothetical case example involving company Y and a new product, product X.

Constructing the Framework

At the outset we need to list in logical order the factors (except long- and short-term profitability) that should be considered in evaluating the intangibles of a new product. Then we should set up standards against which each potential new product can be measured. Let us assume that company Y chooses four major factors, divides each of them into its component subfactors, and defines them as in Exhibit I. Another company with different types of products might break the problem down differently, but essentially the same procedure should be used.

The next step is to study the four major factors and weight them so as to indicate the evaluator's judgment of their importance in relation to each other. These relative weights for company Y are indicated in Exhibit II, column 2. Similarly, each of the subfactors that comprise the four major factors has been weighted in Exhibit III, column 2. (For the sake of brevity, only the subfactors of marketability are used to illustrate this procedure.) At the same time, numerical values are assigned to the definitions transferred from Exhibit I.

What has been accomplished at this point? Very simply, company Y has constructed a framework that enables it to evaluate the over-all problem of new products more objectively by breaking it into its component parts, the factors and the subfactors. Weights have been assigned to these components to indicate their relative importance. At different times, the relative importance of these components may vary; if so, the weights will then have to be changed accordingly.

The next step in this procedure is to study more thoroughly the description of each of the subfactors, and to enter in Exhibit III, columns 3 through 7, the estimated probabilities (EP) that the product in question will equal the description of "very good," "good," "average," "poor," or "very poor." This is the first instance in which the company actually evaluates the proposed product. The purpose is to permit an evaluator to express, in numbers, exactly what he thinks the product's possibilities may be. For example, in Exhibit III, the evaluator believes there is at least a 50–50 chance that the merchandisability characteristics of product X will meet the definition of "very good," that there is less chance that it will meet the definition of "good," and that there is an even smaller chance that it will meet the definition of "average." He also believes that there is no chance at all that the definitions of "poor" and "very poor" will describe the merchandisability of the product. He therefore enters probabilities of 0.5 for "very good," 0.4 for "good," and 0.1 for "average," allowing no probability for "poor" or "very poor."

This method of precisely stating one's best judgment will result in a more efficient evaluation than would be possible using a less systematic procedure.

After assigning probabilities to the subfactors, the management evaluator multiplies each probability figure by the numerical value attached to the rating. The results are placed in columns 3 through 7 in the divisions for expected value (EV). Again let us take merchandisability as an example. Since the evaluator has estimated that there is a 0.5 chance that product X's merchandisability will meet the definition of "very good," and the numerical value is 10.0, the expected value is 5.0. This figure, then, is entered in the EV column. The evaluator also estimates that a 0.4 chance

EXHIBIT I. FACTOR AND SUBFACTOR RATINGS FOR A NEW PRODUCT

	VERY GOOD	GOOD
I. MARKETABILITY		
A. *Relation to present distribution channels*	Can reach major markets by distributing through present channels.	Can reach major markets by distributing mostly through present channels, partly through new channels.
B. *Relation to present product lines*	Complements a present line which needs more products to fill it.	Complements a present line that does not need, but can handle, another product.
C. *Quality/price relationship*	Priced below all competing products of similar quality.	Priced below most competing products of similar quality.
D. *Number of sizes and grades*	Few staple sizes and grades.	Several sizes and grades but customers will be satisfied with few staples.
E. *Merchandisability*	Has product characteristics over and above those of competing products that lend themselves to the kind of promotion, advertising, and display that the given company does best.	Has promotable characteristics that will compare favorably with the characteristics of competing products.
F. *Effects on sales of present products*	Should aid in sales of present products.	May help sales of present products; definitely will not be harmful to present sales.
II. DURABILITY		
A. *Stability*	Basic product which can always expect to have uses.	Product which will have uses long enough to earn back initial investment, plus at least 10 years of additional profits.
B. *Breadth of market*	A national market, a wide variety of consumers, and a potential foreign market.	A national market and a wide variety of consumers.
C. *Resistance to cyclical fluctuations*	Will sell readily in inflation or depression.	Effects of cyclical changes will be *moderate,* and will be felt *after* changes in economic outlook.

EXHIBIT I. FACTOR AND SUBFACTOR RATINGS FOR A NEW PRODUCT (*cont.*)

AVERAGE	POOR	VERY POOR
Will have to distribute equally between new and present channels, in order to reach major markets.	Will have to distribute mostly through new channels in order to reach major markets.	Will have to distribute entirely through new channels in order to reach major markets.
Can be fitted into a present line.	Can be fitted into a present line but does not fit entirely.	Does not fit in with any present product line.
Approximately the same price as competing products of similar quality.	Priced above many competing products of similar quality.	Priced above all competing products of similar quality.
Several sizes and grades, but can satisfy customer wants with small inventory of nonstaples.	Several sizes and grades, each of which will have to be stocked in equal amounts.	Many sizes and grades which will necessitate heavy inventories.
Has promotable characteristics that are equal to those of other products.	Has a few characteristics that are promotable, but generally does not measure up to characteristics of competing products.	Has no characteristics at all that are equal to competitors' or that lend themselves to imaginative promotion.
Should have no effect on present sales.	May hinder present sales some; definitely will not aid present sales.	Will reduce sales of presently profitable products.
Product which will have uses long enough to earn back initial investment, plus several (from 5 to 10) years of additional profits.	Products which will have uses long enough to earn back initial investment, plus 1 to 5 years of additional profits.	Product which will probably be obsolete in near future.
Either a national market or a wide variety of consumers.	A regional market and a restricted variety of consumers.	A specialized market in a small marketing area.
Sales will rise and fall with the economy.	Effects of cyclical changes will be *heavy*, and will be felt *before* changes in economic outlook.	Cyclical changes will cause extreme fluctuations in demand.

339

EXHIBIT I. FACTOR AND SUBFACTOR RATINGS FOR A NEW PRODUCT (*cont.*)

	VERY GOOD	GOOD
D. *Resistance to seasonal fluctuations*	Steady sales throughout the year.	Steady sales — except under unusual circumstances.
E. *Exclusiveness of design*	Can be protected by a patent with no loopholes.	Can be patented, but the patent might be circumvented.
III. PRODUCTIVE ABILITY A. *Equipment necessary*	Can be produced with equipment that is presently idle.	Can be produced with present equipment, but production will have to be scheduled with other products.
B. *Production knowledge and personnel necessary*	Present knowledge and personnel will be able to produce new product.	With very few minor exceptions, present knowledge and personnel will be able to produce new product.
C. *Raw materials' availability*	Company can purchase raw materials from its best supplier(s) exclusively.	Company can purchase major portion of raw materials from its best supplier(s), and remainder from any one of a number of companies.
IV. GROWTH POTENTIAL A. *Place in market*	New type of product that will fill a need presently not being filled.	Product that will substantially improve on products presently on the market.
B. *Expected competitive situation — value added*	Very high value added so as to substantially restrict number of competitors.	High enough value added so that, unless product is extremely well suited to other firms, they will not want to invest in additional facilities.
C. *Expected availability of end users*	Number of end users will increase substantially.	Number of end users will increase moderately.

EXHIBIT I. FACTOR AND SUBFACTOR RATINGS FOR A NEW PRODUCT (*cont.*)

AVERAGE	POOR	VERY POOR
Seasonal fluctuations, but inventory and personnel problems can be absorbed.	Heavy seasonal fluctuations that will cause considerable inventory and personnel problems.	Severe seasonal fluctuations that will necessitate layoffs and heavy inventories.
Cannot be patented, but has certain salient characteristics that cannot be copied very well.	Cannot be patented, and can be copied by larger, more knowledgeable companies.	Cannot be patented, and can be copied by anyone.
Can be produced largely with present equipment, but the company will have to purchase some additional equipment.	Company will have to buy a good deal of new equipment, but some present equipment can be used.	Company will have to buy all new equipment.
With some exceptions, present knowledge and personnel will be able to produce new product.	A ratio of approximately 50–50 will prevail between the needs for new knowledge and personnel and for present knowledge and personnel.	Mostly new knowledge and personnel are needed to produce the new product.
Company can purchase approximately half of raw materials from its best supplier(s), and other half from any one of a number of companies.	Company must purchase most of raw materials from any one of a number of companies other than its best supplier(s).	Company must purchase most or all of raw materials from a certain few companies other than its best supplier(s).
Product that will have certain new characteristics that will appeal to a substantial segment of the market.	Product that will have minor improvements over products presently on the market.	Product similar to those presently on the market and which adds nothing new.
High enough value added so that, unless other companies are as strong in market as this firm, it will not be profitable for them to compete.	Lower value added so as to allow large, medium, and some smaller companies to compete.	Very low value added so that all companies can profitably enter market.
Number of end users will increase slightly, if at all.	Number of end users will decrease moderately.	Number of end users will decrease substantially.

exists that the product's merchandisability characteristics will
equal the definition of "good," and that a 0.1 chance of equaling
the definition of "average" exists. Multiplying these probabilities
by the numerical values attached to their respective definitions,
he obtains the expected values that are shown in columns 4 and 5
for merchandisability.

Up to this point we have concentrated on dividing the problem
into manageable segments and allowing objective decisions to be
made. The next step is to add the individual expected values for
each subfactor and enter the total in column 8. This step begins
the process of combining many decisions and judgments that have
been made, with the ultimate aim of reducing them to one major
index number. The numbers in column 8 should represent the
best numerical estimate that can be obtained of the degree to
which the characteristics of the proposed product meet the desired characteristics listed as subfactors in Exhibit I.

The next step is to multiply the total expected values by the
weights that had previously been assigned to their respective
subfactors (column 2). These results are then entered in column
9. The total at the bottom of column 9 represents the value of the
product's marketability as a whole. This major factor value, as
it might be called, is entered in column 3 of Exhibit II.

We follow the same procedure to get the values for the other

EXHIBIT II. SUMMARY SHEET OF INTANGIBLES

Proposed product:	Product X	Evaluated by:	John Smith
I	2	3	4
Factor	Factor weight	Assigned factor value	Final factor evaluation
Marketability	0.4	71.6 *	28.6
Durability	0.3	68.6	20.6
Productive ability	0.1	91.6	9.2
Growth potential	0.2	69.2	13.8
	1.0		
		Final intangible factor index number	72.2

* From Exhibit III.

EXHIBIT III. EXAMPLE OF THE USE OF AN EVALUATION SHEET

Proposed product: **Product X** Evaluated by: **John Smith**

Factor: **Merchantability**

x Subfactor	2 Subfactor weight	3 Very good (10) EP	EV	4 Good (8) EP	EV	5 Average (6) EP	EV	6 Poor (4) EP	EV	7 Very poor (2) EP	EV	8 Total EV	9 Subfactor evaluation (Col. 2 × Col. 8)
Relative to present distribution channels	1.0	0.1	1.0	0.2	1.6	0.5	3.0	0.2	0.8	-	-	6.4	6.4
Relative to present product lines	1.0	0.1	1.0	0.2	1.6	0.4	2.4	0.2	0.8	0.1	0.2	6.0	6.0
Quality/price relationship	3.0	0.3	3.0	0.4	3.2	0.2	1.2	0.1	0.4	-	-	7.8	23.4
Number of sizes and grades	1.0	0.1	1.0	0.2	1.6	0.5	3.0	0.2	0.8	-	-	6.4	6.4
Merchandisability	2.0	0.5	5.0	0.4	3.2	0.1	0.6	-	-	-	-	8.8	17.6
Effects on sale of present products	2.0	-	-	0.2	1.6	0.5	3.0	0.3	1.2	-	-	5.8	11.6
	10.0											Total factor value	71.4

NOTE: EP = estimated probability as judged by management; EV = expected value computed by multiplying the rating's numerical value by the estimated probability.

343

three major factors—durability, productive ability, and growth potential. Let us assume that we get the values shown in Exhibit II.

Now we want to multiply these values by the weights given earlier to the major factors. If, for example, marketability is considered more important than productive ability, we want to "crank" that difference into the final evaluation. Accordingly, each figure in column 4 combines the series of judgments about how well the product will measure up (column 3) with judgments about how important the measure is to the company in comparison with other measures (column 2).

The total at the bottom of column 4 is the index number that represents the final evaluation of how well product X fulfills the intangible requirements for a new product. While it is but one number, it represents decisions on many problems, each of which has been weighted in the light of its importance to the total problem.

Short-Run Profitability

Long- and short-term profit potentials should be evaluated separately. Therefore, the second index number to derive is one that indicates the product's short-run profitability. We can refer to it as the "payback index." We get this index by inserting in a formula the product's probable short-run profit, and dividing this estimate by the development cost. The formula is shown at the top of Exhibit IV. In effect, payback gives the time required for short-run profits to equal the development expenditures.

Once the general concept and purpose of the formula are appreciated, the easiest way to learn the mechanics of its operation is to study the factors used for the numerator and denominator. They are:

> *Probability of commercial success*—estimated by the new-products committee or its equivalent.
>
> *Estimate of average sales units per year*—estimated by sales manager.
>
> *Estimate of selling price per unit*—estimated by sales manager.

EXHIBIT IV. PAYBACK INDEX

Proposed product: **Product X**	Evaluated by:	John Smith

Formula: $\dfrac{A \times B \times (C - D) \times E}{F + G + H + I}$

Factors:

A. Probability of commercial success — 70%
B. Estimate of sales — units per year (average) — $250,000.00
C. Estimate of selling price per unit — $5.00
D. Estimate of cost per unit — $4.00
E. Competitive grace period — 3 yrs.
F. Additional working capital needs — $10,000.00
G. Market development cost estimate — $10,000.00
H. Additional capital expenditures — -
I. Production development cost — $30,000.00

$$\frac{0.7 \times 250,000 \times (5 - 4) \times 3.0}{10,000 + 10,000 + 0 + 30,000} = 10.5 = \text{payback index}$$

Estimate of cost per unit—estimated by engineering or production manager.

Competitive grace period—estimated by new-products committee (this estimate should be no longer than four years).

Additional working capital needs—estimated by new-products committee.

Market development cost estimate—estimated by marketing manager.

Additional capital expenditures—estimated by production manager.

Production development cost—estimated by production manager.

Of the foregoing, the only items that warrant additional explanation are the probability of commercial success and the competitive grace period.

The figure for the probability of commercial success places a limit on confidence in the sales projection. Since the sales figure is to be estimated by the sales manager, the probability figure permits a further judgment to be made by the new-products committee. Thus it results in a more carefully scrutinized index number.

The competitive grace period is defined as the period of time during which no major, adverse changes in the product's market are expected. Because of market uncertainties, I recommend that in most situations the grace period be limited to a maximum of four years. This serves to set a reasonable limit on the length of the payback period to be considered.

Let us assume that management agrees on the values shown in Exhibit IV. Plugging these into the payback formula, we get an index of 10.5 for product X. If we get similar indexes for other new products under consideration, we will have another helpful yardstick to use in making comparisons and in deciding which items should be manufactured and marketed.

Long-Run Profit Margins

The final index number to be derived is one that represents long-run profit margins. (I use "long-run" to mean longer than five years, and "profit margins" to mean the steady margins that can be expected when the product assumes its normal place in the market.) Since this estimate deals with occurrences far in the future, it is not as reliable as some of the estimates for intangible factors and short-run profitability are. For this reason, less emphasis should be placed on this number. However, it does indicate management's evaluation of the long-range potential of the product, and should be used to complete the over-all evaluation.

To illustrate how the index is worked out, let us turn to Ex-

EXHIBIT V. LONG-RANGE PROFITABILITY TABLE

Product:	Product X		Evaluated by:	John Smith
Assume:	$100,000 sales			
1 Profit margin	2 Probability	3 Conditional profit	4 Expected profit	
10%	0.1	$10,000	$1,000	
15	0.1	15,000	1,500	
20	0.3	20,000	6,000	
25	0.3	25,000	7,500	
30	0.2	30,000	6,000	
	Total expected profit		$22,000	
	Total expected profit as a per cent of sales	$\frac{\$22,000}{\$100,000} = 22\%$		

hibit V (for arithmetical convenience, this table assumes sales of $100,000).

Column 1 lists the most logical range of profit percentages that can be expected. In column 2 an evaluator, or evaluating committee, estimates the probability that these different profit percentages will be attained.

The conditional profits are entered in column 3. For a 10% profit margin, the conditional profit would be $10,000; for a 15% profit margin, $15,000; and so on.

Column 4 is the product of the numbers in columns 2 and 3. For example, there is a one-in-ten probability that a $10,000 profit will be made, and therefore the expected profit is $1,000.

The total of column 4 is used as a numerator, and the assumed $100,000 sales is used as a denominator, which fraction is then converted to a percentage figure. Thus, an estimate of the product's long-range profitability is derived.

Here, again, a framework has been constructed whereby an evaluator can express in figures exactly what he thinks to be the product's potential. By applying simple arithmetic, he then combines the foregoing figures into one long-range profitability index.

Conclusion

The words that best describe this system of evaluating new products are "precise" and "flexible." The system is precise in that it allows an evaluator to quantify his exact opinions on many problems and assure their consideration in the final decision. The system is flexible both in structure and in application. At any time, its framework can be altered either to include factors that have increased in importance or to eliminate those which have decreased in importance. For example, if the choice of factors and subfactors in Exhibit I becomes outmoded, the list can easily be changed to suit current conditions. Also, if the range of factors in Exhibit III should turn out not to be applicable to a proposed product, it could be changed to meet the situation without detracting at all from the system's effectiveness.

Thus, the techniques used in this system can be modified in many ways, as well as adapted to decision-making processes in other areas. Also, their application is flexible. For example, prod ucts can be evaluated by one person or by several people. I evaluation by several people is deemed desirable, the index num bers they derive can be further weighted according to the indi vidual evaluators' experience, knowledge, proven record, and so on.

As much or as little importance can be attached to the fina index numbers as circumstances within the company dictate. In some companies, they might be used as just one of many aids in making product decisions, while in other companies they might become the sole determinant of the product line. In any case the company that employs this system is assured that it is using a more scientific and dependable technique than has been used to date. In addition, it is in a position to make better decisions than its less progressive competitors.

15

MATHEMATICS
FOR PRODUCTION SCHEDULING

MELVIN ANSHEN, CHARLES C. HOLT, FRANCO MODIGLIANI,
JOHN F. MUTH, AND HERBERT A. SIMON

Fluctuations in customers' orders create difficult problems for managers responsible for scheduling production and employment. Changes in shipments must be absorbed by some combination of the following actions:

Adjusting the amount of overtime work.
Adjusting the size of the work force.
Adjusting the finished goods inventory.
Adjusting the order backlog.

Since each of these courses of action has certain associated costs, one of the prime responsibilities of production management is to make decisions that represent minimum cost choices. Difficult enough when fluctuations in orders can be predicted, the decision-making assignment is even more complex in the common circumstance of unforeseen changes in demand. But the importance of the fundamental responsibility is clear. Better deci-

The research for this paper was a group study carried out by members of the Office of Naval Research Project on Planning and Control of Industrial Operations at the Carnegie Institute of Technology. All five authors were members of the Carnegie Tech. faculty at the time.

sions within a company contribute directly to its profits. Even more broadly, better decisions in many companies can increase the efficiency with which the nation uses its resources—a fact of growing importance as our arms race with the Soviet Union intensifies.

This paper reports some of the findings of a research team that has been studying the application of mathematical techniques to the scheduling of production and employment. As a result of this work, new methods have been developed for improving the quality of scheduling decisions and for helping managers to make substantially better decisions than they could make by using prevailing rule-of-thumb and judgment procedures. Once a general rule has been developed, the computations required to establish a monthly production schedule can be completed by a clerk in a few hours or on a computer in a few minutes.

In a paint manufacturing plant the new methods were applied with significant results. A comparison of the actual performance of the factory under management's scheduling decisions with the performance that would have been realized if the new technique had been used indicated a cost advantage of at least 8.5% for the mathematical decision rule, with further gains to be derived from improved sales forecasting. The plant was not a large one; there were only 100 employees. Yet the annual saving amounted to $51,000, reflecting reductions in a number of cost items, including regular payroll, overtime, hiring, training, layoff, and inventory.

The specific decision method described in this paper is applicable to other plants with similar production flows and cost structures. Moreover, the general mathematical method can be adapted to production scheduling in plants with different cost structures. Ultimately, the basic technique should be applicable in areas other than production scheduling.

Production & Mathematics

To use mathematics as a tool, one must understand it as a language. Since it differs from the language of production, the essential first step in applying it to a plant problem is to translate the description of production from its familiar vocabulary into the language of mathematics.

350

Such a transformation calls for generalizing, quantifying, and identifying the goals and constraints (limitations or restrictions). Data drawn from financial and cost-accounting systems are useful for this purpose, but they are not ordinarily sufficient. They need to be supplemented by quantitative approximations of production functions that are seldom described numerically. This may call for simplification and aggregation. Fortunately, as the following comments demonstrate, the actual transformation is less formidable than these words may suggest.

At one end of the production process, orders (on hand or anticipated) generate production. At the other end of the process, shipments satisfy orders. Within these limits the process accumulates costs.

Total costs for a given time period are influenced by managerial scheduling decisions. These decisions commonly are taken with reference to selected goals. Certain costs, for example, are associated with the stability of the production schedule over time.

If there is steady employment of a group of workers, costs are lower than if the group fluctuates in size. Costs associated with hiring, training, layoff, and overtime are minimized, as well as the less tangible costs related to undertime operations.

If incoming orders are not stable, however, a level rate of production can be maintained only by accepting fluctuations in the order backlog or by making shipments as required from a buffer stock of finished goods.

A decision to absorb fluctuations through finished-goods inventory commits the firm to direct investment costs and to the expenses associated with storage, handling, spoilage, obsolescence, and adverse price changes. Similarly, a decision to absorb order fluctuations through a buffer backlog also has recognizable costs associated with it, although these are not measured by standard accounting techniques—the costs of customer dissatisfaction, loss of future business, and adverse price changes.

In most work settings, production decisions are further complicated by the movement of several products through common facilities and work groups. Another problem often encountered is the variable procurement costs for materials and parts, which are related to purchase lot size and stability of incoming deliveries.

Finally, decision strategy must consider the effect of errors in forecasting future orders and of the accumulation of scheduling decisions over successive time intervals. Both these considerations compel the adoption of a dynamic strategy that combines a judgment as to the impact of the orders-stock-production-shipment complex on the immediately upcoming time period with a judgment designed to compensate for prior errors in scheduling for preceding time periods.

The best, or minimum-cost, decision in this complicated setting with its multitude of interrelated variables is far from obvious. There is no easy way out. One management may pursue a shifting strategy outlined by rule-of-thumb procedures; another management may adopt a stable strategy designed to realize a single objective, such as level employment or prompt delivery of customers' orders. However, little argument is needed to show that such strategies cannot, except in extraordinary circumstances, produce optimum results.

Since every fluctuation in incoming orders can be met only by a choice among alternatives, each of which carries an inescapable set of associated costs, the scheduler is confronted with a complex and dynamic situation in which optimum performance requires absorption of fluctuations through a carefully weighted allocation among all buffer elements. Part of the impact may be taken by inventory adjustments (in both order backlogs and finished goods), part by overtime and undertime scheduling of workers, and part by changes in the size of the work force.

The best mix of these elements clearly depends on the nature of the production process (for example, the feasibility of smooth rather than one-step-at-a-time adjustments in the scale of operations, the relation of setup costs to length of run, and so on), and the cost structure in an individual plant. Even for a specific plant, the optimum allocation will change with the frequency, amplitude, and predictability of fluctuations in orders.

The mathematical approach to any decision-making problem requires several distinct steps:

(1) Managers must agree on the objective of maximizing or

minimizing a specific criterion. For the firm as a whole this criterion would be profits. For the production-scheduling manager who controls neither sales nor profits, the critical criterion would be minimizing the costs of operations.

(2) All costs must be described quantitatively in comparable units, including intangible costs and those not regularly identified by financial and cost-accounting systems.

(3) A reporting and planning period must be selected for the accumulation and analysis of information relevant to scheduling decisions. The selection of the decision period is itself a problem. The significant factors include the size of errors in forecasting incoming orders, the cost of making forecasts, the time required to gather new information to improve earlier forecasts, the cost of making and administering decisions, and the relative costs of making a large number of small scheduling changes and a small number of large ones.

The process of quantifying intangibles, such as the costs associated with maintaining a buffer backlog of accepted but unproduced orders, is a process of making numerically explicit certain values that are always present in management thinking but in an ill-defined and cloudy form. Actually, precision in doing this is neither possible nor necessary. But it is essential to assign numerical weights to all variables and to recognize that doing this is no more than translating from a language that permits the implicit to a language that compels the explicit.

Further, the general decision problem must be expressed in a mathematical form that is flexible enough to comprehend the full range of production costs and simple enough to permit relatively easy solution. If we consider the nature of the costs associated with production, as outlined above, we will find that a U-shaped curve is a useful general expression.

For example, high costs are incurred in holding both large inventories and inventories so small that out-of-stock conditions are common, with consequent delays in shipments, short production runs to fill back orders, and customer dissatisfaction.

Similarly, frequent scheduling of both overtime and undertime (a less than fully employed work force) is expensive. Such costs are often regarded as intangible and are not explicitly reported in

353

accounting procedures; but they must be explicitly quantified for mathematical treatment. Somewhere between the extremes of overtime and undertime, labor costs are at a minimum.

These considerations indicate the feasibility of achieving a reasonable and workable approximation of the complex of production costs by the simplest mathematical expression that gives a U-shaped curve—a quadratic function.

It should be observed that the mathematical view of the problem does not assume that the costs of hiring workers equal the costs of laying them off, or that changes in costs in either direction are symmetrical. It does not assume that the costs associated with adding to inventory holdings equal the costs of depleting inventory, or that changes in either direction are symmetrical.

One common misunderstanding about the language of mathematics is the belief that precise numerical expression requires equal precision in reporting "facts." Mathematics can be an effective decision-making tool even in circumstances in which the values assigned to costs represent no more than approximations.

In this sense, the mathematical approach is more precise and consistent, and therefore more rational, than judgment based on experience and informed hunch. It compels the scheduler to consider all criteria previously defined as essential, and it compels him to consider them consistently every time a scheduling decision is made. In fact, after the decision rule, expressed as a formula with explicit values for specified constant elements, has been framed, it does the considering for the scheduler as a routine of the mathematical process.

It follows that the ultimate judgment of the efficacy of a mathematical decision-making process in a production setting is not in terms of its ability to schedule for minimum true costs. After all, the truth about all costs probably can never be determined. But it can be demonstrated mathematically that the decisions arrived at by means of the rule are the optimum decisions for the assigned cost values.

The important test thereafter is showing that the decisions arrived at by means of the mathematical tool are better decisions, and that operations are scheduled at lower costs, than decisions arrived at by alternative methods. This can be demonstrated by matching the actual record under established scheduling procedures with the record that would have been made under the mathematical decision rule.

New Methods Applied

To test the application of the general mathematical techniques described above, the research team studied the scheduling problem in a paint factory. To simplify the analysis, without changing its fundamental concept, scheduling decisions were assumed to be made monthly and costs were accumulated over the same period.

First the following kinds of cost components were identified:

Regular payroll, hiring, and layoff.
Overtime and undertime.
Inventory, back order, and machine setup.

These costs were developed as discrete components and then were combined in an expression of the complete cost function for the factory as a whole.

Payroll. With monthly adjustments in the size of the work force, regular payroll costs per month were a linear function of the size of the work force; that is, if they had been correlated on a graph, with payroll costs on the vertical axis and work-force size on the horizontal axis, the resultant diagonal line would have been fairly straight. Payroll dollars for regular work time also varied directly with the size of the work force measured in man-months.

In contrast, hiring and layoff costs were associated with the magnitude of change in the size of the force. Costs of hiring and training rise with the number of workers hired and trained; layoff costs are associated with the number of workers discharged. There is no necessary symmetry between hiring and layoff costs in their relation to the number of workers processed; and random factors, reflecting the tightness of the local labor market or reorganization of the work structure at certain levels of employment, may also be present sporadically. The representation of these costs by a U-shaped curve, therefore, was only an approximation of the average costs of changes of various magnitudes in the work force.

Overtime. Overtime operations in the factory involved wage payments at an hourly rate 50% higher than the regular time rate. Undertime costs, reported only indirectly through the accounting system, reflected waste of labor time measured by the difference between the actual monthly wage bill and the wage bill for the smaller work force that would have sufficed to accomplish the actual production. Actual overtime during any month is determined, of course, not only by a work load in excess of that which can be produced by the regular force in regular hours, but also by such random disturbances as emergency orders, machine breakdown, quality control problems, fluctuations in productivity, and so on.

In setting the production rate and the work force for a month, the scheduler must balance the risk of maintaining too large a work force against the risk of holding a smaller work force but being required to pay overtime compensation. As in the case of hiring and layoff costs, these considerations suggested a U-shaped, possibly unsymmetrical, cost curve.

Inventory. Absorbing order fluctuations through inventory and back-order buffers gives rise to new costs. Holding a good-size inventory incurs costs such as interest, obsolescence, handling, storage, and adverse price movements. On the other hand, a decision to reduce these costs by operating with a smaller inventory invites out-of-stock conditions with the associated costs of delayed shipments, lost sales, and added machine setups for special production runs to balance out stocks and to service mandatory shipments. The analysis pointed to the need for an optimum inventory level at which combined costs were at a minimum.

The complete cost function for production and employment scheduling was developed by adding the components reviewed above. (For its mathematical form see Appendix, reference 1.) The mathematical generalization was then applied to the specific situation in the paint factory by inserting numerical values representing estimates of the various costs involved.

Some of the estimates were drawn directly from accounting data or obtained through statistical treatment of accounting data. Other estimates, such as those for the intangible costs of delayed shipments, were subjective. Here it is important to note that the accuracy of the estimates was not a critical consideration. An analysis of the effect of errors as large as a factor of two—that is, overestimating specific cost elements by 100% or underestimating them by 50%—indicated that use of the resultant decision rules would incur costs only 11% higher than with correct estimates of costs.

At this point the mathematical process led to the development of two monthly decision rules, one to set the aggregate rate of production and the other to establish the size of the work force. (For the mathematical derivation of these rules see Appendix, reference 2.) The two rules are set forth in Exhibit I.

The production rule incorporates a weighted average of the forecasts of twelve months' future orders, which contributes to smoothing production. The weights assigned to future orders decline rapidly because it is not economical to produce for distant shipment in view of the cumulative cost of holding inventory. (This accounts for the negative numbers for the last seven months in the production rule in Exhibit I.) The employment rule also incorporates a weighted average of forecasts of future orders, with the weights projected further into the future before becoming negligible.

The second term of the production equation ($.993 \, W_{t-1}$) reflects the influence of the number of workers employed at the end of the preceding month. Because both large decreases in the payroll and large amounts of unused labor are costly, the level of scheduled production responds to the size of the work force at the start of the month.

The next two terms in the production decision rule ($153. - .464 \, I_{t-1}$) relate the inventory to production. If net inventory at the end of the preceding month is large, the negative term will exceed the positive term, with a resultant downward influence on scheduled production. A reverse relationship would contribute to establishing a higher level of production. This term also functions to take account of past forecast errors, since their effect is to raise the net inventory above, or push it below, the desired level.

The first term of the employment rule ($.743 \, W_{t-1}$) provides for a direct influence between the work force on hand at the beginning of a month and the scheduled employment during

357

the month, reflecting the costs associated with changing the size of the work force. The next two terms $(2.09 - .010\, I_{t-1})$ make provision for the effect of the net inventory position on the employment decision. A large net inventory will lead to a decrease in

EXHIBIT I. PRODUCTION AND EMPLOYMENT DECISION RULES FOR PAINT FACTORY

$$P_t = \begin{cases} +.463\, O_t \\ +.234\, O_{t+1} \\ +.111\, O_{t+2} \\ +.046\, O_{t+3} \\ +.013\, O_{t+4} \\ -.002\, O_{t+5} \\ -.008\, O_{t+6} \\ -.010\, O_{t+7} \\ -.009\, O_{t+8} \\ -.008\, O_{t+9} \\ -.007\, O_{t+10} \\ -.005\, O_{t+11} \end{cases} + .993\, W_{t-1} + 153. - .464\, I_{t-1}$$

$$W_t = .743\, W_{t-1} + 2.09 - .010\, I_{t-1} + \begin{cases} +.0101\, O_t \\ +.0088\, O_{t+1} \\ +.0071\, O_{t+2} \\ +.0054\, O_{t+3} \\ +.0042\, O_{t+4} \\ +.0031\, O_{t+5} \\ +.0023\, O_{t+6} \\ +.0016\, O_{t+7} \\ +.0012\, O_{t+8} \\ +.0009\, O_{t+9} \\ +.0006\, O_{t+10} \\ +.0005\, O_{t+11} \end{cases}$$

Where:

P_t is the number of units of product that should be produced during the forthcoming month, t.

W_{t-1} is the number of employees in the work force at the beginning of the month (end of the previous month).

I_{t-1} is the number of units of inventory minus the number of units on back order at the beginning of the month.

W_t is the number of employees that will be required for the current month, t. The number of employees that should be hired is therefore $W_t - W_{t-1}$.

O_t is the forecast of number of units of product that will be ordered for shipment during the current month, t.

O_{t+1} is the same for the next month, $t + 1$; and so forth.

the scheduled work force, and a small net inventory will have the opposite effect.

The terms of the two rules make explicit the dynamic inter-action of production and employment. For example, production during a month affects the inventory position at the end of the month. This affects the employment decision in the next month, which then influences the production decision in the third month. Again, the influence of net inventory on both production and employment decisions provides a self-correcting force which oper-ates to return inventory to its optimum position regardless of the accuracy of sales forecasts.

It is most difficult, if not impossible, to account for this inter-action without a mathematical decision rule. The manager who makes these decisions on the basis of intuition and experience may hit the right answer some of the time, but he will not do so consistently.

The weighting of the sales forecasts and the feedback factors determines the magnitude of production and employment re-sponses to fluctuations in orders, thereby allocating the fluctua-tions among work force, overtime, inventory, and backlog in the interest of minimizing total costs. While the work force responds to rather long-run fluctuations in orders, the principal response of production is to near-term orders and to the inventory position. Thus, the rule provides for the absorption of short-run fluctuations in orders and errors of forecasting by scheduling overtime and undertime operations.

How much are decision rules of the kind described an improve-ment over the usual methods of scheduling production?

This question was answered for the paint factory by making a hypothetical application to scheduling in the plant and comparing the results with actual performance under established procedures. Production and employment decisions in the paint factory were analyzed for a six-year period. The production and employment decision rules were then applied to simulate the decisions that would have been made if they had been in use during the same six-year period.

Because the same data were used by the research team as by management, hindsight could be of no advantage except in one situation, and here measures were taken to counteract it. A necessary ingredient for the comparison was a monthly series of forecasts of future orders throughout the period under analysis. Because no such forecasts had actually been recorded, the comparison could not be made on the basis of forecasts identical to those implicitly in the minds of management when it made its scheduling decisions. As a substitute, two sets of forecasts were devised which bracketed the forecasts actually used by management.

The first set of forecasts consisted of actual orders received. This was, in other words, a "perfect" forecast, assuming the future to be known in the present; use of it established an upper limit for performance.

The second set of forecasts was derived by assuming that future orders would be predicted by a moving average of past orders. Specifically, orders for a year ahead were forecast as equal to those actually received in the preceding year. This annual forecast was then converted to a monthly forecast by applying a seasonal adjustment based on actual past performance.

A comparison of actual costs under management scheduling with hypothetical costs under the decision rules did not tell the whole story. The figures were not solid; problems of allocating costs between paint and the other products processed in the plant, as well as the absence of a firm accounting underpinning for certain intangible costs, gave a tentative quality to the data. The research team judged, however, that the comparison was a valid one for all practical purposes and that the cost differences shown in Exhibit II were highly significant. The figures cover two periods:

(1) The longest period for which cost figures were available for a three-way comparison between actual performance and expected performance under the new rules using both a perfect forecast and a moving-average forecast, 1949–1953.

(2) The period in which company performance was matched against the decision rule using a moving-average forecast, 1952–1954.

Exhibit II shows that the general effect of the decision rules, with either moving-average or perfect forecasts, was to smooth the very sharp month-to-month fluctuations in both production and size of work force in actual factory performance. Overtime and inventory-holding costs were somewhat higher under the rules with the moving-average forecast (a "backward-looking" forecast) than the actual costs were, but this excess was more than offset by the fact that back orders were consistently held at lower levels. It is worth observing that the costs associated with back orders are particularly difficult to include as significant factors in rule-of-thumb and judgment decisions.

The decision rule with the moving-average forecasts saved $173,000 annually against factory performance. For this stage in the history of this plant, greater savings could have been secured by making optimum use of crude forecasts than by improving forecasts. Note that the decision rule with perfect forecasts had

EXHIBIT II. ACTUAL PERFORMANCE VS. EXPECTED PERFORMANCE UNDER DECISION RULES (*in thousands of dollars*)

		Decision rule	
Costs	Company performance	Moving-average forecast	Perfect forecast
A. Cost comparisons for 1949–1953			
Regular payroll	$1,940	$1,834	$1,888
Overtime	196	296	167
Inventory	361	451	454
Back orders	1,566	616	400
Hiring and layoffs	22	25	20
Total cost	$4,085	$3,222	$2,929
	139%	110%	100%
B. Cost comparisons for 1952–1954			
Regular payroll	$1,256	$1,149	
Overtime	82	95	
Inventory	273	298	
Back orders	326	246	
Hiring and layoffs	16	12	
Total cost	$1,953	$1,800	
	108.5%	100%	

361

lower costs than the same rule with the moving-average forecasts in the 1949–1953 period—by 10%, or an average of $59,000 annually. This difference, which is entirely attributable to better forecasting, is a sizable one but only about a third as large as the other saving.

In the 1952–1954 period actual factory costs exceeded costs under the decision rule by 8.5%, or $51,000 per year on the average. The economies of the decision rule were achieved by (a) reducing payroll costs more than overtime costs increased, (b) reducing back-order penalty costs more than inventory-holding costs increased, and (c) reducing hiring and layoff costs.

Conclusions

While further exploration of the problems involved in applying mathematical decision rules to production and scheduling decisions seems clearly desirable as a basis for definitive conclusions, the study reported in this paper provides firm support for several preliminary judgments. Empirical experience with the rules in the paint factory corroborates the findings of the research team. The methods have been in actual and satisfactory operation in the factory for several years now, and their use is currently being extended to other factories operated by the same company. The same methods have also been adapted to several other production-scheduling situations in other companies and have satisfactorily passed "dry run" tests preliminary to actual installations in these situations. This report of findings is confined to the paint factory study because this is the only one for which the data are publicly available at the present time.

Decision rules supplement, rather than displace, management judgment in scheduling production and employment. As such they are of great value in helping management to:

(1) Quantify and use the intangibles which are always present in the background of its thinking but which are incorporated only vaguely and sporadically in scheduling decisions.

(2) Make routine the comprehensive consideration of all factors relevant to scheduling decisions, thereby inhibiting judgments which are based on incomplete, obvious, or easily handled criteria.

(3) Fit each scheduling decision into its appropriate place in the historical series of decisions and, through the feedback mechanism incorporated in the decision rules, automatically correct for prior forecasting errors.

(4) Free executives from routine decision-making activities, thereby giving them greater freedom and opportunity for dealing with extraordinary situations.

In the case of the paint factory, for example, use of the decision rules permits regular monthly scheduling of production and employment to become a clerical function. Management attention can now be directed to refining cost estimates and periodically adjusting estimates to reflect changes in costs resulting from modifications of work flow and production process.

Beyond this, management has more time to consider nonroutine factors and special situations that might provide reasons for modifying scheduling decisions computed from the mathematical rules. Anticipated changes in raw material availability, in the supply of workers with necessary skills, in customers' procurement requirements, or in the character of competitors' service offerings can get the attention they deserve from executives relieved of the burden of repetitive, complex scheduling decisions.

Management time is also free to develop ways and means of improving sales forecasting, with the knowledge that such gains can be fed directly into the decision rules and thus improve their efficiency.

But it would be shortsighted to think of the decision rules only in terms of the production setting of the paint factory. They can be modified to apply to other types of scheduling problems. The required changes are in the specific cost terms, not in the general structure of the rules. To be sure, the development of the rules in a different kind of plant requires careful study of the costs that are relevant to scheduling decisions, supported by explicit quantification of all cost elements. Subject to this limitation, however, the general technique is applicable to scheduling in any plant in which the relevant costs may be approximated by U-shaped curves.

Decision problems in areas outside production would also appear to be candidates for the application of mathematical decision rules of the type described. The scheduling of warehouse operations, of employment in retail stores, of certain classes of retail merchandise stocks, of working capital, and of some types of transportation operations—all appear to be fruitful areas for research. And with ingenuity management will undoubtedly discover still other applications in the future.

APPENDIX

The broad implications of this study should be of interest not only to those persons directly concerned with production management but also to a wide managerial group. A more detailed, technical presentation of this research can be found in the following references:

1. C. C. Holt, F. Modigliani, and H. A. Simon, "A Linear Decision Rule for Production and Employment Scheduling," *Management Science*, October 1955, p. 1.

2. C. C. Holt, F. Modigliani, and J. F. Muth, "Derivation of a Linear Decision Rule for Production and Employment," *Management Science*, January 1956, p. 159.

3. H. A. Simon, C. C. Holt, and F. Modigliani, "Controlling Inventory and Production in the Face of Uncertain Sales," *National Convention Transactions*, American Society for Quality Control, 1956, p. 371.

4. H. A. Simon, "Dynamic Programming Under Uncertainty with a Quadratic Criterion Function," *Econometrica*, volume 24, p. 74.

16

THE STATISTICALLY DESIGNED EXPERIMENT

DORIAN SHAININ

In a metalworking concern, where a polishing operation follows plating, 90% of the units pass final inspection, but 10% are rejected. Why?

A complex pneumatic device shows exceptional unit-to-unit variation in performance. Why?

Units of a hydromechanical control mechanism vary widely in performance, even though most of its components are being kept to close tolerance. Why?

Making improvements in products or processes can be one of the most challenging—and also one of the most frustrating—tasks confronting management. To solve a single problem, numerous hypotheses may be advanced, tested, and found wanting. Experiments may drag on for years. After every approach has been exhausted, the company still seems to be up against a series of endless and ever-changing variables. If only it were possible to find the right combination, control the right factors, maintain the proper balance, so as to achieve continuous, economical, trouble-free operation!

Is there no better way than trial and error to solve such problems? Cannot the traditional approach be bettered? What is needed is a method that gives assurance that when a change is made in the product or the process, it will be the right change. The improvement created should be adequate and lasting. It should not cost too much or consume too much time.

An approach that fulfills all these requirements is now available in statistically designed experiments. Already these have solved a variety of problems in many industries. The purpose of the present paper is to indicate briefly what this technique is, what advantages it offers over conventional methods, and what kinds of problems it can solve.

Basic Features

The essential feature of the most up-to-date statistically designed experiment is the simultaneous consideration of a large number (sometimes all) of the possible causes for a product or process problem. It can categorically rule out most of the possible causes after a limited number of experiments. This means that the major source of trouble can be more and more closely pinned down until it is finally isolated.

The approach often makes use of but never depends on hunches and guesses in problem diagnosis. If the initial hunches happen to be right, the time for the experiment may be cut down; yet, if the hunches are wrong, as only too often happens, the experimenters' efforts are not held up until new hypotheses can be formulated. Because statistical design can impartially evaluate most or all of the causes of a problem, it is a completely objective device.

Finally, acceptance or rejection of hypotheses and consideration of alternatives can be evaluated in terms of known confidence levels. The risk of wrong decision can be reduced, for all practical purposes, almost to zero.

Following from these basic features are a number of pros and cons worth noting. On the adverse side, it must be admitted that exploiting the new technique is not a do-it-yourself proposition—at least for companies without a well-qualified statistical engineering group. Knowing how to apply these procedures calls for training; knowing which ones to apply in any particular situation calls for experience and judgment. Accordingly, large companies may wish to develop a group for this activity; smaller ones can get along with one or two people who could combine statistical work with other kinds of duties. Consultants could be hired to do the training.

Granting that the need for specialized help may be a drawback, what are the countervailing advantages? These seem substantial, and they should appeal to businessmen who put a high premium on time as well as on money.

(1) Usually the time involved in problem solving by statistical methods is short. It is not impossible for a single week's investigation to come up with an answer that has been eluding a company for years.

(2) Quick problem diagnosis, leading to quick cure, cuts the expenses of a high-cost operation, and the savings realized quickly pay back the initial costs.

(3) The process does not disrupt production; only minor interference is usually necessary. The experiments can be brief; the tests often involve only a relatively small number of units; and tinkering with operating methods on the line and with product specifications is kept to a minimum.

(4) Through training concurrent with problem solving, the company becomes progressively better able to carry on statistical activity at no extra cost with its own personnel.

Because this approach is fast and inexpensive, it is practical not only for well-heeled industrial giants but also for middle-size and small concerns. Thus, unlike many current developments in business techniques, the use of statistical procedures helps rather than hinders the competitive chances of small firms.

The theory and practice of statistical design rest on a series of simple logical propositions. Although these are not all self-evident, I think they will strike anyone who has ever worked on product or process problems as valid.

(1) Every effect has one or, more often, a number of possible causes.

(2) When there are many possible causes, the major portion of

the effect usually comes from one or, more likely, just a few causes.

(3) These few major causes are not constant in their activity; they produce variation in the end product (the effect).

(4) Therefore, if variations in the end product are analyzed and related to their possible causes, one factor (or part of the total variation) may be expected to show up as being more important than the others, and the unknown cause may be associated with that particular factor.

On the basis of this reasoning, it is a fairly straightforward matter to design an experiment that will enable management to isolate and evaluate the reasons for undesired deviations from standard in a product or process. The action—the way the parts of the total variation show up—is made to "tell on itself."

A few case examples will serve to illustrate the possibilities.

A Quality Problem

Let us start with a problem of product quality—one that had bothered a metalworking firm for years, although it proved simple and quick to solve once an objective statistical design procedure was developed.

After a final polishing operation, the company experienced what was believed to be an excessive rate of rejects and consequent expenses for reworking. Polishing followed plating, and too often the hand-held polishing wheels exposed the base metal. Plant supervisors were certain that the difficulty stemmed from variation in skill among the several polishers and/or some inherent differences in the cloth from which the polishing wheels were made.

Believing that the supervisors' hypotheses sounded reasonable, the statistical engineer assigned to the problem decided to begin by determining, with a given statistical confidence level (a fixed per cent of certainty), who were the least and the most successful workers; then a study could be made of their different polishing habits, the results of which would be incorporated into a training program. In addition, the engineer planned to compare polishing wheels in order to see if variations in their material bore any relationship to work quality.

For statistical validity, it was necessary to run a short test during which a random mixture of different parts would be issued to each polisher, and each man would use one polishing wheel. A protective statistical "level of significance" was chosen so as to distinguish between chance variations in output and real differences arising from unequal skills. Interestingly enough, the results of this test showed no significant difference among operators. In other words, the major cause or causes being sought had been distributed about evenly (randomly) among all the polishers.

This unexpected revelation brought on a decision not to guess further about the major causes of trouble without some really objective evidence to indicate their nature.

Freeing his mind of all preconceptions about the problem, and thinking back to the four logical steps outlined above, the statistical engineer now decided to look at the plating process (in contrast to the polishing operation, which had been pretty conclusively proved innocent); to consider the total variation in plating thickness in terms of three of its factors; and then to let the action of these factors tell which one of them was the most important and thus where the cause of most of the variation lay.

The engineer divided thickness variation into that occurring (a) from time to time, (b) from plating tank to plating tank, and (c) within a tank. Following this line of inquiry, a simple experiment was performed.

Parts were identified for a short period according to the side of the tank and tank number in which they were plated, and according to the hour when the plating was done. A small variation in plating thickness showed up in the hour-to-hour figures and in the tank-to-tank figures, but none of the parts plated on the righthand side of the tanks had the plating polished off, while many of those from the lefthand side had thin plating and had been rejected for exposure of base metal. Therefore, something that correlated with "within-tank" variation had to be controlled to move the variation in thickness toward zero.

Discussion with the plating foreman brought forth no clues. Anode to cathode distances and electrical potentials had all been balanced when the tanks had been installed. It seemed desirable, therefore, to observe the plating procedure. The only nonsymmetrical feature seen was a hand valve on a pipe on the righthand side of each of the 14 tanks. This pipe carried steam along the length of the tank at the bottom on the right, across the front, and back on the left, rising up and out. The steam kept the plating solution warm, which was necessary for good results.

A reason for the polishing difficulty now became clear—a reason that fitted the observed facts. The steam must be hotter on entering the tank than on leaving it, so that the right side of each tank was warmer. Since warm water rises, a counterclockwise circulation of the plating solution must have been created. That meant that the plating particles coming from the anodes were in a rising current on the right side and in a falling current on the left. The articles hanging on the left side of each tank, therefore, must be getting less thickness of plate.

The steam valves were then closed. Parts from both sides of all tanks were polished. None were rejected.

The solution to the problem, therefore, was to relocate the heating coils in the tanks in order to avoid a circulation that would affect plating thickness.

Thus, a major quality problem told on itself in less than one week. The answer unfolded as soon as the statistical engineer insisted on an entirely objective approach, unbiased by what the management "knew" to be the crucial factors—operator skill and/or polishing wheel differences. As is often the case, the solution to the problem was almost ridiculously simple once the components of variation were carefully studied.

A Performance Problem

Solving the polishing problem just outlined was relatively simple; a slightly more complex statistical design may have to be worked out for other problems. A representative case in point involves a manufacturer of a complicated pneumatic unit.

An inexplicable unit-to-unit variation occurred in the production of this complex item. For proper operation, some units required considerably higher supply-line pressure than others. This situation was unacceptable to the customer and had been under intensive investigation for months, while company engineers theorized as to first one, then another, possible cause. So far, no changes in dimensions, tolerances, assembly, or test procedures had resulted in the improvement desired.

Feeling that the clue to performance variation lay in some unknown physical differences among the units, but having no idea what these differences might be, the statistical engineer selected two units from a day's production which evidenced the greatest variation in the pressure required for satisfactory operation. One unit was tagged as the "low" unit, the other as the "high" unit.

After a discussion with the engineers on the job, two subassemblies common to both units were selected as possibly accounting for most of the variation in final unit operation. These subassemblies were removed from the units and identified as "A" and "B," while the rest of the unit was identified as "R." The six components ("A" from "high" and "low," "B" from "high" and "low," and "R" from "high" and "low") were then reassembled and tested in the following combinations:

> A-high with B-low and R-high
> A-low with B-low and R-low
> A-high with B-high and R-low
> A-low with B-high and R-high

Tests were run on each combination twice, giving eight test runs in total. These eight test runs were performed in random sequence, to minimize the possibility that chance environmental factors affecting test conditions could "throw off" interpretation of results.

Next, the readings for each test run (in pounds per square inch) were entered on a diagram, known as a "Latin square," opposite the test number:

	A-high	A-low
B-low	R-high (1) 20.40 (2) 20.50	R-low (5) 20.60 (6) 20.40
B-high	R-low (3) 22.90 (4) 23.10	R-high (7) 23.00 (8) 22.90

By averaging the four readings in each vertical column, the effects of A-high and A-low could be measured.

By averaging the four readings in each horizontal row, the effects of B-low and B-high could be measured.

By averaging the four readings diagonally, two ways, the effects of R-high and R-low could be measured. That is, the average of the upper left and lower right boxes shows the effect of R-high; the average of the lower left and upper right boxes shows the effect of R-low.

Significantly, because of this balanced Latin square design, each pair of averages reflects the difference caused by a change in one particular variable. The effects of the other two variables, while included, are exactly balanced and are therefore neutralized.

For evaluating the results of statistical experiments such as this one, special methods have been devised to indicate within a known confidence level (i.e., acceptable margin of error), whether the differences obtained among average figures are large enough to be significant or not. In this case, on examination of the data, it was apparent even without a statistical test of significance that subassembly B was responsible for the relatively large variation among units. The average results of B-low and B-high showed too great a difference to be attributed to chance, or to the influence of other variables which caused differences among the results within each box.

The results of this experiment suggested a careful inspection of the B subassemblies from both the low and the high units. A dimensional difference was found to exist in the length between a fulcrum and an actuating point on an arm—a difference which could easily be controlled in future production.

Thus, once more, when variation was broken down into its components, immediate clues to the nature of the problem came to light. The company's previous experience had led it to believe that the solution lay in redimensioning subassembly A. Fortunately, this expensive and unnecessary course of action was avoided.

In this instance, one of the two subassemblies first selected for investigation turned out to be the source of the company's problem. What if this had not been the case? Under these circumstances, readings from the diagram would have readily disclosed what the next step ought to be.

(1) If the large difference in averages had remained in R, the test would have been repeated using C and D subassemblies rather than A and B. Eventually, this process of elimination would isolate the source of variation involved.

(2) If the large differences were found to be "within box" variations, this would indicate that test equipment or other conditions of environment were at fault. Such "experimental error" would indicate the need for a more carefully controlled test procedure.

(3) If only one of the four boxes had results out of line with any other, and the experimental error was small, this would be evidence of an interaction among two or more components. Or if one R-low box had a pair of noticeably high readings and the other R-low box had a pair of the lowest readings, that also would point to interaction. To track down a problem caused by interaction, the "factorial" design of experiment should be used instead of the Latin square. The two methods are similar in principle, but the factorial design requires that every possible combination be run at least twice.

A Standardizing Problem

A third statistically designed experiment concerns a company's efforts to reduce variation in the output of a hydromechanical fuel control. In order to use this unit in a new application, a 50% reduction in output variation was required, which seemed to present insurmountable problems.

Most of the critical components and dimensions in the assembly, of which there were many, were already being held to closer tolerances than desired for economical production. Furthermore, trial-and-error methods had given no clue as to what changes might lead to the desired reduction of output variation. It appeared that a major redesign, or a new design altogether, was needed.

With no indication at all of what might be the cause of the trouble, the statistical engineer set about to design an experiment that would unearth it. There were literally dozens of critical "characteristics" (such as a hole diameter, a spring load, a concentricity requirement, a critical length, a radius, a spring rate) in the total unit. Any one of these might be at fault—or the fault might lie in an interaction among them. Furthermore, the "value" of each such characteristic could vary, depending on the tolerance to which it had been held in production.

In order to run a full-scale factorial experiment, testing and re-testing several values of all these critical characteristics in every possible combination, the engineer would have had to make literally thousands of tests. He chose rather to take a random sample of these combinations—to conduct a more limited experiment in the hope of solving the problems faster and with less expense:

He chose to run only 30 tests, randomly assigning to each a value for every critical characteristic. Not all combinations would be run; in fact, only a small percentage of the total possible would be tested. But there would be enough to constitute a good sample.

For each critical characteristic he chose three approximate values, "High," "Medium," and "Low." When the characteristic was physically adjustable (e.g., a spring load), only one component part was required to make the tests. When such adjustments could not be made, available fuel controls often provided examples close to all three values. In certain instances, parts had to be manufactured to specific dimensions.

The particular level of each characteristic to be incorporated into the assembly for each test run was selected by using a table of random numbers. The layout is illustrated in Exhibit I.

EXHIBIT I. RANDOM SELECTION OF CHARACTERISTICS FOR TEST RUN

Test run sequence	Critical characteristic					Fuel flow in lbs./hr.
	I	II	III	IV	V etc.	
1	M	L	H	H	L	_____
2	L	L	M	L	H	_____
3	L	H	L	M	M	_____
4	M	M	L	H	L	_____
5	L	H	L	M	M	_____
•	•	•	•	•	•	. . . .
•	•	•	•	•	•	. . . .
•	•	•	•	•	•	. . . .
30	L	M	M	H	L	

374

Test run 1, then, would require that a fuel control unit be assembled that would include characteristic I at medium value, II at low, III at high, IV at high, V at low, and so on. A fuel flow was recorded for this control, and then this unit was disassembled and a second one was assembled to incorporate the requirements of test run 2. This procedure was repeated 30 times, and 30 fuel flow readings were recorded.

To eliminate time-consuming mathematical calculations, the analysis of the results was performed graphically on ordinary squared paper. A group of 30-point scatter diagrams—one diagram for each critical characteristic—was drawn up, with the value of the characteristic plotted on the horizontal axis, against fuel flow on the vertical axis, as shown in the diagram of characteristic II.

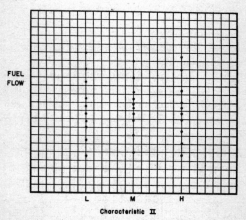

FUEL FLOW

L M H

Characteristic II

In this instance, obviously, there was no correlation between the values of the characteristic and fuel flow. The tolerance specification for this characteristic was relatively unimportant, therefore. Given next is the diagram of another, characteristic IV, which works out differently.

In this instance there was some correlation, but a wide scatter of points occurred about the trend line. The specification affected the results, but fuel flow was influenced much more by values of

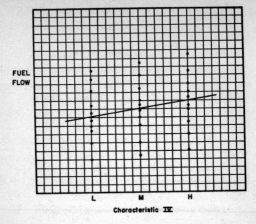

Characteristic IV

other characteristics which were entering the plot in a random manner and were the cause of the large scatter. So let us turn to another one, characteristic VII.

Here there is a good correlation, with a narrow scatter about the trend line. The specifications for this characteristic appeared to have an important effect on the results. In order to validate the finding, this correlation (as well as any other that appeared im-

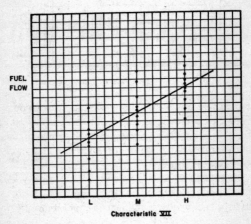

Characteristic VII

portant) was checked by a few additional test runs in a bona fide factorial design, in order to establish valid levels of statistical significance.

It was then a straightforward job to determine statistically the position of two lines, parallel to a trend line, which would include 95% of the points to be expected from a far greater number of runs. Next, from the desired upper and lower limits of fuel flow on the graph, a pair of horizontal lines were drawn (see Exhibit II). The line from the maximum desired fuel flow stopped at the upper boundary of the scatter, that from the minimum at the lower boundary. Perpendiculars were then dropped from these two intersection points. They showed, on the horizontal scale, the real tolerance limits required for characteristic VII to guarantee (with 95% certainty) compliance with the desired fuel flow limits.

This study provided the company with a completely objective evaluation of a highly complex design. Through careful study of the results of only 30 test runs, utilizing components from several fuel controls, it showed where tolerances were too tight, too loose, or just right—but sometimes out of position. Certain important

EXHIBIT II. COMPUTATION OF REQUIRED TOLERANCE LIMITS FOR CHARACTERISTIC VII

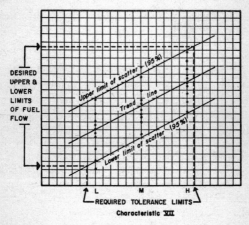

DESIRED
UPPER &
LOWER
LIMITS
OF FUEL
FLOW

Upper limit of scatter (95%)

Trend line

Lower limit of scatter (95%)

L　　　M　　　H

REQUIRED TOLERANCE LIMITS

Characteristic VII

and controlling tolerances had to be held closer in order to avoid the necessity of selective assembly. In some cases, specifications had to be changed to flatten the slope of the trend line so as to provide a practical manufacturing tolerance for those characteristics.

As a result of this experiment, the company was able to make the changes needed to bring the fuel flow within the desired limits without major redesign. In fact, only a few tolerances had to be tightened, and these were amply compensated by the discovery that several others were being held unnecessarily close.

Future Prospects

Statistically designed experiments are increasingly being used to solve production and process problems. But these limited uses by no means exhaust the potentialities of the new technique— potentialities that are still in the early stages of development and exploration and only await the passage of time.

A very large number and a wide range of problems can be attacked by means of techniques based upon the four logical steps enumerated earlier, i.e., letting the action tell on itself. For example, I know of two cases where the unknown but controlling factors in market activities were revealed; of another one in the paper industry where the predominant cause of variation stemmed from the natural uncontrollable characteristics of trees (but could be compensated for); and of an extremely interesting application of the statistical design approach in the area of medical research.

Finally, it seems particularly significant to note that the usefulness of statistical designs is not limited to problem situations. These, after all, are relatively unusual in many industries. Far more common are situations where, for example, products and processes are adequate—but not so efficient or so economical as they could be. Now, through the use of statistical designs, companies at last have a relatively quick and inexpensive way to find out objectively where improvements can be made and what the specific improvements ought to be.

So, for the future, the possibilities for savings in cost and increased efficiency appear to be incalculable.

17

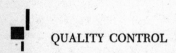

QUALITY CONTROL

THEODORE H. BROWN

Statistical quality control or, more simply, quality control has been called the greatest advance in manufacturing during the last quarter century. Whatever may be the truth of this opinion, the fact is that many progressive companies such as Sheaffer Pen, Gillette Safety Razor, International Harvester, Ford Motor, and General Electric, have installed quality control methods and are firm in the belief that their use secures better products, reduced costs, and improved worker relations. Such prospects always stir the interest of the business administrator and lead him to seek reasons for their success.

The search for controlling ideas in any given situation necessarily leads to questions about the underlying philosophies which are present. In the case of quality control these are largely mathematical and technical in character; consequently the resulting procedures may not be so well understood—and hence not so well or wisely used—as they might be. Only when an administrator really understands the basic reasons why any method, or series of methods, secures the results it does will he apply it effectively, if at all.

Accordingly, it is the purpose of this paper to examine some of the theories of quality control so that businessmen may have a basis for judging both its potentialities and its limitations for use in their own companies' production and purchasing functions, and then to point out some of the practical implications. Of more than incidental interest, at the present time, may be the references to the government's reliance on quality control in its procurement activities.

Basic Concepts

It is common knowledge that in the world about us no two objects and no two actions are identical, even though they may belong to the same given class of objects. Everyone will agree that among the plants or trees of a species no two are exactly the same any more than any two individuals are absolutely identical in all respects. Furthermore, people do not act in the same way on different occasions. Every fan, for example, knows his favorite baseball team does not always play exactly the same kind of game.

Nevertheless, the same fan will try to pick a winner. Tacitly he depends upon a pattern of previous experience from which he hopes to make a better judgment than would be possible with a pure guess. These patterns of experience are to be found everywhere. We say that one person is dependable or that another is erratic. Whenever an individual who was dependable suddenly becomes erratic, some reason is sought for the change. In effect, his quality of "dependableness" has gone out of control.

Such patterns of behavior are particularly in evidence in the goods produced in the shop. It might seem that in precision manufacturing the product from a given process would always be the same. Yet this is far from the truth. A simple example is that of the wrist pin which ties the upper end of the connecting rod to the piston of an automobile engine. Measurements will show that no two of these cylindrical-shaped wrist pins are identical even though machined with the same tools and by the same operator. One may be slightly larger than another in diameter, or the two may differ slightly in their roundness.

From observation we now pass to possible causes. If the pieces were machined from different lots of stock, there might be differences in the quality of the material from which they were made.

If a given machine does not possess the same identical adjustments or have the same sharpness of tools at one time that it does at another, further differences may occur in pieces from the same stock. All of these underlying causes result in products that possess measurable differences, although in size they may be identical to the eye or in weight to the hand. In modern automobile assembly they may have differences so great that one wrist pin will fit satisfactorily while another will not.

The search may be extended far back of the machining processes. We may presume that the finished form of the wrist pin is the result of a number of materials, conditions, and actions which happened long before the semifinished material reached the factory. There was, to begin with, the raw material out of which the final product has been fashioned. Starting with the iron ore, the qualities of the metal have been changed by heat treatments, and the form has been altered by different machines. These are process steps within each of which usually more than one factor has acted. They result in varying qualities of the semifinished stock as received at the manufacturing plant. In the abstract, the whole series of influences and conditions which have been brought to bear upon the original mass of iron to produce the final pin can be summed up in the phrase "system of causes."

Presumably, at each step all along the way there has been the attempt to keep precisely fixed each element in the whole system of causes. Every manufacturer knows, however, that perfect precision is not possible. The best he can do is to control each factor so that it does not vary beyond certain limits; this is the know-how of manufacturing. There is still left a minimum or residual of each causal element which is not eliminated either because the way to do so is not known or because it is too costly.

Within the system of causes, the various elements combine at random to produce variations in the finished product. In the long run, at any particular time they may result in a product which departs from an ideal. The net tends first in one direction and then in another. Clearly it is improbable that such a system of causes will exactly offset one another.

It is also obvious that, if one of these causal factors which has been minimized suddenly gets out of hand, it may become dominant and so cause a radical change in the pattern which a number of the finished pieces will form. It is, therefore, the study of the patterns derived from a series of measurements which provides the quality control engineer with a technique to advise him about conditions among these underlying causes.

A system of causes with its associated pattern of measurements is not unique to this particular case of the wrist pin in the automobile engine. Patterns may be developed wherever the characteristics of an end product can be appraised. These patterns, which are technically known as frequency distributions, represent merely the organization of measurements of a number of objects or actions.

The form of these frequency distributions can be pictured graphically, as has often been done in the shop. Suppose that we wish to study the pattern of measurements for a single outside diameter measurement of a lot of gears which have been manufactured under controlled conditions. Suppose also that in design we are concerned only with this measurement to the nearest thousandth of an inch. After measurement the gears can be stacked in piles, each pile representing a size to the nearest thousandth of an inch. Probably the height of the pile of gears for the smallest diameter will be low, and there will be a correspondingly small pile for the largest diameter measured. In passing from the smallest to the largest measurement, the piles tend to become progressively higher and then lower.

The typical outline of the pattern may not be symmetrical, and frequently is not, because the underlying conditions tend to bias the result toward one or the other extreme. (This is true of the actual data for 30 Telechron clock gears portrayed in Exhibit I.) It is also likely that certain outline irregularities will occur in the plotted pattern. Presumably, however, if the system of causes is maintained for a longer period, such irregularities will tend to become less noticeable with the increased number of cases.

One misunderstanding often turns up in discussions of quality control. It happens that there is a particular case of a symmetrical frequency distribution pattern—often referred to as bell-shaped—which is known to the mathematicians as the "normal" distribution. (See Exhibit II.) The word "normal" is unfortunate because

EXHIBIT I. FREQUENCY DISTRIBUTION OF DIAMETER MEASUREMENTS, SAM-
PLE OF 30 TELECHRON CLOCK GEARS

(performance of machine no. 5377;
position 1, farthest from chuck)

Inches		Frequency
0.4166	x	1
0.4165	xx	2
0.4164	xxxxxx	6
0.4163	xxx	3
0.4162	xxxx	4
0.4161	xxxxxxx	7
0.4160	xxx	3
0.4159	xx	2
0.4158		
0.4157	x	1°
0.4156		
0.4155		
0.4154	x	1°
Total		30

° Coolant supply failed.

many people assume that this word means a pattern which is to be expected in any case. This is not correct. The biases typically present in business situations result in patterns which are not even symmetrical. There is another reason for the word "normal" creeping into use. Statistical theories have been developed on the assumption that the frequency distribution pattern actually is normal, but the patterns dealt with in practical use are not expected to be exactly like it. The theory will be workable, provided the pattern to which it is applied is not too unlike the normal distribution.

In Production

Let us now go on to examine the use of quality control in the production process. Here we shall concern ourselves with two main topics—process research and product control. These represent two different aspects and ought not to be confused as they often are.

Process research. An early study of a pattern of measurements may suggest to the quality control engineer that research is called for in regard to the capabilities of the machine. Not infrequently

383

EXHIBIT II. ILLUSTRATION OF A THEORETICAL "NORMAL" DISTRIBUTION ($\sigma = 4.972$)

Value	1	2	3	4	5	6	7	8	9	10	11	12	13	14	15	16	17	18	19	20	21	22	23	24	25	26	27	28	29	30
Frequency	1	1	2	3	4	7	9	13	17	22	27	31	35	38	40	40	38	35	31	27	22	17	13	9	7	4	3	2	1	1

further studies indicate that changes in the machine or its partial rebuilding may make possible the production of desired pieces within desired tolerances. In other cases, such studies may indicate that the machines are either worn out or are too far out of date to produce the required quality consistently. The studies in such cases should indicate whether the added costs of improving the process will be recovered either through a reduction of scrap or an improvement of quality that will make the goods more salable.

(In some cases, of course, extended research may develop evidence that no currently available knowledge or tools will secure the desired precision. It may become necessary then to proceed with the hope that 100% inspection will succeed in eliminating the poor product until the laboratory has had time to work on the problem and perhaps find a solution.)

Let us look at some practical illustrations where the basic need is process research.

(1) End products often differ radically when two or more systems of causes are operating. For example, in one plant it was desired to control the distance between two holes stamped in a piece of metal. The pattern of measurements for the distance between the centers of the holes for a number of pieces was spread out widely and possessed two humps, much after the fashion of the famed dromedary back. Search disclosed that the pieces were stamped from two different dies. When the product made by one die was separated from that produced by the other and the pattern for each plotted, it was found that the measurements for each followed the pattern of a typical single-hump frequency curve. (See Exhibit III.) The two patterns simply overlapped when the product from the two machines was mixed in one lot. Obviously, the two dies were essentially unlike. The corrective action was to adjust one and set aside the other as a spare.

(2) Another type of problem occurs when the pattern is spread out too widely. For example, when too many wrist pins have a diameter which is larger than that permitted by the engineering drawing and perhaps when some also are too small, the problem becomes one of finding out how to reduce the underlying cause which creates the spread so that the resulting product will be more consistent. The search here may be directed toward studies of the capabilities of machines, the effect of operator action or of changing qualities in the raw material. (This was so in the case of

EXHIBIT III. FREQUENCY DISTRIBUTIONS, DISTANCE BETWEEN TWO HOLE CENTERS, SAMPLE OF 50 DIE STAMPINGS

(drawing tolerances 3.000 ± 0.004 inches)

| | | After Sorting | |
Inches	Before Sorting	Die A	Die B
3.008	x	x	
3.007	xx	xx	
3.006	xxxxxxx	xxxxxxx	
3.005	xxxxxx	xxxxx	
3.004	xxxxxxx	xxxxxx	x
3.003	xxxx	x	xxx
3.002	xxxx	xx	xx
3.001	xxxxxxx		xxxxxxx
3.000	xxxxx	x	xxxx
2.999	xxx		xxx
2.998	x		x
2.997	xx		xx
2.996	x		x

the Telechron gear diameter. The original distribution, shown in Exhibit IV, indicated that changes in the machine were desirable. After adjustments and attachments were built into the machine which cut the teeth on the gear, the pattern was that shown in Exhibit I. Note how the spread of measurements decreases from Exhibit IV to Exhibit I. The target was a maximum spread of 0.0010 inches.)

(3) A final illustration of need for attention to the process follows from the presence of excessive scrap. There is the likelihood that prior to the use of quality control as much as 20% scrap will be found among manufactured pieces, even after they have had a 100% inspection. In many cases the application of quality control will reduce this scrap to somewhere around 1%. The practical working lower limit seems to be ½ of 1%, with an upper limit of 1½% or 2%. (These figures are good bench marks even for manufacturers who pride themselves on the quality of their merchandise.)

It may come as a shock and a surprise to the administrator that there can be so much waste among pieces which have been 100% inspected. One serious difficulty is to be found in the monotony of routine inspection, where judgment quickly becomes dull, resulting in the passage of many pieces judged acceptable when in fact

EXHIBIT IV. FREQUENCY DISTRIBUTION OF DIAMETER MEASUREMENTS,
SAMPLE OF 50 TELECHRON CLOCK GEARS

(performance of machine no. 5377;
position 1 = farthest from chuck)

Inches		Frequency
0.4161		
0.4160	xxx	3
0.4159	xx	2
0.4158	xx	2
0.4157	xxx	3
0.4156	xxxx	4
0.4155	xxxx	4
0.4154	x	1
0.4153	xx	2
0.4152	xxxxx	5
0.4151		
0.4150	xxxxxx	6
0.4149	xxxx	4
0.4148	xxxx	4
0.4147	x	1
0.4146	xx	2
0.4145	x	1
0.4144		
0.4143	xx	2
0.4142		
0.4141	x	1
0.4140	x	1
0.4139		
0.4138		
0.4137		
0.4136		
0.4135	x	1
0.4134		
0.4133		
0.4132		
0.4131		
0.4130	x	1
Total		50

they are not. Thus, in the absence of quality control, bad pieces
are both produced and accepted even with 100% inspection.

It should be recognized that quality control methods are pre-
ventive in character rather than curative; the objective is to eliminate bad work before it is done, rather than to find and remove
bad work from the total product after it is manufactured.

387

Product control. It is obvious that as long as the process is out of control, the product will be also. The first part of a quality control program, therefore, is to make sure, as described, that the process can consistently produce a product of the desired quality. Subsequently, control of the product may be obtained. If there is a suspicion that the process can get out of adjustment—for example, through the careless handling of dies or the dulling of a cutting tool—an "X-bar" chart and an "R" chart may be called for. (To simplify our discussion, only the X-bar chart will be explained here.)

The symbol X-bar is usually written $\overline{X}$, which is the engineering terminology for the average of X's. This represents the average of measurements for a small number of pieces used as a sample to indicate what the process is doing. A chart of three parallel lines is drawn, with the middle line indicating an ideal condition. This mid-line corresponds to the mid-point between the limiting engineering tolerances. Two lines, whose positions are computed, are drawn above and below this middle line to indicate limits within which the average of measurements of samples of a given size should fall. When the plotted average for a sample falls outside these limits, it is recognized as a danger signal. Also, when a series of successive points falls either above or below the mid or average line, a call for attention is indicated. (Exhibit V shows the X-bar chart for the same Telechron gear problem for which earlier questions have been discussed.)

An illustration of a condition calling for the application of an X-bar chart is to be found in the case of a cutting tool where the sharpness affects the quality of the product. Here the plotted average of measurements for samples taken at given intervals, such as on each hour during the working day, will move toward the upper control limit as the tool becomes dull. Whenever the cutting edge of the tool begins to break down, the average value of the successive samples plotted at regular intervals tends to rise rapidly. As these plotted points approach the upper control limit, the operator can judge when he needs to replace a tool with a sharper one. Again, it is to be noted that operator judgment and corrective action presumably take place before defective products are made. (The X-bar chart in Exhibit V shows this situation,

EXHIBIT V. $\overline{X}$ CHART FOR TELECHRON CLOCK GEAR; HOBBING OPERATION

Drg. No 4126-64	Part GEARS	Material BRASS	Dimension & Tolerance 4166 ±.000 ±.002	Shift 7-5
Order No. 51201	Machine No 5631	Operator R. GURNEY	Inspector G.F.U.	Date 2/2/48

MEASUREMENTS

.4161	.4155	.4159	.4158	.4162	.4163	.4162			
.4161	.4156	.4161	.4161	.4159	.4170	.4161			
.4163	.4158	.4161	.4161	.4161	.4168	.4163			

AVERAGES

where "NM" indicates a new move to sharp teeth on the cutting tool or hob.)

If there is reason to believe that no important shifts in the underlying system of causes are likely to occur, perhaps only an occasional sampling check may be necessary. Whether one simply makes a running check like this is a matter of judgment. Statistical routines must not be followed blindly. Statistics provide information; wise action comes only through the administrative use they make possible.

The application which has just been described is fundamentally that of providing the operator at a given machine with objective information from which he can judge whether he is turning out a good product. Without such information, workmen are inclined to adjust and readjust their machines continually in the hope of turning out perfect work. They work blindly on hunches. Such subjective opinions have no place in modern precision methods

389

where tolerances are often held to a few ten thousandths of an inch.

Furthermore, it has been seen that product control is predicated upon a process under control. Out of process research it is, of course, hoped that there will come the know-how by which products with only small amounts of scrap can be made day after day. When this goal has been reached, product control is the job of holding things in line. It must, of course, be recognized that the discussion presents a desired goal which cannot always be reached. Nevertheless, many manufacturers have found success here.

From what has been said, it is obvious that the whole procedure is dependent upon the availability of a series of measurements. Because of the high precision of modern manufacturing, these can be obtained only through the use of better and often expensive gauges, such as dial gauges and comparators. Cases have been known where there has been a refusal to buy higher price dial gauges when an old-style snap gauge could be purchased at a fraction of the cost. (From dial gauges a series of measurements can be obtained, but from snap gauges only the acceptance or rejection of each piece is possible.) This may seem good financial control, but the equivalent sum of money can be wasted many times through failure to have adequate gauging and the resulting statistical data needed for control.

In Procurement

The problems of industrial procurement are closely associated with the questions of quality control because of two interrelated conditions.

(1) It is obvious that some of the underlying causes for poor final products are to be found in the variations present in the raw or semifinished materials out of which those products are made. It is the work of the inspection department to see that the qualities of this incoming material are consistently in agreement with the standards set up by the manufacturing needs. In this sense, also, the passing of material from one department to the next involves an acceptance problem by the receiving department. There is, consequently, a succession of steps where the initial acceptance

of material is of importance if a high quality of the finished product is to be secured.

(2) The technique by means of which the quality of all pieces in an incoming lot is appraised is an associated part of the technique used for quality control. The receiving inspector can either check every individual item or depend upon the information gained from a sample. The use of a sample naturally reduces the cost of a complete inspection, but it raises additional questions. Among these are: "Is my sample a good or a bad picture of the whole?" "What risk am I taking when I accept the evidence of the sample?" "Does a sample favor the vendor or me and to what extent?" There are serious questions for which we need some background ideas. But before these are presented, another aspect of this vendor-vendee picture should be noted.

The buyer or the receiving department does not have to assume the burden of extensive inspection for the desired quality whenever quality control has been used by the manufacturer of the purchased products. For example, one manufacturer of coiled springs provides with each purchased lot a quality control description of the springs in that lot. If the purchaser demands better springs in the sense that the quality of individual pieces in the lot shall differ from one another by smaller amounts, he can get them, together with a quality report, but it will cost him more.

Probably the most conspicuous example of the required use of quality control by the supplier occurs currently in the rearmament program. The armed services are basing many of their purchases upon Military Standard 105-A. These regulations include sets of tables which prescribe a quality control sampling procedure. Moreover, these regulations may be identified as a part of the contract. What the armed services seek is evidence that the materiel which they receive will be of the required quality. They know that when goods are made under conditions of quality control and checked by methods of acceptance sampling, the probability is that the materiel will be better than would be true under any other known control procedure.

Acceptance sampling. What is the basis for acceptance tables or, in general, what is an acceptance plan?

In the use of a sample to check a lot, two things are known exactly: the size of the lot and the size of the sample. For example, suppose that in the delivery of iron castings a lot is under consideration which includes 200 pieces, and suppose that it is proposed to test the lot by selecting at random ten of these pieces.

Now, if we imagine that 8% or 16 pieces are defective, what is the chance that our sample will not include any one of these 16, so that the judgment based on the sample will be that the lot is perfect and therefore is acceptable? This question is one of elementary probabilities. The value of this probability happens to be 0.43. This means that in the long run 43 out of every 100 samples—one sample from each lot—will not include a defective piece.

Again, if the number of defective pieces in the lot was 9% or 18 pieces instead of 8%, what would be the corresponding probability? The answer here is 0.38. The chance of not finding a defective piece is smaller than before. This makes sense because there are more defectives in the lot.

These are but two of a whole series of questions which can be asked about a lot and sample of the sizes named, but in each question assuming a different number of defectives in the lot. It is possible to plot on a chart for each assumed percentage of defectives the probability that the sample will not include any of the defective pieces, that is, the probability that the lot will be accepted. After a series of plottings, a curve can be drawn through the plotted points. Such a curve is known as the operating characteristic curve for a lot and sample of these sizes. (Exhibit VI is a fairly simple case, with the lot and sample sizes both small for the purpose of convenient discussion.) These operating curves are infinite in variety because they depend upon the lot size, the size of the sample, and the number of defectives that may be permitted in the sample for an acceptable lot. For each such set of conditions, they picture the risk of accepting a lot and of judging it perfect even though it contains some defectives.

Everyone is aware that there are certain dangers involved in the use of a sample. After all, probabilities are different from guarantees. The sample of ten from the lot of 200 just cited might include no defective pieces, although defectives actually were

EXHIBIT VI. OPERATING CHARACTERISTIC CURVE
(lot 200; sample 10; no defectives allowed)

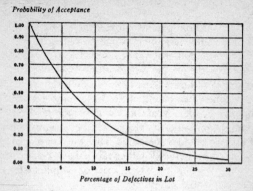

Probability of Acceptance

Percentage of Defectives in Lot

present in the lot. If the purchaser buys on the basis of the sample, he has assumed the risk arising from the possibility that his sample will not contain defectives. This is known technically as the consumer's risk. The consumer usually will attempt to minimize such a danger.

On the other side of the picture, a number of defective pieces might turn up in the sample of ten even though, actually, there were very few in the lot. The buyer would then conclude that the lot was extremely bad. This is the producer's risk. Closely associated with these ideas are three additional elements: the buyer's acceptable quality level, the desire to have a limiting value for the percentage of defects in any lot which the buyer will accept, and the quality level at which a given manufacturing process is performing.

All of these factors and ideas have been merged in the computation of Sampling Inspection Tables, developed by H. F. Dodge and H. G. Romig.[1] These tables prescribe for various lot sizes the size of the sample which on the average will enable the buyer to limit his risks. They do not provide certainty in purchasing. But they do provide a definite plan for acceptance sampling and

[1] See, for example, their *Sampling Inspection Tables* (New York, John Wiley & Sons, Inc., 1944), or "Military Standard 105-A," *Sampling Procedures and Tables for Inspection by Attributes* (Washington, D.C., Government Printing Office, 1950).

thereby take some of the guess out of the otherwise unknown qualities of materials. Moreover, the tables keep the size of the sample at a minimum and so reduce the expense of inspection.

The Dodge and Romig tables provide figures for what is known as single and double sampling. Single sampling is that just described. Double sampling simply calls for two successive samples. If the first passes the lot, the process stops. If it does not, a second sample is added to the first, and the decision is then made. Double sampling has the advantage that, for the same degree of risk, the first sample is smaller. Many lots will be accepted on the first smaller sample, and additional lots will be accepted on the evidence of the two samples combined. Thus the cost of a single large sample tends to be reduced. Other tables have been constructed to extend double sampling into a series of sampling steps, called multiple or sequential sampling.

Military Standard 105-A adds another feature. Two levels of sampling standards are indicated in these tables: one for normal inspection, the other for tightened inspection. The idea is that when the government procures material from a new supplier, a tightened inspection may be required. This means that the probability of locating any lots with an unwanted number of defects will be increased. It is expected that, after the supplier proves that his materiel is of high quality over a period of time, normal inspection will be used. Here the probability of finding defective pieces in otherwise acceptable lots will be reduced. If such a supplier offers for acceptance too many lots with an excess amount of defectives, he may be put back on the probation status of tightened inspection.

Administrators may object to acceptance sampling procedures on the grounds that they are technical, not understandable, and ineffective. Practical experience, however, shows that the reverse is true. Techniques have been reduced to usable tables. The practitioner does not need to understand the mathematical theory. Both parties to the transaction appear to profit in the long run. The purchaser profits because over a period of time he accepts a product on the basis of known risks. This is good business, for it minimizes the uncertainties which would otherwise be present. On the other side of the transaction, the producer is encouraged to raise the quality of his product and to maintain that quality with a high degree of consistency.

Control of Attributes

The material presented here has been based upon the assumption that the qualities to be controlled can be measured. It has been noted also that instruments of measurement are being developed so that it is increasingly possible to obtain measurement data. In many products, however, measurements are not possible or significant. Here simply the presence or absence of a given defect is the determining factor. Thus, for automobile bodies on the assembly line, one notes that the paint is chipped or is not chipped; a particular bolt is or is not in place. These facts cannot be measured, but they can be counted.

For such a situation there are companion theories of quality control which parallel those described for measurement data, known as quality control for per cent defective and number of defects. The control techniques are not so precise as those for a series of measurements, but they do provide substantial help under conditions where measurements are not possible. For this paper it is only necessary to note that the appropriate theory and practice have been developed and are in practical use.

In Research and Development

Reference already has been made to the use of the simple statistical frequency distribution patterns. In some manufacturing processes, notably those in the chemical, paper, and textile industries, a simple cause-and-effect relationship corresponding to those simpler patterns cannot be used because often several uncontrollable elements are operating at the same time.

Take the case of a manufacturer of pharmaceuticals who desired to find out whether the variations in the laboratory test results of one of his products were caused by the differences between the laboratory workers or the variation in the quality of their work from day to day or in the quality of the product itself. All of these elements were operating simultaneously. A frequency distribution pattern similar to those we have discussed was of little value because in that form it pictured a comprehensive summary of the variation in the test results caused by all of these elements acting together. Some means was needed to break down this total pattern into subordinate parts. Students of the theory have shown how to design experiments so that the total variation present in the data might be apportioned among each of the several causes under study.

Accordingly, a sample from one set of apparatus was divided into two groups of eight subsamples each. Each of four laboratory workers was given, unknown to himself, two of the eight subsamples, and the process was repeated on a different day with the second group of subsamples. Similar sets of subsamples were taken from a second set of apparatus. Thus, on each of two days, each laboratory assistant tested four samples—two from each apparatus set. So far as each laboratory worker knew, the samples which he tested were merely parts of the routine process in the daily checking of the manufacturer's product. Moreover, because the process was repeated on two different days, the day-to-day variability in the laboratory appraisal could be separated from the variability between the laboratory workers, between their actions on different days, and between the qualities of the product from the two sets of apparatus.

Thus the 32 subsamples provided a basis for judgments about the relative importance of apparatus, laboratory assistants, and different days by classifying the data in several ways as follows: 16 subsamples for each of the two apparatus sets, eight subsamples for each of the four laboratory assistants, four subsamples for each of the four laboratory assistants on each of the two days, and sixteen subsamples for each of the two different days.

The theory shows how to compute the relative effect of each cause and the residual errors from the obviously completely and exactly organized set of measurements. In the illustration just cited, not only did the product vary as expected between the two sets of apparatus, but it was also found that the laboratory assistants were not consistent in their work between days or even within any one day. The results of the statistical analysis suggested that a series of conferences with perhaps some practice in the testing procedure was necessary to bring the laboratory work itself into a condition of consistency for the testing procedure.

It is important to remember that a comparison of the results from two samples cannot prove that the causes in back of both of them are or are not the same. The statistical analysis can only indicate that as the averages between readings from two samples show wider differences, there is first the judgment that the sources may be different and then, as the spread increases, an increasing confidence that this is probably so. If, on the other hand, the two samples agree with due allowance for the variation present, one can say only that there is no evidence to show that the two samples came from different sources. If the experimenter still believes that in fact the sources are different, he must continue his experimentation either until he is convinced that he cannot distinguish between them or until his added evidence makes it probable that the sources are different.

What this all adds up to is that modern statistical methods provide valuable new tools but that administrators should not expect too much of them. Moreover, it should be remembered that the theory about small samples is less than half a century old and that the largest part of its application in industry has taken place only within the last decade. As a result, ideas and cases are still scattered through professional and trade journals. Ultimately, of course, this material will be brought together into a plan of presentation which will make the attack on the whole problem much easier. Until that event, the administrator must expect applications to his own problems will be slow.

Obtaining maximum value. Usually the maximum value in the application of these modern statistical tools cannot be obtained unless the researcher designs his experiment for the analytical methods that he plans to use. It is extremely difficult and at times impossible to apply these new critical statistical methods to data already collected or to data from experiments which have not been designed wisely.

Suppose, in the case of the pharmaceutical company, a haphazard plan of experimentation had been followed—one of the laboratory assistants making two analyses on one day, another six analyses over three days, and so forth. Under these circumstances one would not know whether the work of the two analysts mentioned was likely to vary from day to day since the data for the work of one was done within one day. The work of the other could be examined, but it would include a compounding of his own work habits and the unspecified effect of different days on the test results. Moreover, if the samples for the three days had different sources, this factor would again create a mixture of causes.

It follows that appropriate designs of experiments tend to reduce the amount of data needed for a suitable analysis. This in turn saves costs. In a factory where work continues during the search for the reasons for unsatisfactory quality, a determination of such reasons at the earliest possible moment may mean large savings.

Effect on Personnel

In some instances the introduction of the methods of quality control has had the direct support and interest of the wage earners. Undoubtedly, some of these situations have been caused by a wage plan based upon the number of good pieces which the workman made. For such an individual, quality control in itself is desirable because it helps him reduce the amount of defective material to a minimum. His take-home pay is thereby increased.

Aside from this, there are some observations of shop conditions which possibly have significance. In plants where a quality control program is in operation, the workmen appear to be quite secure in their attitude toward their jobs. Undoubtedly in these plants a partial cause is to be found in good management-employee relationships. When one watches the machine operators checking from time to time the quality of their work on the nearby control charts, one has the feeling that another influence may be present. The control charts seem to provide the needed tools by means of which each man can consistently make an acceptable product. Each man here, in effect, is manager of his own job.

In one shop, where the quality control engineer had selected a particular workman to determine on a trial basis whether the methods could be applied in a given department, the workman at first objected, then became interested, and subsequently was given the opportunity to try out the procedure. After using a control chart for a few days, he saw the quality control engineer apparently about to take it away. The workman protested this action. Maybe it was just a new gadget which had stirred the workman's interest. Maybe it was the opportunity to try out a new method which had pleased his vanity. Maybe he had found a device which told him how well he was performing and so increased his job interest and security.

There is also the contrary reaction of personnel to a device which seems to lead toward the automatic machine and which seems to reduce the number of jobs. Working people for generations have been opposed to labor-saving devices—an objection caused directly by the fear that their jobs may thereby become unnecessary. Management knows, however, that, in the long run, the contrary is true. As one well-known manufacturer has expressed it, his chief problem in his business life has been to find more efficient production methods so that he could get rid of each employee, and the only penalty he has suffered is that instead of having the few hundred employees he started with, he now has some fifteen thousand to get rid of! His is an effective illustration of the fact that more and better production tools and methods create more jobs, not fewer. The problem is to sell this idea and keep it sold.

Costs and Savings

The subject of specific costs and dollar savings is one which quality control engineers at times carefully avoid. The reason seems to be that a consistently good final product made under a system of quality control may cost more than a product of less dependable quality made by haphazard methods. It is unfair, however, to look at the problem solely from this point of view. Surely the ultimate consumer has some interest in the quality of what he purchases. Reliability and freedom from repairs even under hard usage are the qualities which he seeks. Merchandise of low quality in the long run is likely to be unsatisfactory. From the manufacturer's point of view, the competitive system of free enterprise tends to force him into the acceptance of quality control if he is to satisfy his customers and so maintain his standing in his markets.

399

Perhaps another reason for avoiding questions of costs often is the indirect nature of the savings—for example, those which result when workmen suggest new procedures and better tools. There is reason to think that at times this search for better ways of manufacturing is simulated because of the help of the quality control engineers, yet it is hard to assign cost savings to the use of quality control alone.

There are some manufacturers, however, who believe they have direct evidence on the cost savings which the application of quality control has made possible. Many of these savings are nothing short of fantastic. Figures in the order of $25,000 to $50,000 for a single department of a large plant are not unknown.

In one particular instance the author asked the quality control engineer whether he was still keeping an estimate of the savings which his department was making. The reply was that after a year and a half they had passed the million-dollar mark, and everyone from the president down had become so convinced of the value of quality control that records of cost savings no longer were of immediate interest.

Training Methods

In a subject which is so new and which is so unlike previous experience in manufacturing, the element of training becomes a problem of major importance.

It might be assumed that training should be undertaken among the workmen alone. This position, however, is unwise. Workmen must necessarily possess some knowledge of the methods of recording the qualities of the work which they do. Their supervisors need a broader understanding of the reasons why the procedures are carried through in a certain way. In their turn, the executives require some inkling as to the techniques, but, more important, an understanding of the objectives which are being sought so that they may wisely direct the development of quality control usage in their plants. There is evidence to show that trouble may develop when a quality control program is turned over to someone in the shop or to a statistical technician who lacks understanding of factory know-how; without administrative interest and guidance the program is likely to be unsatisfactory or to fail.

In many plants where quality control has been introduced, it is fortunate that able men with many years of experience in manufacturing have had the interest to pick up the task of learning the methods of quality control, organizing classes, and then teaching them with enthusiasm. Often they have had little training in the mathematics of the subject or in teaching, but they have understood how the working man thinks. For the training courses they have created many devices to make clear the points which they were trying to teach.

A word of caution is in order here: the wisdom of using too elaborate devices in teaching is doubtful. Have these devices become so elaborate that they cease to impart a maximum of instruction? Do they replace instruction with the triviality of amusement? The psychological dividing line between good and bad teaching aids is often so intangible that an appraisal must be made only after extensive experimentation. It is known, for example, that in certain classes where the elements of factory production are taught, the use of moving picture films is very helpful; but if the presentation begins with a few bars of music, the instructional value is very definitely lowered. Again, if the room is completely darkened in order to use a projection apparatus and screen, the psychological setting for leisure and amusement is established immediately, and the impact of instructional material is diminished.

The Future

The administrator has a valid right to ask whether these new methods of quality control are likely to be permanent. We do not know. Certain trends, however, are discernible.

Process research inevitably results in machine capabilities which steadily produce a more nearly uniform product. It may happen, therefore, that a continuing quality control procedure becomes unnecessary in a particular situation, since good work under easy tolerances can be maintained. From an economic and merchandising point of view, however, such a situation may not be permanent, since changes are always occurring. Everyone is aware that better qualities of old products and types of merchandise are in demand by consumers. The development of new prod-

401

ucts is a habit of aggressive manufacturers. For instance, the creation of television calls for new demands on machine capabilities. These in turn provide new opportunities for statistical quality control.

Underlying all advances in improved quality is to be found the rapidly expanding development of the instruments of measurement. Progress here lies in the direction of instruments created to measure physical properties which have never been measured previously, or toward substantially increased precision of measurements which now in some cases run to millionths of an inch, or to measuring devices coupled to automatic sorting of parts by size after they have been measured. The use of electronic gauges and radio isotopes is not uncommon. Manufacturing is becoming a scientific process.

It is only a step from such devices of measurement which control automatically the accuracy in the machining of parts to the electronic controls which tie together whole series of machines. Many evidences of such procedures are already in existence. We are getting close to the automatic factory, although there will remain a mass of work out of reach of the completely automatic process.

It may be that one or another part of the procedures in statistical controls as they are now generally recognized will disappear, but the underlying statistical procedures used in process research or in the analysis of data derived from a complex situation will continue to be of increasing value. This guess is not so extreme as it may sound, since the use of statistical techniques by which numerical information is analyzed is a part of any scientific procedure.

LIST OF CONTRIBUTORS

Melvin Anshen, professor of marketing and business policy, Graduate School of Business, Columbia University

H. Igor Ansoff, development planning specialist, Lockheed Aircraft Corporation

William J. Baumol, professor of economics, Princeton University; member of the consulting firm Mathematica

Edward G. Bennion, professor of economics, Graduate School of Business Administration, Stanford University

Robert Beyer, managing partner, Touche, Ross, Bailey & Smart

Robert G. Brown, operations research group, Arthur D. Little, Inc.

Theodore H. Brown, professor emeritus of business statistics, Graduate School of Business Administration, Harvard University

Gerald A. Busch, vice president and director of market research, Lockheed Propulsion Company

Alexander Henderson, late professor of economics, Carnegie Institute of Technology

Cyril C. Herrmann, vice president for urban and regional economics, Arthur D. Little, Inc.

James C. Hetrick, in charge of operations research, Midwest Division, Arthur D. Little, Inc.

Charles C. Holt, professor of economics and research associate, Social Systems Research Institute, University of Wisconsin

Benjamin Lipstein, vice president and associate research director, Benton & Bowles, Inc.

John G. McLean, vice president for international and financial operations, Continental Oil Company

Richard B. Maffei, lecturer in industrial management, Massachusetts Institute of Technology, and partner, Harvey N. Shycon Company

INDEX

405

Other MENTOR Books of Interest